Clark Ashton Smith, 1958

Photo by Wynn Bullock

Selected Letters of Clark Ashton Smith

Edited by
David E. Schultz and Scott Connors

Arkham House
Sauk City, Wisconsin
2003

Contents

To Donald Sidney-Fryer

Introduction

C LARK ASHTON SMITH DELIGHTED IN RELATING HOW HE was born on a Friday the Thirteenth, in January 1893, "under the influence of Saturn"(letter 15), which supposedly predisposes one toward the uncanny and mystical. He was born to Timeus Ashton Smith and Mary Francis ("Fanny") Gaylord in the home of his grandparents in Long Valley, California, a rural community just outside the Gold Rush town of Auburn. Smith's father was an Englishman, son of a wealthy industrialist, who spent his inheritance on world travel before settling in Placer County. He had possibly been drawn there by the presence of a sizeable English colony at the nearby town of Penryn, whose upper-crust lifestyle (complete with fox hunts!) induced jealousy among many of their neighbors. Timeus was not wealthy, quite the opposite in fact, and earned his living as a night clerk in an Auburn hotel, a gold miner, and a fruit and chicken rancher before ill health left the burden of caring for the family to his wife. He was, however, well educated and well mannered, and he regaled his son with tales of trips down the Amazon and adventuring in Macao.

Smith's parents were more than forty when he was born. An only child, he was also lonely, for few children lived nearby and those by no means were necessarily congenial. Like many a lonely child, he learned to read early, delighting in fairy tales and the *Arabian Nights*. A bout of scarlet fever lasted longer than usual, possibly having developed into rheumatic fever. While this would have important implications for his later health, it delayed his attendance at the local one-room school. There his bookish manners, sickly physique, and withdrawn nature made him a target for bullying. Smith later admitted that he suffered "from a sense of isolation . . . when I was younger, and am inclined to think that solitude is often harder to bear in youth" (letter 219). Denied the company of others, Smith took solace in the beauties of nature and of the stars. His first book, *The Star-Treader and Other Poems* (1912), abounds with images of the socially isolated individual: secluded forests, mountain tops, the spaces between the stars. Later, as he began to write his mature weird fiction, a perceptive critic of his stories remarked: "They are, perhaps unconsciously, autobiographical" (Parker 74). Although Smith was admitted to the local high school, he declined to attend, feeling that he could do better with self-education. To that end, he read the *Encyclopaedia Britannica,* at least one unabridged dictionary, and every volume in the local Carnegie library.

The nearby town of Auburn also left its mark upon the young Smith. Mary Eulalie Shannon, California's first woman poet, had lived there and attracted such visitors as Joaquin Miller and Bret Harte. Ambrose Bierce held court for a time at the Freeman Hotel, satirizing the local gossips in his poem "The Perverted Village." At the age of thirteen, Smith discovered the works of Edgar Allan Poe, and as his reading expanded he found that California literature, at the time synonymous with San Francisco literature, owed much to Poe. Sam Moskowitz has documented how the literary world of San Francisco contained much of "mystery and imagination," with writers such as Ambrose Bierce, W. C. Morrow, Gertrude Atherton, Emma Frances Dawson, and Jack London contributing imaginative tales to such periodicals as the *Argonaut* and the *Overland Monthly.*

The pivotal event in Smith's life was his discovery of the poetry of George Sterling, a pupil and friend of Bierce. They began corresponding in January 1911, beginning a friendship that would last until the elder poet's death in 1926. Until that time, Smith had written mainly fiction, including at least two novels, influenced heavily by the *Arabian Nights,* William Beckford's *Vathek*, Poe, and Kipling. The work was colorful and fast-paced, displaying a taste for the exotic and the macabre. Four of Smith's stories achieved professional standards of competence, as witnessed by their sales to the *Overland Monthly* and *Black Cat*. After Smith began to correspond with Sterling, he largely put aside the composition of short stories until 1929, a brief experiment in writing sophisticated irony for the romance pulps in the early 1920s notwithstanding. Smith now defined himself a poet, and it was as a poet that he earned his first fame.

It is perhaps difficult for the modern reader to understand that the word *poet* once had certain almost mystical implications. Sterling's poetry has been described variously as *fin de siècle*, Symbolist, and Decadent, but fundamentally it was Romantic. One hallmark of Romantic poetry is its emphasis on the Imagination, defined by Coleridge as "the living Power and prime Agent of all human Perception, and as a repetition of the eternal act of creation in the infinite I AM" (Coleridge 516). Poetry had previously been regarded as mimetic, being merely an imitation of that which existed in Nature. In this new scheme, the Poet evoked the same Ideas or Archetypes that God did, so that, in M. H. Abrams's words, "of all men the poet is likest God because he creates according to those patterns on which God himself has modeled the universe" (42). It was for its imaginative power that Ambrose Bierce extolled "Kubla Khan" as the greatest poem, ranking Sterling's "A Wine of Wizardry" as its peer. The concept of the Poet as Man-God eventually would reveal itself in Smith's work in the various near-omniscient sorcerer-necromancers of his stories and poems, beginning as early as "Nero."

Sterling influenced Smith chiefly by introducing to him the cosmos as it was then understood by modern science. Since most poetry at the time was didactic, such a subject was almost certain to fail to find a wide audience. Smith's first efforts at cosmic-astronomic themes met with little understanding:

> I am astonished to find how few really grasp the sublimity and vastness of the stars and star-spaces. One acquaintance did not think such things suitable for poetic treatment, and from the indifference or bewilderment with which most who have seen it regard my cosmic work, I must regard those fitted to understand such things as being very rare. (letter 2)

He was always pleased when he found an appreciative reader, but he made it clear that he did not seek popularity. "Poetry, particularly work like mine, which is so far removed from the everyday interest of the immense bulk of mankind, stands in little danger of being overestimated in these days" (letter 11).

Smith had no use for "human interest" in his poetry, which in his mind implied a concentration upon the pious, the prosaic, and the personal. In his contemplation of the cosmos, its immensity made the insignificance of human aspirations clear to him, and the endless cycle of life and death found expression in poems such as "Retrospect and Forecast," causing one reviewer to label Smith's work "ghoulish" (Jury 2). But what Smith found "morbid" was "realism": the "exaggerated prying into one's own vitals—and the vitals of others" (*PD* 12). He wrote Sterling, "Personally, I'm getting a wee bit sick of the introspective element which so dominates modern literature. . . . There's a frightful lack of dignity and reticence, so that the public seems even to resent these qualities when it does find them" (letter 14). Smith was doing no more than observing Wordsworth's observation that poetry is "truth, not individual and local, but general and operative" (25).

To say, as some have, that Smith was out of step with the literature of his time implies a degree of regimentation that might not be inappropriate considering the industrial civilization that gave it birth. This issue has been discussed elsewhere (Connors), but the success of such movements as Imagism and the New Humanism had important implications for Smith and his mentor. Toward the end of his life, Sterling's confidence in his work had begun to crumble under the attacks of Harriet Monroe and others, leading him to express to Smith a wish that he had devoted more of his efforts to "themes as have some relation to life, some vital significance" instead of "on 'impossible' stuff" (Sterling to Smith, 9 November 1926; 3 October 1926; mss., NYPL). Although publicly supportive of Smith, Sterling privately remarked that Smith's work was "very colorful and imaginative—and utterly inhuman, as probably he intends it to be" (quoted in Dumont). Sterling even went so far as to have George Douglas, literary editor of the *San Francisco Bulletin*, publish Sterling's unsigned review of *Ebony and Crystal*—a book to which he himself had written the preface—in which he stated Smith's art was "inhuman, almost unearthly . . . a deliberate evasion of reality" (Sterling 8). Smith's response to such criticisms was that "Anything that the human imagination can conceive of becomes thereby a part of life, and poetry such as mine, properly considered, is not an 'escape,' but an extension" of life (letter 86). To H. P. Lovecraft, Smith wrote more ardently: "there is absolutely no justification for literature unless it serves to release the imagination from the bounds of every-day life" (letter 107). In his essay "On Fantasy," Smith lamented that

> Only the Real, whatever that is or may be, is admissible
> for treatment; and writers must confine themselves to
> themes well within the range of statisticians, lightning
> calculators, Freud and Kraft-Ebbing, the Hearst and
> McFadden publications, NRA, and mail order catalogues.
> Chimeras are no longer the mode, the infinite has been
> abolished; mystery is obsolete, and sphinx and medusa are
> toys for children. (*PD* 38)

In passages such as this Smith anticipated J. R. R. Tolkien, when
the Oxford don wrote that he found "the notion that motor-cars
are more 'alive' than, say, centaurs or dragons . . . curious" (81).

Sterling's suicide in 1926 affected Smith profoundly, but the
emptiness left by his passing was filled in part by Smith's developing friendship with Lovecraft. Although Smith is sometimes
referred to as a member of the "Lovecraft circle," Lovecraft as well
might be recognized as a member of a "Smith circle," since Smith
had become acquainted with such figures as Samuel Loveman and
George Kirk far earlier than Lovecraft did, and Smith in fact introduced Lovecraft to Donald Wandrei. It was Lovecraft who recognized in Smith a kindred spirit when Samuel Loveman introduced
him to Smith's work in 1922, and Lovecraft initiated a correspondence with Smith that would last until his death in 1937. Despite
his early success, Smith initially found the idea of composing short
stories uncongenial, cleaving as he did to the Romantic view of
prose being an inferior form of expression. His admiration for
Baudelaire's poems in prose, followed by his own experiments in
the form as published in *Ebony and Crystal,* eroded this prejudice,
and his admiration for Lovecraft's work showed him the artistic
possibilities offered by weird fiction. It was the necessity in 1929
to find a way to support his aging parents that convinced Smith to
resume the writing of fiction.

Beginning with "The End of the Story" in the October 1930
issue of *Weird Tales,* Smith began a nearly unbroken run, distinguished as much by its quality as by its abundance. In fact, until
the December 1935 number, Smith was the most frequent contributor to the self-styled "Unique Magazine," leaving even the
prolific Seabury Quinn at the gate. He also became a leading contributor to Hugo Gernsback's *Wonder Stories* and actively sought
other markets, although the two pulp magazines remained his
chief venues.

Smith's career as a fiction writer was not without conflict. Just
as his otherworldly poetry was misunderstood, some readers

objected to his "impossible" stories, leading him to remark that if one particularly outspoken commentator "were transported to some alien world, I fear that he would find the reality far more incredible, bizarre, grotesque, fantastic, horrific, and impossible than any of my stories" (PD 26). The editor of Wonder Stories had told Smith that he wanted "a play of human motives, with alien worlds for a background." Smith responded: "if human motives are mainly what they want, why bother about going to other planets—where one might conceivably escape from the human equation?" (letter 112). His stories, like his poetry, were efforts to "offer a welcome and salutary release from the somewhat oppressive tyranny of the homocentric, and correct the deeply inverted, ingrowing values that are fostered by present-day 'humanism' . . ." (PD 14).

Smith's short stories were in many ways extensions of his earlier work, with themes, images, and techniques from his poems and prose-poems reappearing. For instance, "The Chain of Aforgomon" deals with the final of a *chain* of incarnations, invoking an image used earlier in "The Star-Treader." The prose-poems "From the Crypts of Memory" and "The Flower-Devil" were further developed as "The Planet of the Dead" and "The Demon of the Flower." Likewise, in "The Last Night" we see the vision that gave birth to Zothique, that last continent of Earth beneath the dying red sun. Poems such as "Medusa" and "The Medusa of the Skies" led to stories such as "The Gorgon," achieving a continuity of interest in mythological themes.

Smith was most comfortable when he could "weave the entire web" of a story "on the loom of fantasy" (letter 219). Curiously, this preference had sprung from a desire to achieve accuracy of setting, since by controlling the creation of what Tolkien called a "secondary world," he eliminated opportunities for error that might affect the reactions of his characters. In his flight from a "literature of quotidian detail" (letter 109), Smith raced to the opposite pole, which Northrop Frye identified as myth (51). Smith himself recognized this when, later in life, he gave a lecture on the mythological basis of science fiction. Myths, according to Joseph Campbell, are public dreams, opening the world "to something beyond speech, beyond words, in short, to what we call transcendence" (40). In a rare moment of perception, L. Sprague de Camp titled his biographical sketch of Smith "Sierran Shaman," recognizing that a shaman is a mediator between the land of dreams and what we call reality.

In a letter to Lovecraft, Smith admitted "I sometimes suspect that the wholly *unconscious* elements in writing (or other art) are by far the most important" (letter 109). In a prose-poem written around the time he began his great fiction period, Smith implored: "Tell me many tales, O benign maleficent daemon, but tell me none that I have ever heard or have even dreamt of otherwise than obscurely or infrequently" ("To the Daemon," *PP* 38), the daemon being a Platonic spirit-guide that corresponds to the unconscious mind. In myth as in dream, the element of mystery is paramount, along with its connotations of "that which is hidden and esoteric, that which is beyond conception or understanding," which can develop in a *mysterium tremendum*, leading to an "annihilation of self" and its replacement by the "transcendent as the sole and entire reality" (Otto 13, 21).

It is Smith's use of language that distinguishes him from his contemporaries. Just as Ezra Pound and Amy Lowell eschewed the "grand style" in poetry, so too did Ernest Hemingway's "machine-gun staccato" dominate fiction. Critics such as Isaac Asimov and Marjorie Farber have mocked Smith's Latinate vocabulary, but it represented much more than the indiscriminate usage of a thesaurus (see Connors). Smith himself felt that "the modern intolerance toward what is called 'painted speech,' toward the 'grand manner,' springs too often from the instinctive resentment inspired in vulgar minds by all that savors of loftiness, exaltation, nobility, sublimity, and aristocracy" (*BB* 104), a view echoed by the mystery novelist Rita Mae Brown in the *New York Times Book Review* where she observed that the use of a Latinate English dates back to the Norman aristocracy, which resulted in class distinctions affecting the choice of words. For every objector to Smith's "highfalutin' " style, there are many admirers who exult in his use of language—admirers such as Ray Bradbury, Michael Chabon, Clive Barker, Tim Powers, and Fritz Leiber.

So dazzling is Smith's power with words that it is sometimes thought that there is no depth to his work. Let us examine just one aspect of Smith's use of language. Critics as divergent as Harriet Monroe and Harlan Ellison have remarked upon his ability to evoke a scene visually. Traditional mimetic theories of art echoed the acceptance of Simonides' maxim that "painting is dumb poetry and poetry a speaking painting" (Abrams 13). In Smith's case, what we have is the ability to make the reader visualize that which never was anything but the fruit of his imagination. Smith himself did extensive painting and drawing in the 1920s, and he rejected technical instruction from a recognized portrait-painter on the grounds that this "would be of little help in teaching me how to paint landscapes in Cocaigne, or Saturn, or Antillia" (letter 81). The ability to express the creations of his imagination, whether in poetry or prose, in paint or stone, is Smith's great achievement.

Smith once told a girlfriend that "most letters, even by men of genius, are interesting mainly to their writers and recipients" (letter 122), but many have felt a need for publication of his letters. In fact, there is sufficient interest in his work to justify an edition of his letters but apparently not those of Harriet Monroe, Amy Lowell, and "H. D." (Hilda Doolittle). An obvious parallel is the case of the letters of H. P. Lovecraft, the publication of which being in large part the purpose for which the current publisher was established; however, no special effort was made after Smith's death to preserve his correspondence. That so many of his letters survive is in large part due to his status as a regional literary figure, so that much of his correspondence with other writers was deposited among their papers in various repositories. Many members of the Lovecraft Circle scrupulously preserved Lovecraft's letters, yet Smith's letters to Duane Rimel, Robert Bloch, J. Vernon Shea, and others were lost in various moves and other domestic upheavals. The whereabouts of his correspondence with Benjamin De Casseres, Lilith Lorraine, Stanton Coblentz, Eric Barker, Madelynne Greene, Vachel Lindsay, and others is unknown. Likewise, many letters have disappeared into private collections. One cache, the correspondence between Smith and Samuel Loveman, recently was purchased by the Bancroft Library but is not available for study. One letter, a thank-you note that Smith sent to critic Herbert Bashford for a favorable review, was found by a fan laid into a copy of The Star-Treader, duly copied, and transcribed in his letter to Smith.

If Smith's letters lack the epistolary brilliance of Lovecraft's, they nevertheless reveal heretofore hidden facets of his life, character, and work. The attentive reader can see the swift development from hesitant apprentice to confident cosmic master and mentor. The letters reveal his crushing loneliness, poverty, and sense of alienation from his environment. They also show his familiarity with the work of other poets and weird fiction writers, especially when he extends succinct and penetrating appraisals of their work. Most important, they reveal Smith to be a man of integrity. Though sometimes forced to rewrite or cut his work to ensure a sale, he did so on his terms, and only of necessity to provide for his parents. Aside from that dire circumstance, Smith wrote, painted, and sculpted to satisfy his own muse.

It is fortunate that his career as a writer of weird fiction coincides precisely with his greatest voluminousness as a correspondent. For his earlier life, we have only the letters to George Sterling, supplemented by brief notes to George Kirk and Albert Bender. After the death of his father, Smith did "more living than writing" (letter 230), so there are few letters after 1937. The present selection of letters attempts to cover all periods of his long life while focussing on the letters most pertinent to his best work.

Smith remained a legendary figure in the realm of the fantastic, and received letters from discerning fans, some of whom became close friends and whose visits somewhat alleviated his loneliness. He married Carol Dorman, a widow with three teenage children, late in life, and died of a stroke in Pacific Grove on 14 August 1961. His ashes were interred beneath a boulder at the site of his home in Auburn, which had been destroyed earlier by an arsonist. This boulder recently was moved to Auburn's Centennial Park, where a plaque celebrates and commemorates Smith's life. Smith knew that ultimately we are all ciphers in the Book of Vergama, but he had an abiding faith that his work would survive, if only as "no more, alas, / Than a frail shadow on the glass / Before some latter conjurer" ("Song of the Necromancer," *LO* 81), referring to such writers as Philip K. Dick, Gene Wolfe, Brian Stableford, and other admirers, and that "my volumes and my philters shall abide" ("The Sorcerer Departs," *RA* v). Smith's reputation as an important writer of weird fiction of the last century, second perhaps only to Lovecraft, and his growing reputation as a regional poet in his native California, has drawn increasing attention from readers, scholars, and collectors in both areas, and his works always have remained somewhere in print.

—SCOTT CONNORS
DAVID E. SCHULTZ

Works Cited

Abrams, M. H. *The Mirror and the Lamp*. 1953; rpt. London: Oxford University Press, 1971.

Asimov, Isaac, ed. *Before the Golden Age*. Garden City, NY: Doubleday, 1974.

Brown, Rita Mae. "You Say Begin, I Say Commence—To the Victor Belongs the Language." *New York Times Book Review,* 20 December 1987: 13.

Campbell, Joseph. *The Hero's Journey.* Ed. Phil Cousineau. San Francisco: Harper San Francisco, 1991.

Coleridge, Samuel Taylor. *The Portable Coleridge.* Ed. I. A. Richards. 1950; rpt. New York: Penguin Books, 1978.

Connors, Scott. "Gesturing Toward the Infinite: Clark Ashton Smith and Modernism." *Studies in Weird Fiction* No. 25 (Summer 2001): 18–28.

Dumont, Henry. *A Faun on Olympus.* Unpublished manuscript. Library of Congress.

Ellison, Harlan. "*Out of Space and Time* by Clark Ashton Smith." In *Horror: 100 Best Books,* ed. Stephen Jones and Kim Newman. New York: Carroll & Graf, 1998. pp. 135–39.

Farber, Marjorie. "Atlantis, Xiccarph." [Review of *Lost Worlds.*] *New York Times Book Review,* November 19, 1944; rpt. *Klarkash-Ton* No. 1 (June 1988): 26–27.

Frye, Northrop. *Anatomy of Criticism: Four Essays.* 1957; rpt. Princeton, NJ: Princeton University Press, 1971.

Jury, John. "'The Star-Treader:' A Book of Verse by Clark Ashton Smith." *San Jose Mercury and Herald Magazine,* 8 December 1912: 2.

[Monroe, Harriet.] [Review of *The Star-Treader and Other Poems* by Clark Ashton Smith.] *Poetry* 2, No. 1 (April 1913): 31–32.

Moskowitz, Sam. *Science Fiction in Old San Francisco: Volume I, History of the Movement.* West Kingston, RI: Donald M. Grant, 1980.

Otto, Rudolf. *The Idea of the Holy.* Tr. John W. Harvey. 1923; rpt. London: Oxford University Press, 1950.

Parker, Robert Allerton. "Such Pulps as Dreams Are Made On." *VVV* (March 1943); rpt. *Radical America,* Special Issue (January 1970): 70–77.

[Sterling, George.] "Recent Books of Fact and Fiction" [as by George Douglas]. *Bulletin* [San Francisco], 19 December 1922: 8.

Tolkien, J. R. R. "On Fairy-Stories." *The Tolkien Reader.* New York: Ballantine Books, 1966.

Wordsworth, William. *Wordsworth's Literary Criticism.* Ed. Nowell C. Smith. London: Oxford University Press, 1905.

Editorial Practices

The sources of Smith's letters are given in brackets following the name of the recipient at the head of each letter, save that owners of letters not held in public institutions are not disclosed. Abbreviations used to designate institutions are given below.

Many letters are printed in their entirety. Those that are not have been edited to remove material that is repeated or of little importance. Smith's use of ellipses is preserved. Editorial omissions are indicated by ellipses in square brackets. In order to save space, the editors' ellipses represent any removal of text—to the beginning or end of a paragraph, of a single paragraph or many, or combinations thereof. Postscripts that have been omitted are not so indicated with editors' ellipses. Virtually all of Smith's letters originated either from his home in Auburn or, late in life, Pacific Grove. His return address in the former case was simply "Auburn, California" or slight variations thereof. Thus, to save space, his "return address" is provided only in those rare instances where he used something different; his Pacific Grove address is given in full only once.

Smith's method of indicating the titles of books, magazines, poems, stories, and other works was very inconsistent. The editors have elected to use the modern style of doing so throughout. Likewise, Smith was not consistent in matters of punctuation or in indicating accents in foreign terms. The editors have employed a consistent style based upon Smith's predilection, discerned primarily from his typed letters.

Explanatory notes elucidating references to persons, historical events, works by Smith and others, and other such matters are printed following respective letters. In preparing our notes, we generally did not annotate matters that can be found easily in standard reference works, focusing instead on points where specialized expertise is required. Citations of Smith's works are usually abbreviated, and reference is generally made to first editions as opposed to paperback reprints. Our bibliography lists publications (chiefly Smith's own work) that were consulted in preparing this edition, but a list of articles that may be useful to the interested reader is also provided.

—DES & SC

Acknowledgments

We are grateful to the following institutions for permission to print the letters of Clark Ashton Smith in their possession: Bancroft Library, University of California (Berkeley, CA); the Wisconsin Historical Society; the John Hay Library of Brown University, Providence, RI; the Berg Collection of English and American Literature, The New York Public Library, Astor, Lenox and Tilden Foundations; the Minnesota Historical Society, St. Paul; the University of California, Los Angeles; Mills College Library, Oakland, CA; and Arkham House. Permission to publish the text of the letters has been granted by CASiana, the Estate of Clark Ashton Smith.

We are also grateful to Steven C. Behrends, Geoffrey Best, Anthony Bliss of the Bancroft Library, Janice Braun of Mills College Library, Oakland, California, Ned Brooks, Rusty Burke, Glyneth Cassidy, T. G. L. Cockcroft, L. Sprague de Camp, Gerry and Helen de la Ree, William Dorman, Stefan R. Dziemianowicz, Robert B. Elder, Alfred Galpin, Mara Kirk Hart, Don Herron, Mike Horvat, Ronald S. Hilger, Margerie Hill, Rah Hoffman, S. T. Joshi, Frank Belknap Long, Terrence McVicker, Rob Preston, Christopher Puckelwartz, Samuel J. Sackett, Gene Scott, Roy A. Squires, Helen and Marion Sully, and the staffs of the California State Library and Placer County Library for their assistance in preparing this volume and for their general support of our work.

Abbreviations

ALS	autograph letter, signed
TLS	typed letter, signed
AJ	*Auburn Journal* (newspaper)
AY	*The Abominations of Yondo* (1960)
BB	*The Black Book of Clark Ashton Smith* (1979)
DC	*The Dark Chateau and Other Poems* (1951)
DS	*The Double Shadow and Other Fantasies* (1933)
EC	*Ebony and Crystal: Poems in Verse and Prose* (1922)
GL	*Genius Loci* (1948)
HD	*The Hill of Dionysus: A Selection* (1962)
LO	*The Last Oblivion: Best Fantastic Poetry of Clark Ashton Smith* (2002)

LW	*Lost Worlds* (1944)
Nero	*Nero and Other Poems* (1937)
OD	*Other Dimensions* (1970)
OS	*Odes and Sonnets* (1918)
OST	*Out of Space and Time* (1942)
PD	*Planets and Dimensions: Collected Essays of Clark Ashton Smith* (1973)
PP	*Poems in Prose* (1965)
RA	*A Rendezvous in Averoigne* (1988; rpt. 2003)
S	*Sandalwood* (1925)
S&P	*Spells and Philtres* (1958)
SL	H. P. Lovecraft, *Selected Letters* (Sauk City, WI: Arkham House, 1965–1976; 5 vols.)
SP	*Selected Poems* (1971)
SS	*Strange Shadows: The Uncollected Fiction and Essays of Clark Ashton Smith* (1989)
ST	*The Star-Treader and Other Poems* (1912)
TSS	*Tales of Science and Sorcery* (1964)
WT	*Weird Tales* (magazine)

AB	Ambrose Bierce
AWD	August W. Derleth
CAS	Clark Ashton Smith
DAW	Donald A. Wandrei
FW	Farnsworth Wright
GS	George Sterling
HPL	H. P. Lovecraft
RHB	R. H. Barlow

BL	The Bancroft Library, University of California, Berkeley
JHL	John Hay Library, Brown University, Providence, Rhode Island
MCL	Mills College Library, Oakland, California
MHS	Minnesota Historical Society, St. Paul
NYPL	New York Public Library
SHSW	Wisconsin Historical Society
UCLA	University of California, Los Angeles

Selected Letters of
Clark Ashton Smith

Dear Mr. Sterling:

I've received your letter of the 19th, returning my "Ode to Music." You've certainly added something to the debt I owe you for praise and helpful criticism. I don't think the poem will ever receive a higher compliment than the one you pay it in saying you wish that you'd written it yourself. That is a whole lot more than the "Ode," or anything I've written or am liable to write, deserves.

I've adapted most of your suggestions as to changes, with a few more alterations that occurred to me. I am glad to enclose the copy that you asked for. That was another compliment, and I only wish the thing were more worthy.

Some of your suggestions have more than doubled the value of the lines in question, particularly the line: "Her forms divine expressed in melody," in which you suggested the substitution of diverse for divine, thus introducing the idea of reconciliation. And there are others, which wouldn't have occured to me in a hundred years, and for which I can't thank you enough.[2]

I think I write too hastily, and don't work hard enough over my things. I seem to have a "deadly facility" for turning out verse, – of a kind.

I've been trying my hand at some cosmic verse lately, and a month's work, and a lot of spoiled paper have led me to the conclusion that your "Testimony of the Suns"[3] is about the last word in that line, and that the subject is too big for me to handle, anyway. I'd better stick to butterflies and roses, etc. (I don't mean that these subjects are less worthy) instead of trying to wipe out half the constellations (on paper) and put the rest askew. This is about what I've done in four poems, varying in length from 112 to 56 lines.

One of the things—an "Ode to the Abyss,"[4] has about all the sparks of originality in the collection. That's a deep subject, isn't it? (Forgive the rotten pun.) I'll send it to you, afterwhile, when I've pruned it a bit more, and sweated out as much of its crudity as I can.

I'm sorry to hear that you won't be able to write any more poems before Autumn. If it weren't for you, American poetry would hardly have the wherewithal to clothe its nakedness. Of course, there is Markham, but he doesn't seem to have done anything lately.⁵ At least, I haven't seen it. I hope his silence means that a long poem will be forthcoming.

I've written a few short nature lyrics during the last few days, treating simple subjects in the simplest manner that I can. They should be about the most saleable work that I have done. The "Ode to the Abyss," setting aside its length, is rather too tart for the magazines. It might "gall the kibes"⁶ of the blatant optimists among their readers. [. . .]

I hope you'll enjoy that eastern vacation. I hardly think that I could have come down to Carmel this summer, on account of my father's ill-health. It may be different next year, when I fervently hope to accept your kind invitation.

It's about time to put an end to this dissertation, and it might as well stop one place as another.

Yours, most sincerely,
Clark Ashton Smith

1. George Sterling (1869–1926), the California poet and unofficial poet laureate of San Francisco who strongly opposed the Modernist movement in American poetry. A protégé of Ambrose Bierce (1842–1914?), GS himself became CAS's mentor.
2. "Ode to Music," ST 28–30 (omitted from SP). Line 65 ultimately was rendered "And diverse forms expressed in harmony:".
3. GS, "The Testimony of the Suns," a long poem included in The Testimony of the Suns and Other Poems (1903). CAS quotes ll. 93–96, 101–104 as an epigram to the Star-Treader section of SP.
4. In ST, SP, and LO.
5. Edwin Markham (1852–1940), a colleague of AB and GS who gained celebrity with the publication of "The Man with the Hoe" (1899), although AB, GS, and CAS all disdained the poem because of its didacticism.
6. Hamlet 5.1.150. A kibe is an ulcerated chilblain.

[2]   To George Sterling [ALS, NYPL]   Oct. 6th, 1911

Dear Mr. Sterling:
Your card and letter at hand. I am glad you like the photograph, but really, it isn't a very good one. To me the eye of a camera always looks like the mysterious, murderous muzzle of a thirteen-inch gun, and I am apt to look like the enemy.

I have heard nothing from the *North American Review*. It quite knocked me over to hear that you had sent my "Ode to the Abyss" to such a big magazine. If it's accepted, I'll probably lose what little reason I have left.

How I wish I were down in Carmel with you! I am not at all certain whether I can get away this winter or not. If I do come, it probably won't be before December. I am so tied down that the way is not at all obvious now. I'd rather be able to accept your invitation than have the "Abyss Ode" accepted—even by the "high and mighty" *North American Review!* Auburn is nothing but a cage, and with little gilding on the bars at that.

I am enclosing some more poems, which you must consider at your leisure. Don't worry about my feeling "neglected" if they are not returned for a month or two. I really do not know what you'll think about the "Star-Treader."[1] It was written in a mood of mid-summer fantasy, and altogether to suit myself. It is frightfully irregular, both in thought and form, and probably a little obscure. I have begun to doubt the propriety of such a lack of regular form in a narrative or semi-narrative poem, but this was the way it presented itself to me, and I have not the courage to try working it over.

The "Song From Hell" is a subject that it would take Browning to do rightly.[2] I do not remember to have seen anything of the kind before. I think you will admit, after reading these two poems, that I do not lack courage in attacking difficult subjects!

I have several others as good, or for aught I know, better than the poems enclosed, but I lack the nerve to load any more upon you. [. . .]

I am glad that Mr. Markham liked the "Abyss" thing. The poem must be fearfully esoteric if he did not quite grasp the theme. It seems quite plain enough to me, but I have had others (people who read and understand most poetry) own up to being puzzled by it. I am astonished to find how few really grasp the sublimity and vastness of the stars and star-spaces. One acquaintance did not think such things suitable for poetic treatment, and from the indifference or bewilderment with which most who have seen it regard my cosmic work, I must regard those fitted to understand such things as being very rare.

Your younger-brother-poet,
Clark Ashton Smith.

1. "The Star-Treader" is the title poem of CAS's first book; in *SP* and *LO*. The title echoes Robert Browning's epitaph on Shelley in *Pauline* (1833): "Sun-treader, light and life be thine for ever" (l. 151), and CAS had first titled the poem "The Sun-Treader."
2. Published posthumously in *A Song from Hell* (Glendale, CA: Roy A. Squires, 1975).

[3]   To George Sterling [ALS, NYPL]   March 24, 1912

My dear Friend:

I've just received your letter, at the end of a day of tussling with inveterate boulders, and an even more stubborn ploughman, who has a prejudice against doing anything except in his own way. He likes to plough straight lines, and insisted on taking in a nest of half-ton cromlechs in one corner of the field. So they had to be removed from his lordly path. I'll have to write an "Ode to a Boulder" to get even. Really, though, it should be a good subject, when you think of the cosmic evolution that every stone of the earth must have passed through. The big black brute that persisted in rolling back into the hole every time I got a good leverage upon it, may at one time have formed part of the inmost core of some forgotten sun.

I am rather at a loss to understand the previous note you wrote to me. You said in that (at least so I understood) that Robertson[1] was to give you the proofs on my book in a week or so. But from your last letter it seems that it was only the poems in Ms.

I did not receive copies of the sonnets you speak of; but I hope you'll send them to me soon, if it's convenient. "The Muse of the Incommunicable"[2] sounds particularly good. That's the kind I have to wrestle with most of the time . . . I talk your poetry to every one I can get to listen to me, and am glad to say that I have made three converts, which is pretty good for Auburn. You'd appreciate my efforts if you knew the place. It's peopled with particularly impenetrable (and impenitent) Philistines, whose Goliaths are Bierce's "champions of offended dulness."[3] I'm to tackle a bunch of them, who form a debating-club, with a paper on "The Philosophy of Literary Criticism."[4] It will be rather a hot tamale for them, I expect, and there should be some good fun. This paper is about all that I have had time to write lately. I have any number of ideas for poems, but neither time nor strength to work them out.

I am extremely sorry to hear that you have written so little of late. Aren't you going to have a try at Mitchell Kennerly's *Lyric Year* Competition?[5] That $1000 sounds pretty good, particularly to me, who am as poor as a Scotch mouse. But of course I can't get even a smell at it. Was there ever a contest in which the prize was rightfully awarded? I am especially suspicious of this one. William Stanley Braithwaite, who is announced as one of the judges, writes critical eulogies on Richard G. Badger's publications, and a man who will do that is capable of anything.[6] I suppose a review by Braithwaite, in *Poet Lore,* is part of the contract Badger gives to his victims. I can always tell when one of my poems has appeared in the magazines, by the resultant letter from Badger, asking me to submit some of my work.

It's a devilish age for poets, this, with the sharks of publishers on one hand, the lions of critics on the other, and such part of the public as is not away at the nearest baseball park, sitting around trying to look Romanesque while they watch the battle. Don't think that I'm beginning to squeal, though. I'm going through with it now, and have no present intention of taking Nora May French's method of escape. By the way, can you tell me who publishes her poems, and also the title and price of the volume?[7] I intend to add it to my little collection of present-day poetry as soon as I can. Besides your books, I already have Alfred Noyes' *Drake* and a volume of Bliss Carman.[8] By the way, what do you think of *Drake?* It seems to me to be a great poem. Second to you and Markham. Noyes appears to me to be the foremost living poet who writes in English. Stephen Phillips hardly ranks with him.[9]

I'm enclosing a "Dedication" which you might add to my poems if you think it good enough.[10] That sort of thing is particularly hard to write: even Tennyson fell down on it. Mine has a certain merit—its briefness. [. . .]

Please forgive this slipshod, fag-end letter; and send me your sonnets. You don't know how much I'd appreciate them.

Most sincerely, as always
Clark A. Smith

1. A[lexander] M[itchell] Robertson (1855–1934), San Francisco bookseller; publisher of most of GS's poetry and publisher of *ST* (1912).

2. The other sonnet was "The Coming Singer." Both are in GS, *Beyond the Breakers and Other Poems* (1914); "The Coming Singer" also appears in *Thirty-five Sonnets* (1917) and *Sonnets to Craig* (1928).

3. AB, "An Insurrection of the Peasantry," *Cosmopolitan* 44, No. 2 (December 1907): "When the cause to be served is ignorance, the means of service is invariably misrepresentation. The champion of offended Dulness falsifies in statement and cheats in argument, for he serves a client without a conscience. A knowledge of right and wrong is not acquired today, as in the time of Adam and Eve, by eating an apple; and it is attained by only the highest intelligences" (p. 222). AB's essay is his celebrated defense of GS's "A Wine of Wizardry," which had been rejected by all the major magazines and was finally published in *Cosmopolitan* 43, No. 5 (September 1907): 551–56.

4. CAS refers to the Monday Night Club, a group that included several of his friends, including Dr. John Franklin Engle of the Placer Union

High School; the poet Harry Noyes Pratt; and Emily J. Hamilton, the teacher who introduced him to GS. CAS delivered his address on "The Philosophy of Literary Composition" on 25 March 1911, "a remarkably able production for a young writer" ("Amusements," *Placer Herald* [30 March 1912]: 5). Notes for CAS's address survive on the typescript of his poem "Copan" (JHL).

5. The *Boston Evening Transcript* conducted a competition offering a $500 first prize and two $250 second prizes (GS won one) and published the 100 best poems in the anthology *The Lyric Year: One Hundred Poems*, ed. Ferdinand Earle (1902). See letter 6, n.1.

6. William Stanley Braithwaite (1878–1962) was a noted African American critic and anthologist who served as literary editor of the *Boston Evening Transcript* and editor of the annual *Anthology of Magazine Verse* (1913–29). Richard G. Badger was a publisher in Boston, known for publishing the work of poetical novices.

7. Nora May French committed suicide in 1907 at the age of 26 (see also letter 20). Her *Poems* (San Francisco: The Strange Company, 1910) was published by George Sterling, Jack London, Harry Lafler, and Porter Garnett.

8. Alfred Noyes (1880–1958), *Drake, an English Epic: Books I–XII* (1906–08); Bliss Carman (1860–1929), American poet.

9. Stephen Phillips (1868–1915), British poet and dramatist.

10. Roy A. Squires notes that the poem "To George Sterling" (that beginning "High Priest of this our latter Song,") is "dated 1910 on the ms. A later ms. carries the word 'Dedication'. Concerning that the printer can proffer no guess which will not occur to the reader" (*To George Sterling* [Glendale, CA: Roy A. Squires, 1970], n.p.).

---

[4]   To George Sterling [ALS, NYPL]   Apr. 12th, 1912

My Dear Friend:

I must first thank you for your lovely sonnets. I blush to think that "The Coming Singer" is meant for me, for I have not the courage to hope that I may fulfil such a prophecy. Nothing could be more sublime than the ending of that sonnet[1] and I think it the better of the two, though the last lines of "The Muse of the Incommunicable" have been chanting themselves in my ears all day, to a ghostly music. You are one of the few masters of the sonnet.

I am extremely sorry that you think it necessary to withdraw the Dedication and the personal poems. But I understand the situation well enough, and have observed the temper and characteristics of the "many-headed beast." Only I had not expected that you would be required to act as my press-agent—and I don't like the idea any too well. But as you, in your friendship and kindliness, have offered to do so, I cannot be so ungrateful as not to accept it. The only way that I can repay the debt will be by living long enough to pass it on to someone else.

Of course, I understand how it is with Mr. Robertson—and I am not including him among the "sharks." But I have one remark to make on publishers in general: Their principal defense is that they must give the public what it wants—but are they not in many ways responsible for the taste of the public—are not they, in company with the periodicals, theaters, etc, largely the creators of the present depraved standards? If all were to band together to refuse the publication of the torrents of wish-wash—and worse—that are rotting the appreciation of anything *better* in so many minds— could they not educate their readers (and audiences) to something higher? Most people are neither better nor worse, mentally or any other way, than their environment—and literature and its counterparts are a potent part of environment. Perhaps, though, I am overestimating the latent capacities of the public, perhaps it's as imbecile as the publishers seem to think it is. If it is imbecility, it's a dangerous and violent form. But its present literary diet must be having some effect on the Beast, if only to impair its digestion. There is not a volume of Ambrose Bierce among the two thousand-odd in the local Carnegie Library—and I suppose Auburn is average enough in its tastes. I told a local debating-club that Bierce was the greatest living American of letters, and they were too much surprised, I suppose, to dispute me. Possibly they thought it safer to humor the lunatic! But what's the use? Demoralization has the stronghold, and you and I and a few other eccentrics to whom no one pays attention, are on the outside.

I do not care so much for "Drake" on re-reading it. The faults are all painfully evident, but still I think it notable work. I have not read much else of Noyes. I spoke of Phillips from a reading of three plays—*Nero, Ulysses,* and *Paolo and Francesca.*[2] I thought *Nero* much the best of the three. If Noyes is "playing to the gallery," it counts a great deal against him. I fear I speak of current poetry from too little knowledge. I have to depend too much on *Current Literature* and *The Literary Digest,* for I can't afford to buy much, and the books are most unobtainable here otherwise.

As you suggest, I shall transfer the Dedication of *The Star-Treader* to my parents. But my second book will certainly be dedicated to you—and I shall try to write a better poem to go with it.[3] Who is Mr. Ross?[4] He was in Auburn some time ago, and

introduced himself to me as a friend of yours and of Mr Robertson's. He talked mostly on political economy.

    In all sincerity and gratitude,
        Your friend,
            Clark Ashton Smith

1. "Behold! his feet shall take a heavenly way / Of choric silver and of
chanting fire, / Till in his hands unshapen planets gleam, / 'Mid murmurs
from the Lion and the Lyre."
2. *Nero* (1906); *Paolo and Francesca* (1900); and *Ulysses* (1902).
3. The volume was in fact dedicated only "To my mother." CAS dedicated his fourth book, *S* (1925), to GS.
4. Ross is unidentified, but GS had written: "Ross is a man whom I
once met at the Bohemian Club's midsummer 'Jinks,' up in Sonoma
County. I don't recall him; but some time ago I got a letter from him urging me to write Socialistic verse. I have been too busy to answer the letter,
and probably shall not. He's a 'well-meanin' cuss'" (GS to CAS, 21 April
1912; ms., NYPL).

---

[5]   To George Sterling [ALS, NYPL]   Apr. 28th, 1912.

My Dear Friend:
    Many thanks for your sonnets! Both are good, and I can't
criticize except to say that I like "Respite" a little the better of the
two.[1] If it isn't ungrateful of me to say it, I think that you would
better be writing poems of your own than reading and criticizing
my out-put. You are writing altogether too little. (This is putting it
mildly!)
    Your friend Ross was after me to write Socialistic verse, too;
but I can't see it. The chief trouble is that it wouldn't be anything
but verse—and to make it at all effect[ive] one would have to write
down to the straitest capacity of that economically-brained animal, the Mob. Edwin Markham is an example of what it leads
to—and there are others. I have a poet-friend on a San Francisco
newspaper who is going the downward path.[2] Besides, what's the
use, anyway? Even if one could advance the cause of socialism,
(which I theoretically believe in), the tides of things are so regu-
lated that everything would swing back afterwhile, and be all the
worse for the added momentum. The thing called civilization, as
the history of the past shows conclusively enough, is only a dog
chasing its own tail. As Bernard Shaw points out: There is an

accumulation of inventions and mechanical knowledge (the work of exceptional men, but not requiring exceptional men for their appliance) and this gives the illusion of progress—this, and the wave-like integrations of material wealth—, which by their own excess, tend to become disintegration. The history of nations is the same as that of worlds and individuals—birth, youth, maturity, age, and Death—or, more scientifically, integration and disintegration.

To get back to the starting-point, I don't see that I owe anything to the mob anyway. Bierce says that the present state of things is all the crowd's own fault; but I suppose one might go further back and lay the blame on the law of gravitation, which is as good a place to let it rest as any. In either case, I don't see that I'm "obligated" to attempt the amelioration of the muddle by the composing of Socialist rhymes. It won't matter so very much, anyway, whether I did or didn't, in the days when the world begins to bleach and shrivel, and the sun is blotched with death. Socialist and Individualist, they'll all be a little dirt lodged deep in the granite wrinkles of the globe's countenance.[3] (There's nothing like a cosmic perspective for cheering one up!)

I am doing a certain amount of work, but it doesn't seem to me that I am putting much inspiration into it. Most of my best work has been done in the months between May and September. I have finished a narrative poem entitled "Saturn," dealing with the fall of the Titans, which runs to about 250 lines. It's rather an experiment, and I don't feel very sanguine about it. I have also written a dramatic monologue, "Nero,"[4] which is even more of an experiment. It's the emperor's soliloquy after he has watched the burning of Rome. I suppose one has to do a lot of inferior work to pay for the privilege of writing something really good on occasion. I am trying another poem, "The Shadow of the Unattained," but it doesn't seem to take shape at all easily.[5] Sometimes I get clear lines like these—

"Fainter than winds that breathe
The folds of twilight's drapery."

and, again—

"Beauty, whose lyric laughters hold
A sadder music learned of old,
An echo from the halls of Death"—

but, on the whole, what I have done so far is rather unsatisfactory.

I entered the Kennerly contest, and got paid for my temerity. The editor told me that if I'd re-write the poem I sent in,[6] according to his notions (he was so kind as to send me a version of his own to work on!) he might use it. I spent the most of one perfectly good Sunday trying to re-write the poem without undue violence to my own conception of it, but I take it from what the editor said that I'll have to be one of the goats omitted from the Kennerly fold. Why is an editor? Perhaps like red motor-cars, church-bells, mosquitoes, and the saltatory flea, they are sent upon us as a judgement for our sins.

Most sincerely, your friend,
Clark Ashton Smith.

1. In *Beyond the Breakers and Other Poems* and also *Thirty-five Sonnets* (1917).
2. I.e., Ernest Jerome Hopkins (1887–1973), later known as a Bierce scholar.
3. In "Vulthoom," the extraterrestrial villain, after receiving a "temporary" 1,000-year setback at the hands of two Earthmen, taunts them with their own impermanence: "[Y]ou, who dared to interfere, will lie beside me then as a little dust . . . and the dust will be swept away" (*GL* 82).
4. CAS apparently read Stephen Phillips's play *Nero* (1906) only weeks previously. Both "Saturn" and "Nero" are in *ST, SP,* and *LO.*
5. Nonextant.
6. I.e., "Nero."

———————————•———————————

[6]   To George Sterling [ALS, NYPL]   May 26th, 1912.

My dear Friend:

I've just received your letter, and the clipping from the *Transcript.*[1] Your ode seems to me by all odds the best of the lot; the first two stanzas of it are particularly great, and all of it, indeed, is good. Markham's sonnet is good, too, but I don't care much for the others. I don't like to say that you have overinformed your subject; I like Browning, and think he is a great poet. But to me (perhaps I don't understand him well enough) it seems that he is not a poet of the very first rank, like Poe, Milton, and Keats. I measure a poet largely by his imaginative powers; and to me, "human interest" is not in the least essential. Most people who see my work complain that it lacks the human note; but that is something I have not tried to put in it. Perhaps imaginative insight into human life (like Browning's) is just as valuable as the more sidereal kind; but I don't see it that way. For that reason, there are stanzas in your "Testimony" that seem to me to outweigh in poetic value any whole poem that I have ever read of Browning's. However, my reading of him is rather limited, so I won't pass absolute judgement.

I am almost afraid to send you "Nero." About four-fifths of it is prose, and not particularly good prose at that. However, I'm sending it. I hope you're not expecting too much of it. It has psychological value, I suppose; pathological might be a better word. The human interest (if it has any of what is usually meant by that term) is sinister and abnormal. It has a few great lines (according to my taste) such as "The vampire Silence at the breast of worlds,"[2] but I am not at all hopeful about it.

I have been trying other poems; but the "Uncontrollable" (as someone has called it) does not seem to be on the job. Consequently, it's been slow and painful work for me to piece any thing together at all. It's unpleasant, to say the least, to *want* to write some thing with all your might, but not to be able to do it. The state is not unfamiliar to me, though; I don't think I've ever had more than three or four straight, clean attacks of inspiration. One of them was when I wrote the "Abyss Ode;" I did practically all of it at a sitting . . . My nerves, too, are giving me hell as usual; it's a sort of musical toothache.

I, also, have heard nothing from Mr. Robertson. I understood, a month or so ago, that he was to send me a contract soon; but nary a word. I suppose he'll dump the proofs on me without warning some day when the mercury is trying to climb out of sight.

You mention Neihardt.[3] I have seen some of his work, and it's certainly fine stuff. I hope he'll do some yet that's even better; I think he has the power.

I saw something of Shauffler's in *Current Literature* awhile ago.[4] I think it was a plea for the European immigrants—the "scum of the Earth," which is about what most of them are. I don't think he has a very good case. It's the low European, the anarchist and King-ridden, who is going to bring about America's downfall, and that at no very distant day, either. The criminally insane and viciously imbecile thing called American civilization can't stand many more of the breed. They're like rats gnawing at the foundations of a rotten barn. Well, let it go with the rest,—with these "tribes of slaves and Kings"[5] that have kept the world's dust astir for awhile. It won't affect the "cost of living" in the worlds around Antares and Canopus, I suppose—this collapse of a pseudo-republic, built mostly of paper, and mortared with ink. They won't even know about it in the other planets of *this* system, unless they have rather better telescopes than ours. It seems of importance here, though; I suppose that the social upheavals of the ant-hill are of importance to the ants, too. But all colors will look alike in the night of Death. In the meanwhile, the race goes merrily on. I think the motor-car should be the symbol of American civilization, with the motto, "speed, dust, noise, and stink." Joy-riding, if it's kept up long enough, and fast enough, generally has but one end.

I wish I could meet Bierce when he comes out; but I don't suppose it will be possible. Possibly he wouldn't care so much about meeting me.[6]

Well, I must close. May the muse attend you!

    Ever your friend,
      Clark Ashton Smith

1. "An Ode to the Centenary of the Birth of Robert Browning." *Boston Evening Transcript* 83, No. 107 (4 May 1912): Sec. 3, p. 3.

2. "Nero," l. 58.

3. John G[neisenau] Neihardt (1881–1973), Nebraska poet who later gained celebrity as the author of *Black Elk Speaks* (1932). At the time, he was corresponding with GS.

4. Robert Haven Schauffler (1879–1945), poet, music critic, and friend of GS. His poem "Scum o' the Earth" appeared in *Atlantic Monthly* (November 1911); rpt. *Current Literature* (January 1912).

5. Unidentified. But GS's "'Omnia Exeunt in Mysterium'" in *Beyond the Breakers and Other Poems* contains the lines: "Slaves, seamen, captains, councillors and kings, / Gone utterly, save for those echoes far!" (II.9–10).

6. AB visited California from June to October (he had been living in Washington, DC, since December 1899), arriving in Oakland 26 June, leaving to spend time in Lake Tahoe from 1–17 July, and returning again to Oakland. AB and CAS did not meet.

---

[7]   To George Sterling [ALS, NYPL]   Aug. 18th, 1912.

Dear George:

I haven't done much since my return here, except to read the surprising newspaper accounts of myself. Robertson's just sent me one from a Stockton paper, which describes me as being nine years old, and as having written poetry ever since I was eight. This advertising has had a good effect, though: Robertson tells me that he's going to get my book out about the middle of September, instead of in November, as he originally intended.[1]

Thank Mr. London for his kind invitation.[2] I sincerely hope that I'll be able to accept it; but I'm not sure that I can. [. . .]

I saw Bierce's letter in *Town Talk*.[3] The old boy treated me pretty well, under the circumstances. It must be maddening to be misquoted as he has been. I don't think he's the only sufferer, though. Schauffler was quoted in the San Francisco *Post* as saying that I was the greatest American poet to date;[4] but he never said anything of the sort to me.

We had a forest-fire near here the other day—just across the American River in El-Dorado Co. I went out and watched it from the canyon edge in the evening. It was something of a sight—a long line of flaming trees that seemed to move over the hills like the swaying torches of titans, and behind it a great burnt-over space blue with twilight and a low haze of smoke, through which scattered glowing fires made me think of your line about the "coals of Tartarus."[5] They were like the strange red cristallations of some imagined firmament.

Ever yours, affectionately,
Clark

1. The book did not in fact appear until November.

2. GS had conveyed Jack London's invitation for CAS to come to London's ranch at Glen Ellen, CA. CAS did not go.

3. A letter by AB appeared in the column "The Spectator" (*Town Talk*, 3 August 1912) praising CAS but protesting against extravagant comments on CAS placed in his mouth by journalists.

4. Sophie Treadwell (1890–1970), "Makers of Books and Some Recent Works," *San Francisco Post* (10 August 1912): 12, quotes Schauffler as calling CAS "the greatest poet ever produced in America."

5. GS, "A Wine of Wizardry," *A Wine of Wizardry* (1909), l. 29.

———————— • ————————

[8]   To George Sterling [ALS, NYPL]   Sept. 11th, 1912.

Dear George:

It's tremendously good of you to have corrected my proofs for me—rather more than I'd have had the nerve to ask you to do. I surmise that they were an awful job. To get even with me, you'll have to let me take a turn at the proofs of your next book.

It's queer that "Saturn" wasn't in the bunch. I sent a copy of it to Robertson several weeks ago, after receiving it back from the *Atlantic*. The editor said it was "an interesting poem."

The amount of work in my book descriptive of the death of suns and worlds, is, I confidently expect, the chief thing the critics are going to slam me for. I was surprised myself, the other day on going over a lot of copies of my stuff, to find how much work of that nature I really had written. Not that I at all regret the writing and publication of these poems. But I'm conscious that they'll lay me open to some unfavourable criticism. I'll get the reputation of being a sort of cosmic decadent—a sidereal Baudelaire.

To my imagination, no other natural event seems half as portentous as the going out of a sun. I admit that I have been, and still am, obsessed by visions of stupendous dooms—of blotching suns and whitening worlds hushed and slow in the black night of space. But I agree with you that I'd best quit writing about such things, at least for awhile. I think I shall make a few ventures into the realms of wonder and terror; also, of course, I shall write some nature-verse. [. . .]

Affectionately,
Clark

───────────── ◆ ─────────────

[9]   To George Sterling [ALS, NYPL]   Sept. 26th, 1912.

Dear George:

I've gone over the proofs of "Saturn," and have returned them to Robertson, with a few changes. For the last line, to which you objected, read: "Against their march, with the diminished stars."

The weather here has been uncomfortably warm for the last few weeks, though the housefly, in his swift and musical multitude, doesn't seem to mind it at all. My inspiration seems rather sodden under the influence of the weather, and the cold that's been hanging to me ever since I returned here from San Francisco. The latter has sapped my vitality a bit, I suspect.

I sent a bunch of poems to the new poetry magazine, and have just received a letter from the editor saying that she intends to accept several of them.[1] That's one rift in the grey, at least. Also, the Board of Education here has decided to put my book in the libraries of all the schools of the county. Doesn't that appeal to your funny-bone? I'm not altogether without honour here, other-wise: one of the local citizens was heard to admit lately that I might be able to write if I had a good education . . . They can't get over the fact here that I never attended High School.

I feel tempted to do a little road-agenting myself. The Sacra-mento motor-cars that I have to pass every day, make me feel like a red anarchist; and the blatant optimism of the Bromide is an unctuous and unremitted offense to my nostrils.

I wish there were a hell for magazine-editors and their public, in which, for a few hundred thousand years, they could be made to see themselves as you and I see them.

I'm enclosing a couple of new poems, the best of the few that I've written lately.

    Lovingly,
    Clark.

1. *Poetry,* a Chicago-based magazine edited by Harriet Monroe (1860–1936), published a few poems by CAS and GS, but the magazine was devoted chiefly to the avant-garde and was a major forum for the Modernist poets of the 1920s.

---

[10]   To George Sterling [ALS, NYPL]   Nov. 13th, 1912.

Dear George:

I've just received several copies of *The Star-Treader* from Robertson, and am sending you one of them. It's a relief to have the book out at last, for I've had it hanging over my head ever since September, the first date that Robertson set for bringing it out.

The poems read rather better to me in book-form. The binding is surprisingly good—much more beautiful than I really expected it to be. I found only one error persisting in the text—"contrained" for "constrained" in "To the Sun."[1]

Thanks for your good sonnet. It is good—but not very, very good.

Your remarks on "The Titans in Tartarus"[2] are entirely just. The thing is decidedly inferior to "Saturn." However, I believe I shall do some better work presently.

I wish you *would* drop in on me, before January. Really, why can't you? I'd like to have you here for Christmas. Believe me, my father can make an English plum-pudding that's worth while.

I got up at half-past six this morning, and saw a good sunrise over the Sierras—a long rose-red sky above a hundred odd miles of indigo mountains. It looked like the Judgement Day climbing over the outermost rim of things. I wish you could have seen it.

Now that I'm laid open to the critics forevermore, I wonder how many of them will damn *The Star-Treader*. It might be interesting to know—to a crank on statistics . . . I shall watch the poetry columns of *Current Literature* with a rapt interest, though, to see if the editor says what I'm quite sure that he will say. I'll bet you a bone collar-button that he'll quote "Averted Malefice" and "The Medusa of the Skies,"[3] and let the book go at that.

> Affectionately,
> Clark.

1. Line 13; the word is correct in *SP*.
2. Published posthumously in *The Titans in Tartarus* (Glendale, CA: Roy A. Squires, 1974).
3. CAS refers to "Recent Poetry," *Current Literature* 53, No. 10 (October 1912): 472. The column quotes "The Abyss Triumphant" (from *Town Talk*) and "Nero" (in part, from the *San Francisco Call*), and does not acknowledge the impending publication of *ST*.

---

[11]   To Herbert Bashford[1]   Jan. 15th, 1913

Herbert Bashford, Esq.

Dear Sir:

I wish to thank you for your appreciative review of my book in the *Bulletin*. I was delighted—surprised—at such praise and appreciation, after the stupid or narrow-minded criticisms which I had previously seen in the periodicals of the Coast. In publishing my work, I had little expectation of immediate praise, or of much save misunderstanding and severe criticism: this from the essentially unpopular nature of most of my poems, of which I am, of course, fully aware. Poetry, particularly work like mine, which is so far removed from the everyday interest of the immense bulk of mankind, stands in little danger of being overestimated in these days. Therefore I am so much the more grateful for your appreciation, and desirous of thanking you for it.

> I remain,
> Yours, most sincerely
> CLARK ASHTON SMITH

1. Herbert Bashford (1871–1928), newspaper critic, surprised GS by reviewing *ST* favorably ("Clark Smith's Poems. Wonderful Lyrics Deserve

Recognition with World's Best," *San Francisco Bulletin* (30 November 1912): 14.

[12]   To George Sterling [ALS, NYPL]   Feb. 3rd, 1913

Dear George:

I like "The Thirst of Satan" best of the three poems that you enclose. It's a strong sonnet. And I like the thought of "Scrutiny" . . .[1] You're right enough, I suppose, about the things I sent you; there isn't much thought-content in them.

Thanks for the *Times* review.[2] It isn't so bad, except for the generally flippant tone and the execrable English. How can a poet be a "note in a symphony of arts"? A poet isn't an *art*. And is the phrase "caressing hills" a bit of the Celtic mysticism recommended to my study? The phrase is mystic enough, I'll confess. I'd like to find a way to put a crimp in the self-satisfaction of such critics. But there isn't any way. And the English language has few champions these days to protect her.

I've just read *The Land of Heart's Desire*, by W. B. Yeats. I've heard it praised highly; but I can find little in it. I rather prefer Anna Branch's *Rose of the Wind*, which is similar to the Yeats poem.[3]

I've also been reading *The City of Dreadful Night*, by James Thomson.[4] It's a tremendous thing in its way, and rather different from anything else that I've read. The thing is about the last word in the literature of despair and pessimism.

Who wrote a book called *The Ape, the Idiot, and Other People?*[5] Someone who wrote to me mentioned it among several books which she thought had influenced my work. The title sounds like Bierce; but I've never heard of the book before.

Current Literature has just noticed my book, quoting two poems from it.[6] I suppose you've seen it, too. I think there are forty or fifty better things in the book that they might have quoted from.

I'd like to have been there when you caught that octopus!

Affectionately, Clark.

1. Both in *Beyond the Breakers and Other Poems*.
2. [Shamus O'Sheel (1886–1954)]. "A Young Poet. He has Quality, but Also the Faults of Youth," *New York Times Review of Books* (26 January 1913): 38.
3. William Butler Yeats (1865–1939), *The Land of Heart's Desire* (1903), a verse drama; Anna Branch (1875–1937), *Rose of the Wind and Other Poems* (1910).
4. James Thomson ("B. V.") (1832–1882), *The City of Dreadful Night and Other Poems* (1886).

5. W. C. Morrow (1853–1923), *The Ape, the Idiot and Other People* (1897). Morrow was a fellow journalist and friend of AB.

6. "Recent Poetry," *Current Opinion* [formerly *Current Literature*], 54, No. 2 (February 1913): 150. The review compares the work of two new poets, CAS's *ST* (quoting "Cloud Islands" and "Retrospect and Forecast") and *Renascence* by Edna St. Vincent Millay (1892–1950). The reviewer's rhetorical question is telling: "But where is the critic keen enough to calculate the flight of imagination and tell us just where in the heavens these two youthful prodigies will be shining a dozen years hence?"

---

[13]   To George Sterling [ALS, NYPL]   May 11th, 1913

Dear George:

It doesn't seem likely, at present, that I can come to Carmel, in July. I've too much on my hands, for one thing—plans for a score or so of poems which I'd like to at least draft out before I forget them. And the early summer is my best time for work. I'd rather come down in the fall, anyway, if it's all the same to you. It'll be quieter then. Your saying that Carmel will be livelier this summer, is no inducement to *me:* You know I don't care much about meeting people. [. . .]

I don't suppose you'd care for the few things I've written lately. Here are some of the titles: "The Medusa of Despair," "Gothic Nightmare," and "The Doom of America."[1] The last is a sort of Bible prophecy, in about fifty verses. I don't suppose it's poetry. It's a sort of round-up of all my grudges and kicks against the present age. I even took a swat at the suffragettes. I'm glad it's out of my system.

I've some prose-poems planned; the idea of one of them is about as perfect a nightmare as I ever got hold of: it's to be a description of the carnivorous, half-animal plant and tree-life of an imaginary world—huge jungles of rooted serpents and vampire orchids, and things, monstrously luxuriant in the ghastly and exuberant light of some vast green sun. There's no reason why there shouldn't be such things, in the worlds of other systems; but think of being caught in the octopus-like tentacles of some enormous plant—and slowly absorbed by its innumerable leech-like mouths! I shall call the thing "The Forest of Strange Horror."[2]

Just before receiving your letter, I returned the French translations which you lent me, to Carmel. I suppose you'll get them all right, tho.

> Yours, affectionately,
> Clark.

1. "The Medusa of Despair" (*OS, EC, SP,* and *LO*); "Gothic Nightmare" (i.e., "Nightmare"; *EC, SP,* and *LO*); "The Doom of America" (unpublished).
2. CAS produced a prose poem ("The Flower-Devil," *EC* and *PP*), a poem ("The Hashish-Eater," *EC, SP,* and *LO*), and a short story ("The Demon of the Flower," *LW*) that each use this setting and imagery.

---

[14]   To George Sterling [ALS, NYPL]   July 1st, 1913

Dear George:

I think I've delayed sufficiently in answering your last letter. But you needn't worry about owing me letters: I'm never offended by that, for I know you've much less time for correspondence than I have.

I like your "Past the Breakers," tho I don't think you're so successful with the three-syllable meters as with the iambic. I'm even less so— That's an especially fine line, "The hissing ridges ran like dragons driven by gods—"[1]

I'm surprised by your judgement on "The Medusa of Despair." I hadn't thought so much of it myself. Personally, I'm getting a wee bit sick of the introspective element which so dominates modern literature. So many present-day writers are like the diseased beggars at the gates of Eastern cities, exposing their sores to public pity and benevolence. There's a frightful lack of dignity and reticence, so that the public seems even to resent these qualities when it does find them. That's one reason why people accuse my work of wanting "human interest," I suppose. Another reason is that I've no soothing-syrup for 'em.

I've a new poem or two, but shan't send them now. "The Witch in the Graveyard" is the title of one.[2] 'Tis a sweet subject, as I'm sure you'll agree.

Miss Monroe of *Poetry* has just returned a bunch of my late things with a gentle intimation that she doesn't think much of 'em. What do you think of that editor and that magazine, by the way? *Poetry* seems to be getting badder and badder, what with the Whitmanesque "Hasidu" in the last number.

I received five dollars for "The Nereid," from *The Yale Review* the other day.³ The editor spoke of the check as a "modest honorarium(!)"

I agree with you as to the desirability of the changes which you suggest, in the "Medusa" and the other poems. But I've no suitable alternatives at present.

      Affectionately yours,
        Clark.

    1. In *Beyond the Breakers and Other Poems.*
    2. GS had written of this "great" poem (in *EC, SP,* and *LO*) that it was "a truly terrible poem" and "clearer than most of your sonnets, and ends wonderfully" (GS to CAS, June 22, 1913). In the same letter, GS announced that "Personally I've quit what Sheffauer called 'marching under Ambrose's black banner of despair,' and think America is getting more intelligent and decent yearly, though I've neither leisure nor inclination to discuss the matter with pen and ink."
    3. "The Nereid," *Yale Review* (July 1913); in *EC, SP,* and *LO.*

---

[15]   To George Sterling [ALS, NYPL]   Jan. 27th, 1914.

Dear George:

I hope you'll be able to arrange the "stop-over." I must see you soon; and I fear there's little likelihood of my being able to meet you in San Francisco.

I've no news worth mentioning. I continue, I am sorry to say, in my usual frame of mind—dispirited, and a prey to the most abject doubt and self-distrust. I am unable to write a line; peace of mind is one of the prime necessities in poetic composition; and mine is a divided kingdom. [. . .]

The thirteenth of the month was my twenty-first birth-day. I was born on a Friday, too, by the way, and under the influence of the planet Saturn. A rather ominous combination, don't you think?

      Affectionately as ever,
        Clark.

[16]   To George Sterling [ALS, NYPL]
                              Manzanita Springs,
                              Weimar, Cal.
                              July 27th, 1914.

Dear George:
     I'm staying for a few days with some English friends of mine,
on their ranch twelve miles or so above Auburn. The country is
quite different here, considering the smallness of the distance, and
the temperature is a few degrees cooler. The scenery is much
wilder, and is full of ravines which are deep and steep enough to
be called canyons. I'm told that there are rattlesnakes in the vicinity. But I've neither seen nor heard one during the five days that
I've spent in scrambling up and down the manzanita-covered hills
roundabout. And the genus homo is well nigh as scarce as the rattlesnakes.
     You're quite right about the resemblance of the first line of my
poem to the one in the *Rubaiyat:*—"Before the phantom of false
morning died," which begins the second quatrain of that poem.[1]
It's strange that I'd not noticed the reminiscence before. I've not
thought of a new line, so far. [. . .]
     I've done very little, myself, and marvel at your industry. My
health is to blame, I suppose: I can't digest anything, it would
seem, and have been suffering from the curse of constipation to
boot.
     I shall enclose a prose-poem that I have with me, if it seems
good enough on re-reading. My faculties are too relaxed for composition in verse.
     I wish you could see this place. The scenery is not unlike some
of the Carmel country, tho steeper, on the whole. There's rather a
variety of conifers—the sugar pine, the spruce, the cedar, the yellow pine, and a sort of fir whose name I forget, besides the common grey and green pines. The golden-rod is beginning to appear,
and there are a few other flowers. I found some columbines in the
canyon the other day—a flower that I've never seen before. The
only objectionable thing is the omnipresent tar-weed: one's shoes
become fairly coated with the tar from walking thro whole fields
of it.
     Don't address me here when you write:—I shall probably
return to Auburn before the middle of the present week.
                         Affectionately,
                              Clark.

1. Cf. "A Phantasy of Twilight": "Ere yet the soaring after-fire was flown"; in *The Potion of Dreams* (Glendale, CA: Roy A. Squires, 1975); other mss. have "Ere yet was Day's immense red phantom flown," and "Ere the red phantom of the day was flown."

———— • ————

[17]   To George Sterling [ALS, NYPL]   Oct. 16, 1914.

Dear George:

[. . .] I've just received a letter from Robertson,—the first I've had from him for over a year—enclosing a fifty-dollar check to cover the first royalties on *The Star-Treader*. I'm very much surprised that the book has done so well. Robertson doesn't say how many copies have sold, but the number must be close to nine hundred, since I was to receive no royalty at all on the first five hundred.

I'm glad to get this money, since I'll at last be able to repay the ten dollars which I owe you. I shall enclose a postal money-order with this letter.

The sonnet ("Bombardment")[1] which you send, is good, tho I'd rather see you use another word than the clichè, "screaming." Why not "hurling," which can be used intransitively? There's enough about sound-effect in the preceding line, it seems to me.

I've little to send you in return, I fear, except the fragment of an "Ode to Beauty," which I've not had the strength to complete.[2] I may try to finish it some day, if you think it worth while.

My father and I are sinking a shaft on our land at present—ostensibly for water. But I hope to hell there'll be more at the bottom of it than that. Poverty grows monotonous after a time; and for me, it would seem, the only way out leads thro a gold-mine. We may strike "bedrock" before so very long.[3]

Did you ever use a quill-pen? I'm writing this letter with one—the wing-feather of a hawk. It moves more easily and lightly than a steel pen—

          Affectionately,
               Clark.

1. In GS's *The Caged Eagle and Other Poems* (1916).
2. In *SP* as "To Beauty (a Fragment)."
3. In April 1961, CAS was compelled under court order to fill the shaft, an event of great sadness for him (see letter 274).

[18]   To George Sterling [ALS, NYPL]   March 11th, 1915

Dear George:

I hope you'll be able to stop over and visit me for a few days on your return. You'll come in the height of the season here, when the flowers are all out, and the months of long sunlight are assured. I want to see you, and have a long, long, leisurely talk with you—something that I seem never to have had. [. . .]

Your comments on "The Psalm to the Desert"[1] are quite just. Still, why shouldn't the thing be written? It's quite true, and even original, since no one ever wrote anything really like it on the subject before, to my knowledge—Why shouldn't the Abyss be the dominant theme of my work? Other poets have made their main work a series of expatiations on some central subject, and no one has risen up to rebuke them for monotony or self-repetition. Poe really had but one theme—the death of a beautiful woman. And how about Rossetti and Swinburne, whose work deals mainly with passion, and sexual passion at that? However, it may be well to vary the images and symbols a bit, and I shall write less about the gulf for awhile. I've plenty of other themes, tho the ideas of change and death and evanescence will continue to be the ground-tones of my work. I shall write other things, tho—a "Psalm to the Sea" considered as the source and reservoir of all planetary life, and a few poems illustrative of certain of the less-handled Greek myths, such as that of the god Somnus . . . I think of doing a "Psalm to the Moth and the Worm," as the ministers of time and change, who liberate the atoms in decaying bodies, and deliver them over to the processes of new life. I shall tell of how these atoms dance and sing, and weave strange harmonies from dissolution—of how they jubilate in their freedom from the broken bonds of form—

Here are a few alterations for "The Psalm to the Desert," which I sent to you in a rather crude state: For the sixth verse read: "Thy breasts are fallen from roundure, they are flat and rivelled: marah is all the milk thereof." In the eleventh, "terrible sighing of voidness." In the thirteenth, "a ban is proclaimed." And for the 15th "Thy womb shall conceive but of death, the teeming thereof shall be dissolution, and the seed of corruption." You'll note that these changes simplify the grammar and help to explicate the sense.

I enclose a few short poems—nothing very good, I'm afraid. My main conceptions seem to hang in the air as yet.

I've been corresponding a good deal with Loveman[2] of late.

He's an odd genius—which I mean in the most complimentary sense,—and seems to have an inexhaustible supply of books (he sends me something with nearly every letter) and a treasury of praise to lavish on the few trifling poems that I give him in return—

>Affectionately, as ever,
>Clark

1. Published posthumously in *Klarkash-Ton and Monstro Ligriv* (Saddle River, NJ: Gerry de la Ree, 1974).

2. Samuel Loveman (1887–1976), poet and friend of GS, AB, Hart Crane, and HPL. CAS dedicated *EC* to him. Loveman introduced HPL to the work of CAS, and it was through Loveman that HPL began corresponding with him.

---

[19]   To George Sterling [ALS, NYPL]   Apr. 23rd, 1915.

Dear George:

I'm sorry that you can't stop over on your return. The country won't be nearly so inviting a month or so from now, because of the drying-up of the grass, which usually begins to "turn" early in May. However, I'll be hellishly glad to see you, anyway.

I've little enough that's worth recording. I have just answered a letter from Loveman, who speaks of being a bit "under the weather." I've had a touch of Spring fever myself, but have managed to write a few things—three or four prose-poems, and a few indifferent verses. I'll not bother to send them now—you can read them all when you're here, and I'll have more and perhaps better things to show you by that time. I seem to do most of my writing in the months between May and September.

The flowers are past their prime now, tho the Mariposa lilies are still to come—also the leopard lilies. I wish you could be here in time to see them. They're a gorgeous, barbaric blossom.

I've sold nothing at all to the magazines, and gave my "Harlot of the Generations" to *Town Talk*.[1] It was "impossible," I suppose, for any of the respectable eastern publications. I'll probably have to write some stories before long—it seems imperative that I should make a little money in some way or another. Damn the planet, anyway—it's fit only for the habitation of hogs, who enjoy rooting.

I've no intention of playing a "harp of one string." There'll not be nearly so much of the spacial element in my second book as in the other. Most of the things I plan are in the vein of the gorgeous or the ghastly,—anything but the ordinary, conventional type of nature-verse, for which I've come to realize that I don't care a whoop. But no more about that—we'll have time enough for literary argument when you're here.

Have you heard anything about Bierce? I've seen stories in the papers both affirming and denying his re-appearance. Loveman, who met him just before his departure for Mexico, seems to think that he may have disappeared merely for purposes of mystification.[2]

Affectionately,
Clark

1. "The Harlot of the World" (*Town Talk*, 27 March 1915; in *OS, EC,* and *SP*).
2. AB had disappeared late in 1913. Loveman corresponded with AB but never met him.

———— ♦ ————

[20]   To George Sterling [ALS, NYPL]   Aug. 16, 1915

Dear George:

It's good to write you a letter after so long. As usual, I've delayed thro lack of subject-matter, and, it would seem, might delay till doomsday for the same reason. Also, I've nothing to send you, except some prose-poems, and I've no extra copies of these, since my typewriter is temporarily out of order—However, you won't miss much.

I'm addressing you at Jack London's, since I presume you've reached there by this time. I fear it's impossible for me to join you, for I'm poorer than a Scotch mouse, and, even if I weren't, could scarcely find the time.

I'm glad you liked the sonnets. I plan to write some more presently, in a similar vein.

Here are some of my attempts at drawing. I hope they don't bore you. I like to draw, but really know very little about the art, and, I fear, have no very conspicuous talent for it. I've drawn a number of things in the vein of the weird and the grotesque, and will make copies of a few of them for you presently. There's one of a ghoul that you'd probably like—everyone thinks it too horrible to have around. "The Lich," "The Red Death," "The Vampire," "Abaddon," "The Abyss"—these are a few other titles.

Things have been even duller than usual this summer. I've not visited the local town in weeks, and have been too indolent to shave. Can you fancy me with the beginnings of a beard ala Swinburne?

You ask if I've ever written anything on Nora May French.[1] I'd like to, but I fear I've no talent for personal or memorial verse. I've long intended to write an ode in honour of Poe, but have done nothing with it.

Please return good for evil, and write to me before so very long. Here are the drawings, among them a silhouette of yourself that I've drawn from memory. It may interest you.

> As ever,
>   affectionately,
>   Clark.

1. CAS eventually did write "To Nora May French" (*EC, SP,* and *LO*).

---

[21]   Albert M. Bender[1] [ALS, MCL]   Nov. 6th, 1915.

My dear Mr. Bender:

You make it impossible for me to refuse your kind offer.[2] To do so would be ungracious. I shall be happy to accept the invitation proffered by yourself and your friend, if only for a few days. It will, I fear, be impossible for me to devote a full week, or ten days, to seeing the Exposition.

I expect to be in San Francisco by next Friday or Saturday— I am not sure of the precise date, and shall call upon you at my first opportunity.

> With sincere thanks, and kindest regards, I am,
>   Cordially yours,
>   Clark Ashton Smith.

1. Albert Maurice Bender (1866–1941), San Francisco businessman, patron of the arts, benefactor and friend of GS and CAS. CAS dedicated "Memnon at Midnight" to him.
2. Bender had invited CAS as his guest to attend the Panama-Pacific International Exposition in San Francisco. See "A Poet Sees the Fair," *Town Talk: The Pacific Weekly,* 26, No. 1213 (November 20, 1915): 11.

[22]   To Albert M. Bender [ALS, MCL]   Feb. 9th, 1916.

My dear Albert

[. . .] My health is better than it has been on the whole, tho I'm by no means rid of my nervousness. My ill-health has been more a matter of the mind than the body, I think. The change in my handwriting of which you speak, is due to the fact that I've been learning to write with the wrist-movement, which, of course, makes for a more free and even hand. [. . .]

I sincerely hope that the "pensiveness" expressed in some of my poems, is not a matter of personal grievance, but merely the outcome of deliberate philosophical speculation. My physical health, good or bad, would hardly affect that.

    With regards to you and to Miss Bremer,[1] believe me,

      Most sincerely, your friend,

        Clark Ashton Smith

1. Anne M. Bremer (1868–1923) was Bender's cousin. A talented artist, she won a bronze medal at the 1915 Panama-Pacific Exposition. Her portrait of CAS appears on the inside front cover of CAS's *Grotesques and Fantastiques* (Saddle River, NJ: Gerry de la Ree, 1973).

[23]   To George Sterling [ALS, NYPL]   April 5th, 1916

Dear George:

I seem to have left your last letter unanswered for even longer than my usual period of procrastination. It isn't often that the calendar steals such a March on me!

However, you haven't missed much through my writing. There's little or nothing for me to put on paper, excepting trivialities.

I've done a little gardening lately,—we're going to have a few pears, and strawberries, and other vegetables. I wish you could be here to eat some of them, in a month or so. Can't you remind Dr. Abrams[1] of his plan for motoring up to Auburn with you in the Spring?

I'm eager to see your new book.[2] By the way, I wish you would find out from Robertson when he will be ready to publish my next volume. I'd like it to come out in the autumn, if possible. I've not found a title for it as yet. I'd like something that would denote the mixed nature of the collection, if possible. *Ivy-Leaf and Orchid-Flower* might do, if floral titles weren't so common. I'd rather not use a title-poem, unless I have to.[3]

I've had a few malarial symptoms lately, and haven't felt at all well—This eternal state of semi-sickness is a dreadful bore to me. I wish I could either die or get well—anything for a change.

Tell Stella[4] that I wish she had kissed me a few more times! Kisses don't seem to come my way in Auburn.

Affectionately,
Clark.

1. Dr. Albert Abrams (1863–1924), a quack doctor in San Francisco, inventor of "radionics." He later did examine CAS.

2. GS, *The Caged Eagle* (1916).

3. CAS considered various titles, but ultimately settled on *Ebony and Crystal*, which he published at his own expense in 1922 after numerous rejections by major publishers. See letters 46, 47, 50, and 52.

4. Estelle Tuttle was a dancer with whom GS had a long-term relationship after his divorce.

———————◆———————

[24]   To George Sterling [ALS, NYPL]   June 15th, 1916.

Dear George:

As usual, I find it necessary to preface my letter with an apology for not having written before. You aren't the only one who has reason to complain, tho—my other correspondents don't fare any better, indeed, most of them fare worse. Considering the limited amount of my correspondence, I ought to hold the record for dilatoriness.

I've been expecting, from day to day, to hear that your book was out. But I've seen nothing so far. Robertson's procrastination seems to be constitutional.

I wish my next volume were off my mind—and off my nerves. I dread the ordeal of proof reading. *Poppy and Cypress,* which you suggest, seems a much better title than the other.

I enclose a few things—nearly all that I have written of late. When one writes without caring to write, the result is not likely to be very good. I seem to have developed a deadly indifference toward my work, partly through my inability to please myself, but more, through my increasing personal unhappiness. Misery is not a stimulant to me, as it is to some. With me, it has more the effect of a narcotic, of a deadly drug.

Some of the poems enclosed may interest you, since they are more personal than most of my work. Personal expression seems peculiarly difficult for me. I would prefer to write such things, if I could only do them well enough. . . . Love and death are the only things worth writing about.

Give my affectionate regards to Bender, and assure him that I'm not such a scoundrel as I seem. I'll write to him very soon.

Affectionately,
Clark

---

[25]   To George Sterling [ALS, NYPL]   Oct. 11th, 1916.

Dear George:

I'm ashamed to find that I've had your last letter lying by me unanswered for a whole month. I always have to preface my letters with an apology—so here's another one. But I'll try to do better next time.

There are beautiful lines and images in the poem that you enclose. The conception is very similar to that of something I had once planned to write. I've not much to send in return, excepting the draught of a companion poem for "Coldness." I've burnt most of my late work, and might do just as well to burn the rest. I write more to distract my thoughts than for any other purpose, and hardly care whether the result is good or bad. The intense technical preoccupation keeps me from thinking about things that I don't want to remember.

My mother is recovering very slowly, and may not be able to get around much for another month. My father is better, tho. We haven't been able to do much with our mine this year, and it will soon be too late, since the first heavy rain will fill the shaft with water.

My physical condition is better, temporarily at least. Abrams may have been right about my lungs—I've had more than one symptom suggestive of it.[1] However, the sort of life I lead is an ideal one for lung trouble, so any tendency of the sort isn't likely to develop much.

My best friend here is very ill. She seems to have developed an attack of brain fever in addition to the consumption from which she has suffered for years. I don't know whether she will live or not. If she dies, I think I will go mad with grief and a guilty conscience.[2]

This isn't a very cheerful sort of letter, so I'll have to beg you to carry my troubles lightly. My life seems to be turning into a story of the sort that Poe might have written. I'm sure that some of the situations in it would have given him a gruesome delight.

Write before long, won't you? My love to you and Stella.

Affectionately,
Clark.

1. Abrams had diagnosed CAS as having tuberculosis.
2. See CAS to GS (26 July 1917; ms., NYPL): "I've not been able to write—every thing seems frozen at the source with me—a matter of a broken heart that doesn't mend. Why should a hopeless and impossible passion have power to disorganize and disrupt one's entire existence?" Carol Jones (Dorman) Smith's uncompleted memoir of CAS states that "he lavished his love upon his first, hopelessly ill beloved, who died of consumption before she was thirty[. . . .] And always, after the first tragedy of love for the beautiful blonde separated from her husband, [CAS] chose brunnettes for his deepest loves" (ms., JHL). Several poems seem to memorialize this loss: "Brumal" (*AJ*, 1 November 1923), a brief untitled item (in Steve Behrends, "Song of the Necromancer: 'Loss' in Clark Ashton Smith's Fiction," *Studies in Weird Fiction*, 1 [Summer 1986]: 5), and the unpublished "For Iris." CAS's poem "Requiescat in Pace" [c. April 1918], dedicated to one "M. L. M." in *SP*, could be about the woman in question.

---

[26]   To Samuel Loveman [ALS, JHL]   Oct. 24th, 1916.

Dear Sam:

Your card, and the volume of Flecker's poems[1] are both at hand, but no letter, as yet. I've delayed writing because I expected one from day to day, but I'm ashamed to put it off any longer.

I enjoyed the volume of poems greatly—many of Flecker's things are very much to my taste, tho some are perhaps too colloquial, and others somewhat obscure. I particularly like "Felo de Se," "Mary Magdalen," "Mignon," "Tenebris Interlucentem," "Gravis Dulcis Immutabilis," and the translations from Baudelaire—also certain parts of the "Town Without a Market," the poems on Helen of Troy and the fascinating (tho not perfectly intelligible) sonnets of Bathrolaire. My sincerest thanks to you for the volume. By the way, there's an interesting article on Flecker in a late (I think the October) number of the *Bookman*. This article quotes from a later volume, entitled *The Golden Journey to Samarkand, and Other Poems*. Some of the quotations are very fine.

I've written nothing new since the last poems I sent you. Everything seems to hang fire with me. I've not sold anything lately—my one recent sale seems to have been pure accident—"the exception that proves the rule." I hope things are better with you.

Have just been reading the *Journal of Marie Bashkirtseff*[2] for the first time. Are you familiar with the book? It saddens, fascinates me, stirs my sympathy, tho certain portions are tedious or trivial, as they could hardly help being, in a transcript from life.

Good luck to you! I'll try to send you something in the way of poetry, or at least prose, before long.

   Affectionately,
   Clark

1. Presumably *The Collected Poems of James Elroy Flecker*, ed. J. C. Squire (1916). Flecker (1884–1915) was a British poet and playwright. The other volume referred to is *The Golden Journey to Samarkand* (1913).

2. *Journal of Marie Bashkirtseff*, trans. from the French by A. D. Hall (1908; 2 vols.), the first intimate diary of young womanhood ever published, was the diary of French-Russian girl who lived in Paris in the mid-1800s. It caused a publishing sensation in Europe and America when it was published shortly after its discovery.

---

[27] To Albert M. Bender [ALS, MCL]   Jan. 19th, 1917.

Dear Albert:

[. . .] It's quite out of the question for me to come to the city again at present. Besides, I don't see the necessity—I'm not sick enough to go to a hospital, and won't be for a long time, even if my disease progresses—which it probably won't. Consumption is one of the commonest of infections, and many people recover from it without knowing that they've had the disease.

To-day (the 19th) is Edgar Allan Poe's birthday. The 13th was mine. I celebrated with a lemon pie!

   Ever your friend,
   Clark.

[28]   To George Sterling [ALS, NYPL]   Feb. 28th, 1917

Dear George:

I've had your letter lying by me for several days, hesitating as to how I could answer you. I'm sorry, but the sanitarium idea is as repugnant to me as ever. Besides, the expense would be so unnecessary; my health is already much improved, and people tell me that they never saw me looking so well. My real problem at present is the financial one—and a few months in the hospital wouldn't solve that. The mortgage on our place (a matter of seven hundred dollars, including unpaid interest), is due, and if not paid or transferred very soon, will necessitate our selling out to meet the debt. Possibly, tho, my people may be able to obtain a loan from someone in Auburn. Otherwise, we will certainly have to sell out.

I wish I could have a talk with you—also with the lady of whom you speak.[1] I fear that I haven't explained matters fully enough to you before. A loan of $1500 or better still, $2000, to pay off the mortgage and give us a little capital to "go on," is about all that would really help me. I can take care of my health— my getting so run down at times has been partly my own fault, and partly a matter of too much emotional and nervous tension. You are mistaken, too, in thinking that I would be happier at the sanitarium. I would fret and chafe all the time, balk at most of the rules, and be considered a cantankerous nuisance—Dr. Abrams, if you will remember, told me that I would probably not do well in a sanitarium.

Please believe that I am deeply gratified to you for all the trouble you have taken—also to the kind lady who has offered to help me. You make it so embarrassing, so difficult for me to refuse, as I feel that I *must* do.

Am I to return the check? I'm holding it till I hear from you again, since I can't use it for the purpose for which it was sent.

I wish you were here. The Spring has been coming on by leaps and bounds, these last few days. The almonds and plums are already beginning to blossom. I feel as if I could write a little now—I've hardly tried for a long time.

    Affectionately,
        Clark.

P.S. I'm sending you a copy of my book, for the lady of whom you speak. I suppose it's out of print now.

1. GS had written "I have just arranged with the wife of a very rich man to have your parents taken care of while you are at Dr. Rochschild's sanatorium. He makes a specialty of cases like yours, and you will find your surroundings very pleasant. Of course all your expenses there will be taken care of by this lady. I've explained to her that you prefer to hold the financial assistance as a loan, and she will so assume it, thoroughly understanding" (23 February 1917; ms. NYPL). The couple were Charles W. Clark, the mining magnate, and his wife Celia.

---

[29]   To George Sterling [ALS, NYPL]   March 3rd, 1917.

Dear George:

Your letter came yesterday, and I'm answering it immediately, to settle the business details. My parents think that the person who holds the mortgage on our place, would be willing to let it run on if the interest, (one hundred dollars), were all paid up. As to the amount per mensem for our household expenses, I hardly know what to say. Do you think $60. or $75. a month would be too much? Our bills are very light, and we could put aside capital for the poultry venture on such a sum.

I can't say how deeply indebted to you we all feel, for the trouble to which you have been. And will you not convey my gratitude to the lady who is willing to do so much for me? I shall certainly try to repay the debt when I get on my feet financially.

Don't worry about my health. I'm a lot harder to kill than most people seem to think (else I wouldn't be alive now). My weight is back to normal, and I think that the temporary loss (due mainly to my not eating enough for a long time) was good for me rather than otherwise, thro the elimination of much effete matter and certain digestive poisons. I feel much more buoyant and cheerful, and my skin is much clearer than it used to be.

I wish you could come up some time during the spring. May or April would be the best month. Couldn't you make it? My father and I are planning a little trip to the mountains during the summer. How about coming along with us, if you can't make it earlier?

Affectionately,
Clark—

P.S. Raine Bennett has offered to publish my next book without expense to me, if I'll give him the exclusive rights. What do you think of the idea? Robertson is so eternally slow and cautious, that, personally, I feel like accepting the offer. But of course, I shan't, if you advise me to the contrary.[1]

1. Raine Bennett (1891–1987) was the publisher of *Bohemia,* which used several of CAS's poems. See also "Clark Ashton Smith, Virgin," *Studies in Weird Fiction* 18 (Winter 1996): 34–36.

[30]   To George Sterling [ALS, NYPL]   April 14th, 1917.

Dear George:
    This is a rather belated acknowledgement of your last letter, and the check; but I've had so little to write about, that, as usual, I've kept putting it off from day to day. So perhaps you'll excuse me, considering that you haven't missed much.
    I keep in good health, physically, but so far, I've not felt like doing any literary work. I fear the rest cure is making me lazy. I wrote a few tentative verses the other day, and then gave up, partly from discouragement, and partly, I am afraid, from sheer indolence.
    Have you heard from Loveman lately? I've not had a letter from him for a month, and am beginning to wonder what is wrong. Letters miscarry, tho, sometimes—especially when they have to pass thro the Auburn postoffice.
    Robertson writes me that he was mistaken about the sale of my book. Only *half* the edition has been sold, the other half still lying unbound at the printers'. How's that for a come-down? And so far, I've not learned anything definite about the publication of my new volume. Bennett hasn't even written to me about it yet—I merely heard that he *intended* to make me an offer of publication. I shall call the book *Ebony and Crystal*—if it ever is published. The title is appropriate enough, and is more to my taste than any of the floral titles proposed.
    Have you read any of the books of Edgar Saltus? I've just been reading *The Philosophy of Disenchantment*—a fascinating and finely written exposition of the history and theory of pessimism. I'm trying to obtain another book by Saltus, entitled *The Anatomy of Negation.*[1] I've been reading a great deal lately—*De Profundis,*[2] the dramas of John Webster and Cyril Tourneur,[3] the *Journal of Marie Bashkirtseff,* Dostoevsky's *Journal of an Author,*[4] James Thomson's *City of Dreadful Night,* and two or three books by

Lafcadio Hearn, among many others. Hearn, Wilde, and de Quincey (aside from Poe and Bierce) are the prose-writers to whom I seem to take most naturally.

Affectionately,
Clark—

1. Edgar Saltus (1855–1921), *The Philosophy of Disenchantment* (1885) and *The Anatomy of Negation* (1886).
2. Oscar Wilde (1854–1900), *De Profundis* (1905), a tract written in Reading Gaol.
3. John Webster (1580?–1625?), English dramatist most noted for *The White Devil* (c. 1609–c. 1612) and Cyril Tourneur (1575?–1626), English dramatist most noted for *The Atheist's Tragedie* (1611).
4. Fyodor Dostoevsky (1821–1881), *A Writer's Diary* (1873–76).

---

[31]   Albert M. Bender [ALS, MCL]   Jan. 15th, 1918.

Dear Albert:

[. . .] As to my health, for which you inquire, I've no great reason for complaint. I seem to keep well enough, physically speaking. Mentally, I suffer from depression most of the time; and I have not written, or tried to write, for months. What use is a poet who can't work?

Thanks, many, many thanks for your efforts in regard to the Book Club volume.[1] I only wish that my poems were more worthy of so fine and sumptuous attire.

Wishing you a thousand good things for the coming year, I am,
As ever, your friend,
Clark.

P.S. The 13th was my 25th birthday! I feel unutterably ancient.

1. Bender was Secretary of the Book Club of California, which published *OS* in 1918.

---

[32]   To George Sterling [ALS, NYPL]   Feb. 25th, 1918.

Dear George:

Many, many thanks for the check, which I should have acknowledged more promptly than this. I am sorry to hear that Mrs. Clark is ill, and hope that she is better by this time.

No news, in especial. I've written nothing, but have drawn a great deal, by way of avocation. I keep pretty well, and have gained considerably in weight, partly, perhaps, through lack of exercise.

Bender tells me that I've been made an honorary member of the Book Club. They've presented me with a beautiful bronze placque, of which, naturally, I feel very proud. But I shall feel even prouder of your preface for my book.[1]

I've had two letters from Loveman during the past fortnight, with the promise of a third in a few days. He is certainly what you called him—"a spasmodic correspondent."

By the way, have you, or would you care to have, Symons' translation of Baudelaire's prose-poems?[2] I happen to possess an extra copy, and could turn it over to you just as well as not.

> Affectionately,
> Clark.

1. GS had written a brief preface for *OS*.
2. *Poems in Prose from Charles Baudelaire,* trans. Arthur Symons (1905).

---

[33]   To George Sterling [ALS, NYPL]   April 8th, 1918

Dear George:

Your welcome letter, enclosing the check, arrived last week. A thousand thanks! I am sorry to hear that Mrs. Clark has not been well.

I mailed you the Baudelaire last Friday. Symons' translation is, of course, excellent, tho by no means superior (in my opinion) to that of Stuart Merrill,[1] which I also possess.

I've done a little writing lately; also a number of drawings, from which (even if they are valueless artistically) I get considerable amusement. I enclose two prose-poems and a sonnet.

I like both of the sonnets you send—"Infidels" best, even tho I agree with the dictum of the bonzes.[2] Even pleasure (from my experience) is not enough to redeem the wrong of existence.

Have you heard from Loveman lately? He has been drafted, and expects to be called up this month. Perhaps I may go yet!

I've been very good the last two months, and have kept unusually quiet, with no long walks or over-exertion of any kind. The trouble about the rest-cure is that one gets so infernally "soft." I feel tired and nervous most of the time, in spite of the gain in weight. The nervousness, however, may be due to digestive poisoning.

The flowers are beautiful now—pansies, popcorn-balls, shooting-stars, faun-lilies, wild hyacinth, and a score of others. I wish you were here to see them.

As ever, affectionately,
Clark.

1. *Pastels in Prose* (1890) by Stuart Merrill (1863–1915), an American poet who wrote nearly exclusively in French, contains translations of the work of twenty-three French authors, including Baudelaire. Merrill's work may have suggested CAS's own "prose pastels." CAS translated, but did not publish, a handful of Merrill's poems.
2. In GS, *Sails and Mirage and Other Poems* (1921). The dictum is "Life is evil."

---

[34]   To George Sterling [ALS, NYPL]   Aug. 10th, 1918.

Dear George:

I'm wondering if you received my last letter, written sometime in the fore-part of July. I've been expecting to hear from you any time, so your silence makes me think that my letter may have miscarried. However, there was nothing of importance in it.

I was terribly shocked to read of Mrs. Sterling's death,[1] and fear what it may mean to you. Mrs. Clark, in a letter I have just received, speaks of your feeling so keenly on the subject. She (Mrs Clark) is wonderfully kind to me, and I feel as if my debt were more than a matter of dollars.

Everyone seems to be dying, these days. Andrew Dewing's brother, Walter, died last month, of consumption—a shock and surprise to me, since he had not seemed any worse than usual. Andrew, as you doubtless know, has been drafted. He is coming back to Auburn for a visit, and I'll probably see him tomorrow.[2]

Have you ever found time to write to Loveman? Even a note from you would mean a great deal to him, I think. His life in the training-camp is a hard and unhappy one, since his poor eyesight debars him from any prospect of service over sea,

I have been better, on the whole, since my visit to the city, and think that it really did me good. My "Katzenjammer" was two-thirds physical exhaustion and lack of sleep. I take better care of myself now, though it's hard for me to make myself eat enough. However, I've gained a little, the last few weeks, and don't look quite so much like a starving Belgian as when you saw me.

Our weather is wonderfully cool and pleasant, on the whole. The thermometer stands at 70° as I write—early this morning it was down to 50°, or less. I never knew such weather in August among these dry foothills.

When do you expect to return? Can't you stop off at Auburn, when you come through? I'd love to have you, for any length of time you could stay, or would care to stay.

As ever, affectionately,
Clark—

1. Carrie Sterling, who had divorced GS in 1913, committed suicide on 7 August 1918.
2. Andrew Dewing (1897–1977) was a friend of CAS from Auburn.

---

[35]   To George Sterling [ALS, NYPL]   Aug. 31st, 1918.

Dear George:

I should have written you before this, had it not been for the extreme heat. Even letter-writing is a severe mental effort, when the mercury is flirting with the hundred-mark. I do little but lie around and read, these days, though I feel much stronger than I did last month, in spite of the debilitating weather.

As usual, there's no news, in particular, unless it's the fact that I've actually sold a poem ("The Desert Garden") to *Ainslee's* magazine.[1]

Andrew is here, and expects to stay on the ranch for several months. What is his trouble? "Tobacco heart?"[2]

I am extremely distressed, and very much puzzled, over the rumour concerning which you wrote to my mother. The income I have received (as she is writing you separately) has been more than ample for all our necessities, and even for a few luxuries. I can think of only one person from whom such a story might have emanated—a young musician in Red Bluff, with whom my mother and I both had some correspondence, anent the melodies he had composed for certain of my poems, and whose publication he wished me to finance, on a profit-sharing basis.[3] This I declined to do . . . How anything that my mother said, or that I said, could have been construed into a profession of abject poverty, I am totally unable, or, at least, unwilling to imagine.

Can't you run up for a few days, when the weather grows a little cooler? I want very much to see you.

> Affectionately,
> Clark.

1. "The Desert Garden" (later "Song of Sappho's Arabian Daughter"), *Ainslee's* (February 1919); in *EC* and *SP*.
2. A hypertropy and dilation of the heart attributed to the use of tobacco.
3. The composer Henry Cowell (1897–1965).

---

[36]   To George Sterling [ALS, NYPL]   Oct. 13th, 1918.

Dear George:

I should have written you long before this; but there seemed to be nothing in particular to write about; and I know how burdensome and voluminous your correspondence has become. So I've spared you my tale of platitudes and trivialities till now.

Have you written much of late? I haven't. One sonnet (which I enclose) makes up the sum total of my work during August, September, and the present month.[1] Nor have I been able to sell anything since the poem that found lodgment in *Ainslee's*. I've not felt like writing, and have been tired and depressed most of the time. I eat more than I did, and have gained in weight, but, somehow, not in strength.

I see Andrew fairly often, which breaks the monotony of my solitude. He told me himself (in secret) about his real malady. I'm not surprised (his elder brother died recently of the same disease) but I don't think that he stands in much danger of a breakdown . . . Still, one never can tell.

Loveman writes me regularly. He doesn't like the training-camp life, and seems to suffer greatly from depression. His address is: Corporal Sam Loveman, Co. H., 4th Infantry Replacement Reg't., Camp Gordon, Ga.

The news to-day is disgusting and appalling. But it hardly seems possible that we can make an armistice with Germany; to do so would be a crime against the whole future of civilization. However, our pusillanimous president, and his Congress of cowards, are capable of anything.

Give my best regards to Bender, if you see him. My parents wish to be remembered to you. Can't you manage to run up, some time? My parents join me in the most cordial of standing invitations.

> Affectionately,
> Clark.

1. "The Chimera" (*EC* and *SP*).

---

[37]   To George Sterling [ALS, NYPL]

> East Auburn, Cal.,
> Nov. 16th, 1918

Dear George:

I inscribed the copy of my book for Mr. Bekeart,[1] and mailed it to you yesterday. I should have written you before, but, as usual, there was little or no news. I've been keeping to my hill-top pretty closely, since the mask ordinance went into effect (the wearing of one is a Chinese torture to me) and have only been in Auburn once or twice in the past month.[2] So I've had a rather quiet and peaceful time of it.

I submitted a few sonnets to Fisher, who has accepted two of them ("The Mummy" and "In Saturn").[3] He returned "The Chimera" and "Eidolon," both of which, in my opinion, are superior to "The Mummy."

I like the triad of sonnets you enclose ("Ocean Sonnets") but think the second one the best. Your river-poem is strong, like everything of the sort you have written.[4]

Have you written to Loveman? He has been in hospital with a severe and protracted case of bronchitis, and had just been released when he wrote me last.

I haven't seen Auburn for nearly a fortnight, so you can surmise the completeness of my isolation. I don't feel any too well, and avoid walking and tiring myself any more than I can help. Physical exhaustion or over-exertion seems to hurt my nerves in a way that it didn't use to. I suffer from depression and insomnia when I fatigue myself too much.

To-day, I've been making clean and revised copies of some of my unpublished work. I shall go on, and put together everything that I care to have preserved in book-form, under the general title, *Ebony and Crystal.* If anything were to happen to me, you'd have one hell of a time editing my mss. as they stand. I've been very careless in the past, and have even neglected to keep typewritten copies of some of my things.

> Affectionately, as ever,
> Clark.

1. Philip Baldwin Bekeart (1861–?), a book-collector and patron of the arts.

2. Presumably to protect against the flu epidemic of 1918–19, which killed 15 million worldwide and about 450,000 in the U.S. (see *AJ,* 21 November 1918).

3. Mahlon Leonard Fisher (1874–?) was the editor of the *Sonnet,* which published "In Saturn" (January–February 1919; *EC, SP,* and *LO*) and "The Mummy" (May–June 1919; *EC* and *LO*).

4. "Ocean Sunsets," in *Sails and Mirage and Other Poems.* The "river-poem" has not been identified.

---

[38]   To Samuel Loveman [ALS, JHL]

> East Auburn, Cal.,
> April 1st, 1919.

Dear Sam:

Our weather has turned warm and fair, all of a sudden, as it usually does. Lady April promises to be a buxom sort of lass. I've more than a touch of "spring fever," and have found nothing better or more pleasurable than to lie around and read the con-signment of Conrad books that you sent me. With the exception of *Youth* and *Falk,* all of these are new to me. I like the *Tales of Unrest* in especial.[1] "Karain" is worthy of Flaubert, and at least one other story in the volume ("The Idiots") has all the best qualities of de Maupassant. "Romance" is well-named, and I wish I had read it in the days when I first read *Treasure Island,* and other books of the same ilk. In all ways, it is far superior to Stevenson.

I've made a few purchases lately—Hearn's *Japanese Fairy Tales* in the Penguin series of B. & L., *The Private Papers of Henry Ryecroft,* by George Gissing, and Hearn's translation of *The Crime of Sylvestre Bonnard.*[2] The fairy tales are charming, but only four of them are by Hearn; the rest are by Basil Hall Chamberlain and others. I've not found time to read the other books as yet. I notice that Boni and Liveright announce a translation of *The Flowers of Evil* among the next additions to the Modern Library,[3] and I shall certainly obtain it; also, a new selection, *Love and Other Stories,* from de Maupassant.[4] Things begin to look more hopeful, when such books are published in a "popular" edition.

Why in Hades are you destroying any of your work? I like nearly all of your prose-poems, and am haunted recurrently by several of the unpublished lyrics you have sent me. I earnestly advise you against destroying any of your work. Moods of depression are not to be trusted,—I know them too well, since I have been tempted several times a month, at least, to make a holocaust of my own writings.

The editor of *The Thrill Book* is a "good sport"—he "raised the ante," to use his own phrase, and paid me seven dollars for "Dissonance"[5]—double the price I expected. I'm investing the boodle in books, though, with the Great National Drouth impending,[6] I was sorely tempted to add a few more demijohns to my hoard of liquid treasure. The G. N. D. is no joke—things are bad enough now, with the prohibitive taxes on wine and brandy. Harry Leon Wilson, in an article in the *Saturday Evening Post,* predicts that coffee and tobacco will also be prohibited in a few years.[7] I don't care about tobacco personally, since my smoking is confined to an annual, or semi-annual cigarette, but, damme, if coffee is banned, I'll stow away on the first hooker that leaves for Java!

Dewing (the young rip!) has gone to San Francisco for a few weeks. I wish I were with him—the vie de Boheme has its allurements even for me. Bohemia will be a dull and tawdry sort of place when the light of wine is faded from its walls and tables. It's hard to imagine S. F. "on the wagon." I'll contrive to visit the old burgh, for a day or two at least, before June 30th, if I have to go hog-stealing to raise the funds!

Here's hoping that you are in a brighter mood by now. I feel better myself, apart from the languor due to the changing weather. Much of my nervousness is due to indigestion, I believe, though, of course, the lack of companionship you mention is an aggravating factor. I should go mad with loneliness were it not for my books—those tongueless but eloquent friends—friends who never accuse or betray!

Well, an end to this long-winded letter—a rigmarole of trivialities.

You must pardon me, for there's nothing else. Life seems an endless chain of banalities—even pain becomes banal with repetition. And all roads lead to the hell of boredom—that 10th circle which Dante never penetrated, and, apparently, never suspected. Lucky Dante, for whom the inferno was only flame, and slime, and ice!

As ever, your affectionate friend,
Clark

1. Joseph Conrad (1857–1924), *Youth* (1902); *Falk* (1903); and *Tales of Unrest* (1909).

2. *Japanese Fairy Tales,* by Lafcadio Hearn (1850–1904) et al. (1918); George Gissing (1857–1903), *The Private Papers of Henry Ryecroft* (1903); Anatole France (pseudonym of Jacques Anathole Thibault [1844–1924]), *The Crime of Sylvestre Bonnard,* trans. Lafcadio Hearn (1890).

3. Presumably *Baudelaire: His Prose and Poetry,* ed. T. R. Smith (New York: Boni & Liveright, 1919).

4. Guy de Maupassant (1850–1893), *Love, and Other Stories,* trans. Michael Monahan (New York: Modern Library, 1920?).

5. "Dissonance" (*The Thrill Book,* 15 September 1919). The editor of the short-lived magazine (sixteen issues between 1 March and 15 June 1919) was Harold Brainerd Hersey (1893–1956), later editor of *Ghost Stories.*

6. I.e., Prohibition, which went into effect in July 1919.

7. "Here's How" (*Saturday Evening Post,* 5 April 1919).

———————◆———————

[39]   To George Sterling [ALS, NYPL]

East Auburn, Cal.,
June 10th, 1919

Dear George:

I certainly enjoyed your satire on "The Modern Muse."[1] Many of the stanzas are tremendously clever . . . The badness of much of the "new poetry," is almost unbelievable. Certainly, the Bolshevists have taken Parnassus, and the Muses have fled to some happier and more peaceful planet. Helicon is contaminated with filth and spittle.

I've tried to work, but with small success. However, I enclose the result—two prose-poems, a lyric, and a sonnet. I've sold a few things during the past month—one poem to *Ainslee's,* one to *The Thrill Book,* and two more ("Palms" and "Flamingoes") to a beautifully printed geographical magazine entitled *Asia,* which pays 50¢ per line. Oddly enough, three of these four poems were in the alexandrine form—the measure you dislike so much.[2]

Things are quieter than ever, if possible. Andrew is serving a term of hard labour on the ranch, and I've not seen him for three weeks or more. I amuse myself in all ways that happen to be unavailable, i.e., the reading of unpopular fiction, the shooting of cotton-tails out of season (and without a license) and the manufacture of cherry wine. The last involves a double felony, since I'm making the stuff from stolen cherries.

I may come down for a few days, before the end of the summer. My health is improving, in spite of a mouthful of bad teeth. I weigh close to 130 lbs, and feel much stronger, in a physical sense. Mentally, I still feel as if I were dead and damned, but even that is improving.

I wish you could see the tiger-lilies—I gather them by the armfull in the canyon. They fairly startle one at first sight, growing as they do on the dry hillsides. Their flowers are so exuberantly gorgeous and savage, that they give the impression of a more than vegetable vitality.

The wild black berries will begin to ripen in a week or so, and I expect to gather them by the bucket-ful, for preserves and wine. Also, I'm planning an expedition in search of wild goose-berries. Think of all the innocent rural pleasures that you're missing!

Affectionately,
Clark.

1. There is a poem by GS titled "The Modern Muse" among his mss. at *BL*.

2. "In November" (*Ainslee's*, December 1919); "Dissonance" (*Thrill Book*, 15 September 1919); "Palms" (*Asia*, April 1920); "Flamingoes" (*Asia*, November 1919); all in *EC* and *SP*.

---

[40]   To George Sterling [ALS, NYPL]

East Auburn, Cal.,
Aug. 28th, 1919

Dear George:

Thanks for *The Hill of Dreams*, the reading of which has given me considerable pleasure. Much of it is very beautiful and subtle. Am I to keep the book? . . . I have another of Machen's books, entitled: *Hieroglyphics*,[1] one of the best things on literature and literary values that I have seen for a long time, apart from the writings of John Cowper Powys.

Have you written during the summer? I've not felt up to much, and have done nothing, with the exception of a few indifferent sonnets. I feel worn-out, after the long and tedious hot spell—the temperature here has risen above ninety every day for the past three weeks.

Nearly everyone seems to be sick, or ailing, these days. My father and mother are unwell, and so are Andrew's parents. You may see Andrew in a few days—his mother is in Oakland, and wants him to come down.

Loveman writes me pretty often. He, too, has been ailing—heart-trouble, perhaps, since he was laid up with something of the sort while in Georgia.

Thanks for the clipping from the *Bulletin,* which I am returning at last. It must have been tremendous—that last and culminative night in the city. I can't imagine what the place is like now, even with such oases, and "wells amid the waste"[2] as will continue to exist.

Here are the sonnets I mentioned.[3] I wonder that I ever attempt to write—nothing of the sort seems worth while in these days. The whole world seems crumbling into chaos—I'm not even sure that you'll receive this letter,—I'm told there was no mail from the city yesterday, on account of the railroad strike.

    Affectionately,
    Clark.

1. Arthur Machen (1863–1947), *The Hill of Dreams* (1907), on loan from Leslie Nelson Jennings (1890–1972), poet and friend of GS, best known for his poem "Lost Harbor"; *Hieroglyphics: A Note upon Ecstasy in Literature* (1902).
2. *Rubáiyát,* stanza xlviii: "A moment's Halt—a momentary taste / Of BEING from the Well amid the Waste—."
3. "Heliogabalus" (two sonnets), first published in *SP* under "Translations and Paraphrases: From Christophe de Laurières" (who is CAS himself).

---

[41]   To George Sterling [ALS, NYPL]

East Auburn, Cal.,
Nov. 1st, 1919

Dear George:

Have you been arrested yet? The Prohibition Enforcement act is so complete and all-comprehensive, that millions of people must be liable to prosecution under it. It'll be a case of "safety in numbers," I suppose, for people who have made wine or other liquor at home. However, there's no telling to what length these pestilential puritans may go in the future—they may establish an Inquisition, with racks and thumbscrews for anyone who is suspected or accused of knowing how to make wine!

The poem you send ("The Queen Forgets")[1] is one of your best lyrics, in my opinion. You have caught the very essence of mystery, in a few lines as magically simple as those of "La Belle Dame sans Merci." I wish I had something to send in return—but I have felt, and still feel, totally unfit for work.

How are you coming on with *Lilith?*[2] Andrew tells me you were at work on the proofs when he saw you last.

The Heliogabalus sonnets were written for Loveman, who has a tremendous admiration for the strangest and most "decadent" of the Roman emperors. I've no compunction or concern regarding the "ethical" aspect of the matter—ethics are an illusion, like everything else. Virtue and vice are but veils of Medusa . . . No, I don't care to write a series of sonnets on the Roman emperors— I'm tired of that vein of thought and imagery.

The t.b.s appear to have given me up—there's no loss of weight or strength, at least. Otherwise, I feel damnably unwell—my nerves, brain, eyes, teeth, and stomach are ill in a conspiracy against me. Perhaps a doctor would diagnose the trouble as common, everyday ennui—but that's bad enough. It isn't drink, at any rate, since I've been on the wagon for weeks, and have taken little enough at any time for a year past. I've manufactured more than twenty gallons of assorted vino during the summer and autumn, but my father is the principal consumer. Some of the stuff I've made is quite promising—it ought to be the real thing, if it gets a chance to age.

When are you coming up? I can give you a bunk, and something to eat and drink, at any time.

Affectionately yours,
Clark—

1. In *Sails and Mirage and Other Poems.*
2. GS, *Lilith, a Dramatic Poem* (1919), a verse drama.

[42]   To George Sterling [ALS, NYPL]

East Auburn, Cal.,
Jan. 29th, 1920.

Dear George:

Thanks for the clippings—O'Day's review of *Lilith* was very good, I thought. I'm glad he quoted my opinion, and am sorry I didn't say more,—as I might well have done.[1] The poem is packed with beauties—I find something new every time I take it up.

I don't think much of Cale Young Rice's classification of modern poets.[2] I'm sick of classifications, anyway. . . . He'd call me a "romanticist," I suppose. Well, at a pinch, I'd rather be called that than a "realist"—it sounds much less offensive.

I enclose a philosophical fantasy "The Ghoul and the Seraph."[3] Bender complains of the "pessimism" in it—which I can't "see." The philosophical thesis is a plain statement of scientific fact—the immortality of matter, and the evanescence and commutation of its forms.

I've been at work on a much longer poem, "The Hashish-Eater," but am "stuck" at the end of three hundred lines. It will take another hundred to finish the thing. I'm afraid it's too long and incoherent. It has some monstrous images—"Boulder-weighted webs of dragons' gut," "plagues of lichens" that overrun empires, "Continents of serpent-shapen trees, With slimy trunks that lengthen league on league,"[4] etc., etc. I've left the poor devil of a Hashish-eater in mid-air, fleeing on the back of some providential hippogriff, from a python as big as a river.

I suppose you're right about my odes. I've long meditated an ode in honour of Poe, and another for Swinburne. Also, an ode on the seven prismatic colours. I might "do" one in honour of Dionysus, too, for the delectation of our friends the prohibitionists.

I enclose a note for Lafler,[5] since I don't know his address. He surprised and naturally delighted me with his letter—I had scarcely expected anyone to become excited over "Omar."[6]

Don't apologize for not answering my letters sooner. I know what your correspondence is like.

Affectionately,
Clark—

1. Edward F. O'Day quoted from a letter by CAS in his column "Men and Women in the Mirror" (as by "The Clubman"), *Oakland Enquirer* (10 January 1920): 8.
2. Cale Young Rice (1872–1943), poet and friend of GS.

3. In *EC* and *SP*.

4. Respectively, l. 80; l. 124; and ll. 14–15 (as in *SP* and *LO;* also in *EC*).

5. Henry Anderson ("Harry") Lafler, San Francisco businessman, poet, and friend of GS.

6. Presumably "To Omar Khayyam" (first title, "To Omar"), written 13 December 1919 (in *EC, SP,* and *LO*).

———————————◆———————————

[43]   To George Sterling [ALS, NYPL]

East Auburn, Cal.,
March 29th, 1920

Dear George:

I hope you won't be overwhelmed by the bulk of the enclosure! —the draught of my interminable hashish-poem, which I've finished, after a fashion. Loveman, the only person who has read it so far, thinks it "the greatest imaginative poem in the language"— an amazing judgement. The poem is imaginative, but, to me, the technique is so intolerable that I can take no pride or pleasure in it. I would revise it, if I could; but for the past month, the nerves of my head and eyes have been so troublesome that I find it difficult to concentrate to any purpose.

I am sorry to hear of your mother's death, and sorry that you have been laid up. But you have not been idle, it would seem! I'm tremendously interested in that new dramatic poem you mention, and have a "hunch" that you've been doing some great stuff. You know my opinion of *Lilith*. *Rosamund* seems all right as a title; Swinburne's drama of that name was an early and minor performance, anyway.[1]

Your resignation from the American Academy of Arts and Letters, is the best bit of news that I've heard for a coon's age![2] Mencken[3] summed it up very felicitously, I think—the episode is certainly "rich and stimulating!" Possibly, some of these purveyors to Demos, these panders of stupidity, may surmise that there is a difference between literature and hog-wash—Anyway, they will be forced to know that there are people in America who hold that such a distinction exists.

Sam Loveman intends to start a magazine in Cleveland—a sort of semi-private affair—for the publication of his own work and mine. He spoke of calling it *The Decadent;* but I've suggested *The Satanist* or better still, *The Saturnian,*[4] as alternatives. I've no particular wish to be identified with any "school"—even the

"Decadent"—a word that critics have forced to serve in too many senses, often contradictory or conflicting.

I'm pleased that you found something good in "The Ghoul and the Seraph." I planned a series of these fantastic dialogues, many years ago.[5] "Asmodeus and the Gargoyles" was one of my titles. The scene is the Paris of Villon's time. Asmodeus, in his flight through the midnight heavens, pauses to chat with the gargoyles of Notre Dame, who tell him the news of the city, and receive all the current gossip of Hades in return. Perhaps I shall write it some day. A fine subject for an etching by Felicien Rops, or Meryon.[6] I don't think there is any living artist who could draw the scene to my taste . . . I had other titles, too, such as "The Colloquy of Christ and Belial," and "The Girl from Venus." All of the dialogues were to contain a philosophical import, under their guise of fantasy and grotesquerie. [. . .]

As you say, there are tremendous possibilities in hashish. The subject has been touched upon very little, at least in poetry. Bailey Aldrich has a poem with the same title as mine, and Symons a lyric entitled "Hashish,"[7] the last stanza of which is truly great:

> "Who said the world is but a mood
> In the eternal thought of God?
> I know it, real though it seem,
> The phantom of a hashish-dream,
> In that insomnia which is God."

A lot of Baudelaire's imagery is undoubtedly reminiscent of his visions and sensations while under the influence of the drug. But no one seems to have attempted anything on the order of my poem. Possibly, I'm at a disadvantage, in having no personal knowledge of the effect of hashish. But I remember your telling me that the effect was often disappointing, at least to Occidentals.[8]

I hope all this doesn't bore you too much. I rarely see anyone that I can talk to, and must take out my loquacity in correspondence—when I feel loquacious, which is seldom enough.

            Affectionately,
            Clark—

1. GS, *Rosamund: A Dramatic Poem* (1920). Algernon Charles Swinburne (1837–1909) had published a verse drama, *Rosamund, Queen of the Lombards,* in 1899.

2. GS declined membership in the American Academy of Arts and Letters because it included such writers as Robert W. Chambers (see letter 191 n.2) and William Lyon Phelps.

3. H. L. Mencken (1880–1956), American literary critic and editor of *Smart Set* (1908–1923).

4. Loveman edited three issues of the *Saturnian* in 1920–22.

5. CAS's lists of titles for possible future short stories (or prose poems) include "The Satyr and the Courtesan," "Venus and the Village Priest" (in *SS* as a fragmentary play), "The Statue and the Picture," "Valdez and the Daughter of Hesper," and "The Lady, the Maid, and Salabub."

6. Felicien Rops (1833–1898), Belgian Symbolist engraver; Charles Meryon (1821–1868), French artist.

7. American poet and fiction writer Thomas Bailey Aldrich (1836–1907) wrote a poem entitled simply "Hascheesh" in *Pampinea and Other Poems* (1861); British poet and critic Arthur Symons (1865–1945) wrote "Haschish" in *Images of Good and Evil* (1899).

8. Cf. the first sentence of CAS's uncompleted "In a Hashish-Dream" (formerly "A Tale of Hashish-Land"): "The first effects of hashish, like those of opium, are often disappointing to the Occidental" (*SS* 101).

---

[44]   To George Sterling [ALS, NYPL]

East Auburn, Cal.,
July 10th, 1920.

Dear George:

I hope *Rosamund* is ready for her debut by now. Can you get me an extra copy of it? I've promised one to Loveman, and will gladly pay for it.

The second issue of *The Saturnian* will probably appear in August. Two of my drawings are to be reproduced as illustrations.[1] Loveman is coming out to California in December, to take a position at Paul Elder's. I imagine he will find S.F. much more congenial than Cleveland, in spite of Paul Elder.[2]

I liked all the poems you sent me. The one to Untermeyer[3] is terrible, and the other two are filled with pure lyric beauty and melody. I wish I could send you something good in return; my blank verses on Nora May French appear tedious, rambling, and uninspired. Pass them on to Lafler, if you care for them at all. Possibly they are not as bad as I think—I'm no competent or impartial judge of anything at present, since I feel disgusted with everything I have ever written. I've turned more seriously to drawing than ever before, and am working steadily at it. I illustrated the "H. Eater," among other things, and am making a set of designs for Poe at present. The Poe drawings are better than most illustrations of Poe that I have seen—which isn't much of a brag, after all.

I'm sorry that people think "The H. Eater" a mere extension of "A Wine of Wizardry." That's no mean compliment, however—

The "Wine of Wizardry" has always seemed the ideal poem to me, as it did to Bierce. But the ground-plan of "The H. E." is really quite different. It owes nearly as much to *The Temptation of Saint Anthony*[4] as to your poem. But few American critics will prove sufficiently well-read and perspicacious to notice the former debt. After all, what's the diff? My literary ambitions are almost dead, and I may not write again, except in prose.

That Democratic convention must have been horrible.[5] It sickened me to read the headlines in the papers. America is putrid to the point of utter dissolution—it reminds me of M. Valdemar, in the story by Poe. How long till the liquefaction of the corpse?

I don't know when I'll be able to visit S.F. I'm up against the money-problem, and am hesitating between bank-robbery and shortstory-writing. I've a faint hope (perhaps without foundation) that I may be able to sell some of my drawings. It would be a case of reaching the right people,—people with a taste for the weird and the bizarre, and a *distaste* for conventional technique. "Rare birds," I dare say—I meet very few of them, and they never have money, by any chance.

Affectionately, as ever,
Clark—

P.S. Don't worry about my tampering with hashish. Life is enough of a nightmare without drugs, and I feel content to take the effects of h. on hearsay.

1. The second number of *The Saturnian* (August–September [1920]) noted "It is with regret that we postpone our original intention of dedicating this number to the work of Clark Ashton Smith, until the next issue. This will contain reproductions of two or three of the imaginative drawings, notably the magnificent 'Fear'." The third (and final) issue likewise contained nothing by CAS.

2. David Paul Elder (1877–1948), well-known specialty publisher in San Francisco.

3. Louis Untermeyer (1885–1977), well-known American poet and critic of poetry. GS's "To Louis Untermeyer" is unpublished.

4. Gustave Flaubert (1821–1880), *The Temptation of St. Antony* (1848–49; revised 1856, and again before publication in 1874), a long poem in prose that portrayed exotic subjects in a heightened lyrical fashion.

5. The Democratic National Convention took place in San Francisco from 28 June to 6 July 1920.

[45]   To George Kirk[1] [ALS, private collection]

Sept. 16th, 1920.

Dear George:
    [. . .] I'm glad you enjoyed the visit. It was a great pleasure to
me, and I wish you could have stayed longer. I, too, seldom meet
anyone whose tastes are at all congenial. I am sure we will be good
friends; you must write me when you can.
    I had a letter from Sam yesterday. His artist-friend, Nelson, has
been "cracking up" my pictures; he thinks them better than the
symbolist-drawings of Odilon Redon,[2] the famous French artist,
who deals, as I do, in the weird and fantastic. Set that against the
judgement of my work in S.F.! What do you do when critics disagree? I know what I'd do, if I could. I'd take three fingers of
Scotch, if I had it; after that, another three fingers!
    My parents join me in the best of remembrance and regards.
        Cordially, your friend,
        Clark Ashton Smith

    1. George [Willard] Kirk (1898–1962), publisher of Samuel
Loveman's book *Twenty-one Letters of Ambrose Bierce* (1922) and
proprietor of the Chelsea Bookshop in New York. He was a close friend
of HPL and presented HPL with a copy of OS.
    2. Odilon Redon (1840–1916), French Symbolist painter, lithog-
rapher, and etcher.

---

[46]   To George Kirk [ALS, private collection]

East Auburn, Cal.,
Oct. 3rd, 1920.

Dear George:
    [. . .] I've sent my whole collection, some ninety titles in all, to
Alfred A. Knopf. Sterling advised me to try him, and it's not a bad
idea. Mencken, one of Knopf's advisers, is pretty well disposed
toward me. I'll try Brentano's if K. doesn't "come through." I don't
think there'd be any use in submitting my work to the more conservative publishing houses, like Scribner's and Houghton Mifflin.
My very titles would scare them!
    There's no news. I am horribly idle and restless, and have done
nothing at all . . . To-day is Sunday, and I'm going to church for a

change—I've not entered one in years. Picture the wolf in the sheep-fold!

I hope you had a pleasant trip. Doubtless you will have seen Loveman by this time.

My parents join me in the best of wishes and remembrances. Write me when you can.

> Your friend,
> Clark.

---

[47]   To George Sterling [ALS, NYPL]

> East Auburn, Cal.,
> Oct. 19th, 1920.

Dear George:

My congratulations on *Rosamund!* As you warned me, it lacks the poetic beauty of *Lilith;* but nevertheless, it is a great drama. What action! It should make a tremendous "film" if you don't mind my saying so: I don't mean that as a slam, in any sense. "The Iris-Hills" is very beautiful; in the setting in which it occurs, it is like a sapphire on a breast-plate of bronze.[1]

I've nothing to send you this time; I can't create in my present mood—a mood in which no art, no creation seems worth the price one pays for it. You are right—the world is "clogged with great poetry." And I've written nothing that satisfies me at all; and feel the impossibility of doing so in the strait-jacket that circumstances have made for me.

Knopf is "unable to consider the publication" of *Ebony and Crystal*—I doubt if they even read the poems. However, I'll try some of the other firms, B. & L. and John Lane, anyway. Can you think of others worth trying?

I'm cutting fire-wood when the weather permits. Otherwise, there seems nothing that I can do, at present. I've an idea or two for short-stories, and may try to work them up.

I went out to see the Herkomers a couple of weeks ago, and showed H. a few of my drawings.[2] Like most painters, he is horribly unimaginative, and could see nothing in them but their shortcomings from the stand-point of the usual studio-technique. I feel absolutely certain that some of my work possesses great imaginative value; but few people seem able to see it. As to "bad drawing"—they used to charge Beardsley with that. The indictment has been brought against almost every imaginative artist.

Are you writing?
    Affectionately,
        Clark—

1. "The Iris-Hills" first appeared in *Songs: Lovingly Dedicated to Nellie Holbrook* (with "Lawrence Zenda") (1916); then later in *Rosamund* and *Sails and Mirage and Other Poems.*
2. Herman Gustave Herkomer (1865–1935), California painter of portraits and interiors.

———————— ◆ ————————

[48]   To Samuel Loveman [ALS, JHL]   Dec. 6th, 1920.

Dear Sam:
    The doctor has ordered me to stay in bed for a few days, but I'm disobeying him long enough to write you this letter. I disgraced myself by collapsing in public yesterday, and had to be carried home. I'm better to-day, but still a bit weak. I dare say it's my old nervous trouble,—with a few new and quite unmentionable symptoms.
    Fortunately, my eyes are better, and I can read a little. I read Adams' novel, but really didn't care much for it, except in spots. Yes, I received *Resurrection,* and purpose to look it over before long. Conrad's *The Rescue,* which you mention, is a fine book.[1]
    All I know of Casanova is from Havelock Ellis' essay.[2] The man certainly does seem to have "gone the limit" in sexual matters. But, after all, should one blame him? It's a generous vice. To me, gluttony and avarice are the only intolerable vices.
    I've not heard from George for months, and have an intuition that matters are not well with him. Margaret Nicol hinted as much. Prohibition (and prohibition booze!) is terrible for a man who has drunk heavily for many years. He needs a certain amount of alcohol to keep him normal. And the stuff they sell now is worse than squirrel-poison! (You'd appreciate the comparison if you knew the dope that farmers put in ground squirrel-holes to asphyxiate the creatures.)
    Write soon, if you can.
        Affectionately,
            Clark

1. The Adams novel is unidentified. The other works are Leo Tolstoy

(1828–1910), *Resurrection* (1920; 2 vols.) and Joseph Conrad, *The Rescue: A Romance of the Shadows* (1920).

2. Giovanni Giacomo Casanova (1725–1798) writer, soldier, spy, and diplomatist, whose surname is synonymous with "libertine." An essay by H. Havelock Ellis (1858–1939) on Casanova appears in his book *Affirmations* (London: Walter Scott, 1898).

---

[49]   To George Kirk [ALS, private collection]

East Auburn, Cal.,
Feb. 4th, 1921.

Dear George:

Please forgive my long silence. I've been a little under the weather part of the time (nothing serious) and haven't had much to write about, anyway.

I envy you those books you mention. Casanova has always interested me. I like Nietzsche—he and Schopenhauer are the only writers of German represented in my little library. You'll notice that I don't class them as *Germans*.

I've wanted to make you a book-plate, but thought I'd better ask if you have any particular design or motif that you would prefer. I have one in mind—the figure of a woman representing Beauty or the Muse, poised on a great globe supported by dragons. I'm not sure that you'll care for the idea—there ought to be something better.

Our spring has already begun, if the shooting-stars, buttercups, and pussy-willows are to be trusted as indications. We've had a most phenomenal rain-fall.

I've made some new drawings—the latest of them a series of women's heads, done mostly in bronze-green. "Charmion," "Sappho," "Clarimonde," and "Victoria Fulton" (the heroine of *A Bed of Roses*)[1] are the best.

Have you seen Sam lately? I've not heard from him for nearly a month, and feel a bit worried. Of course, it's possible that his letter may have miscarried.

I sent a number of my poems to Mrs. Meynell,[2] but have not heard from them as yet. I shall do some more writing before long —something that I can *sell*, if possible. I don't believe *anybody* will publish "The Hashish-Eater." I shall never attempt another long poem. Love-lyrics, and odes (Horatian odes!) are about my limit at present.

My parents wish to be remembered to you. My very best

regards to you, and to your wife. I hope to see you back in California, some time.

Write me when you can.

Most sincerely,
Your friend,
Clark Ashton Smith

1. Walter Lionel George (1882–1926), *A Bed of Roses* (1919).
2. Alice Meynell (1847–1922), British poet and feminist. Meynell had written CAS re his poetry and was impressed by *ST* and *OS*. She was very conventional and withdrew her support of Fisher's *Sonnet* after it had published GS's "To Science" (July–August 1919). CAS had submitted his ms. to her as a "last resort," but because of illness she was unable to place it with a British publisher.

---

[50]   To George Kirk [ALS, private collection]

East Auburn, Cal.
Sept. 1st, 1921

Dear George:

I was glad to get your letter, and sorry that things have not been so well with you. Don't worry about the drawings: I meant them as a gift; and certainly I owed them to you! They have no market-value, anyway. I have given up the idea of selling them, and, indeed, have almost given up drawing itself.

Wish I had more news for you; but there is little—at least that I can tell. My life at present is like a novel by Balzac or Flaubert. Highly romantic—but it's necessary to dodge the censors!

I was in San Francisco last July, and saw Sterling and some other old friends. Prohibition seems to have affected nothing but the price . . . G. S., though, is on the water-wagon, and intends to stay on,—till somebody offers him champagne! The sybarite!

My poems are under consideration by the Houghton Mifflin Co. at present. The president of a local woman's college offered to recommend me to them.[1] A rash offer—since she had not seen my unpublished work! So far, I've heard neither from the lady nor from the Mifflin Co. . . .

I wish I could buy some of your books; you have many items that tempt me. Perhaps I'll be able to, later on. I may go to work this month, typing bills in a water-office. I tried it for a week in July. Nothing could be more hellishly monotonous; but all work is monotonous.

Tell Sam to write me. I wrote him twice, and got no answer.

Best wishes and remembrances to you. I hope the luck will change for all of us: it's about time, is it not?

Your friend,
Clark.

1. Aurelia Henry Reinhardt (1877–1948) was president of Mills College, a school for women. The college owns several of CAS's mss.

———————————— ◆ ————————————

[51]   To George Sterling [ALS, NYPL]

East Auburn, Cal.,
Sept. 5th, 1921

Dear George:

I return the excerpt from Mrs. Crane's letter.[1] Yes, I heard from the lady. She seems to have misunderstood me in more ways than one—which was perhaps inevitable . . . Don't tell people that I am a cynic—it isn't more than half-true. I am incurably romantic—and prove it by falling in love every six months. . . . But even cynicism might not protect one against that.

I have been very idle, lately, and have seldom felt so listless and effortless. I am not very well—"nerves," eye-strain, and a disordered stomach. I don't know when I will go to Roseville—or whether I will go at all. "Everything is in the air."

I like the poems you enclose—particularly the sonnets on Beauty. I've nothing to send in return,—except a prose-poem written last spring.[2]

No, I have heard nothing from T. R. Smith[3]—which doesn't prove that he hasn't written me! The local post-office is run by a bunch of congenital idiots, and I get everyone's mail but my own. Two of "Cleopatra's" letters have gone astray.

I have not heard from Loveman for a long time. Had a letter from Leo Mihan[4] yesterday; he tells me that you have induced him to try Abrams' treatment. I wish I could have seen Abrams when I was in the city; but I'll be down again before the end of the year, if I have any luck.

Can you induce one or two others to contribute ten a month? It would be a great help. The forty dollars I receive now is barely enough; but we could get along on sixty.

[. . .] Marriage is an error I was never tempted to commit: I have not been in love with an unmarried woman since I was fifteen! Anyway, I object to marriage on moral grounds.

Ever yours,
Clark.

1. Estelle P. Crane. GS had asked CAS to send her a copy of *ST*.
2. "In Cocaigne" (*EC* and *PP*).
3. T[homas] R[obert] Smith (1880–1942) assembled three volumes of *Poetica Erotica* (1921–22). It contained six poems by GS but none by CAS.
4. A friend of GS and CAS.

---

[52]   To George Sterling [ALS, NYPL]   Dec. 17th, 1921.

Dear George:
    [. . .] I've heard nothing about the fate of my own book, which is, or should be, in the hands of the Houghton Mifflin Co. . . . The "literary shambler" of Keats' day (his own phrase)[1] wasn't a circumstance to that of the present. I have been reading Upton Sinclair's *Brass Check*,[2] and feel more in sympathy with the Bolshevists than I have ever been before. I fear there's no chance for me. I could print a small edition myself, if someone would loan me a couple hundred dollars. There should be no difficulty in selling enough copies to pay for the cost of production. I wish something could be done: My inability to publish puts me in a false position, and disappoints the few people who care for my work. It has even affected my last love-affair:—the lady accused me of being a failure! If it weren't for my people, I'd hoof it out of this —! —! —! rotten country to-morrow, and stow away on a steamer for England or France. As it is, I may come to the city for awhile next spring: I've had nearly all I can stand of Auburn at one stretch.
    Forgive this diatribe: it eases my mind a little.
    The enclosed article, from an Auburn paper, may amuse you. It shows the estimation in which literature is held locally. The promising young journalist who wrote it, gives me a paragraph, and barely mentions Bierce. Gregory, who heads the list of luminaries, writes western tales of the Jesus-Christ-and-cowboys type. He isn't as bad as Harold Bell Wright, and doesn't sell more than half as well.[3]
    I'll dig up some verses to enclose with this also. And next week I'll mail you two or three of my drawings (the ones you liked best.) I wish I had something better to send.
            Affectionately,
                Clark.

1. This phrase has not been identified.

2. Upton Sinclair (1878–1968), *The Brass Check* (1919), a book exposing the press.

3. "Placer County Scribes and Artists Shine Brightly Among the Stars of California's Literary Firmament" (*AJ*, 15 December 1921): 8. Harold Bell Wright (1872–1944) was the first author to make $1 million as a novelist, and the first American writer to sell more than one million copies of a single novel. Jackson Gregory (1882–1943) was an author of popular westerns.

---

[53]   To George Kirk [ALS, private collection]

April 11th, 1922.

Dear George:

I want to thank you for the books, which came a couple days ago. The book on B. is Sam's gift, is it not? Gautier's memoir is very fine.[1]

I've been hoping to hear from you or Sam, but nothing has come so far. I hope things will "pick up," now that the beastly winter is about over.

One of the local printers has promised to bring out a small edition of *Ebony and Crystal* for me. I'll have all my poems (except the most daring of the erotica) between covers by July, if the promise is kept. The edition will be a small one—not more than three hundred copies.

The London Mercury took one of my sonnets some time ago. And *The Lyric West* (do you ever see it?) continues to buy my stuff.[2] They actually *pay,* at the rate of $5 per page. But I need all I can pick up, and more too: I'm poorer than ever, and will have to pick fruit this summer to keep things going.

Affectionate regards to yourself and Sam.

　　　Ever yours,
　　　Clark.

1. Presumably Théophile Gautier (1811–1872), *Charles Baudelaire: His Life,* trans. Guy Thorne (London: Greening & Co., 1915).

2. "Symbols" (*London Mercury,* July 1922; as by "A. Clark Ashton Smith"; *EC* and *SP*). *Lyric West* published eight poems by CAS.

---

[54]   To George Sterling [ALS, NYPL]   April 11th, 1922.

Dear George:

I like your new poems—especially "The Gulls."[1] I wish *I* could turn things out whenever I want to. [. . .]

I've planned a new book, which oughtn't to be so hard to dispose of. It will be made up entirely of love-poems, and the colouring will be sensuous rather than sensual. *Sandalwood* ought to be a good title, since the imagery and the setting will be largely exotic. [. . .]

I seem to be more isolated than ever. Oh, h-ll—what a life! My "Cleopatra" has thrown herself into newspaper-work (in an effort to "forget") and her successor (?) seems to [be] nursing a mortal grudge against me. I'll either have to leave the town—or steal Andrew's girl!

Aff., Clark

1. GS, "The Gulls," *Nation* No. 2959 (22 March 1922): 345 (un-collected).

———————◆———————

[55]   To George Sterling [ALS, NYPL]   June 25th, 1922

Dear George:

I sent you a box of Lambert cherries by express last Friday. Hope you received them promptly, and made good use of them! Don't worry about *paying* for them—they didn't cost *me* anything apart from the expressage.

The cherry-picking will be over in a few days. I've been earning $3.50 per day at it. Plums are the next fruit; and I understand the wages are better for picking them. Of course, the work is a bore; but it's preferable to most other forms of wage-slavery. As to writing—I don't feel in a creative mood at present, anyway. I, too, am in a "rut,"—the opposite kind from the one of which *you* complain. Too much of the same thing is always deadly, I suppose.

If you want solitude, why not come up and spend a few days or weeks with me? You won't have to see *anyone* most of the time, if you don't want to. I haven't many friends; and they're all busy at present. And I'll be off at work most of the time, myself.

I *am* to have a book published at last! One of the local printers offered to do the job for me—on credit! They're setting up the type now; but I don't know just when it will be ready. The book will include nearly all the unpublished work that I care to preserve, aside from half-a-dozen of the more "daring" erotics. Those should have gone into T. R. Smith's anthology!

My friend Mrs. Hemphill (whom you met last summer) has published a book of short stories (mining tales of the days of '49.)[1] It came out in time for the '49 celebration at Sacramento, and sold very well, I believe.

There are two ex-bartenders on the cherry-picking "force" with which I work! Almost the only entertainment I've had lately, comes from over-hearing the reminiscences they exchange!

Aff.,

Clark.

P.S. Thanks for the check from *Snappy Stories*![2] It just came.

1. Vivia Hemphill, *Down the Mother Lode* (Sacramento: Purnell's, 1922).
2. For "Plum Flowers," see letter 56.

---

[56]   To George Sterling [ALS, NYPL]   Sept. 29th, 1922.

Dear George:

I know how hard it is to write, when one has nothing to write about. *I* haven't very much, myself; but I'm making a clean sweep of my correspondence, so here goes.

Ebony and Crystal ought to be ready before long. The type is all set up, and the paper has been ordered for it. The book ought to create something of a row, even if I *did* leave out a few of the most sensual love-poems. There are ninety-four poems and twenty prose-pastels in the collection. It will be printed on a good quality of rough paper, and bound in boards or cloth.

The poems you sent me are all good. I liked the sonnets best,— "Ephemera," and the one on Shelley.[1]

Miss McIlvaine accepted "Plum-Flowers"; and "Song" and "Artemis" are included in my book. You might send "Chance" to Mencken, however.[2] He never takes anything of mine unless *you* send it in! [. . .]

As to my love-affairs—the two that you knew about are over and done with. It's about time for another, now . . . A. and I are planning a wild picnic down in the river hills when my book comes out. I haven't decided who I'll pick for *my* partner in the affair. There are three "possibilities"—all safely married!

Here are my latest verses—a song for a projected play.[3]

Aff.,

Clark

P.S. Yes, the fruit-picking is over. Wood-cutting is the hardest work that I'm doing now!

1. GS, "Ephemera" (*All's Well,* January 1923; uncollected); "Ode to Shelley" (*Scribner's Magazine,* July 1922; in *After Sunset* [1939]).

2. Ellan [*sic*] McIlvaine was an editor at *Snappy Stories.* It is not known if "Plum-Flowers" appeared in *Snappy Stories,* but it did appear in *L'Alouette* (March 1924), an amateur journal. *Smart Set* did not publish "Chance," which CAS published in his column in *AJ* (14 June 1923).

3. "The Song of Aviol" from *The Fugitives* (*AJ,* 5 April 1923 and *Lyric West,* March 1924; *S* and *SP*). The play was not completed.

---

[57]   To George Sterling [ALS, NYPL]   Nov. 23rd, 1922

Dear George:

These are finished pages,—not proof-sheets—that I am sending you! Any alterations that I make now will have to be written in by hand. Sorry I didn't send you the galleys—I had such a h-ll of a time with misspelled words, omitted lines, etc., that I failed to give proper attention to the punctuation. My punctuation is rotten, anyway; but I don't think the linotyper improved it. Also, he repeated errors, and even made fresh ones, in attempting to correct! However, I suppose I am lucky to get this stuff into print at all.

Here is a proof of your preface, which you can send back at leisure. 90 pages of the book are done and folded ready for stitching; but I think it will take at least a fortnight more to finish the job. The binding will be done in Sacramento. . . . I enclose pages 57 to 80.

I have done all the folding myself, to expedite matters!! It's a lot of work; but, even at that, I keep up with the printers, and have time to call on one or two ladies besides.

Most of the blind-pigs in Auburn (eight or nine, at least!) were raided last Sunday and their proprietors consigned to the hoosegow! But they haven't done anything to the boot-leggers, who supply these places with hootch. I heard that one of the local Supervisors had made ten thousand by bootlegging, within the past year!

Snappy Stories has accepted a little prose-sketch of mine, entitled "The Flirt."[1] They pay 2 cents a word for prose. Maybe I'll do some more whore-mongering, at that price.

A. Dewing is as well as usual. One of my principal occupations consists in furnishing alibis for him. And occasionally he gets a chance to return the favour!

> Affectionately,
> Clark

1. This appearance not located (see *SS* 197–8), but a tearsheet exists among the CAS papers of Genevieve K. Sully.

---

[58]   To George Sterling [ALS, NYPL]   Dec. 13th, 1922

Dear George:

I've only received a few copies from the binders so far, but will probably get the rest in a day or two, and will send you a bunch of them in care of Robertson as quickly as possible. In the meanwhile, I am sending you a copy for yourself. You will note that the book has no fly-leaves, in addition to its other eccentricities! The printer only allowed for one at each end, and apparently it never occurred to anyone that the binders would have to paste these onto the cover!

I am also sending you the Bierce letters.[1] Kirk, the publisher, only sent me two of them, though I *thought* I ordered three. I'll send the other to Bender. These two are about all my purse will stand, anyway, (they're $2.00 apiece) so if I get one for Newbegin,[2] somebody else will have to pay for it. I insist on *giving* the other two.

The *Chronicle's* official jester is a fool in more senses than one.[3] I don't mind. I hope, however, that some of the others will be fairly decent.

> Aff.,
> Clark.

1. See letter 45, n.1.
2. John J. (Jack) Newbegin was a well-known book dealer in San Francisco.

3. "San Francisco Poet Treads New Worlds. Earth Fetters Cast Off by Star Rover," *San Francisco Chronicle* (10 December 1922): 59.

———————◆———————

[59]   To George Sterling [ALS, NYPL]   Dec. 17th, 1922

Dear George:

The d——d binders only sent up fifty of my books in the first consignment, and I needed most of these to fill advance orders, many of them local. I didn't receive any more till yesterday afternoon, and tried hard to get fifty of them ready in time to send off. But it took hours to number and autograph them, and correct the worst of the misprints, and the express-office had closed by the time I had them boxed up. They'll go down Monday morning, and I'll get off another fifty Monday afternoon. I'm addressing them to you in care of Robertson. I'm sorry about the delay; but, as you see, it was not my fault . . . Certainly, I'll authorize you to collect on delivery! I've paid my printer a hundred dollars, but I still owe him about four hundred more!

I was delighted with the *Argonaut* review—I hadn't expect[ed] anything half so intelligent and sympathetic from a San Francisco reviewer. *Thanks* for the extra copies! I'll write a letter of thanks to Mr. Todd.[1]

I'm not sending any copies east, except to places where I *know* they will be reviewed. One will go to Canada, for a Professor Allison of the University of Manitoba, who reviewed *The S.-T.* two or three years ago in a string of Canadian newspapers.[2] He was very enthusiastic. Also, a new correspondent and admirer of mine, Alfred Galpin, Jr., has been commissioned to write me up in *The New Republic*![3] Galpin (who is a college student at Madison, Wis.) must have a "pull" somewhere! Anyway, he is clever, and very appreciative, and will probably do the job quite well.

No, I wouldn't bother Mencken with the book. I can't think of any one in New York who would be likely to do anything for it, with the possible exception of Beni Casseres.[4] He should be the man to appreciate it. Can you get me his address? . . . I haven't much use for *The Bookman*. The editor wrote, asking me to submit some poems, and sent them back with the usual printed rejection-slip, after holding them for two or three months.

Don't forget to send me the *Examiner*'s write-up![5] They may not put it in the "rural" edition of the paper. The *Chronicle*'s little send-off was apparently confined to the city edition.

Affectionately,

Clark.

P.S. I'll send some mistletoe and toyon during the week.

1. Morton Todd, "Clark Ashton Smith's New Volume 'Ebony and Crystal' Marks Another Stage in the Development of a California Genius," *Argonaut* (16 December 1922): 387–88.

2. Prof. William Allison's review has not been located.

3. Alfred Galpin, Jr. (1901–1983), a protégé of HPL, was an amateur journalist. He wrote a review of *EC* and *ST* titled "Echoes from Beyond Space," *United Amateur* 24, No. 1 (July 1925): 3–4 (as by "Consul Hasting"). HPL claimed this piece was rejected by a dozen different magazines.

4. Benjamin De Casseres (1873–1945), "And a Little Book Shall Lead Them," *Art and Decoration* 19 (August 1923): 47 (which also reviewed GS's *Selected Poems*). De Casseres is the author of the preface to *SP*.

5. "Boy Publishes More Poems," *San Francisco Examiner* (17 December 1922): 20 (unsigned).

———————— ◆ ————————

[60]   To George Sterling [ALS, NYPL]   Feb. 9th, 1923.

Dear George:

I hope you don't think I have fallen off the map! But I seem to have had nothing that was worth putting into a letter. I hope things are not so dull at your end of the line as they are here.

I haven't heard from anybody in S.F. None of the booksellers have deigned to write me, so I presume that my book is something of a "frost." There are no letters of appreciation, even, except from people to whom I have sent copies. Publishing poetry is a thankless business.

I haven't written anything, myself; but here is a story sent me by a correspondent of mine, H. P. Lovecraft, who is a friend of Loveman's. He writes in the Poe-Bierce-Dunsany style, and his best things are astoundingly imaginative. Please return "Dagon," and tell me what you think of it.[1] The stuff is hard to publish, of course. One of Lovecraft's stories, "The Lurking Fear," is appearing as a serial in a magazine called *Home Brew*—which is somewhat on the order of *The Whiz Bang!* The editor (through Lovecraft) commissioned me to do eight drawings for the story—the first drawings that I've had published.

My father is "laid out" with a lame back at present; and I'm suffering from eyestrain, and a bad case of the "blues." Life doesn't look very rosy: my "girls" are all married, and their husbands all have me on the black-list!

Phelan sent me his book, *Travel and Comment*.[2] I haven't read much of it (I've had to spare my eyes lately) but it looks interesting.

> Aff.,
> Clark

1. In reply, GS wrote "I've a suggestion to make—a valuable one, I think. The tale is disappointing at it's climax, because there's not enough detail, enough suspense, enough action. It's all over in ten seconds, like a rabbit's amour. My advice is that he have the monster uprear, approach the monolith with horrible sounds of worship, and prostrate itself. Then have the mire quake and Dagon fall upon the monster, slaying it, just as other heads of its kind rise from the slime" (GS to CAS, 13 February 1923; ms, NYPL). Though HPL's response to CAS was cordial, he wrote a tart comment to the editor of *WT*, which had accepted the story for publication (*WT*, October 1923): "A friend of mine—Clark Ashton Smith [. . .] shewed this yarn to George Sterling, who declared he liked it very much, though suggesting (absurdly enough, as I view it!) that I have the monolith topple over and kill the 'thing' [. . .] a piece of advice which makes me feel that poets should stick to their sonneteering" (HPL to Edwin Baird, c. June 1923; *WT* 2, No. 3 [October 1923]: 82). To his horror, the comment was published in the magazine's letter column. He later wrote Baird, "I hope . . . that Messrs. Starrett and Sterling won't start gunning for me because of the allusions I make in those letters!" (HPL to Edwin Baird, c. October 1923; *WT* 3, No. 1 [January 1924]: 86, 88).

2. James Duval Phelan (1861–1930), *Travel and Comment* (San Francisco: A. M. Robertson, 1923). Phelan had been a banker, mayor of San Francisco for three terms, and U.S. Senator for one term; he was one of CAS's financial benefactors. Phelan quotes from CAS's poem "Psalm" in the final section of his book.

---

[61]   To George Sterling [ALS, NYPL]   June 23rd, 1923.

Dear George:

No, I have heard nothing from Mrs. Spreckels. But I think I told you that Armsby remitted.[1] And I have earned a few dollars by fruit-picking, so the bean-sack is never quite empty.

Your poems were all excellent, as usual. No one else can keep on turning out good work the way you do. I enclose some more of my own verses: There's no inspiration in them; but they're better than I could have done a few years ago without inspiration. Facility can be acquired, I suppose, if one keeps at it long enough.

There is a new magazine called *Weird Tales,* which is publishing hell-raisers that no other periodical would print. They wrote asking me to send in some verse![2] "Dagon," the tale by H. P. Lovecraft that I showed you some time ago, was accepted by them.

Lovecraft tells me that I am mentioned in Braithwaite's last anthology. Methinks the honour is a dubious one.

My mother is going to a family re-union in Monterey at the end of the month. Probably she will be in S.F. about the second week in July.

I don't know when I will be able to come down. But I don't care much at present: life promises to become a little more amusing than it has been. Perhaps I'll bring a *new* lady-love with me, when I do come, instead of the one you inquire about.

What do you think of the stationery? My printer gave me a whole ream of it for nothing!

    Aff.,

      Clark.

1. The wife of Rudolph Spreckels (d. 1958), the sugar magnate, had been a benefactor of CAS. Raymond Armsby has not been identified.
2. The editor had decided not to publish poetry in *WT,* but when HPL lent him samples of CAS's work, he relented. CAS's first appearance in *WT* was "The Red Moon" [="Moon-Dawn"] and "The Garden of Evil" [="Duality"] (July–August 1923), thus antedating HPL's first appearance (save for a published letter).

---

[62]   To Frank Belknap Long[1] [ALS, private collection]

                                July 7th, 1923.

My dear Long:

It seems incredible that I have had your last letter on my desk for over a month without answering it. I have been busy, for one thing . . . Not, however, at poetry-writing—only at what the 100 per cent American would call "useful labour." Personally, I agree with De Gourmont[2] that work is only a "sad necessity" at best. I can't understand the popular tendency to exalt and deify something that is usually disagreeable—or worse. . . .

I suppose you are right about the northern peoples and their distrust of colour. Why don't you work out the theory in an essay?

You could prove that poetry—like morality—is largely a matter of latitude.

I have seen a book called *The Hasheesh-Eater,* which was published by Harpers back in the fifties or sixties. The author called himself "The Pythagorean"; and the book was obviously written in imitation of De Quincey.[3] I wonder if it is the name that you refer to . . . I remember one passage in which the author described himself as hovering in the air above a floor lined with red-hot needles! . . . No, I shouldn't advise you to tamper with hasheesh. The reaction is terrible, especially in those of a nervous temperament. I have never taken it myself, but I know several people who have. My friend George Sterling had a lot of the stuff in his possession at one time.

The poem you sent me ("Nostalgia")[4] is melodious and haunting. I like it all, except the word "jellied." Why not use something like "woven," or "plighted," or "pleachèd" if you don't mind the suggestion.

Here are some more of my own verses.

    Yours,
        Clark Ashton Smith

1. Frank Belknap Long (1901–1994), fiction writer and poet and one of HPL's closest friends and correspondents.

2. Remy de Gourmont (1858–1915), French philosopher and essayist then enjoying a vogue. The comment is probably from *A Night in the Luxembourg,* trans. Arthur Ransome (New York: Modern Library, 1923).

3. Fitz-Hugh Ludlow (1836–1870), *The Hasheesh Eater; Being Passages from the Life of a Pythagorean* (1857); Thomas De Quincey (1785–1859), *Confessions of an English Opium-Eater* (1822).

4. Not located; perhaps unpublished.

---

[63]   To George Sterling [ALS, NYPL]   Nov. 4th, 1923.

Dear George:

This is an unusual lapse even for me—it must be two or three months since I received your last letter. But I guess you'll forgive me: there has been little or nothing to write about, anyway.

De Casseres' review came out in September. It was very "brief mention," though favourable enough to *me,* as you surmised. I'll enclose it with this. . . . I sent a copy of *E. & C.* to Arthur Symons some time ago, in care of his London publisher. I hope it will reach him in one of his lucid intervals.

I have not written any verse this fall, with the exception of the enclosed ("Barrier.")[1] Latterly, I've amused myself by making a lot of epigrams, and am letting the *Auburn Journal* print the milder ones.[2] Many people think the stuff might easily be syndicated; certainly, I hope so: it's about the only *possible* way for me to ever make any money—unless I marry a rich wife. And I've known too many married women to think highly of marriage.

Life isn't so rotten as it was, apart from eyestrain, and having to milk the cow for my nearest neighbour's widow! I seem to be almost popular, of late, with the Auburn ladies. There's nothing like having a bad reputation!—at least, for a poet.

You *did* give me a copy of your *Selected Poems:*[3] my mother brought it home from the city with her. The selection was excellent, for general purposes: Doubtless not nearly so many people would buy the selection I would make.

Andrew spoke of meeting you one night in the city . . . I'll *never* have a chance to come down again, unless I syndicate my "column"![4]

   Aff.,
    Clark.

1. "The Barrier" (*AJ*, 13 September 1923; rpt. in *Step Ladder*, May 1927; *S* and *SP*).

2. Most of CAS's epigrams appeared in *AJ* between 4 October 1923 and 11 June 1925. They are gathered in *The Devil's Notebook* (Mercer Island, WA: Starmont House, 1990).

3. GS, *Selected Poems* (New York: Henry Holt & Co., [May] 1923).

4. *AJ* published "Clark Ashton Smith's Column" and other items from 1923–1926. It consisted primarily of poetry and epigrams.

---

[64] To George Sterling [ALS, NYPL]   July 21st, 1924.

Dear George:

You owed *me* a letter—but I'll forgive you. Thanks for the various notes from magazine editors that you forwarded me. I was surprised that any one would even consider "The Pagan."[1] I tried Benet with "On the Canyon-Side" and "The Witch with Amber Eyes,"[2] but apparently they were too strong for him.

Hope you received the *Ten Story Book* containing a storiette of mine.[3] I received $6.00 for it—on publication! But the story was rotten, anyhow—except for the spanking—which was what I *ought* to have administered, some time back, to a certain badly spoiled female person.

The magazines are always welcome. My lady friends get a great kick out of some of them—particularly *The Chicago Literary Times*.

I ought to work, but don't seem to get anything done in a literary way. Doubtless I'd be in better shape if I could afford a few hundred dollars worth of treatment from doctors, dentists, and oculists. As it is, I'm cutting live oak wood for a little money to live on next winter. Armsby seems to have dropped out again, though Phelan and Crocker[4] keep on remitting . . . I'll have to go in for bootlegging or blackmail if I'm ever to make any money!

As ever,
Clark.

1. "The Pagan" appeared in *S&P*, but was to be published first in *SP* as a "translation" by Chrisophe des Laurières.
2. "On the Canyon-Side" (*AJ*, 27 September 1923; in *SP*); "The Witch with Eyes of Amber" (*AJ*, 24 May 1923; in *DC* and *SP*). William Rose Benét (1886–1950) was editor of *Saturday Review of Literature*.
3. "Something New" (*Ten Story Book*, August 1924; in *OD*).
4. C[harles] Templeton Crocker (1884–1948), philanthropist, patron of the arts, and benefactor of the California Historical Society.

[65]   To George Sterling [ALS, NYPL]   Jan. 20th, 1925.

Dear George:

I have been laid up for the past week with an injured toe, and am learning to curse by more gods than you could find in a book of cross-word puzzles. I ought to be out cutting wood to help pay off the family mortgage! (which falls due next winter.) It's a merry life . . . Also, my best friend has left the neighborhood (including her husband) and things are upset, and likely to be more so. [. . .]

If this d——d toe doesn't improve pretty soon, I'll have it amputated! It was bruised (not broken) by a falling block of wood; and a bruise of that sort is worse than a break, sometimes. I can't afford to be laid up for any length of time.

Aff.,
Clark.

[66]   To Ina Coolbrith[1] [ALS, BL]   March 12th, 1925

Dear Miss Coolbrith:

Thank you for your kind letter, which I had meant to acknowledge long before this. Diffidence more than anything else, has
restrained me: But I *would* have written a little sooner, if I had
known that you had a birthday in March. I was delighted by the
account in the San Francisco papers: it is good to know that one
true poet, at least, is "not without honour." Surely you deserve it—
and more.

Miss Ahern[2] tells me that you are having difficulty in finding a
publisher. Truly, I am fitted to sympathize, since I am engaged in
the same elusive and exasperating search. The publication of my
last book was due to the generosity of a local printer who, I am
afraid, has barely cleared expenses . . . In your case, surely the difficulty is due to the present day confusion of poetic values—or (one
is tempted to say) the almost total lack of them. "Bedlam [is] loose,
and the bars are down." But perhaps there will be a lucid interval,
some day.

I am very much on the shelf at present, with a lame foot (a truly
Byronic impediment!) but some day I mean to send you a few of
the local wild-flowers, if you will accept them.

With thanks for your appreciation, and all best wishes, I am,
dear Miss Coolbrith,

        Your admirer,
            Clark Ashton Smith

1. Ina Donna Coolbrith (1841–1928; born Josephine D. Smith, niece
of the Mormon prophet) was an editor of the *Overland Monthly* and
the first poet laureate named in the U.S. (1915–1928).

2. Mary Eileen Ahern (1860–1938) was a librarian along with
Coolbrith at the public library in Oakland.

———————————•———————————

[67]   To George Sterling [ALS, NYPL]   March 15th, 1925.

Dear George:

No, I didn't kick a boulder over the cabin: I was sawing
wood—and a block rolled off the pile, and struck me on the little
toe. I'm still laid up—any effort to get around only sets me back;
and Satan only knows when I'll be able to wear a shoe and set the

village husbands to worrying again . . . But I guess poets are always more or less unlucky: Their ill-luck begins with the fact that they *are* poets, in a world of pigs and pawnbrokers.

Don't apologise for the magazines you send. The worse the merrier, from my viewpoint. I find a Satanic amusement in some of them,—especially Miss Monroe's monthly assortment of canary-droppings.

The confinement is "getting my goat," and I don't feel very creative. My latest diversion is paraphrasing a few of the Baudelaire translations by F. P. Sturm and others.[1] I don't know how close my versions come to the original; anyway, French verse (B. included) *seems* infernally banal, from what little I can make out . . . Probably I have superadded a good deal . . . Anyway, I have tried to avoid such pusillanimous banalities as "woman frail and weak" in Sturm's translation of "The Remorse of the Dead."[2] Compare the second half of his octave with mine:

"And when the stone upon thy trembling breast
And on thy straight sweet body's supple grace,
Crushes thy will and keeps thy heart at rest,
And holds those feet from their adventurous race—"[3]

I've never seen the original; but it seems to me that my version is more *Baudelairean*. B. *might* have written something of the sort.

There isn't much news to record, as far as I know. Hardly anyone comes near me. I begin to think that the person who would most like to come is being kept in a room with barred windows! Drew was here the other day. He seemed to be on the sick-list, but was rather vague concerning the nature of his malady.

If you know any superfluous virgins, you might give them my address. But tell 'em to bring enough money for return fare!

Affectionately,
Clark—

1. Frank Pearce Sturm (1879–1942), *The Poems of Charles Baudelaire*, selected and translated from the French by F. P. Strum (London: The Walter Scott Publishing Co., 1906; rpt. AMS Press, 1981). The other translators are unknown.

2. "The Remorse of the Dead," p. 30. In his translation (*The Measure*, April 1925), CAS instead used the phrase "unslumbering wantons."

3. CAS's reading of these lines (5–8) is:
Yea, when the ponderous carven shaft unshaken
Is the one weight your passionate nipples know,
And grinds you down and will not let you go
To find again your faithless lechers . . .

[68]   To H. P. Lovecraft[1] [ALS, JHL]   March 20th, 1925.

My dear Lovecraft:

I was indeed glad to hear from you, and to infer that you took no offense at my prolonged silence. Also, I was glad to hear that *Weird Tales* is still running, since the local news stand no longer buys it, and the proprietor seemed to think that *W.T.* had ceased publication.

Here is "Yondo,"[2] in which you will probably find some ideas and images. This is my best copy—and I wish you would forward it to *Weird Tales* for me after you have read it. I have lost the present address of the magazine, having given all the late copies to a fair friend who has since left the neighborhood—and her husband. The last copy I bought contained your "Festival" and (I think) something of Long's, "The Desert Lich?"[3] "The Festival" (as I have doubtless said before) is a masterpiece of sepulchral horrors, in which the powers of corruption attain forms of unimaginable menace. I liked "The Desert Lich" (the only contribution of Long's to *W.T.* that I have seen so far). It is wonderfully imaginative, but I have the feeling that Long could do better in point of style, if he tried.

I should like very much to see Long's critique of my work, and hope you will send me a copy of the magazine containing it.[4]

I am glad Loveman and Kirk have pulled out from Cleveland, which must have been an uncongenial sort of place . . . I mailed a batch of typescripts to Loveman's Cleveland address a few days before your letter came, and hope it will be forwarded.

Here are two of my crossword puzzles, which you can keep indefinitely, though I should like them returned some time, since they are my only copies. The ones you would like best have been loaned to others; but the smaller of these two is fairly demoniacal,—and the larger one is an unholy goulash containing everything from Mediterranean thirst-provokers to Chinese dynasties. Many of the two-letter words, "ab," "ar," "oc," "Fo," "Ve," etc, are complete in themselves! If these two don't give your puzzle-fiend[5] "the Molossian pip" (to use George Sterling's phrase in describing the effect of archaic words on magazine editors) I'll send you some that will!

Weird Tales may not care for "Yondo." I'll have to shed some of my exotic diction to produce anything saleable . . . And there were one or two audacities ("large as the body of a gravid she-goat," etc.) which may serve to "queer" the story, apart from the language.[6] I haven't finished "Sadastor," which will be utterly unsaleable, anyway. But I will finish it presently.[7]

I have a story based on the effects of hashish, also half-finished.[8] Prose-writing comes hard with me—but I am beginning to think that I might do something in that line, if I set myself to it. There are some good paragraphs in "Yondo,"—at least, comparatively good . . . But English (as Joseph Conrad observed) is a rotten medium for prose, and a marvellous one for poetry. I find it impossible to understand why so few people care for English verse.

I am still crippled, and may be for some time. I don't know anything more tiresome than a bone-bruise: a clean break would heal more quickly.

Remember me to Loveman, Kirk, and Long.

As ever,
CAS

1. H. P. Lovecraft (1890–1937), the great American author of weird fiction, corresponded with CAS from 1922 until HPL died. This letter is the earliest surviving letter to him from CAS.

2. *WT* rejected "The Abominations of Yondo" (*Overland Monthly*, April 1926; *AY*).

3. *WT* (January 1925) contained HPL's "The Festival" and Long's "The Ocean Leech." "The Desert Lich" had appeared in *WT* (November 1924).

4. CAS refers to Alfred Galpin's review of *ST* and *EC* in the *United Amateur*; see letter 59, n.3.

5. I.e., HPL's friend James Ferdinand Morton (1870–1941), curator of the municipal museum in Paterson, NJ; see letter 195.

6. This phrase occurs in the magazine appearance of the story.

7. "Sadastor" (*WT*, July 1930; *OST* and *PP*).

8. The uncompleted story, "In a Hashish-Dream" (*SS*).

---

[69]   To George Sterling [ALS, NYPL]   May 21st, 1925.

Dear George:

Thanks for all those magazines! The more contemporary verse I read, the more highly I think of my own productions!

Have you written to me in the past two months? I've been losing mail, in addition to my other troubles.

Here are some more Baudelaires. I feel frightfully stale and un-creative—the natural result of being laid up so long. I get around a little on the ranch; but it may be months before I can walk to town without doing myself up. Of all the putrid luck—!!!

However, the village is still talking about me! One of my fair friends has brought suit for divorce; and some of the local tabbies seem to think that I have an interest in the case. In reality, no one is to blame,—except the husband, who is an ass of the first magnitude. But the lady and I have been seen together pretty often . . . There was one yarn going around, to the effect that we used to meet every day at the local post-office! That's a h-ll of a rendez-vous! [. . .]

I notice that Gelber is publishing books of verse.[1] Does he do it at his own expense—or only in the customary way?

> As ever,
> Clark.

1. The publisher Gelber Lilienthal of San Francisco, presumably under the imprint of The Lantern Press.

---

[70]   To George Sterling [ALS, NYPL]   July 1st, 1925.

Dear George:

My copy of the B. C. Anthology arrived last week. Your preface is about the best thing it contains—from my point of view. Many of the poems are meritorious, or at least clever; but not one of them is *pure poetry*. Yours and Lafler's are probably the best. One of Scheffauer's was good, too.[1] But I don't "get" this vitalistic school. Some of their stuff is clever (but, lacking the preservative of fine art, it will look—and smell—like a lot of dead cabbages the day after to-morrow).

Here are some more Baudelaires. I have been digging the stuff out of the original French—and find it well worth the effort. Most of the poems are new to me (Sturm only translated about a third of them, and his rendering is a bit Bowdlerized in places ("flood" for "slime," "wanton" for "lecherous woman," etc., etc.) And I don't think he gives an adequate impression of the style and technical qualities. The manner is peculiarly formal, glacial, armor-like—but often with a red-hot content! There are many beautiful things,—and one, at least, that is ghastlier even [than] "The Corpse." It describes a room where a woman has been murdered (decapitated,) by her lover, who has left the naked body lying on the bed, and placed the head on the table! There is more than a hint of necrophilism in the poem—it is more awful than Poe's "Berenice."[2]

I am so disgusted with everything and everybody, that I would write my own poems in French—or Latin,—if I knew either language well enough.

I walked to town yesterday, for the first time since January—and my feet are so blistered as a result that I can hardly toddle today! I'm certainly in no condition to pick fruit.

By the way, I'd be glad to type some of your poems for you if you'd care to send them up. I'd return them promptly—and you wouldn't have to pay a typist.

I'll send my new collection of verse (*Sandalwood*) to Seymour[3] in a few days. I've been holding it to polish up some of the Baudelaires; but my brain refuses to work in this devastating torridity. I hope this Seymour isn't a stickler for "modernity." Anyway, I'm leaving out all the lascivious ones. If he rejects the collection, I'll put 'em all in again, and send it to Pascal Covichi![4]

> As ever,
> Clark.

1. *Continent's End: An Anthology of Contemporary Poets,* ed. GS, Genevieve Taggard, and James Rorty (San Francisco: Book Club of California, 1925), contained "On the Canyon-Side" and "Transcendence" (*EC, SP,* and *LO*). The poet Herman George Scheffauer (1878–1927) was a friend of GS and another of AB's disciples.

2. CAS refers to "Un Martyre."

3. George Steele Seymour (b. 1878), of the Bookfellows of Chicago.

4. Pascal Covici (1888–1964), book publisher in Chicago known for publishing daring books sometimes banned for obscenity; champion and publisher of John Steinbeck.

---

[71]   To Donald Wandrei[1] [ALS, MHS]   July 10th, 1925.

Dear Mr. Wandrei:

I am greatly indebted to you for the loan of the *Book of Jade,*[2] which I will return in a week or two. You are right about the mortuary poems being the best: some of them, such as the "Sonnet of the Instruments of Death," "Sepulchral Life" etc. are truly impressive, and, it seems to me, very original. There is a tremendous idea in the "Grotesques," also, in the second of the "Fragments." In the first section, the sonnet "Ennui" impressed me as being perhaps the best, or at least, the most perfect. Ennui and sheer corruption are both extremely difficult subjects to handle. If I am ever in a position to edit an anthology, I will certainly include at least half-a-dozen of these poems.

There is no *certainty* that *Sandalwood* will be accepted by the publisher to whom I am sending it. Most of the poems are not in my best style; so maybe it will have a chance! "Reve Parisien," one of my Baudelaires, is the best poem in the book. There are fourteen other attempts at Baudelaire; but I'm not sure yet whether most of them are good or bad. As far as I know, I am the only translator who has done them in the original metres. It is far harder to write good alexandrines in English than in French.

No, there is hardly any one who writes poetry of the imaginative type any more. There is a book called *Vanitas* by one Paul Eldridge,[3] which is *said* to be in the Baudelaire style; but I've never seen it. It is easier to find imaginative prose. You should read the earlier books of Lafcadio Hearn, particularly *Fantastics* and *Stray Leaves from Strange Literature,* if you have not seen them.[4] And you might find something in Lord Dunsany's *Book of Wonder and Dreamer's Tales.*[5]

I am planning a new book which will contain nothing but pure poetry, no sentimentalities, no philosophical aridities—nothing but the strange, the magical, and the gorgeous! *Incantations* might be a good title for this book . . . which, in all likelihood, I will have to print at my own expense.[6]

Thanking you again for *The Book of Jade,* and for the magnificent compliments you pay me, I remain,

> Very sincerely,
> Clark Ashton Smith

1. Donald A. Wandrei (1908–1987), poet and author of weird and science fiction. He and AWD founded Arkham House to publish the work of HPL; they ultimately published numerous books by CAS.

2. David Park Barnitz (1878–1901), *The Book of Jade* (New York: Doxey's, [1901]); rpt. Durtro Press, 1998 (the author's name appears nowhere in the first edition).

3. Paul Eldridge (1888–1982), U.S. educator and poet, *Vanitas* (Boston: The Stratford Co., 1920).

4. Lafcadio Hearn, *Fantastics and Other Fancies* (1914); *Stray Leaves from Strange Literature: Stories Reconstructed from the Anvari-Soheili, Baital Pachisi, Mahabharata, Pantchatantra, Gulistan, Talmud, Kalewa, etc.* (1912).

5. Edward John Moreton Drax Plunkett, 18th baron Dunsany, (1878–1957), *The Book of Wonder* (1912); *A Dreamer's Tales* (1910).

6. The book never was published. RHB, first through his Dragon-Fly Press, then through the The Futile Press of the Beck brothers of Lakeport, CA, had intended to publish it in the late 1930s, but CAS withdrew the ms. after a falling out with RHB. CAS ultimately included a section in *SP* entitled *Incantations.*

[72]   To Donald Wandrei [ALS, MHS]   Aug. 25th, 1925.

Dear Mr. Wandrei:

Many thanks for the loan of *Dreams after Sunset*. I agree with you that some of the poems are good, but most of them are more or less disappointing. Saltus seems to have written about ten times too much. I have never seen *Shadows and Ideals* (a good title) but will certainly keep an eye out for it. *The Bayadar* [sic] *and Other Sonnets* is the collection I have.[1] Speaking of sonnets you should see the *Collected S. of Lloyd Mifflin*,[2] which contains between three and four hundred! Some of them are fairly good, though not highly imaginative.

No, I have not seen *Les Paradises* [sic] *Artificiels*, which is, in part, a translation of De Quincey's "Opium Eater."[3] The original portion is a monograph on the effects of hashish. One of Baudelaire's translators—F. P. Sturm—speaks of it as showing a deterioration in his style.

Robert Chinault Givler is a new name to me.[4] I note that a book of poems called *The King of the Black Isles* by someone named Nicholson (I forget his initials) has been published in Chicago.[5] The title is attractive, and the specimen of the contents that I saw quoted, was uncommonly musical. Also, the book was severely "slated" by Harriet Monroe, editor of *Poetry* (?), which is a recommendation in itself.

It will cost at least a hundred dollars to print a pamphlet of the sort that I am contemplating. Printers charge by the page; and I doubt if the material I have can be crammed into less than fifty pages, even by printing it continuously, with the shorter ones two to a page. But there should be no great difficulty in disposing of so small an edition as 200 copies. It will be a rare and precious item for collectors, some day!—if I can get the necessary hundred dollars.

As to the inadequate praise received by *Ebony and Crystal*— well, you ought to know that connoisseurs are few and far between. However, the world usually accepts the judgement of the experts in the long run. There were few published reviews of the book, and most of these were more or less laudatory. Benjamin de Casseres was one who praised it highly. . . . Many copies, however, were sold locally, to people of the Babbitt type, who purchased it more from curiosity than any other motive. About all they could understand, was the erotic imagery in a few of the poems,—which gave the book a reputation for impropriety among the village Methodists!

My Baudelaires have been highly praised by people who know the original. It was hard to make anything of "La Fontaine de Sang," which I enclose. The last two lines, *literally* translated, ran thus: "But love for me is only a mattress of needles, / Made for to give a drink to the cruel girls!" Surely my last line is an improvement![6]

I'll return the Saltus in a few days.

    Cordially,

      C. A. S.

1. Francis S. Saltus (1849–1899), *Dreams After Sunset: Poems* (1892); *Shadows and Ideals: Poems* (1890); *The Bayadère and Other Sonnets* (1894).

2. Lloyd Mifflin (1846–1921), *Collected Sonnets of Lloyd Mifflin* (1905).

3. Baudelaire's *Les Paradis Artificiels* (1862) is an account of the dreamlike visions he experienced under the influence of alcohol, opium, and hashish.

4. Robert Chenault Givler (1884–?), author of *The Ethics of Hercules: A Study of Man's Body as the Sole Determinant of Ethical Values* (1924). But see letter 73, n.2.

5. J[ohn] U[rban] Nicolson (1885–1944), *King of the Black Isles* (Chicago: Covici-McGee Co., 1924).

6. CAS's polished ending reads "But love for me is a mattress that sharp needles fill, / Whereon, for thirsty girls, my blood pours many a rill" (*SP*).

---

[73]   To Donald Wandrei [ALS, MHS]   Sept. 12th, 1925.

Dear Mr. Wandrei:

It is princely of you to offer to assume even half the expense of printing *Sandalwood!* I can't raise *all* of the remainder at present; but the printer, who is a good fellow, is to go ahead, anyway, and you will be glad to know that the linotyping of the book has already been begun. It will be bound in a heavy, bluish-green art-paper, tied with cord; and will, I think, present a fairly attractive appearance. I am including 43 new lyrics and sonnets, together with 19 of my Baudelaires. Many of the poems are so brief that they can be printed two to a page.

When you send me your checque, I suggest that you register the envelope containing it. Some of my mail (including the typescript of a short story) has gone astray during the past year.

I enclose two more Baudelaires. It is remarkable how few modern English poets have used the alexandrine at all. Dowson has the best ones; and Arthur Symons and Lionel Johnson have also used the line to good effect. There is an excellent specimen ("Ante Aram") in Rupert Brooke, too. Most of Bergen Applegate's Verlaine alexandrines don't impress me as being any too good; but then, Verlaine is far harder to translate even than Baudelaire.[1] Symons did the best ones on the whole; but they are more Symons than Verlaine. Thanks for the book of Givler's poems! There seems to [be] a genuine poetic impulse in the "Dream-Flowers"; but most of the others are banal and didactic.[2]

I will return *Shadows and Ideals* next week. A few of the poems are excellent; and the ones in French are quite pretty.

If the books you name were included in the Auburn library, they would all be relegated to the back closet—and would have a considerable circulation, since people could find them without hunting all over the shelves! However, you forget Balzac's *Droll Stories,* the *Novellino* of Masucchio, and Louys' *Aphrodite.* I possess copies of these; and the ladies are always borrowing them. They think the *Heptameron* dull by comparison![3]

I have tried to be faithful to the thought and mood of the original in my translations. But you will notice, in several instances, that I have varied the images a little. However, I do not think that I have *essentially* altered, or falsified anything, as the other translators of B. have sometimes done. Even W. J. Robertson[4] offends in this respect. "Tu contiens dans ton oeil le couchant and l'aurore" is rendered "Thine eye is filled with dawn, with twilight dwindles"—which is miles away from Baudelaire's meaning—also sheer nonsense. My version of the fourth stanza in this poem ("Hymne à la Beauté") is perhaps more lurid than the original, since I have used "rosary" in place of "bijoux" and "jewelled crucifix" in lieu of "breloque" (trinket, or charm).[5] However, the substitution seems "Baudelairian" enough.

Thanking you a thousand times in advance for the loan of the fifty, I am

Cordially yours,
Clark Ashton Smith

Have you ever read "The Sphinx" of Oscar Wilde? You would like it, I think.

1. The poets are Ernest Dowson (1867–1900); Lionel Pigot Johnson (1867–1902); Rupert Brooke (1887–1915); and Bergen Weeks Applegate. CAS himself translated a few poems of the French lyric and Symbolist poet, Paul Verlaine (1844–1896); in *SP.*
2. *Poems* (n.p., n.d., 143 pp.), an exceedingly rare book.

3. Honoré de Balzac (1799–1850) *Contes drolatiques* [*Droll Stories*] (1832–1837; CAS's projected novel of Zothique, *The Scarlet Succubus*, was said to have taken its inspiration from a story in this book); Salernitano Masuccio (15th cent.), *Novellino*; Pierre Louys (1870–1925) *Aphrodite: Ancient Manners* (1925); Queen Marguerite of Navarre (1492–1549) *L'Heptameron* (Arthur Machen's translation [1886] was published by Knopf in 1924).

4. William John Robertson (1846–?), *A Century of French Verse: Brief Biographical and Critical Notices of Thirty-Three French Poets of the Nineteenth Century with Experimental Translations from Their Poems* (1895).

5.   "Thou tramplest on the dead with mockeries eternal;
    Horror is half thy jewel-laden rosary;
    And Murder is a precious amulet infernal
    That on thy bosom burns and trembles amorously." (*SP*)

---

[74]   To George Sterling [ALS, NYPL]   Sept. 14th, 1925.

Dear George:

Thanks for the review,—which, however, I have seen before. It was submitted to me in ms. by the author, a student at the University of Minnesota, named Alfred Galpin.[1] Some of his criticism were quite amazing; but not all of them were sincere: he tried to get the article into The *Nation* (or *Freeman*, I forget which) and qualified his praise in an effort to obviate suspicion. However, they refused to "bite."

I have had to break my back lately, to earn a few miserable dollars, and have done very little writing. Damn the economical system: I ought to have a rich mistress.

I am printing a small edition (250 copies) of *Sandalwood*, myself. A new admirer (in St. Paul, of all places) very generously offered to assume half the expense; and the printer is willing to give me credit on the rest. The book will be bound in art-paper, tied with cord, and certainly ought to present a more attractive—and saleable—appearance than the last one. It contains 43 new lyrics and sonnets and 19 of my French translations. I have taken the liberty of dedicating it to you.

No, the *Mercury*[2] is not obtainable in Auburn. I don't imagine anyone in these parts would buy it, except me—and I'm too poor, at present.

Stella was a great girl! I'd like to have seen her.
        Aff., Clark.

1. See letter 59, n.3. CAS has mistaken Alfred Galpin for DAW.
2. H. L. Mencken's *American Mercury* magazine.

[75]   To George Sterling [ALS, NYPL]   Dec. 1st, 1925.

Dear George:

Thanks for the *Argonaut* review[1]—which, like the other, amused and disgusted, but did not surprise, me.

I sent *Sandalwood* to de Casseres, and he wrote me a letter shortly after mailing that card to you. His praise of *E. & C.* is certainly munificent; and I don't know of anyone whose opinion I value more.

I can't agree with the high-brows that the "weird" is dead—either in poetry or anywhere else. They're all suffering from mechanized imaginations. But, I, for one, refuse to submit to the arid, earth-bound spirit of the time; and I think there is sure to be a romantic revival sooner or later—a revolt against mechanization and over-socialization, etc. If there isn't—then I hope to hell my next incarnation will be in some happier and freer planet. Neither the ethics or the aesthetics of the ant-hill have any attraction for me.

Here is my latest. I'm in no mood to write madrigals. Some of the fantasies I am planning will have an ironic undercurrent of the deadliest kind. The enclosed is mild.

Your poem *might* get the *Nation's* prize—good luck to it. I may be "naive"—but not sufficiently so to submit any of my verse in that contest! As to "Yondo"—*Weird Tales* (which pays ½ cent per word) *might* have taken it under the former editor, who actually published Lovecraft's "Dagon." The present editor is more commercial;[2] but he did take two of my Baudelaires, and will pay 25¢ per line for them on publication.[3] I may write some shockers for him, with more action and less poetry than "Yondo." Lovecraft's tales are appearing in the magazine every month.

My mother has an injured hand, which may take quite a while to heal. The Lord certainly favours the poor!

As ever,
Clark.

1. [Morton Todd], "The Bard of Auburn," *Argonaut* (14 November 1925): 9.
2. Farnsworth Wright (1888–1940) replaced Edwin Baird (1886–1957) as editor of *WT* in November 1924.
3. "Spleen" (*WT*, February 1926; *SP*); "Horreur Sympathétique" (*S*; *WT*, May 1926; *SP*).

[76]   To George Sterling [ALS, NYPL]   May 8th, 1926.

Dear George:

Here is a copy of "The Envoys" for *The Overland*. I hope it will get a few more goats. "Yondo" must have had a kick in it, after all, if it aroused so many protests.[1]

Ben De C. has sent me his new book, *Forty Immortals*.[2] It is great stuff, like everything else of his that I have read. I understand that he intends to do one some day on you, Jeffers, and myself, under the title of "Three California Poets."[3] I appreciate the prospective honour, though, in my present mood, I feel inclined to deny that I am a Californian . . . But I suppose one might as well be that as anything, since one can't emigrate to Saturn. . . . Moronism, unhappily, is not confined to California.

I've gone back to the wood-pile, and may pick fruit later. Would have written before, but I get so beastly tired after a few hours' work. The "freak" rain-storms are giving me a day or two of respite. I got caught in a cloud-burst yesterday, coming home from the village. The cherry-crop must be pretty well ruined (by the rain) for commercial purposes: I'm glad I've no fruit to worry about.

Send me that new poem—the perverse one—when you have a copy . . . You and Jeffers won't leave me anything to express, except a complete reaction against sex, à la Odo of Cluny.[4] The attitude should have a certain novelty, in this age of satyriasis! I have a perfectly plausible and defensible theory that we live and act in order to learn the worthlessness of life and action.

Don't forget to look up George Moore's address for me. Also, the address of any one else you can think of who might appreciate my stuff. I have about a hundred copies of *Ebony and Crystal* left—apparently unsaleable. My stock of *Sandalwood*, though, has dwindled to about thirty.

Thanks for the clippings. I note that Lewis has refused the Pulitzer prize—but I'd refuse it, too, if my work sold as well as Lewis'.[5]

As ever,
Clark—

1. "Your 'Yondo' awoke many protests from the mentally infirm, I'm told" (GS to CAS, April 18, 1926; ms., NYPL).

2. *Forty Immortals* (New York: J. Lawren [1926]).

3. (John) Robinson Jeffers (1887–1962), a controversial U.S. poet of the early 20th century. His third book, *Tamar and Other Poems* (1924),

brought him immediate fame. He was a friend of GS, and subject of GS's *Robinson Jeffers: The Man and the Artist* (1926).

4. Published as *Strange Waters* [San Francisco: Privately printed, August 1926], a poem with a Lesbian theme, written in the manner of Jeffers.

5. Sinclair Lewis (1885–1951) had won the Pulitzer Prize in 1925 for his novel *Arrowsmith*.

———•———

[77]   To H. P. Lovecraft [ALS, private collection]
May 9th, 1926

Dear H.P.L.:

It is good to know that you found so much in my latest paintings. I, too, consider them an advance on my earlier work. I don't suppose my "technique" will ever be perfect; but, by dint of practice, I am acquiring a little more of the artist's touch than I used to have . . . Few have managed to excell [*sic*] in two arts—Blake and Rosetti are almost the only ones that come readily to mind. Poetry and painting are *not* interchangeable—what you express through one you *cannot* express through the other. For this reason, I contend that my verses and paintings are complementary to each other.

I can readily imagine the contrast between Brooklyn and Providence. All the big cities are becoming more or less polyglot— and lots of the small ones, too, for that matter. But I suppose New England has suffered less from foreign invasion than most of the U. S. My mother's people were New Englanders, by the way—the family (Gaylord) has been in America since 1630. They were descendants of Huguenot refugees driven out of France at the time of the revocation of the Edict of Nantes—the name was Gaillard originally. Oddly enough, some of my father's people, the Ashtons, were English Catholics! The mixture should make for non-conformity.

I trust you will find the home atmosphere more conducive to literary work than Brooklyn and turn out a number of new masterpieces. I have not forgotten my own project for some short stories and prose fantasies.

Hope something can be done with the paintings! There must be collectors somewhere who would appreciate and buy them. [. . .]

I wrote to Long the other day. Regards to all the "gang." I'll be interested to hear their reaction to the pictures . . . . Incidentally (as I told Long) I am an ignoramus concerning phallic symbolism, and seldom "do" a picture with a consciously symbolic intention of any kind. The drawings simply represent a quest for exotic beauty, weirdness, and fantasy—"anything out of the world." But, of course, they may have an unconscious symbolism. I am not a psychoanalyst—and don't think much of psychoanalysis, anyway.[1] As ever,

> Cordially yours,
> CAS

1. See CAS's satire "Sonnet for the Psychoanalysts" (*SP*).

---

[78]   To Benjamin De Casseres [ALS]   May 22nd, 1926.

Dear Ben:

Thanks! There are many splendid things in your new book; I have read it over twice, and find something new and superlative every time I dip into it. Indeed, we have been working in the same thought-stratum; but your epigrams are richer than mine. You have a tremendous vision of the phantom-flux of time and matter, the masques and mummeries of the infinite, and the ineluctable trans-substantiation of suns and monads, of opals and coprolites, of microbes and seraphim. You break the bottles of the Djinns, you tear the swaddlings of Ialdabaoth[1] and the mummy-cloths of Maya. You are a cosmic eagle who can carry worlds aloft and let them drop in the carapace of God.

I am glad you liked my epigrams; but many of them were light-weight. I gave up writing them—my worldly wisdom seems to have been a passing phase. I should like to do a volume of short stories in the fantastic vein. Hope you received the *Overland* containing my "Abominations of Yondo." It was strong enough to "evoke many protests" according to G. S.

No news. I have gone back to the wood-pile, and may pick fruit later on, to make a few dollars . . . $ and ¢ are among the great phallic symbols, according to a friend of mine. Have you ever noticed that the numeral 1 is a lingam, and the nought—0—is a yoni? This should help us to understand the mysteries of finance; also, the relations of Astarte and Mammon . . . But to hell with symbology, in any serious sense—I'm not D. H. Lawrence. There are more things in heaven and earth than are dreamt of in phalli-cism or psychoanalysis.[2]

I thank you again for the precious volume. You might also have called it "Forty Immoralists."

Yours for two hundred per cent hooch.

CAS

1. Ialdabaoth is, according to the Sethian Gnostics, the creator of the physical world.

2. *Hamlet* 1.5, 166–7: "There are more things in heaven and earth, Horatio, / Than are dreamt of in your philosophy."

——— ◆ ———

[79]   To Donald Wandrei [ALS, MHS]   July 4th, 1926.

Dear Donald:

Many thanks for your fine essay on my work, which I have enjoyed immensely.[1] Portions of it are prose-poetry. Of course, I want to keep this copy, if I may. I liked best the portion beginning with the phrase about "shadowed gold." Also, the paragraphs touching specifically on *Ebony and Crystal.*

My comparative non-productiveness during the ten years given to *E. & C.* was due largely to ill-health. Also, I destroyed much imperfect work. But this is inessential. The essay needn't be altered to include such details. I have no technical criticism to offer, except that the word "literature" is used with noticeable frequency in the first two pages. It might be better to vary it with "poetry." Flaubert, I believe, made it a rule never to repeat the same word on the same page. But one needn't go so far as that, even in prose. In poetry, repetitions may have a distinct value.

Glad you liked my paintings. Some day I will loan you a lot of the best ones. Four have been sold privately in New York, though at a poor price ($5.00 each). An exhibition, if it could be managed, might uncover a few patrons. But the market for pictures (outside of commercial art and illustrating) is pretty limited in America. Anyway, there are few connoisseurs of the exotic and bizarre.

Misanthropy is the inevitable end, if you have both sense and sensibility. But it's a waste of spiritual energy: people aren't worth despising. They seem to exist for the same reason that Coventry Patmore[2] said the Cosmos existed: "To make dirt cheap."

Write me when you feel like it. I always enjoy your letters.

As ever,
C A S

1. DAW, "The Emperor of Dreams," *Overland Monthly* 84, No. 12 (December 1926): 380–81, 407, 409; rpt. *Klarkash-Ton: The Journal of Smith Studies* No. 1 (1988): 3–8, 25.

2. Coventry Patmore (1823–1896), British poet and critic.

——— ◆ ———

[80]   To Donald Wandrei [ALS, MHS]   Sept 27th, 1926.

My dear Donald:

I have your letter, and the revised copy of the essay. I think you were wise to "tone down" superlative adjectives, and I have no fault to find with the alterations. The whole paper seems excellent to me. As to bettering it, I fear I have no suggestions that would be worth offering. More criticism and less eulogy would make the paper more acceptable to editors and readers. However, you wanted to express your own reaction (which doesn't seem to include fault-finding!) as clearly and sincerely as possible. And it seems to me that you have done this.

I mailed you a picture last week—one of three experiments on a black fabric. It was necessary to lay the colours on quite thickly, and the result is more fragile than I had hoped. In future, I shall add white of egg to the mixture, to fix the paint and bronze powder more firmly.

I haven't had much difficulty in painting on fabrics, even with washes of ink and water-colour, since I use only fabrics that are close-woven. The colours *would* run, in an ordinary weave. Many of the old Chinese and Japanese masterpieces were painted on silk. But I can't afford a silk that would be suitable for the purpose. The cloth that I use is known to the trade as "Venetian sateen."

The difference between Oriental and Occidental art is most significant, it seems to me. The former is spiritual; the latter, with its insistence on literal form and realistic detail, springs from the infernal materialism of the western peoples. Ideal design and colour are sacrificed to produce, at any cost, the illusion of "reality."

However, there are some European and American painters that you should like. If you have not seen them, I should advise you to look up any originals or reproductions that you can find, of Gustave Moreau, John Martin, Felicien Rops, and Sime, the London artist of the grotesque. Odilon Redon (I have been compared to him, but don't know his work) might be worth investigating; also, the American Romantic painter, Arthur P. Ryder.[1]

As ever,
C A S

1. Gustave Moreau (1826–1898), French symbolist painter; John Martin (1789–1854), British painter of Biblical themes; Sidney Sime (1867–1941), British illustrator, known for his work in the books of Lord Dunsany. CAS means Albert Pinkham Ryder (1847–1917), American painter whose subjects were Biblical and mythological.

[81]   To George Sterling [ALS, NYPL]   Sept. 28th, 1926

Dear George:

[. . .] Of course, I lack technical training, in the academic sense. But I don't care much more for the literalness of academic painting than I do for the geometrical abstractions of some of the modernists. What I am after is imaginative (some would say emotional) expression through organized design and colour with novel decorative values. Realism is not aimed at, and I reserve the right to paint in perfectly flat colours, if I wish. The decorative screens and panels of R. W. Chanler,[1] which show an Oriental influence, are more to my taste than the work of most American painters. As to getting instructions, I doubt if my ideals would be understood or sympathized with, by the average art teacher. I'll have to work it out in my own way. Certainly Herkomer, who is, or was, a portrait-painter, would be of little help in teaching me how to paint landscapes in Cocaigne, or Saturn, or Antillia. Like most people, he wouldn't get the idea at all.

Not much news here. I sold a picture locally for ten dollars, which seems to be the top price. Two others went at five apiece, some time ago. [. . .]

I enjoyed your last column in *The Overland,* on the progressive dementia of the mob.[2] You might have said that the world was going from general imbecility to absolute idiocy.

Miss Lee is safe, as far as I am concerned.[3] What I want is an old-fashioned Parisienne.

As ever,
    Clark.

1. Robert Winthrop Chanler (1872–1930), known for his portraits, murals, and wildlife paintings.
2. GS, "Rhymes and Reactions," *Overland Monthly* 84, No. 10 (October 1926): 325–26.
3. B. Virginia Lee was an editor at *Overland Monthly.*

---

[82]   To William Whittingham Lyman[1] [ALS, BL]
                                          Oct. 10th, 1926

My dear Lyman:

[. . .] I have a few copies (fifteen or twenty) of *Sandalwood* left [. . .] It will be the first of my books to go out of print—due, of course, to the small edition. The volume was only a phase, generally speaking, and the next will be quite different. I want to write somewhat longer poems of a purely imaginative character, and steer clear of the sentimental, erotic bog in which Occidental literature is floundering. Of course, the result will be highly unpopular. Nothing goes but exhibitionism, nowadays!

I await your wife's volume with great interest.[1] It surprises me that she cared at all for my stuff. I'm not popular with Miss Monroe, who evidently thinks me a hopeless case!

My parents join me in remembrances and best wishes.

Cordially yours,
Clark Ashton Smith

1. William Whittingham Lyman (1885–1983) taught English at Los Angeles Junior College. His wife was the poet Helen Hoyt (1887–1972), author of *Apples Here in My Basket* (New York: Harcourt Brace, 1924).

---

[83]   To George Sterling [ALS, NYPL]   Oct. 11th, 1926

Dear George:

I agree with all that you say about Wandrei's essay; but after all, his "reaction" is obviously sincere, and it seems to me that he is entitled to a hearing. You might run the essay, if *The Overland* will stand for it. I won't mind the hee haws of the local tame asses. Anyway, W. means to print and circulate it at his own expense, if he can't get it into any magazine.

I always thought, and still think, that Bierce merely gave "A Wine of Wizardry" its just due. But good judges of poetry are almost rarer than poets, it would seem. [. . .]

As to my pictorial technique, I'll admit that it falls far short of my own ideal. However, I can't see that my pictures are so terribly rough, compared to much of the stuff that gets over nowadays. I may screw up courage to send some of my late work to Bender, with a request that he recommend it for exhibition somewhere, if he finds merit in it. Ray Boynton,[1] who likes my stuff, would probably do something, even if Bender wouldn't. Do you ever see Boynton?

Too bad you have to write prose. It's a beastly occupation. As to the length of poems, it seems to me that most brief ones don't have much driving-power. Too many people can write a good lyric, anyway. But few can write a hundred, or two hundred lines of sustained poetry.

As ever,
Clark.

1. Ray Boynton (1883–1951), California painter, known for his town and landscape paintings and murals.

---

[84]   To Donald Wandrei [ALS, MHS]   Oct. 26th, 1926.

Dear Donald:

Here is a letter for you from George Sterling. He had loaned your article, with address, to Miss Lee of the *Overland,* so sent me the letter to mail.

I advise you to accept his offer, since I am convinced, myself, that no Eastern magazine would run your article. A far briefer and much less enthusiastic review of my work, written by one Alfred Galpin, was turned down everywhere. But the *Overland* will be glad enough to run your paper. It will call attention to them as well as to me. Doubtless, as George says, there will be much derision and incredulity; but I take it that you care as little as I do. Anyway, few people around San Francisco can even have read my work if the S. F. sales are any indication. A hundred copies of *E. & C.* and thirty of *Sandalwood* seem to have glutted the market.

Don't mind what G. says about your presumptive youth. As I'm pointing out to him, there are others, such as De Casseres and H. P. Lovecraft, men of middle-age, who would back you up, in substance. Everyone thinks your article well-written, especially Lovecraft, to whom I loaned my copy not long ago. He was curious about you, and wanted to know if you had written anything else. I'm asking his permission to loan you the typescripts of some new horror stories that he sent me.

Glad you liked the picture, which was at least imaginative enough. I thought of leaving out the back-ground rocks, but a similar trick has been done before. Goya has a picture of some people sitting on a rotten limb, over an abyss, with no suggestion of background or bottom. It will make you giddy, if you look at it long enough.

As ever,
Clark

[85]   To William Whittingham Lyman [ALS, BL]
                                              Oct. 26th, 1926
Dear Jack Lyman:
     [. . .] Of course, I hold no brief for prudery either. But it seems
to me that the literature of the time (perhaps as a reaction) shows
a too exclusive preoccupation with erotic themes. I, for one, am a
bit tired of the subject, literarily speaking. Anyway, I agree with
Sterling, de Casseres, and others, who think that my strongest and
most distinctive poems are the ones in a vein of speculative cosmic
phantasy. Others have done as well, or better, in love poetry. I have
more than a streak of the pioneer or adventurer in me, and hate
familiar fields and beaten paths. My ambition is to explore the
Hyperborea beyond Hyperborea. [. . .]
          With all best wishes,
               Cordially yours,
               Clark Ashton Smith

I am enclosing a poem from *The Overland*. It had no less than ten
misprints![1] *The Overland* may run a long article on my work by
one D. Wandrei of St. Paul. It is very rhapsodic and extravagant,
but ought to make people sit up and take notice.

     1. "The Envoys" (*Overland Monthly*, June 1926; rpt. with corrections
July 1926; *SP* and *LO*).

———————————◆———————————

[86]   To George Sterling [ALS, NYPL]   Oct. 27th, 1926
Dear George:
     I forwarded your letter to Wandrei. He's a strange fellow, but
much more critical than you imagine. I don't know just how young
he is; but it's only fair to say that there are men of middle-age
(enough of them for a jury, almost!) who would back him up in his
contention that my eventual place will be a very high one. He
doesn't really contend that I am greater than certain other poets,
and the excess of his essay is more in the manner than in the substance. Doubtful though I am, myself, I think that the people who
will laugh at him are fools, and are deaf and blind to all the lessons
of literary history. Literary tastes and standards are in a state of
perpetual flux, and the narrow, hide-bound "humanism" of the
present may seem absurd in some future age. It is absurd to me,
and to a few other free spirits. I've no quarrel with the slogan of

"art for life's sake," but I think the current definition or delimitation of what constitutes life is worse than ridiculous. Anything that the human imagination can conceive of becomes thereby a part of life, and poetry such as mine, properly considered, is not an "escape," but an extension. I have the courage to think that I am rendering as much "service" by it (damn the piss-pot word!) as I would by psycho-analyzing the male and female adolescents or senescents of a city slum in the kind of verse that slops all over the page and makes you feel as if somebody had puked on you. [. . .]
    Yours, in the quest of the Holy Grail,
    Clark—

---

[87]   To George Sterling [ALS, NYPL]   Nov. 4th, 1926.

Dear George:
    Why don't you write an essay on the prevailing trend in thought and aesthetics? You might call it "The Americanization of Intellect." I'd do the article myself, if I knew where Bierce had left his cat-o'-nine-tails.
    I suppose I'm hopelessly "inadaptable;" but I simply can't attain to that faith in material values professed by the humanists and other Babbitts.[1] Many attempts have been made to convert me; but I still fail to see that the "impossible"—or problematical—is any more futile than anything else as a poetical topic. Indeed, my fondest dream is to find a *Hyperborea beyond Hyperborea,* in the realm of imaginative poetry. I have the feeling that my best and most original work is still to be done.
    However, I didn't mean to start an argument by what I wrote. We both know the futility of argument. But—whenever you begin to feel that you have wasted your time in writing imaginative verse, remember that poetry such as yours and mine would have found as little favour in the 18th century as it does to-day. Dr. Johnson and the other Henry Seidel Canbys of his time would scarcely have understood "A Wine of Wizardry."[2] And I'll be damned if I can see that the present age, for all its scientific discoveries, psychoanalysis, etc., is any smarter or more sophisticated than the 18th. It is, however, equally cock-sure, and materialistic;—or more so. But the present orgy of materialism will exhaust itself sooner or later, and perhaps end in some great social *debacle.* After that—since history never does anything but plagiarize itself—there may be a revival of interest in imaginative literature, and a new Romantic epoch, like that which followed the French Revolution.

Yes, I get the *Overland,* and always look for your page in it. I'd appreciate an extra copy or two of the issue in which W.'s article comes out. Wandrei has a theory that the literature of the future, since purely human topics are pretty well worked out, will concern itself more and more with the fantastic and the cosmic. Hence, in part, his enthusiasm for my stuff. Of course, neither he nor I, nor any body else can *prove* anything about the literary tastes and trends of posterity.

Dam'me, I believe I'll do an article myself, in defense of imaginative poetry.[3] One could attack the current literary humanism, with its scorn of all that has no direct anthropological bearing, as a phase of the general gross materialism of the times. If imaginative poetry is childish and puerile, then Shakespeare was a babbling babe in his last days, when he wrote that delightful fantasy, *The Tempest.* And all the other great Romantic masters, Keats, Poe, Baudelaire, Shelley, Coleridge, etc., are mentally inferior to every young squirt, or old one, who has read Whitman and Freud, and renounced the poetic chimeras in favour of that supreme superstition, Reality.

Ben says somewhere that poets pay their debts in stars and are paid, in wormwood. But I'll pay some of mine in nitric acid.

Affectionately,

Clark.

1. Irving Babbitt (1865–1933), Harvard professor, literary critic, and proponent of the New Humanism, not the materialistic businessman of Sinclair Lewis's novel.

2. Henry Seidel Canby (1878–1961), critic and book reviewer.

3. Such an essay is listed among the CAS papers at JHL, but the manuscript currently is lost.

———————◆———————

[88]   To Helen Hoyt [ALS, BL]   Nov. 7th, 1926

Dear Helen Hoyt:

Excuse my delay in writing to thank you for the gift of your book. I have been busy, and wanted to read it over thoroughly before I wrote.

I have gone through the poems several times, and found more in them at each perusal. My present preference, if it would interest you, is for the following ones: "We Were Together," "Detachment," "We Never Left Our Love Unsaid," and "Love is a Burden." These, to me, seem remarkably finished of their kind. Some of these reminded me (I don't know quite why) of Arthur

Symons, a little-appreciated poet whom I consider one of the best among the moderns. I think your book, as a whole, does very much what you want it to do; and I have picked out the above-mentioned poems, which are only links in a chain, because of my bent towards formal perfection.

I *do* like the cover of the book—a favourite colour-combination with me. I wish my own books were as well-bound and printed!

I hope we will meet some day. Remember me to your husband, whose visit was a rare pleasure. Tell him not to take my anti-humanism too literally.

Thanking you again for the book, I am
  Cordially yours,
   Clark Ashton Smith

---

[89] To James D. Phelan [ALS, BL]   Nov. 19, 1926

Dear Mr. Phelan:

I am glad you selected "Autumn Orchards."[1] It was, I thought, the best of the three poems. Don't bother to return the others—one has been published in book form, and I have several typescripts and clippings of the second.

I am desolate and heart-broken over the terrible news.[2] George was easily the first of living American poets, and there is no one left now to carry on the classic tradition. His work, I feel sure, will outlive most of the verse that has been written in English since the beginning of this present century. Sooner or later, there is bound to be a reaction in favour of pure poetry.

Some day, I hope to write an elegy that will not be too unworthy of him. I can't do it now. But Shelley alone (remember "Adonais") could write such a threnody as it should be written.

With all best wishes,
  Very sincerely yours,
   Clark Ashton Smith

1. The poem appeared in *A Day in the Hills,* ed. Henry Meade Bland (San Francisco: Taylor & Taylor, 1926), a souvenir booklet commemorating the second annual meeting of the Edwin Markham Chapter of the English Poetry Society. The meeting was held at Phelan's villa on 18 September 1926.

2. GS had committed suicide on 16 November.

[90]   To Donald Wandrei [ALS, MHS]   Dec. 6th, 1926.

Dear Donald:

George's death was a great shock to me. We were intimate friends, and I have always had the highest admiration for his poetry. But I suppose he took the best way out. As Benjamin De Casseres wrote me: "We are all waiting to get out of the pig sty." I enclose a clipping from *The San Francisco Chronicle.*

I think his poetry (not the best of it, however) will come in for considerable appreciation now. "A Wine of Wizardry" had great influence on my own poetic development, and helped to confirm my flair for the fantastic. I think it is the longest poem that I know entirely by heart. I first read it when it appeared in the old *Cosmopolitan,* about 1907, with an accompanying eulogy by Ambrose Bierce, who ranked it among the greatest imaginative poems in literature.[1] To this I subscribe whole-heartedly, in the teeth of all the popes and Grand Moguls of poetic (?) realism. I have all of George's books, and would be glad to loan you anything you have not seen. The drama *Lilith* is one of his best works, and *Sails and Mirage* contains much fine work. My prime favourites, though, are the first three volumes, of which *The House of Orchids* was the third.

Your article on me is out, and reads even better in print, despite two or three typographical errors. I think you will receive five copies—the only payment that *The Overland* makes.

I have gone through *Ebony and Crystal* of late, and am struck by what Edgar Saltus would call "the resonant merit" of the poems. There is something invidious, beyond a doubt, in the way my book has been passed over. Many presentation copies to literary notables, such as William Rose Benet, Conrad Aiken, and Stuart P. Sherman,[2] were not even acknowledged by the recipients. In fact, Markham and De Casseres were the only "notables" who really welcomed the book. You can draw your own conclusions, knowing the "trend of the times." "Vested Interests" are not confined to business and religion.

Note George's mention of *The Hermaphrodite*[3] in his "Rhymes and Reactions" in the Dec. *Overland*—probably the last thing that he wrote. The author is an old friend of mine, Samuel Loveman, *not* "Tweman," as the name is spelled by the *Overland*'s linotypers, who ought to be taken out and launched from the parapet of the S. F. Ferry Bldg. The poem is a marvellous achievement, and has inspiration, beauty, and melody in excelsis. In it one may wander

"With halcyon feet by seas of rose
Against whose foam the ilex grows."[4]

It should be another "wild hair" in the eyes of the "vitalists," if any of them read it.

I am ordering ten *Overlands* for distribution among people who will appreciate your article. Lovecraft wanted two. The editor's note prefixed to your essay was not in any too good taste. George was somewhat brow-beaten by the realists, toward the end, and even doubted the value of his own best work.

You shall have my epigrams before long.

As ever,
Clark

1. See "George Sterling: An Appreciation" (*Overland Monthly,* March 1927; *PD*). AB's first article on the poem was "A Poet and His Poem," *Cosmopolitan* 43, No. 5 (September 1907): 575–77.

2. William Rose Benét, editor of *Saturday Review of Literature;* Conrad Aiken (1899–1973), critic, poet, and author; Stuart P[ratt] Sherman (1881–1926), professor at the University of Illinois and editor of the literary section of the *New York Herald Tribune,* was a conservative who quarrelled at length with H. L. Mencken.

3. Samuel Loveman, *The Hermaphrodite* (Athol, MA: W. Paul Cook, 1926).

4. *The Hermaphrodite,* ll. 53–54.

———————◆———————

[91]   To Donald Wandrei [ALS, MHS]   May 7th, 1927.

Dear Donald:

Your letter was forwarded to me in Berkeley, but I was caught in a "mad whirl"—a round of musicales, luncheons, walks, rides, picnics, etc, etc., and found it impossible to answer letters. I returned to Auburn day before yesterday, and am now trying to clean up my accumulated correspondence. [. . .]

I have arranged for an exhibition of my paintings at the Claremont Hotel, in Berkeley. It will give me some local publicity, at any rate. The exhibition (two weeks) will begin June 19th.

I hope your eastern trip will do something to relieve your boredom. You might like San Francisco, which has more individuality than most cities. My happiest hours there were spent in Golden Gate Park—a place that one could not exhaust in weeks. Much of it has been permitted to run wild, and there are spots where one can forget that one is in a public park. Portions of Berkeley are charming, too, and I had some wonderful walks in the neighboring hills, which are crested with groves of eucalyptus. But (apart from my hostess) I met no one who interested me. The mob is the same everywhere.

However, I *did* meet Mrs De Casseres, who was travelling in California with a friend, and we had a wonderful evening together. She is one of the most remarkable women I have ever met. I met Edwin Markham, also, and thought him a bit of a poseur. He was the roaring lion of a luncheon at the St. Francis Hotel (S.F.) which I attended.

I'll try to enclose some verses with this.

As ever,
Clark

---

[92]   To Donald Wandrei [ALS, MHS]   July 9th, 1927.

Dear Donald:

I envy you that tramping-tour! Sooner or later, I intend to do something of the sort, myself.

I didn't imagine you would care much for New York. All big modern cities (or little ones, either) are monstrosities, anyhow. I never feel at home in them, myself. Like the stranger in Baudelaire's prose-poem, "I love only the clouds—the clouds that pass—over there—the marvellous clouds."[1] [. . .]

I worked hard for awhile—and now I'm playing hard. Next week, I shall go on a camping-trip in the Sierras, with a harem of three women.

As ever,
Clark

1. Paraphrase of Charles Baudelaire, "The Stranger," trans. Stuart Merrill, *Pastels in Prose from the French* (New York: Harper, 1890), p. 164.

---

[93]   To Donald Wandrei [ALS, MHS]   Sept. 18th, 1927.

Dear Donald:

[. . .] Believe me, I appreciate what you say, and obviously feel, concerning the labour that one can, and indeed must[,] put into such work. There are times when I simply haven't the courage to attempt it, foreknowing, as I do, the cost in nerve-strain, the toll that it takes of eye and hand and brain. But even at that, I find the paintings easier to "do" than poetry.

I wish I could *give* you one or more of these pictures, but I don't feel able to do so at present, since I no longer have the time that I once had for making new ones. If you feel able to buy any of them, I won't "sting" you on the price.

Oddly enough, I have seen little of the work of any of the artists you name as having congenerate tendencies. Perhaps I have seen more of Nielsen than of the others; but have never encountered *anything* of Redon's till lately, and then not in colour. I was compared to him years and years ago by a Cleveland artist (a friend of Loveman's) who thought my work superior. Harry Clarke I admire greatly, since finding (only a few months ago) some specimens reproduced in an art magazine, *The Studio*. Wallace Smith I know only by the single drawing in De Casseres' *The Shadow-Eater*.[1] So you can see how little I owe to pictorial influences, apart from Oriental art, of which I have seen and studied a fair amount.

Perhaps I *may* yet achieve an exhibition in New York, since Bio de Casseres is still trying to get one for me. She is a woman of indomitable strength and energy—perhaps the most striking feminine personality that I have ever encountered. Out here, there is no hope: galleries are closing, and some of the best-known artists in the state are starving. S. F. becomes more hog-tied and hide-bound commercial every minute.

I've written nothing very recently. One needs the cream of one's energy for creative effort; and I've had to do some money-making (never mind what). Any way, it takes the edge off of me, and I'm not getting rich, either. Damn the U.S., and hurrah for Denmark, where worthy poets actually receive a salary from the state after they have given proof of their abilities!

Yours for the second coming of Casanova,
Clark

1. Kay Nielsen (1886–1957), Danish book illustrator. In 1934, RHB gave HPL a copy of Poe's *Tales of Mystery and Imagination* (New York: Tudor Publishing Co., 1933), illustrated by Harry Clarke (1890–1931). Following HPL's death, RHB presented the same copy to CAS. Wallace Smith (1888–1937) was an author and artist, illustrating, among many other things, De Casseres' *The Shadow-Eater* (New York: Albert & Charles Boni, 1915; ill. ed. New York: American Library Service, 1923) and Ben Hecht's *Fantazius Mallare* (1922).

[94]   To Donald Wandrei [ALS, MHS]

Apr. 20th, 1928.

Dear Donald:

Many, many thanks for your volume,[1] which should be a source of pride to both yourself and Cook. It is beautifully printed; and as is usual, the poems impress me as being even better in print than in typescript. I like in particular "Ecstasy," "On Some Drawings," "Sanctity and Sin," and "Valerian," by whose dedication I feel highly honoured. I do hope the sale will re-imburse you for the expense of publication.

I wrote you not long ago, enclosing some more Baudelaires. Have just finished my draft of *Les Fleurs,* all but the poems in decadent Latin, which I am unable to read. Of course, a lot of these are sorely in need of revision.

Did I mention that two of my paintings on black cloth, done about the same time as the one I gave you, have been on exhibition at the Independent Show in New York? These pictures, it seems, have attracted the favourable attention of two visiting art-critics from France; and I am in receipt of letters from two Parisian magazines, *Les Artistes D'Aujourd'hui,* and *Revue du Vrai et du Beau,* asking for information concerning my artistic aims and aspirations—also, for any clippings of press-notices, photographic reproductions of paintings, etc, with which I may be able to furnish them. These critics, Mr. Henri de Montal-Faubelle[2] and M. Comte de Chabrier, have signified their intention of writing articles upon me and my work—surely an honour which is not likely to be accorded to all the exhibitors at the Independent Show,—which, I understand, is not taken seriously by New York critics. Recognition of this sort is truly significant, and may open the way to almost anything.

I hope you'll write before long, and send me some more poems. There's no question in my mind that you have unusual gifts and potentialities as a poet.

As ever,
Clark

1. *Ecstasy and Other Poems* (Athol, MA: Recluse Press, 1928). The book's publisher was W. Paul Cook (1881–1948), a colleague of HPL.
2. Henri de Montal-Faubelle, "Clark Ashton Smith," *Les Artistes d'aujourd'hui* (1 August 1928): 17. CAS translated this review for a news article, "Paintings by Auburn Poet," *AJ* (20 November 1941): 5.

[95]   To Donald Wandrei [ALS, MHS]   Oct. 21st, 1928

Dear Donald:

I found your letter awaiting me on my return last week from Berkeley, where I visited for nearly a month. It was good to hear from you, and to learn that you are so ambitious and so full of fine literary projects.

As for myself, there is little enough to report at present. I am now starting to overhaul and re-type my Baudelaires, with the intention of preparing them for possible book-publication. I have had no time or energy, so far, for original literary work. I made seven new paintings in September (you would like some of them, particularly the three on a black [back]ground) and have left them on display together with some old work, at an art-store in Oakland.

Good luck with the publishers! I haven't even tried anyone with *Incantations,* but may sometime muster up sufficient courage to send to Pascal Covici, of Chicago. Just at present, I don't even feel like expending the postage, since my last round of dissipation in the Bay region has left me practically "broke"!

While in Berkeley, I saw a copy of Poe's *Tales of Mystery and Imagination* with the illustrations by Harry Clarke. They impress me as the best Poe designs I have yet encountered. The ones in colour, especially, are full of true Poesque horror—he seems to catch the very tints of psychic decomposition, morbidity, fear, and death.

Here's wishing you all manner of good luck. And remember me to the "gang." I have just written to Lovecraft, who is certainly faithful and patient with my epistolary irregularities and short-comings. I've owed him a letter for nearly two months. I liked his "Dunwich Horror," which is truly Lovecraftian.

Tell Long that "The Space-Eaters" was *great.*[1]

As ever,
Clark.

1. HPL, "The Dunwich Horror" (*WT,* April 1929), read in ms.; Frank Belknap Long, "The Space-Eaters" (*WT,* July 1928).

---

[96]   To Donald Wandrei [ALS, MHS]   March 20th, 1929

Dear Donald:

As usual, I am in arrears—and I had honestly meant to answer your letter before this.

I think that a period in Carmel might be an interesting and worth-while experience for you. The cost of living is moderate, the scenery is full of varied beauty and rugged sublimity, and—if you cared for such—you could have the society of people whose aspirations, at least, are more or less artistic. Personally I prefer scenery that is unpopulated—but that is a prejudice, which I don't recommend to others.

As for my plans—well in the present state of my affairs, emotions, sensations, fatigues, desires and ennuis, I find it almost impossible to formulate, or, at least, adhere to any. I have written a few poems (one or two of which I'll enclose) and have put my new volume of verse, which I have entitled *The Jasmine Girdle and Other Poems*,[1] in the hands of a N. Y. literary agent who thinks he might inveigle some publisher into bringing it out.

I can well understand how N. Y. impresses you—since to me any city, any crowded place, partakes too much of the nature of Baudelaire's "cauchemar multiforme et sans trêve."[2]

Remorse seizes me when I think of all the poems, prose-poems and stories that I should have written. I begin to suspect in myself some fatal depressing of will or energy—or of both. But perhaps it is a hopeful sign that I begin to blame myself rather than circumstances.

Write when you feel inclined.

  As ever, your friend
   Clark.

Did I send you "Nyctalops?"[3]

1. The Grace Aird Agency of New York was unsuccessful in placing *The Jasmine Girdle; SP* contains a section by that title.
2. "Le Gouffre," l. 8.
3. "Nyctalops" (*WT,* October 1929; *SP* and *LO*).

---

[97] To H. P. Lovecraft [ALS, JHL]   Nov. 26th, 1929.

Dear H.P.L.:

By far the best news in your last letter is the intimation that you may do some new original work. I think you would be wise to do this, for more reasons than one; and I hope you will loan me copies of the results, which I am indeed eager to see. I haven't really enjoyed anything in the realm of weird writing since your "Call of Cthulhu" and "The Dunwich Horror."[1] As I said in a letter to Wright, no one else living has your command of primordial and abysmal horror.

The Hervey Allen biography[2] certainly "sounds good," from your description. I have been re-reading most of Poe lately: his best things seem even better, and his poorer ones worse, after a lapse of years.

I am quite elated over the placing of my longest story, "The Venus of Azombeii," for which Wright is offering me 75 bucks. I enclose a carbon of "Satampra Zeiros," which you should like.

I have two sizeable affairs under way, one of them a brand-new conception with illimitable possibilities, which I am calling "The Monster of the Prophecy."[3] It concerns a starving poet who is about to throw himself into the river, when he is approached by a stranger who befriends him and afterwards introduces himself as a scientist from a world of Antares, who is sojourning briefly on earth in a human disguise. The Antarean is about to return to his native planet, with the aid of a vibratory device which annihilates space, and offers to take the poet with him. When they reach their destination, it develops that he has a little game of his own to play. For he uses the poet to bring about the fulfillment of an ancient prophecy, to the effect that a mighty wizard will appear in a certain place at a certain time, accompanied by an unheard-of white monster with two arms and two legs, and that this wizard will then become the supreme ruler of half the planet. The Antarean adventures of the poet will, I think, be something absolutely novel in interplanetary fiction. He ends up, after incredible perils and experiences that bring him to the verge of insanity, as the lover of an ennuied princess with three legs, five arms, and an opalescent skin, and realizes that, even though he is universally looked upon as a monstrosity, he is no worse off in this respect than he was in his own world. For once, I think, the side-lights of satire will not detract from the fantasy. [. . .]

Yours ever,
CAS

P.S. Our dry fall is becoming a drouth. I hear that conditions will become serious if there is not rain before long. The atmospheric conditions here strike me as being genuinely abnormal: among other things, our sky (though the stars are very bright) has a peculiar iron blackness at night which I have never seen before. And a woman-friend of mine tells me that she saw the noon sky actually whiten the other day, as if there were some intense momentary radiation. That sort of things sets one's imagination to working.

1. "The Call of Cthulhu" (WT, February 1928).

2. Hervey Allen (1889–1949) Israfel: The Life and Times of Edgar Allan Poe (New York: George H. Doran Co., 1927 [2 vols.]).

3. The stories CAS refers to are "The Venus of Azombeii" (WT,

June–July 1931; *OD*); "The Tale of Satampra Zeiros" (*WT*, November 1931; *LW* and *RA*); and "The Monster of the Prophecy" (*WT*, January 1932; *OST*).

---

[98]   To H. P. Lovecraft [ALS, JHL]   Dec. 10th, 1929.

Dear H.P.L.:

I am delighted to know that "Satampra Zeiros" impressed you so favorably. Indeed, there was no hurry about its return. I usually make more than one carbon copy, anyway. I'll certainly be glad to hear from Long. His "Red Fetish" in the last *W.T.* was a clever piece of writing, and was the best story in the issue.[1]

I am astounded at the *scope* of some of your "revisory" labors![2] I fervently hope you will soon have time for something you can publish under your own name. The idea at which you hint, for an interplanetary story, is superb. I think the psychic, rather than physical, precipitation of your hero into an alien orb should have infinite possibilities. Odd—or perhaps not odd—my own imaginings have run at times along a somewhat similar channel. I had an idea for a yarn to be called "The Planet of the Dead,"[3]—dealing with a world in which there remained very few living beings, and where these few were carrying out a sort of memorial and mortuary existence, overwhelmed by, and absorbed in, the monstrous shadow of the past and its innumerable sepulchers and ruins. In a way, it would be an expansion of an old prose-poem of mine, "From the Crypts of Memory"; but would differ from this in having an earthly hero, drawn to this planet by his spiritual affinity with the inhabitants. I am sure, though, that you could handle the idea with a more genuine command of the sources of shadowy horror than I could. [. . .]

I have finished "The Monster of the Prophecy" and have mailed it to Farnsworth Wright. The thing is really what would be called a novelette, since it runs to 15,000 or 16,000 words. I am mailing you a carbon of it, which can be returned at leisure—no hurry at all about it. I think you will like certain portions, at any rate. It struck me on re-reading the thing that I had consciously, or unconsciously satirized pretty nearly everything. Even science, and the pseudo-scientific type of yarn now prevalent, are made a josh of in the first chapter, in the creation of the absurd "space-annihilator . . ." But of course the profoundest satire is that which is directed at intolerance of all kinds. I seem to have put far more *intellectual* ideas into the story than into anything else of mine—which, of course, may have ruined it from a purely artistic stand-point.

Our phenomenal drouth has at last been broken by a warm, heavy rain, which is still continuing after two days. Every one is singing hosannas, I imagine, since conditions were bordering on the serious . . . The cold in New England must indeed be terrible, and I sympathize with you. I, too, am unable to endure cold. [. . .]

A poet-friend of mine, Susan Myra Gregory of Monterey, sister of the novelist Jackson Gregory, asked me to write a preface for a little collection of her verse which is being brought out in Southern California. She has a real lyric talent, of the true feminine Sapphic type, and I was glad to do the preface—an odd interlude in the writing of my Antarean novelette.[4]

I was fool enough to send "Satampra Zeiros" to *Amazing Stories*, before I had seen a recent copy of the magazine. It hasn't come back yet, which surprises me. I suppose Wright will use it some time, but I don't want to crowd him with too much stuff. I'm praying that he'll take "The Monster," which really ought to attract attention. I'm sure it's the first interplanetary story on record, where the hero didn't return to earth at the end!

I bought a copy of *Science Wonder Stories*, which is not dissimilar to *Amazing Stories*. There was one yarn, however, called "The Vapor Intelligence,"[5] which didn't reek so much of the laboratory. I may try them with something, presently. I can see that if I am to make a real living out of fiction, I am in for a certain amount of quasi-hackwork.

By the way, have you ever thought of trying any of the British magazines? Some of them, such as *The Strand*, are, or used to be, not so hide-bound in regard to excluding the weird as American publications.

I am going to wish you a happy holiday with this. And may Thoth be auspicious in granting you the time for some work of your own. By the way, if you have any old typescripts around that I haven't seen, I'd appreciate a peep at them. I don't know anything that would refresh me so much. I take out the typescript of "Dagon" that you once gave me, and re-read it every so often.

As ever, your friend,
CAS

1. Frank Belknap Long, "The Red Fetish" (*WT*, January 1930).
2. HPL was revising "The Mound" (*WT*, November 1940) for Zealia Bishop.
3. "The Planet of the Dead" (*WT*, March 1932; *LW* and *RA*).
4. The introduction CAS refers to was for *Shadows of Wings* (San Diego: Troubadour Press, 1930) by Susan Myra Gregory (d. 1939); rpt. in *SS*.

5. Jack Barnette, "The Vapor Intelligence" (*Science Wonder Stories,* January 1930).

———————— • ————————

[99]   To H. P. Lovecraft [ALS, JHL]   January 9th, 1930.

Dear H.P.L.:

You should have heard from me long before this; but I fell into a round of holiday dissipation, and am only just now beginning to recuperate, and resume my normal routine.

I enjoyed your last letter hugely—also, F.B.L.'s improvisation, his design for "Satampra Zeiros," and your two poems. As to the latter, I am inclined to agree with Wright in preferring "The Ancient Track," which is a fine mixture of eerie fantasy and realism. I might be inclined to reverse the judgment, however, if all of "The Outpost" were equal in quality to the first stanza. These poems obviously give you a high place on Parnassus.[1]

Wright has not yet reported on my "Monster." *Amazing Stories* returned "Satampra Zeiros" without express comment, which was what I expected. By the way, there is now a new magazine, *Astounding Stories of Super-Science,* one of the Clayton publications. It seems to require a technical twist, like the others of the same ilk, but might be worth looking into. I imagine that it pays well, and on acceptance. I had no luck with the two English magazines that I tackled—maybe they're too plum-duppy after all. I'll hunt up one or two addresses for you, and send them on later.

I was delighted by your additions to the Tsathoggua myth. Too bad you aren't publishing the story under your own name. It sounds most fascinating! By the way, here is a clipping about the Carlsbad Caverns in New Mexico. I'd certainly like to be in that expedition which is planning to plumb the nether depths!

Thanks for the nice things you say about "The Monster." I am inclined to think well of it myself, and look upon it as the result of a definite inspiration. At present, I am wondering at the energy which enabled me to do the thing at all. I haven't completed any more stories, though I am dragging on at present with "The Metamorphosis of the World,"[2] and am now engaged in killing off an odious bunch of scientists. I wrote 8 or 10 prose-poems just before Christmas, and will try to enclose some of them for you. And I ended the year by making half a dozen new pictures. At present, I am still torn by the desire to paint, which I don't feel that I should indulge, for financial reasons. My best pictures seem so amazingly good, that I am rendered morose and sorrowful by such an exigency. I'd like nothing better than to fare forth on a debauch of form and color for the next few weeks.

Your idea for an interplanetary story is great—of course, transportation to an alien world would be an experience of the utmost terror and strangeness for human nerves, and the probable result would be delirium and madness. I hinted at this in "The Monster," where Vizaphmal had to keep Alvor under the influence of a drug so that he wouldn't break down. I hope you will soon find time to work out your superb idea. I shall begin my "Planet of the Dead" before long; and I agree with you that there is little danger of parallellism. I think you underestimate the element of sheer fantasy in your own work, though I agree with you that your best things show evidence of the closest literal observation. The blending of qualities is simply marvellous in its effect. I, too, am capable of observation; but I am far happier when I can create *everything* in a story, including the milieu. This is why I do best in work like "Satampra Zeiros." Maybe I haven't enough love for, or interest in, real places, to invest them with the atmosphere that I achieve in something purely imaginary. [. . .]

There is six inches of snow on the ground this morning, and I am revelling in the aesthetic spectacle, which is rare at this altitude. But I abominate the cold, and suffer from it, even though it never drops more than a few degrees below the freezing point.

I'd appreciate a re-reading of "Hypnos" and "Randolph Carter," if you have copies that you can loan me.[3] Later, I'll name some others. You can keep the enclosed poems in prose.

As ever, your friend,
        CAS

1. "The Ancient Track" (*WT,* March 1930); "The Outpost" (*Bacon's Essays,* Spring 1930).
2. Early title for "The Metamorphosis of Earth" (*WT,* September 1951; *OD*).
3. "Hypnos" (*WT,* May/July 1924); "The Statement of Randolph Carter" (*WT,* February 1925).

---

[100]   To H. P. Lovecraft [ALS, JHL]   Jan. 27th, 1930.

Dear H.P.L.:

"The Statement of Randolph Carter" is even better than I had remembered it as being—which is saying a good deal. The atmosphere and suggested horror are simply tremendous; and I certainly can't find any trace of immaturity in the style. I took the liberty of showing it to a woman-friend whose opinion I value highly,[1] and she was greatly impressed.

I'd be glad of the loan of almost any others that you have on hand, particularly "The White Ape" and "The Nameless City." I have copies of "Erich Zann," "The Lurking Fear," "Dagon," "The Picture in the House," and "The Cats of Ulthar."[2] Apparently I have lost or given away my printed copies of some others that were in *Weird Tales*. I was looking over "The Picture in the House" not long ago, and thought it a most consummate masterpiece of its kind. Ugh!!! I can see that plate of the cannibal butcher-shop, and the horrible old man, and the spreading blood-stain!

Here is the address of the *Strand Magazine:* Southampton St, Strand, London, W.C. 2. I haven't seen a copy of it in years, but there used to be an occasional tale with a weird trend in its pages. Doubtless there are other possibilities in England. I'll see if I can't get a line on them, and if I have any luck, will let you know.

Wright surprised me by returning "Satampra Zeiros," which is therefore apparently hopeless from the view-point of salability. I enclose his letter. I have abbreviated the opening of "The Monster," and have re-submitted it. Perhaps I'm doing well to "put over" a novelette on any terms at this early stage. I couldn't altogether grasp Wright's objection, though. The full text can be restored, if the tale is ever brought out in book-form.[3]

I finished "The Metamorphosis of the World," and am trying it out on the "scientifiction" magazines. I don't know that you would care for it: probably the best element is the satire. I think, however, that you would like my latest, "The Epiphany of Death," which was inspired by "Randolph Carter" and was written in about three hours, the day after my re-reading of your story. You are to keep the copy enclosed; but you can return "The Resurrection of the Rattle-Snake" sometime. This latter is pretty punk, except for the touch of genuine horror at the end—which by the way, I owe to the same friend who liked "Randolph Carter" so much. It was she who suggested the finding of the bloody rattles in Godfrey's clenched hand. Apart from this the tale owes something to Bierce.[4]

Glad you liked the prose-poems—I'll send you some others later on. I await *Fungi from Yuggoth* with vast interest.[5]

Probably I shouldn't have said that I am indifferent to places, since I am very sensitive to the charm of wild and uninhabited spots at any rate. Ever since childhood, I have been subject to an odd mental phenomenon: often, in conjunction with an emotional mood, an idea or a train of ideas, the image of some particular landscape will arise before me and persist, without any obvious relation to my trend of thought. Probably I would feel the historic charm of places like New England, where there is a multitude of accumulative associations. But here, everything is too raw and recent in that sense. Also, I became disenchanted about gold-mining, the pioneer industry of these parts, by growing up on a ranch that had several alleged gold-mines scattered over it.

I heard from Wandrei not long ago—he is taking some post-graduate courses.

Our snow melted away long ago, but there has been an abundance of rain, fog, and drizzle, far more than we commonly have in January. I can't imagine what real zero weather would be like—any approach to freezing is bad enough, as far as I am concerned.

I am beginning "Marooned in Andromeda," which will be a wild tale about some mutineers on a space-flier who are put off without weapons or provisions on an alien world.[6] The idea will form an excellent peg for a lot of fantasy, horror, grotesquery, and satire. I have so many ideas for stories that I find it impossible to catch up with a tenth of them. Here are some titles I have noted down—each of which represents a more or less definite conception: "The Satanist," "The Ghoul from Mercury," "The Moon-Specter," "The Lord of Lunacy," "The Transformation of Athanor," "The Trilithon," and "Hecate." "The Transformation of Athanor" will, I think, be about a million times more hideous than Mr. Stevenson's well-known "Jekyll and Hyde." And "The Satanist"[7] won't deal with ordinary devil-worship, but with the evocation of absolute cosmic evil, in the form of a *black* radiation that leaves the devotee petrified into a sable image of eternal horror. "The Ghoul from Mercury" is an extra-planetary entity like a globe of fire, which hides in caverns by day and breaks into morgues and graveyards by night, where it devours corpses. Finally it develops a predilection for mummies, and breaks open all the cases in museums. It grows bigger and bigger with all the bodies it devours, and is finally seen to fly away, just after sunset, in the direction of Mercury.

I hope you will loan me "Hypnos" some time.

As ever, your friend,
CAS

1. The friend to whom CAS refers was Genevieve K. Sully (1880–1970).

2. "Facts concerning the Late Arthur Jermyn and His Family" (*WT*, April 1924; as "The White Ape"); "The Nameless City" (*The Wolverine*, November 1921); "The Music of Erich Zann" (*WT*, May 1925); "The Lurking Fear" (*Home Brew*, January–April 1923, illustrated by CAS); "The Picture in the House" (*WT*, January 1924); and "The Cats of Ulthar" (*WT*, February 1926).

3. CAS deleted a foreword to "The Monster of the Prophecy" (*OST*) and removed several descriptive passages from the first third of the story. The 1,500 words he excised were restored in *The Monster of the Proph-*

ecy, ed. Steve Behrends (West Warwick, RI: Necronomicon Press, 1988).

4. "The Epiphany of Death" (*Fantasy Fan,* July 1934; *AY*). "The Resurrection of the Rattlesnake" (*WT,* October 1931; *OD*).

5. HPL's sonnet sequence, written in very late 1929 and very early 1930. HPL presented CAS with a typescript of the first thirty-three sonnets.

6. "Marooned in Andromeda" (*Wonder Stories,* October 1930).

7. I.e., "The Devotee of Evil."

---

[101]   To H. P. Lovecraft [ALS, JHL]   April 2nd, 1930.

Dear Éch-Pi-El:

It has been a privilege to re-read the stories you sent, both of which I like immensely. I can't see why Wright should have rejected "From Beyond." You *might* try *Science Wonder Stories* with this tale,—also, *Astounding Stories.* Neither of these magazines, however, seems to have any feeling for literary style, to judge from the stuff they publish. *Weird Tales* is a compendium of classics, in comparison—even at its worst.

You might re-loan me "The Quest of Iranon," "The Unnamable," and "The Outsider," when you next write, if you have them on hand. I hope, also, that "Arthur Jermyn" and "Celephaïs" will soon be available.[1] You can't imagine the sheer *refreshment* and *stimulation* that I get from your stories. They create an atmosphere that I have never found anywhere else.

My own activities have been somewhat intermittent of late, since I have had a certain amount of out-door work to do. "Andromeda" is still unfinished; and "The Planet of the Dead" is about half-written. I have completed one shortish tale, "The Satyr," and will send you a carbon of it as soon as it is re-typed. Wright accepted "The Phantoms of the Fire," but rejected "The Devotee of Evil" and "A Murder in the Fourth Dimension."[2] He thought the first part of the latter was "unconvincing." "The Devotee" he liked—"but not quite well enough."

I note your sonnet in the current issue—a fine imaginative conception. My "End of the Story"[3] doesn't look so bad in print, and I hope it will get at least a corporal's vote. I don't see how Wright could turn down *anything* of yours, and then print such abominable junk as "The Land of Lur," which is really a consummate model of what prose-writing ought not to be. I think the author must have cooked it up as a joke![4]

My portrait may not be so bad—particularly when it is retouched by Herman Herkomer, who lives near here, and who has been giving Matlie some instruction and overhauling. Herkomer is about the most competent of living portraitists, and I can't see that he is very much inferior to the celebrated Sargent.[5] I had the privilege of watching him re-touch Matlie's picture of my friend Mrs. Sully, not long ago. The picture was a hopeless mess, and looked about as much like the lovely and subtle original as a panful of dough; but Herkomer, in about half-an-hour, brought order out of it and established the basis of a likeness. It was marvellous to watch him.

I hope earnestly that you will soon get around to some original work. Even from a strictly practical standpoint, it would be more than worth your while. You certainly have a public waiting for you, if the letters in the "Eyrie" form any indication. Their frequent mention of you certainly gives me a heightened estimate of the *Weird Tales* public.

You can keep all the enclosures. The literature from *S.W.S.* will give you some idea of their requirements. I think I missed one or two articles about the Carlsbad Caverns. What an underworld for the delvings of imagination! When you write your tale about the dinosaur, you should describe the last return of Tsathoggua, mounted on the great monster, to these inframundane depths.

By the way, I think of adding to the Hyperborean mythology, by writing a tale to explain why "Jungle-Taken" Commoriom was deserted. The tale will be told by the public headsman of Commoriom, and will relate how he was compelled to behead a certain notorious outlaw seven times, and how this outlaw (who was connected with Tsathoggua on his mother's side, and also had a very peculiar sub-human strain in his ancestry) managed to *leak* or *ooze* from the tomb on each occasion, and re-appear on the streets of Commoriom; till, after the seventh re-appearance, the population migrated in a body, and Athammaus the headsman, albeit somewhat regretfully (since this was the one failure of along and honorable career) gave up the hopeless job and followed them. The tale should make a rollicking hell-raiser.[6]

Yours, in the Black Mass,
CAS

Perhaps you have seen photographs of the new planet—but I enclose this anyhow. Did you hear that the planet has been named "Pluto" by the Italian government?

1. "The Unnamable" (*WT,* July 1925), "The Outsider" (*WT,* April 1926), and "Celephaïs" (*Rainbow,* May 1922). At this time "The Quest of Iranon" was unpublished.
2. "The Satyr" (*La Paree Stories,* July 1931; *GL*); "The Phantoms of

the Fire" (*WT,* September 1930; *GL*); "The Devotee of Evil" (*DS* and *AY*); "Murder in the Fourth Dimension" (*Amazing Detective Stories,* October 1930; *TSS*).

3. "The End of the Story" (*WT,* May 1930; *OST* and *RA*).

4. *WT* for May 1930 also contained HPL's "Recapture" and "The Land of Lur" by Earl Leaston Bell.

5. Charles Matlie, a local artist; John Singer Sargent (1856–1925), American painter.

6. "The Testament of Athammaus" (*WT,* October 1932; *OST*).

———————◆———————

[102]   To H. P. Lovecraft [ALS, JHL]   April 23rd, 1930.

Dear Éch-Pi-El:

"The Outsider" is a masterpiece of shadowy cobweb horror, with illimitable suggestive values and overtones. Honestly, I think it more successful than two-thirds of Poe! I like the dramatic "Unnamable" too, as I do everything of yours . . . But "The Outsider" is a classic, in the Gothic genre.

Your southern *pasear* sounds marvellously inviting, and I know you will enjoy it. I wish you were coming out my way—perhaps you will sometime. Wandrei writes me that he may visit California this summer.[1]

Thanks for your gratifying praise of the "Satyr." The tale hasn't sold, but I scarcely expected that it would. Yes, I might write a whole series, with Averoigne for the milieu; but I have so many ideas, with geographical locations in widely scattered realms of myth and fancy, that I may not get around to Averoigne again for awhile! But certainly it's a temptation to repeat some scene or character; and among other things, I shall certainly write another tale about Vizaphmal, the Antarean scientist in "The Monster of the Prophecy." I think the title will be "Vizaphmal in Ophiuchus"; it will be full of fantastic contingencies and perils.[2]

Here are my two latest. Wright took "The Planet of the Dead," somewhat to my surprise. "The Uncharted Isle" should be salable;[3] though, as you say, one can never tell. "Andromeda" is still unfinished, but the "action" is improving! The mutineers have been picked up from the waters of an inland sea, by a monstrous bird something between a pterodactyl and a pelican, which has stowed them away in its pouch and is about to carry them to the environs of a forest of intelligent, half-animate trees.

Thanks, too, for what you say about "The End of the Story." Wright tells me it was "very popular" with his readers. [. . .]

Some of the yarns in *Science Wonder Stories* aren't bad, of their kind, though none of them really attain a literary level. "The City of the Living Dead," in the last issue, was an interesting conception of the ultimate lengths to which mechanical devices could be carried.[4] The magazine is a shade better than *Astounding Stories,* which is the crudest of the pseudo-scientific group. By the way, Wright hints that he is starting a new magazine; but he didn't give me any particulars.

As ever,
Ci–Ay–Ess, the evangelist of Tsathoggua,
and the archivist of Mu and Antares.

1. DAW first visited CAS in November 1934, then again in March 1943 and November 1950.
2. CAS never wrote this sequel. See *SS* for a synopsis to "Vizaphmal in Ophiuchus."
3. "The Uncharted Isle" (*WT,* November 1930; *OST* and *RA*).
4. Laurence Manning and Fletcher Pratt, "The City of the Living Dead" (*Science Wonder Stories,* May 1930).

---

[103]   To Helen Hoyt [ALS, BL]   May 16th, 1930

Dear Helen Hoyt:
        I have just submitted a volume of my verse, entitled *The Jasmine Girdle and Other Poems,* to Harcourt, Brace and Co., I am wondering if you would care to write them a line recommending my work. If you feel like doing that, I should certainly be grateful. I am anxious to have a volume brought out by some regular publisher.
        The poems enclosed are representative of the collection. *The Jasmine Girdle* itself is not a single poem, but a sequence of love-lyrics. I haven't written any verses lately, and may not for a long time to come. I have done a lot of prose-writing (fiction) and have sold ten of my stories since last fall. They are all in the fantastic genre, and hardly represent the fashionable thing among the "intelligentia." But they are the only sort of fiction that amuses me. I may even make a little money, if they should become popular with the public that reads *Weird Tales* and *Amazing Stories.* The former magazine is my chief market, so far.
        I have been re-reading your *Apples,* and like it even better than I did at first. The poems have the charm of true simplicity and emotional directness—a very difficult thing to achieve, as I know. I doubt if I have any real gift for it—I am usually pre-occupied with creating a picture or a tone-poem, regardless of strict veracity; and

have seldom revealed myself, except by indirection. At present, I am as tired of masks as I am of my real self.

Give my best regards to Jack Lyman. Some day, I hope to see you both.

As ever,
Clark Ashton Smith

---

[104]   To H. P. Lovecraft [ALS, JHL]   July 30th, 1930.

Dear Éch-Pi-El:

I received the stories some time back, and have re-read both of them several times with renewed appreciation. I think "Cthulhu" is my favorite—it makes the super-terrestrial and the monstrous so terrifyingly credible; and after reading about the dreams of the sculptor Wilcox, I begin to wonder what unholy arcanic significance some of my own nightmares may have had! I read also the appended "Eyrie" containing your letter (which somehow I had not seen before) with great interest and approval. Galpin's criticism of your endings seems captious and ultra-sophisticated to me: I have no fault to find with any of them—least of all on the score of obviousness.

Thanks for your suggestion about "The Necromantic Tale"! I think so highly of it that I am re-typing a page of the story with an additional sentence or two about the mysterious footnote at the very end of the old record, saying that they saw Sir Roderick disappear when the flames leaped high; and that this, "if true, was the moste damnable proof of hys compact and hys commerce with the Evill One." This emendation I shall submit to Wright, who has already accepted the tale. Wright ought to approve—the change almost "makes" the story.[1]

What you tell me about Belknap's experience with the Gernsback[2] crowd is indeed amazing. I don't see how they do business on a basis of that sort. Certainly Dr. Keller, Arthur B. Reeve, Starzl, and a lot of other people whose work they use aren't writing just for the glory of seeing their names in print. I suppose their game is to cheat the more obscure or occasional contributors, if they can "get away" with it. There ought to be some way of getting at them. Anyway, let me know how the affair works out! They have not yet reported on my "Andromeda" (after nearly two months) and I am writing to make a rather curt inquiry.

Ghost Stories still reeks of McFaddenism, to judge from a cursory examination.[3] Let's hope for the best. I have nothing at present that is properly classifiable as a "ghost story," anyway. My last three yarns are interplanetary fantasies of varying types. I am sending you one of them (along with "Andromeda") and will mail the others presently. You will note that in this one ("The Door to Saturn") Tsathoggua is brought in under the name of Zhothaqquah, by which he was known in Mhu Thulan, (ancient Greenland.) "A Voyage to Sfanomoë," (which deals with two Atlanteans who went to Venus in a space-vehicle just before the sinking of the last remnant of Atlantis) has been taken by Wright. The third tale "The Immeasurable Horror," which is about Venus, I am peddling among the scientifiction magazines.[4]

I hope to see "The Whisperer in Darkness," when your program admits of the proposed changes. In the meanwhile, you might re-loan me "The Horror at Red Hook" if you have an extra copy available.[5] Your tales are almost all that I have read lately: the great welter of current books and magazines simply overwhelms me with boredom. The way in which the well-known human sewage is blithely hashed-up for the seventy-millionth time is really beyond my comprehension.

I trust you will get around to a novel sometime–it ought to be worthwhile from the financial angle anyway. I haven't made a start on anything myself–the idea of spinning anything out to book length rather appalls me. But I suppose I could do it if I tried. I've thought vaguely of a yarn to be called "The Interstellar Changelings," dealing with some entities from an alien universe who substitute one of their own offspring for a human child, and take the human to their own world. It would involve a two-part narrative, detailing the respective fates of the substituted infants; and I don't feel energetic enough at present.

I will return your tales in a few days.

In the name of Cthulhu, "who waits dreaming in his house at R'yleh [sic],"

Yr friend,
Klarkash-Ton

1. CAS's letter of 30 July 1930 was in reply to HPL's of 18 July, parts of which have been reprinted in Roy A. Squires' *Catalog* No. 19 (1985). In particular, HPL is quoted as saying: "I wonder how it would have been to have the ancient wizard *disappear* at the stake, before the eyes of all spectators, just as the flames flare up?" (p. 25). CAS worked this suggestion into "The Necromantic Tale" (*WT*, January 1931; *OD*).

2. Hugo Gernsback (1884–1967), Editor-in-Chief of *Wonder Stories*.

3. *Ghost Stories* was owned by Bernarr MacFadden from 1926 until 1930, when it was sold to Harold Hersey; it folded in 1931.

4. "The Door to Saturn" (*Strange Tales*, January 1932; *LW*); "A Voyage to Sfanomoë" (*WT*, August 1931; *DS*, *AY*, and *RA*); "The Immeasurable Horror" (*WT*, September 1931; *OD*).

5. "The Whisperer in Darkness" (*WT*, August 1931); "The Horror at Red Hook" (*WT*, January 1927).

[105]   To H. P. Lovecraft [ALS, JHL]   Aug. 22nd, 1930.

Dear Éch-Pi-El:

Your letter, enclosing "The Horror at Red Hook," arrived just as I was starting on a camping-trip in the mountains. I mailed you "The Immeasurable Horror" before I left—also your ms. of "Pickman's Model" and the printed copy of "Cthulhu."

I'm glad the new stories were so much to your liking. "Andromeda" appears next month in *Wonder Stories* according to the editors. Also, they want me to do a series of tales about the same crew of characters (Capt. Volmar, etc.) and their adventures on different planets, saying that they would use a novelette of this type every other month. I have asked them to name a rate of payment, and shall not submit anything more without a definite understanding, since (apart from the warning conveyed by Long's experience) I have secured some confidential information about the Gernsback outfit, to the effect that it is unwise to do business with them except on a definite basis. In fact, I think I shall wait till they have paid for "Andromeda" before sending in another tale—which may be *never*.

My trip in the mountains was, as usual, a fascinating experience. I drafted nearly all of a new novelette, "The Red World of Polaris,"[1] during the trip. It was written on several mountain-tops, beneath the thousand-year-old junipers on granite crags; and the giant firs and hemlocks by the margin of sapphire tarns. You shall see it later, when it is revised and polished. The writing was good practise in concentration, since tremendous or grandiose scenery is more likely to be a source of distraction than inspiration, except in retrospect.

"The Phantoms of the Fire"[2] is no favorite with me—I prefer nearly all my other tales.

I liked Belknap's "A Visitor from Egypt" very much indeed, and thought it by far the best tale in the last *W.T.*, aside from the reprint of Suter's excellent story. *Your Fungi from Yuggoth* were admirable; and Rankin's head-piece had its points.[3] The new type is certainly an improvement, since it gives a more spacious and less crowded aspect.

I think you underrate "Red Hook," which has, for my taste, a lot of good writing and atmosphere. It isn't *your* best, perhaps, but how far above the best of others! By the way, I read your "Picture in the House" aloud one evening by the light of our campfire in the mountains; and it was received with great enthusiasm by my hostess Mrs. Sully and her daughters.[4] On another evening I read

Merimee's great story "The Venus of Ille;"[5] but it had to divide the honors with your tales.

Have you copies of "Polaris" and "Beyond the Wall of Sleep" which you could re-loan me?[6]

My "Red World of Polaris" is pseudo-scientific with a vengeance: it deals with a race of people who had their brains transplanted into indestructible metal bodies, and who were going to perform the same office for the humans who visited their world. The denouement is terrific, and should certainly be an improvement on Edmond Hamilton,[7] at least in regard to variety. There are possibilities in this type of story, though I'd prefer writing something even more extra-terrestrial, with no human characters at all.

Write me when your revision work permits.

Greetings and valedictions from the outer moon of the Red World, in the hour following the collapse of the atomic vault, the outbreak of the metal-eating monsters from the subterranean realm, and the downfall of the last Babelian tower of the Zophnatars.

Klarkash-Ton

1. "The Red World of Polaris" was completed but never published, and the manuscript for the story may no longer be extant.
2. "The Phantoms of the Fire" (*WT,* September 1930; *GL*).
3. *WT* for September 1930 contained "The Phantoms of the Fire," as well as Frank Belknap Long, "A Visitor from Egypt"; Paul Suter, "Beyond the Door" (a reprint); and HPL, "The Courtyard" and "Star-Winds" from *Fungi from Yuggoth*.
4. Genevieve Sully's daughter Helen (1904–1997) visited HPL and various of his associates on a trip east in the summer of 1933. Her younger daughter was named Marion.
5. Prosper Mérimée (1803–1870), "The Venus of Ille," *Revue des Deux Mondes* (1837).
6. "Polaris" (*The Philosopher*, December 1920); "Beyond the Wall of Sleep" (*Pine Cones*, October 1919).
7. Hamilton (1904–1977) was a popular and prolific author of "weird-scientific" stories for *WT* during the 1930s.

———————•———————

[106]   To H. P. Lovecraft [ALS, JHL]   [c. mid-September 1930]
En route to Aldebaran—
At the dawn of the grey nebula.

Dear Éch-Pi-El:

Thanks for the tales, both of which are like old friends.

"Polaris" is indeed a haunting fantasy; and there are stupendous and supremely original imaginative implications in "Beyond the Wall of Sleep." Yes, the latter was the first of your tales that I read: it was loaned to me by Loveman back in 1919 or 1920. It doesn't say much for editorial acumen that neither of these tales has had professional publication.

Your hints about "The Whisperer in Darkness" are most alluring; and I hope you will have it in its definite form before long. That idea of the brains transported in metal cylinders is excellent! By the way, I note a yarn by Edmond Hamilton in *W. T.*, about some heads that were kept alive by artificial systems after their bodies were destroyed. My own conception of a brain in an artificial physique dates back almost to my childhood!

Here is "The Red World," which I have not yet submitted to *Wonder Stories*. I have received a letter from the editor offering me ¾ of a cent per word as a preliminary basis of payment, with an increase if my tales "go over." In return I am telling him very politely that I can't even take time to finish the next yarn unless I receive prompt payment for "Andromeda." Whether anything eventuates or not will of course depend on the favor which this story finds with the scientifiction "fans." I thought the cover-design about the limit—I could paint a better one in ten minutes. Also there were some irritating misprints, and two or three sentences interpolated by the editor in Chap. VI, which didn't improve the style. But I hope the Gernsback gang will make it worth while for me to do the series,[1] since there are undeniable possibilities in such stories—even though I would rather drop the stale paraphernalia of ether-ships, gas-masks, etc., and the personnel of terrestrial explorers, and plunge into something wholly ultra-terrene and belonging to the Beyond. [. . .]

I find many of the yarns in *Wonder Stories* and *Amazing Stories* interesting for their ideas. One can't even find ideas in the other classes of magazines—all of them, from the *Atlantic* to the wild-west thrillers, are hide-bound and hog-tied with traditions of unutterable dullness. The other day, when I got out the *W.T.* containing your "Dunwich Horror," to loan to a friend, I noticed that it also included a reprint of "The Diamond Lens" by Fitz-James O'Brien, which first appeared in the *Atlantic* back in 1858. I couldn't help musing on what would be the fate of this fine story if it were submitted to the *Atlantic now* for the first time.

Our weather now is the golden, azure, Indian-summery kind, with a mellow warmth that pervades one's being like an elixir. I, too, still work out of doors as much as possible. Probably the mountain scenery was a stimulant to my writing—but it was so tremendous that it temporarily altered and confused my sense of values. Mere words didn't seem to stand up in the presence of those peaks and cliffs. But now, amid the perspectives of familiar surroundings, "The Red World" doesn't seem so bad. The last chapter could afford themes for Doré or Martin, in regard to cataclysmic scope at any rate.

"The Immeasurable Horror" has not yet been submitted to Wright—it is still out with *Amazing*. Wright accepted two poems ("A Chinese Vase" and "Jungle Twilight") for *Oriental Stories*.[2] I shall try to do some prose for this magazine.

As ever,
Klarkash-Ton

Can you let me re-read "The White Ship" some time?[3]

Later—

I have received your card from Quebec, which must indeed be a marvellous importation of old-world charm and antiquity in our hemisphere. I can well understand your feelings—I'm a sort of Tory, too. I mean to see that country sometime; but, like you, I wouldn't care for the sub-arctic weather.

I am enclosing a brief Orientale with "The Red World." Have begun a new novelette, "The Eggs from Saturn," with a realistic local setting for its ultraplanetary mysteries and horrors. Have also worked out a synopsis for another of the Captain Volmar series, to be called "The Ocean-World of Alioth."[4]

Before long you will receive the primordial stone statuette of an unknown deity which I found while in the mountains, on what is known as Crater Ridge, a long, barren, rock-strewn hill with a little lake of unfathomable depth lying almost in its crest. Geologists say that the lake is *not* an extinct volcano, nor the ridge of volcanic origin; but the whole locality is so scoriac in its appearance that I don't believe them. Many of the smaller stones are extremely fantastic in form. Mrs. Sully found one that was reminiscent of a small Aztec idol! She calls it *Tsathoggua,* and refuses to give it up!

plus tard—

I've put off the mailing of this, till it begins to take on the character of a diary as well as an epistle!

Your letter enclosing "Sfanomoë" was received. Glad you liked this story, which is a sort of favorite with me. Your letter, in its rhapsodic descriptions, is the finest prose-poem I have read for some time. And the cards (for which I thank you) certainly give a most astounding impression of continental atmosphere.

I've been sick with a bad cold—unable to sleep for two nights.

It's beginning to break up to-day. And I hope to get out and mail you the pre-human god before long.

By the way, the Gernsback outfit has just remitted a sizable check ($90.00) for "Andromeda," and they seem anxious to see the new story, which I am now submitting. They may have taken me for a compatriot, from the tone of my letter to them! And they are saying to each other, "We will not bamboozle our Jewish brother even if we could."

1. The "Volmar" series.
2. "On A Chinese Vase" (Spring 1932; *SP*); "Jungle Twilight" (Summer 1932; *SP*, *S&P*, and *LO*).
3. "The White Ship" (*WT*, March 1927).
4. Neither "The Eggs from Saturn" nor "The Ocean-World of Alioth" was completed. See *SS* for partial drafts of both tales and a synopsis of the latter.

---

[107]   To H. P. Lovecraft [ALS, JHL]   [c. late October 1930]
Temple of Rhalu, the moon goddess, at the hour
of the blood-sacrifice, in the last cycle of Mu.

Dear Éch-Pi-El:

I hope you have received ere this the nameless, pre-human statuette of a divinity who must have come down from ulterior stars and planets with Cthulhu and Tsathoggua. Perhaps you can give it a name; and I will be glad of any information which you can afford me, regarding its origin and attributes, all of which are undoubtedly dark and awful, not to say sinister.

I was delighted with your letter; and I can picture those fields near the river-bank where you began it in the autumn twilight. And thanks for your commendation of my last tales and the loan of "The White Ship,"[1] which, to my taste, is perhaps the best of your purely fanciful, poetic stories, after "The Silver Key." It has an abiding, undiminishable charm, like a chapter out of Sir John Maundeville,[1] or the voyages of Sindbad; and certainly I do not think it in any wise inferior to Dunsany. I believe you underrate this side of your work; though I agree with you that the quasi-realistic mode of treatment is your best metier. I never cease to marvel at the patient, monumental accumulation of veridic details which, in such stories as "Cthulhu" and "The Dunwich Horror," produces in combination with the unearthly imaginative element an absolutely overwhelming effect. But it is only fair to say that I would not care for the realism without the other element.

I hope to see "The Whisperer in Darkness" before long. I, too, find that the results are more satisfying when composition is not strung out over a long period. If I had the unbroken time I would try to draft all my own tales in as few sittings as possible, since in this way one is more likely to secure a perfect unity, and to utilize the full force of the original imaginative impetus.

My own writing was held up for about two weeks last month by the joint illnesses of my parents, who came down simultaneously with the grippe following my own attack of the same malady, for I have not done anything with the novelettes I mentioned, beyond the first chapter of "The Eggs from Saturn," and a synopsis of the next Volmar story, "The Ocean-World of Alioth." However, I have written a new "short" ("Medusa") which I enclose; and am now doing another which deals with the ancient Lemurian remains on South Sea isles.[2] As soon as I have finished this, I will tackle the Volmar yarn.

Wright accepted "A Rendezvous in Averoigne," which seems to have pleased his fancy. He is also taking "The Immeasurable Horror,"[3] but has asked me to make an alteration or two which will account for two of the characters, who, it seems, I dropped rather summarily before the end. This is now done—it involved only the addition of two brief sentences. I will send you the carbon of "Averoigne" in a few days.

Wright is certainly capricious in his rejections and acceptances; though I, for one, am the last to blame him for trying to please his public. But it seems to me that he makes mistakes even from this view-point. I thought the last issue of *W.T.* rather punk, apart from the verses, the frontispiece decoration by Senf, and one or two *fine* passages in Howard's tale. I couldn't stomach this last as a whole— that bloody battle stuff is so stale that it gives me what Sterling called "the Molossian pip." Still, it was better than Hamilton's *current* re-dishing of his immemorial moth-eaten plot, and the commonplace detective thriller by Quinn. Munn's story was vivid and original in some of its detail, but I didn't get much out of it as a whole. And even the reprint was pretty tame.[4]

By the way, have you seen *Oriental Stories?* It is pleasingly gotten up; though I failed to find anything remarkable in the contents. My "Willow Landscape" was rejected—only "action stories" are desired.[5] If you have not seen this magazine, and would care to have it, I will send you my copy, together with late issues of *Ghost Stories, Amazing, Astounding,* and *The Argosy.* The last-named is a possible market for your fantastic-scientific adventure stories; and I bought the issue for a novelette by Kline.[6] None of these magazines would need to be returned. Two or three tales in *Ghost Stories* were not bad of their kind; though the McFadden drool and drivel is still in evidence. *Astounding* absolutely gags me—in one of the stories, for example, there is a Man from Mars who talks American slang! I shall not buy the magazine again.

As for the problem of phantasy, my own standpoint is that there is absolutely no justification for literature unless it serves to release the imagination from the bounds of every-day life. I have undergone a complete revulsion against the purely realistic school, including the French, and can no longer stomach even Anatole France. God knows what I can find to read, after I have exhausted the last of your re-loaned mss! I must get hold of De La Mare's stories, and those of Montague Rhodes James, if I can.[7]

Speaking of Dunsany, I note that there are stories by him in late issues of *Harper's* and Hearst's *Cosmopolitan*.[8] I read the tale in the last issue, and found it disappointing, with a note of smart sophistication.

The future of phantasy is certainly a most problematic one. You analyze very clearly the reasons backing the present attitude; and I suppose you are right about the purifying process . . . When the novelty of modern discoveries, etc., has worn off, it seems to me that people must go back to a realization of the environing, undissipated mystery, which will make for a restoration of the imaginative. Science, philosophy, psychology, humanism, after all, are only candle-flares in the face of the eternal night with its infinite reserves of strangeness, terror, sublimity. And surely literature cannot always confine itself to the archives of the anthill and the annals of the hog-sty, as it seems to be doing at present.

That picture of me in *Wonder Stories* is a bum drawing from a villainous, passport-like photograph. No one likes it; so please don't get the idea that it looks very much like me.

I read that story by Flagg with much interest.[9] His work, though it is none too distinctive in point of literary style, seems always to stand a little apart from the ruck of magazine fiction. It shows mentality and imagination—both of which are usually lacking.

Our weather has been very changeable lately, alternating from sultry golden warmth to days of high fog and icy gales. The autumn colors are appearing; and I must have a few leisurely weeks before the season is over. I have an idea that the winter will be heavier than usual, with many storms and much rain.

Probably you have seen "The Uncharted Isle" in *W.T.*, which has two or three misprints. The bull about Lima as a sea-port was uncorrected, though I have the impression that I told Wright. Personally, I don't mind—it's like the celebrated "sea-coast of Bohemia!"[10]

I have come to the conclusion that it is hardly worth while to write stories under three or four thousand words. For one thing, anything shorter than this seldom makes any deep or lasting impression, no longer how good or well-done. It doesn't seem to have the requisite "body" and carrying-power.

Write soon. And may I have "The Hound" to re-read? I am returning two of the last ones that you loaned me, and will send "The White Ship" in a few days.[11]

As ever, yr. friend, Klarkash-Ton

1. "The Silver Key" (WT, January 1929). Soon after writing HPL on 16 November 1930, CAS wrote "A Tale of Sir John Maundeville" (Fantasy Fan, October 1933, as "The Kingdom of the Worm"; OD).

2. Original title of "The Gorgon" (WT, April 1932; LW).The second tale is "An Offering to the Moon" (see letter 109).

3. "A Rendezvous in Averoigne" (WT, April–May 1930; OST and RA); "The Immeasurable Horror" (WT, September 1931; OD).

4. WT for November 1930 contained verse by Alice l'Anson ("Teotihuacan"), Frank Belknap Long ("Great Ashtoreth"), and DAW ("The Cypress Bog"); "Kings of the Night" by Robert E. Howard; "Stealthy Death" by Seabury Quinn; "The Master Strikes" by H. Warner Munn; and "Siesta" by Alexander L. Kielland. C[urtis] C[onstantini] Senf (1873–1949) was briefly an illustrator for WT.

5. "The Willow Landscape" (Philippine Magazine, May 1931; DS and GL).

6. I.e., Otis Adelbart Kline (1891–1946), literary agent and author of popular fiction in various genres.

7. Walter de la Mare (1873–1956), British poet and author of weird fiction; M. R. James (1862–1936), British antiquarian and author of ghost stories.

8. Lord Dunsany, "A Queer Island" (Harper's, September 1928) and "Mrs. Jorkens" (Cosmopolitan, October 1930; as "The Mermaid's Husband"), both tales involving the clubman Joseph Jorkens.

9. Francis Flagg, pseudonym of Henry George Weiss (1898–1946), "The Jelly-Fish" (WT, October 1930).

10. A famous error in Shakespeare's The Winter's Tale.

11. HPL, "The Hound" (WT, February 1924; rpt. September 1929).

———————◆◆———————

[108]   To Donald Wandrei [ALS, MHS]   Oct. 9th, 1930.

Dear Donald:

[. . .] I am sorry you could not come to California this summer. I was in the high mountains for ten days in August. You would love it there—also, you would like the country around Auburn . . . The autumn, too, is my own especial season; and everything is about perfect now, as far as I am concerned. Of course, much if not all of the autumn color around here is in the fruit orchards; but it is very lovely and gorgeous . . . Let's hope for better luck next year—also that you will finish your novel, and find a ready publisher in the meanwhile.

[. . .] I have not written any poetry this year, and have the feeling that my vein is at least temporarily exhausted. But there seems to be no limit to the prose, some of which I write with as much facility as if it were being dictated to me! It may seem a bold project to make a living from fantastic fiction of a high literary type; but I believe it can be done. In fact, I shall have to do it—or else take to ditch-digging. I have no other alternative, since I am not fitted for business or any of the professions.

Lovecraft writes to me often; and I have been re-borrowing all of his stories to read. They are almost all that I can read in present-day fiction. I have completely sworn off on the realistic school, and can't even read Anatole France any more. In the name of Hecate, Medusa and Proserpine, please hurry up with your weird novel.[1] I may do one myself, alternating the chapters with the writing of shorts and novelettes. In that way, it shouldn't be so much of a strain. [. . .]

As ever,
Clark

1. DAW, *Dead Titans, Waken!* published as *The Web of Easter Island* (Sauk City, WI: Arkham House, 1948). See also letter 134.

———————————— ✦ ————————————

[109]   To H. P. Lovecraft [ALS, JHL]   [c. 24 October 1930]
In the world Sarkolosh. At the dawn of the
red sun and the setting of the green.

Dear Éch-Pi-El:

I, too, surmised that the simulachre might well prove to be an ultra-mundane and pre-human representation of Tsathoggua, but hardly dared to venture my surmise without the surety of corroboration from more learned pontiffs, and hierophants and hierarchists of superior and paramount adeptness. I await with shuddering avidity the result of the dread divinations and auspices at which you hint. The suggestion of any simulachral relationship or connection with Azathoth (even of the remotest vestigial sort) is simply overpowering in its terror; for is not Azathoth the animating Daemon of that all-encompassing Space which Einstein in his latest theory and a certain unknown poet in a long-forgotten "Ode to the Abyss,"[1] have represented as devouring the material universe?

Your last letter contains far more substance than most magazine articles, and brings up a world of ideas on which I will touch presently. But first of all let me thank you for the re-loan of "The Hound," and your more than gracious offer to loan me your books. I will accept the latter, on condition that you will consider my own library at your service; though I doubt if I have much that would be new or of interest to you. The bulk of it is English poetry, and romantic or realistic fiction. Apart from Poe, Bierce, and some of Lafcadio Hearn's collections of strange folklore, it is really lacking in the weird. There is a set of six volumes, *Mystery and Detective Tales*,[2] containing some miscellaneous "weirds" from many languages, which you may well have seen. The singular continuation of *Melmoth* by Balzac is one of the items. Also, I have a book by Clemence Housman, *The Werewolf,* which is probably as good as that kind of story can be. It failed to make much of an impression on me. I have also Barbey D'Aurevilly's *Story without a Name,*[3]—an atrocious carnal horror for which you probably wouldn't care . . . I have read some of the books you mention; but others I have not read, and have been vainly trying to obtain. I should be vastly grateful for the loan of *The House of Souls*[4]—also, for the books by M. R. James when you get them back. By the way, you don't mention the Bierce-Danziger book, *The Monk and the Hangman's Daughter.* This I also have. A sadistic tale, for which I no longer care greatly. I think you are right in suspecting the "cosmicism" of Bierce, and even of Machen. Bierce's horrors are purely human. "The Death of Halpin Frayser" is probably as good as any. It is certainly the ultimate of its kind.

In spite of your disparagement of "The Hound," I must frankly admit that I enjoyed re-reading it, and find the tale hideously suggestive. I don't mind the weird properties, etc.; though, abstractly, I can see what you mean. The tale is inferior by comparison with many of your others—but doesn't lose by comparison with weird fiction in general.

As I told you in my last, I think your new tale is among your best. It is a capital example of the theory you advance regarding the composition of weird stories—a theory which is undoubtedly the soundest one possible. My own *conscious* ideal has been to delude the reader into accepting an impossibility, or series of impossibilities, by means of a sort of verbal black magic, in the achievement of which I make use of prose-rhythm, metaphor, simile, tone-color, counter-point, and other stylistic resources, like a sort of incantation. *You* attain a black magic, perhaps unconsciously, in your pursuit of corroborative detail and verisimilitude. But I fear that I don't always attain verisimilitude in my pursuit of magic! However, I sometimes suspect that the wholly *unconscious* elements in writing (or other art) are by far the most important. Poe tried to rationalize his processes of composition and explained everything . . . except his own incommunicable secret.

By the way, I have just been re-reading "The Canal"[5], which you mention. It certainly creates a memorable atmosphere; but the one flaw, to me, is the wholesale dynamiting, which seems to introduce a jarring note among the shadowy supernatural horrors. However, this is just my own reaction. I would have had the narrator simply kill himself, overwhelmed by despair at the *irremediable* scourge he had loosed, and leave the horror to spread unchecked. However, I shouldn't be captious: it is the only good vampire story I have ever seen, apart from Gautier's "Clarimonde" and my own "Rendezvous in Averoigne." And the merits of Gautier's tale are stylistic rather than imaginative. You are right about the Latins—they have no imagination except of the most earthbound type. Baudelaire's abysses are those of the soul or the nerves, and his horrors are drawn from the subterranes of human consciousness, and never from the outer gulfs.

Thanks for your intercession on behalf of "Satampra Zeiros"! It seems to me also that Everil Worril's [*sic*] co-editorship should help to counter-balance some of Wright's dunder-headed decisions;[6] and I shall resubmit "Satampra" and perhaps also "The Door to Saturn" at some future date. But even with all his rejections, Wright has certainly accepted a lot of my stuff in the past year. He has taken thirteen stories,—not to mention poems. I certainly need more markets for my "weirds," and am now submitting to *Ghost Stories* (as a preliminary try-out) such tales as "Medusa" and "An Offering to the Moon."[7] But this magazine is not at present a very hopeful or high-class proposition. However, one or two of the *Weird Tales* contributors have had stories in it; so there may be a chance for me. *W.T.* at its worst is a compendium of classics in comparison. [. . .]

I didn't mean to dogmatize when I spoke of my reaction toward realism. My attitude at bottom is precisely the same as yours: I admit the objective claims of such art—in fact, of all good and sincere art; and will even admit that my distaste for the literature of quotidian detail is doubtless co-related with a sort of personal disenchantment with the social world. I am partially, at least, almost in the psychological condition of your own Randolph Carter. With me, though, there is no conscious desire to go back in time—only a wild aspiration toward the unknown, the uncharted, the exotic, the utterly strange and ultra-terrestrial. And this aspiration, as I know with a fatal foreknowledge, could never be satisfied by anything on earth or in actual life, but only through dream-ventures such as those in my poems, paintings and stories.

I don't think I have had anything quite like the pseudo-mnemonic flashes you describe. What I have had sometimes is the nocturnal dream-experience of stepping into some totally alien state of entity, with its own memories, hopes, desires, its own past and future—none of which I can ever remember for very long on awakening. This experience has suggested such tales as "The Planet of the Dead," "The Necromantic Tale," and "An Offering to the Moon." I think I have spoken of the place-images which often rise before me without apparent relevance, and persist in attaching themselves to some train of emotion or even abstract thought. These, doubtless, are akin to the images of which you speak, though they are always clearly realistic.

Certainly, there are not many people with a sense of the cosmic strangeness and mystery. Popular education has effectively killed anything of the sort in the middle-classes; and the only people who retain it are the ignorant, or those who have the spark strongly enough to survive the snuffing-out influence of relative knowledge: so, as you say, the field narrows down to the plebs and the spiritual patricians. I have been interested to find that my own tales are read eagerly by local people with no pretensions to literary taste or culture; and the one person of the opposite sort (a woman) who appreciates them, is of an ultra-aristocratic type.

I am forwarding "The Whisperer" to Derleth as per direction. You should have received ere this my "Averoigne," which I mailed some time ago. And I am enclosing "An Offering" with this letter. Just now I am lagging over a scientific horror, "Like Mohammed's Tomb." The chief merit is that the scientist uses his contraption to commit a highly novel and unique suicide, and also to remove a budding fellow-inventor from the sphere of mundane effort.[8]

By the way, your "Whisperer" suggested an idea which you might develop to more advantage than I could. Why not write a tale about some extraplanetary being who has undergone (either at the hands of his own kind, or of some human plastic surgeon) a facial transformation which enables him to pass as a human. His body, of course, would be "teratologically fabulous" beneath his clothing; and there would be all sorts of disquieting suggestions about his personality. I think you could work this up to perfection if the idea appeals to you.[9]

I have also conceived what I think is a whale of an idea, as illustrating the conditional nature of our perception of reality. A human is transported to some foreign world, where he suffers incredible and utterly unimaginable torture from the nature of the sensory impressions he receives, which are worse than delirium or drug-nightmares. Perceiving his condition, the people of this world subject him to some mysterious process which changes all his nerve and sense-reactions, so that existence becomes at least tolerable for him through a sort of adaptation. He, however, does not realize how completely his sense apparatus has been transformed. He grows homesick for the earth, which he still remembers *as he had known it,* and makes a secret use of one of the cosmic projectors employed by his hosts in interstellar travel, to effect his return. But, with his new sense-reactions, the earth is no less strange and intolerable[10] to him than the other world had seemed before the sensory change. He dies raving and in a hospital, where his case has been roughly diagnosed as delirium tremens. I think there are huge possibilities in this, if it is carefully and graphically worked out. The change in the feeling of time, movement, geometry, the monstrous transmutations and amplifications and distortions and combinations of visual, aural, and other images, could be dealt with in a minutely realistic style. For instance, there might be an extension, or combination of tactility with visions which would cause acute torture from certain terrestrial images. The tale is so damnably possible when you think of what a little fever, or a dose of hashish, can do to one's sensory apparatus. But it will be hard to write—and harder still to sell, since it will be analytic and descriptive rather than actional: which brings me to the reflection that one reason there are so few good weird stories is the damned editorial requirement for "action," which makes it very difficult to build up any solid or convincing background, or to treat the incidents themselves with the necessary fulness of detail. I did what I thought was a fair job of that with "The Red World"—and received the disgusting criticism which I mentioned in my last letter.[11] [. . .]

Later—

I am greatly pleased to learn that the new Averoigne tale was so much to your taste. It is one of my own favorites—in fact, I like it much better than the celebrated "End of the Story." I have an idea for another tale dealing with the seamy supernatural side of Averoigne; and it will probably rise to the proportions of a two- or three-part serial. [. . .]

I sent you that job-lot of magazines the other day. Maybe they'll be utilizable as fuel, when your New England Winter sets in.

Contrary to my expectations, we are having our usual long, dry autumn—not a drop of rain, and hardly the wisp of a cloud. It suits me well enough, since I can be outdoors as much as I like.

I have just been reading *The Book of the Damned,* which I procured from the State Library at Sacramento. (Unluckily, they don't loan fiction by mail—only "serious books.") Fort's volume is certainly fascinating—one of the oddest books I have ever encountered. I don't care for the style—but the assembled data is quite imposing, and worthy of close study.[12]

Here is a tale, "The Face by the River," which I wrote in a single day. There's not much of the cosmic in it; but it might interest you as an attempt at psychological realism.[13]

Yrs.,
Klarkash-Ton

You might re-loan me "The Colour out of Space," which I would like to re-read carefully. I once had a copy of *A.S.* containing it; but some one has nefariously made away with the magazine.[14]

1. CAS refers to himself and his poem

2. In HPL's letter to CAS of 7 November 1930, he identifies this set as Julian Hawthorne (1846–1934), ed., *The Lock and Key Library: Classic Mystery and Detective Stories* (New York: Review of Reviews Co., 1909). HPL's ed. was published in 10 vols.

3. Jules Barbey D'Aurevilly (1808–1889), *The Story Without a Name*, trans. Edgar Saltus (1891).

4. Arthur Machen, *The House of Souls* (1906). Contains: "A Fragment of Life"; "The White People"; "The Great God Pan"; and "The Inmost Light."

5. Everil Worrell, "The Canal" (*WT*, December 1927).

6. Worrell never held an editorial position with *WT*.

7. "An Offering to the Moon" (*WT*, September 1953; OD).

8. Nonextant.

9. HPL considered CAS's idea seriously, for he entered in his commonplace book: "Inhabitant of another world—face masked (perhaps with human skin) or surgically alter'd to human shape, but body alien beneath robes. Having reached earth, tries to mix with mankind. Hideous revelation. [Suggested by CAS]" (entry 181). This entry influenced "Through the Gates of the Silver Key" (1932–33) and "The Shadow out of Time" (1934–35). HPL had used the phrase "teratologically fabulous" in "The Dunwich Horror" to describe Wilbur Whateley's true appearance.

10. See *SL* 3.211–16 and Steve Behrends, "CAS & Divers Hands: Ideas of Lovecraft and Others in Smith's Fiction," *Crypt of Cthulhu* No. 26 (Hallowmas 1984): 31. HPL noted on the margin the following: "Have him find what he thinks to be an utterly strange and hideous planet—recognizing it as the earth (except for vague, disquieting suggestions of familiarity)—only at the last." CAS later wrote this idea as "A Star-Change" (*Wonder Stories*, May 1933, as "The Visitors from Mlok"; *GL*).

11. In a letter written on or about 21 October 1930 (ms., JHL), CAS told HPL that "The Jews want some more 'ekshun' in the first part of 'The Red World,' which they criticize as being 'almost wholly descriptive'." As with "Like Mohammed's Tomb," this story is lost. See *SS*, pp. 269–270.

12. Charles Fort (1874–1932), *The Book of the Damned* (1919). Fort's books were accounts of various weird phenomena.

13. A typescript of "The Face by the River" was once among the CAS papers at JHL in the early 1960s, but its whereabouts is now unknown.

The story involved a murderer who sees in a pool of water a reflection of the face of his victim, and in seeking it drowns himself.

14. HPL, "The Colour out of Space" (*Amazing Stories,* September 1927).

---

[110]   To August Derleth[1] [ALS, SHSW]   Nov. 2nd, 1930.

Dear August Derleth:

Many thanks for sending me your stories, which came to-day. They are just the sort of reading-matter that I had been wishing for—the sort of which I find too little. I have already read "The Panelled Room," and must express my admiration of its artistic handling, its shadowy, terrifying suggestiveness. I want to read "The Early Years" carefully and at leisure. Wandrei has spoken very highly of it; and I feel sure it will be good.[2]

Here is my carbon of "A Rendezvous in Averoigne"—the vampire tale that you wanted to see. I am also sending you under separate cover my originals of two unsold stories, "The Epiphany of Death" and "The Tale of Satampra Zeiros." I fear they are unmarketable unless Wright should at some future time re-consider them. "The Epiphany" may remind you a little of Lovecraft's "Outsider"—but it was written before I had read this latter.

My other unplaced tales are all out or loaned. I will be glad to let you see several recent stories of the occult when I get them back. I've just had the nerve to send one to the *Atlantic*!! [. . .]

Does *Mystic Magazine* plan to use much fiction? I looked it over on the local stand, and most of the contents appeared to be articles or (allegedly) true stories. The field of the occult certainly isn't over-crowded. The Harold Hersey *Ghost Stories* may have possibilities if it ever gets through printing McFadden left-overs.

Cordially,
Clark Ashton Smith

1. August W. Derleth (1909–1971), author of weird tales and also a long series of regional and historical works set in his native Wisconsin. After HPL's death, he and DAW founded the publishing firm of Arkham House to preserve HPL's work in book form. Ultimately, Arkham House published twelve books by CAS.

2. "The Panelled Room" (*Leaves,* Summer 1937). "The Early Years" is the core of AWD's *Evening in Spring* (New York: Scribners, 1941).

---

[111]   To H. P. Lovecraft [ALS, JHL]   Nov. 10th [1930]
                                                —Year of the Black Suns
                                                —In the Tail of Serpens.

Dear Éch-Pi-El:

A tranquil downpour of autumn rain has been succeeded by days of cloudless sunlight. The air is very clear—one might say sparkling; and the glory of the colored leaves is still undiminished. No frost as yet. And I hope that the leaguerment of the cold has not yet begun in your region.

Your letter was highly welcome. Indeed, "The Whisperer" is something to remember—nothing gives me so much pleasure as a fine piece of work like that. I am eager to know what you think of my "Offering to the Moon"—though perhaps it isn't quite my best.

Derleth wrote me not long ago, and loaned me some of his own excellent work to read. Have you seen the *Mystic Magazine,* of which he is associate editor? I've looked it over recently—it seems to consist mainly of articles on astrology, spiritualism, and such like themes, with one or two stories along similar lines in each issue.

Your idea for an interplanetary tale is tremendous. Most interplanetary yarns might as well have been laid on earth—as far as I can see—the characters seem no more affected by their alien milieu than if they were in some exotic terrestrial region. But certainly, the usual editorial requirements militate against any attempt at a sound psychological treatment . . . "The story is too leisurely." "No plot, no complications." "Put some more action in it." Oh, hell! Which reminds me that I am beginning another Volmar yarn for the Jews—"Captives of the Serpent."[1] I'll give them their "action" this time!!!

Here's a little scientific horror for you to read. The anti-gravitation mechanism was put to a good use, I think.[2] By the way, I may tackle the well-worn idea of a time-travelling machine some day, and bring it to its logical denouement. A journey behind or ahead of earth-time would, it seems to me, land the voyager in some alien corner of space, unless he had made special provision for accompanying the movement of the earth and the solar system during the same backward or forward period. If he went far enough into the future, he might find himself in some world of Hercules! But this is an abstruse subject!

I, too, am not taken by the conventional "spell of the East"—though I did feel something of the sort in my teens . . . As to works on Arabic history and customs, I hardly know which to suggest.

Probably the best ones are in French and German. Burton and Doughty[3] might be worth reading in regard to the customs, which are doubtless the same now as they have always been . . . I have thought vaguely, sometimes, of laying a tale in the prehistoric pagan period of Arabia. Also, the Uighur empire (supposedly 17,000 years old) mentioned in Churchward's *Lost Continent of Mu,* should have its possibilities.[4] And all sorts of new claims could be staked out in the pre-glacial or antediluvian epochs of the earth. Interstellar travel and traffic was probably in its prime, as Charles Fort suggests!

I think it would "pay" you from all standpoints to write a new series of stories. And, most assuredly, I and many other appreciative readers would be the gainers thereby!

As ever,
Klarkash-Ton

1. Later titled "A Captivity in Serpens," the story was published in *Wonder Stories Quarterly* (Summer 1931; *OD*) under the editor's title, "The Amazing Planet." It was the second and final tale in CAS's "Volmar" series.
2. "Like Mohammed's Tomb." See *SS,* p. 270.
3. Sir Richard F. Burton (1821–1890), *The Gold-Mines of Midian and the Ruined Midianite Cities: A Fortnight's Tour in North-Western Arabia* (1878); Charles Doughty (1843–1926), *Travels in Arabia Deserta* (1888).
4. Col. James Churchward (1852–1936), *The Lost Continent of Mu* (1926).

---

[112]   To H. P. Lovecraft [ALS, JHL]   [c. 16 November 1930]
From the audience-room of the throned worm,
in the nighted Kingdom of Antchar, on the road that is
no longer used by living men between Abchaz and Georgia.

Dear Éch-Pi-El:

First of all, to thank you for the loan of *The House of Souls,* and for the re-loan of "The Colour out of Space." I have been reading all of these with pleasure. Of the Machen stories I like best "The Great God Pan," and next to it "The White People." The other two, at first reading, fail to impress me so cogently.

I don't wonder at your preference for "The Colour out of Space," which is a most satisfying production from all view-points. It has all the elements of terror, weirdness and insoluble extraterrene mystery with a ground-work of marvellous realism in which no contributory detail has been overlooked. I have been studying it closely, with the keenest relish and appreciation.

I am beginning this on the evening of a rainy Sabbath. A good old-fashioned down-pour has continued all day; and I have just finished the drafting of a new "short,"—"A Tale of Sir John Maundeville," which I am intercalating with my Gernsback thriller. The Kingdom of Antchar, which I have invented for this tale, is more unwholesome, if possible, than Averoigne!

1,500 volumes quite dwarfs my little library, which doesn't contain more than six or seven hundred at the most. I imagine, from your summary, that you have a pretty solid collection, and I'd certainly like to see a list of the weird items, when you have the time and inclination to compile it[1]. Some of my choice volumes are books on art, or illustrated editions, including the John Martin edition of *Paradise Lost,* with drawings of Simeon Solomon, Charles Conder, Kahlil Gibran, Edmond Dulac and others.[2]

I'm glad my last stories seemed passable. Neither Derleth nor Wandrei seemed to be very enthusiastic about "An Offering to the Moon"—and Wright isn't either, to my sorrow. He thought it "wordy" and "unconvincing." *Ghost Stories* has just returned "Medusa" after holding it six weeks, with a personal letter expressing interest in my work and a desire to see more of it. I'm surprised to infer, from this, that they gave the story serious consideration—which was hardly to be expected in view of their standards, which seem to call for a combination of spookiness and raw human interest. I have also had another communication from the *Wonder Stories* editor, posting me further on how he vants I should write dose Volmar stories. "A play of human motives, with alien worlds for a background." But if human motives are mainly what they want, why bother about going to other planets—where one might conceivably escape from the human equation? The idea of using the worlds of Alioth or Altair as a mere setting for the squabbles and heroics of the crew on a space-ship (which, in essence, is about what they are suggesting) is too rich for any use. Evidently *Astounding Stories* is setting the pace for them with its type of stellar-wild-west yarn. There doesn't seem to be much chance of putting over any really good work, and a survey of the magazine field in general is truly discouraging.

I should be very glad to hear from Whitehead,[3] whose work in old issues of *W.T.* I have remarked and admired. He is one of the half-dozen who are superior to the rank and file of its contributors, and is obviously a man of culture.

Later—

I began this a week ago. Now another Sabbath has rolled around—a clear, cloudless day, with all the far mountains, crowned with new snow, visible beyond the fading tatters of the autumn splendor. The past week has been mostly given to some necessary outdoor labor; my writing has gone by the board, and I have been too tired even to write anything very ambitious in the way of a letter. And now, with the coming of your last, returning "Like Mohammed's Tomb," I am your debtor for two fine epistles.

It is good to know that you liked this last story. As to that problem of transmission—well, it seems to me that the author has to be omniscient or nothing: though one might get the story out of the "astral records" (preserved somewhere in the ether, and accessible to adepts) which are mentioned in the literature of esoteric Buddhism! The tradition of Hyperborea, Mu and Atlantis were supposedly preserved in these records! Certainly, if one had to make a choice, something of that sort would be preferable to anything so puerile as "the medium Bayrolles . . ."[4] Personally, I doubt if I can sell this story anyhow—another editorial objection will be on the grounds of subversive pessimism and nihilism. Wright will be the only choice, and since he has a whole raft of stuff under consideration now, I shall wait a while before sending it in.

I haven't gone on very much with the Volmar yarn, but will try to draft a chapter or two to-day. I can't work to good result unless I have a free hand; so I doubt if the series will amount to much. I am glad that Belknap is planning to bring a complaint against that gang of Yiddish high benders.

Your suggestions about a time-voyaging story are great! Thanks for offering me that idea—it could certainly be worked up to advantage. The notion of finding an ancient record, in English, in one's own hand, is tremendous! The *mechanism* of time-travel, in this case, might be a secret vault or adytum in the ruins which the archeologist is exploring—a place designed by some ancient priesthood for the purpose of transportation in time. The hero stumbles upon the adytum *after* finding the records in his own script, and is whirled backward through the ages.[5]

The travels of Palgrave, Burckhardt, and Wellsted[6] might also be of interest to you, in regard to Arabic customs. I want to get hold of a book on the Assassins (I forget its exact title) and will make inquiries before long of the State Library. I have just been reading the Donnelly book on Atlantis, which strikes me as being quite solidly done.[7] The book by James Churchward, *The Lost Continent of Mu* (which I obtained from our State Library) is truly interesting, especially in the mass of data relating to South Sea ruins which is presented. Churchward also gives a purported translation of some ancient Burmese tablets (called the Naacal tablets) which contain a description of Mu, its far-flung colonies and its destruction. Of course, I have no means of knowing how much reliance can be placed upon this interpretation, and on Churchward's reading and co-relation of various ancient symbols which he supposes to have reference to Mu. I have never seen *The Riddle of the Pacific,* nor the book by Scott-Elliot either, and must find out if they are locally procurable.[8]

Irem would be a splendid theme for a story. Do you know of the present-day tradition among the Arabs, that the city still exists in the desert, though invisible, and is occasionally vouchsafed as a brief vision to some favored mortal? One might make a modern tale out of this. By the way, speaking of Orientales, here is one ("The Ghoul") which I have done recently.[9] The legend is so hideous, that I would not be surprised if there were some mention of it in the *Necronomicon.* Will you verify this for me? I seem to have had quite an influx of ghastly and gruesome ideas lately. Some of them will be real terrors, if they are developed properly. One is about a man who dies in two different places at the same moment and leaves *two corpses!* One will have to work in some emotional motive, I suppose—a desire on the part of the man to be in both places. Another idea concerns a dismembered corpse, whose parts the murderer has buried in various spots. But presently he encounters some of the members running around and trying to re-unite and re-join the head, which he has kept in a locked closet! A third—which should really take the palm for macabre grotesquerie—is about two undertakers, business partners, whom (for temporary convenience) we might call Jake and John. John has a very poor opinion of Jake's professional abilities, especially as an embalmer, and tells him one day that if he (John) should die before Jake does, and has to be subjected to the latter's mercies, he will rise up from the dead . . . Well—John eventually dies, and his partner is about to begin operations on the corpse, when John suddenly sits up. Jake drops dead from heart-failure at the shock . . . Next morning, *two* corpses are found laid out in the undertaking establishment; and it is discovered that the corpse of *Jake* has been very efficiently embalmed . . . .[10]

To revert to some things in your earlier letter. I think we are probably more alike than some of my remarks on a desire to voyage in space and time may have led you to infer. This desire, in all likelihood, is mainly cerebral on my part, and I am not so sure that I would care to be "a permanent colonist" in some alien universe—no matter how bored or disgusted I may *seem* to be at times with my environment. And I have had reason to discover, at past times—particularly in times of nervous disturbance—how dependent I really am on familiar things—even on certain features of my surroundings which might not seem very attractive to others. If I am upset, or "under the weather," an unfamiliar milieu tends to take on an aspect of the most distressing and confusing *unreality*—

similar, no doubt, to what you experienced in Brooklyn.[11] So, in all probability, I will do well to content myself with dream projections . . . But doubtless your geographical sense is far more clearly and consciously developed than mine.

The problem of "style" in writing is certainly fascinating and profound. I find it highly important, when I begin a tale, to establish at once what might be called the appropriate "tone." If this is clearly determined at the start I seldom have much difficulty in maintaining it; but if it isn't, there is likely to be trouble. Obviously, the style of "Mohammed's Tomb" wouldn't do for "The Ghoul"; and one of my chief preoccupations in writing this last story was to *exclude* images, ideas and locutions which I would have used freely in a modern story. The same, of course, applies to "Sir John Maundeville," which is a deliberate study in the archaic. The style of a yarn like "The Door to Saturn" forms still another genre; and this tale seemed unusually successful to me in its unity of "tone." Probably the light ironic touch helped to make it seem "unconvincing" to Wright. Of course, there was no attempt whatever to do what I did in "Averoigne" and "Medusa." I suspect, too, that "An Offering to the Moon" was doubtless queered with him by the addition of an element which was far from weird—that is to say, the full development of the stodgy Thorway as a foil to Morley. Of course, the "action" was held up by the archaeological discussion which brought out this difference. But I wonder what Wright would say to Machen's "White People," with its preliminary twelve pages of discussion about the nature and essence of sin!

Thanks, heartily, for your invaluable suggestions concerning the development of my sense-transformation idea! You certainly clarify it for me; and if the result is any good, it will owe much to you. I must do something with this tale, which would be something really worth while in the vein of scientifiction. The possibilities in the Volmar series are going to be pretty slight, I'm afraid. [. . .]

I hope to hear that you have done some new stories before long. That "commonplace book" of which you speak must be a fascinating affair. I have formed more and more the habit of noting down ideas, since otherwise I tend to forget them wholly or in part. I have outlined, among other things, the plot of "Vizaphmal in Ophiuchus," which will not bring in any human beings at all; and the synopsis for a "two-part serial," "The Sorceress of Averoigne."[12]

You are right, I suppose, about the genres of your work; but I certainly hope you will do some more tales of the "Erich Zann" and "Silver Key" types. The Dunsany type of tale is the most difficult of all; and it seems to me that Dunsany himself often fails. No one admires *The Book of Wonder* and *A Dreamer's Tales* more than myself; but I never could work up much enthusiasm over *The Gods of Pegāna*,—apart from the marvellous illustrations of Sime. I still maintain that your "White Ship" is a fine thing.

Thanks again for your offer of books; of which I will be glad to avail myself presently. My time for reading is not unlimited; so one or two items often lasts me quite a while. I want to re-read the Machen book carefully before returning it; also, your "Colour out of Space," which latter I will return next week. I will look forward to the books by James. I have, by the way, the 85,000 word ms. of a novel brought me by a local authoress, and have not yet mustered the courage to tackle it! But I certainly enjoyed Derleth's novel, and agree with you that he has tremendous possibilities.

The Mystic Magazine is indeed impossible—the sort of junk that is illustrated with faked photographs, à la McFadden. Probably it won't even run very long. I can understand how Derleth feels about the job; but nevertheless, anyone who has any kind of a job these days should count himself fortunate. The general condition of things, from what one hears, is a terror. Undoubtedly, modern science, with its labor-saving machinery, is much to blame for the situation of unemployment. Eventually, the only solution will be to reduce the population—or discard the machinery!

I am glad Wandrei liked "The Whisperer" as well, and think that his taste is certainly to be commended. I thought the tale a prime and faultless piece of work; and there will be no doubt about its enthusiastic reception from readers who were appreciative of "Cthulhu" and "The Dunwich Horror."

The trouble with Wright's acceptances, in my case, is that he isn't printing my work as fast as he takes it. I wish he'd get a move on with the longer, more striking—and more remunerative tales! "The Venus of Azombeii" (10,000 words) and "The Monster of the Prophecy" (14,000) will bring in some much-needed cash.

I'm looking forward to Long's two-part serial.[13]

Keep me posted on any divinations relative to Tsathoggua—or Azathoth.

Written under the seal of the lion-headed Ong [. . .]

Yrs, Klarkash-Ton

1. CAS's request may have resulted in HPL's preparation of "Weird &c. Items in Library of H. P. Lovecraft" (see Lovecraft's *Library: A Catalogue* (New York: Hippocampus Press, 2002), pp. 150–154.

2. John Milwarp, a writer of imaginative Oriental fiction, and the main character in "The Chain of Aforgomon" (*OST*), owns a copy of this book.

3. Henry S[t. Clair] Whitehead (1882–1932), Episcopalean archdeacon and writer of weird and adventure fiction.

4. Ambrose Bierce divulged information through Bayrolles in "An Inhabitant of Carcosa" (1886) and "The Moonlit Road" (1907).

5. See HPL to CAS, 11 November 1930 (*SL* 3.216–17).

6. William Gifford Palgrave (1826–1888), *Narrative of a Year's Journey Through Central and Eastern Arabia (1862–1863)* (1865); John Lewis Burckhardt (1784–1817), *Notes on the Bedouins and Wahabys, Collected During His Travels in the East* (1831), among other titles; James Wellsted (d. 1842), *Travels in Arabia* (1838), among other titles.

7. Ignatius Donnelly (1831–1901), *Atlantis: The Antediluvian World* (1882).

8. J. Macmillan Brown (1846–1935), *The Riddle of the Pacific* (1924); W. Scott-Elliot, *The Story of Atlantis and the Lost Lemuria* (1925).

9. "The Ghoul" (*Fantasy Fan*, January 1934; *OD*).

10. These are "The Supernumerary Corpse" (*WT,* November 1932; *OD*), "The Return of the Sorcerer" (*Strange Tales,* September 1931; *OST*), and "A Good Embalmer" (*SS*).

11. Cf. "Remoteness" (*PP*) for a fictionalization of this experience.

12. CAS completed neither story. See *SS* for synopses.

13. Frank Belknap Long's *The Horror from the Hills* (*WT,* January and February/March 1932) contained verbatim a passage from a letter by HPL to Long describing his famous "Roman dream."

---

[113]   To August Derleth [ALS, SHSW]   Dec. 1st, 1930.

Dear August:

You should have received a copy of *E. & C.* by this time. [. . .]

Wright has accepted "The Tale of Satampra Zeiros," which gives him eight unpublished tales of mine, most of them quite sizable, and two of novelette proportions. He tells me, much to my surprise and dismay, that *W.T.* is soon to become a bi-monthly, "owing to conditions in the magazine world."[1] I don't quite understand this. Either his readers are getting sick of the undue proportion of junk, or else *Oriental Stories* is so much of a liability that the other magazine is being sacrificed to it. I'm not a business man; but my instincts, such as they are, have made me dubious from the beginning about the possibilities of this new periodical. The field of specialized adventure story magazines is so damnably overcrowded; and I even note a direct rival to *O.S.* in the shape of *Far East Adventure Stories.* Wright professes to want stuff that is truly Eastern in spirit, but most of the published tales are about the doings of Occidental tourists, beachcombers, etc. Poetic atmosphere and weirdness are to be excluded. It's too much for me . . . But I'm truly sorry about *W.T.* Personally, I can see that I'm doomed to the writing of scientifiction—a genre in which I can work off a lot of satire, though poetic atmosphere is hardly possible. I don't believe Gernsback would print my work, if he realized the Swiftian irony of some of it. In one tale, a human explorer was spewed out as indigestible by a flesh-eating Andromedan plant! And in the one I am writing now, two terrestrial scientists are caught on an alien planet by visiting zoologists from a neighboring world, who take them for rare specimens of the local fauna, and transport them to an interplanetary zoo!2 And the astronomical novelette, "The Monster of the Prophecy," which Wright has, is hilariously sardonic in its implications. [. . .]

As ever,
CAS

1. *WT* did become bimonthly for the period February–July 1931, then resumed monthly publication.
2. "Marooned in Andromeda" (*Wonder Stories,* October 1930; *OD*).

[114]   To Albert M. Bender [ALS, MCL]   Dec. 14th, 1930.

Dear Albert:

I was very glad to receive your letter and the Christmas gift, for which I thank you heartily.

I had been wondering how you were, and meaning to write. I hope you are now in good health—you do not say in your letter.

Things are not so bad with us, though my parents both have colds, and I myself have caught something which is surprisingly like that absurd and atrocious malady, whooping-cough.

As to writing, I have confined myself to prose-fiction during the past fifteen months. The financial returns are slow and inadequate so far, but certainly they help out. I am at present writing a fantastic-scientific novelette for the Gernsback publication, *Wonder Stories.* I enclose a story from the current issue of *Weird Tales.* This magazine has used a lot of my work, and in spite of certain cheapnesses, is about the only periodical in America that is hospitable to imaginative literature of a high class. That is to say, there are several writers contributing to it whose work is superior (as far as I am concerned) to anything that one would find in the more pretentious magazines.

You are right about pessimism—it doesn't get anyone anywhere.

I may try my hand at a novel before long—perhaps something on the order of Wells' *Time-Machine.* My general bent in fiction is toward fantasy—sometimes with a tinge of satire. I don't care much for realism—and I care still less for romanticism.

I hope I can send you the usual mistletoe and toyon. If I don't, it will be because I am unable to get out.

My parents join me in all good wishes and holiday remembrances.

As ever
CAS

---

[115]   To H. P. Lovecraft [ALS, JHL]   [c. early January 1931]
From the dark companion of Algol, at the perihelion
of innermost and uttermost occultation.

Dear Éch-Pi-El:

Salutations to a companion in misery! Measles and chicken-pox (I managed to have those at the proper age, along with scarlet fever) are surely an off-set to the whooping-cough. The latter has been a tiresome business, though; and the cough still lingers, albeit far less frequent and severe than it was.

My greetings and genuflections to It for the New Year (Azathoth alone knows *what* year it is in the reckoning of the elder cycles) and may the fumes of appropriate sacrifice and the murmurs of prescribed prayer be still acceptable to the Dark One of the doubtful, unspoken name; and may it continue to withhold the ultimate horror and direness of Its oracular utterance . . .

Let's hope for the best in regard to *W.T.* Wandrei says that the magazine tried going on other than a monthly basis back in its earlier years; and I seem dimly to remember something of the sort, though I did not buy it very often in those days. But I guess there won't be much chance for *Strange Stories* under the circumstances[1] . . . As to delayed remittances—I notice that the delay began coincidentally with the starting of *Oriental Stories*—before that, checks had been coming promptly on publication.

I have finished the time-travelling yarn, "An Adventure in Futurity" (47 p.!) and have sent it off.[2] But I am still hung up on the final chapter of the Volmar opus. I'll send these tales on presently, if they seem to pass muster at all. Just now, the time-story strikes me as an awful piece of junk. The Venusian slaves and their Martian abettors are left to divide the earth at the end, while the remainder of humanity (which has been driven to the polar regions) takes flight for the farther asteroids. I agree with you that inter-cosmic immigration will never do! The Martians might smuggle in the Black Rot, which devours whole cities and turns half the elements known to chemistry into a fine black powder. Also, there is the Yellow Death, that microscopic aerial algae from Venus, which grows in the air, turning it to a saffron color, and causing all terrestrials who breathe it to die of slow asphyxiation with violent pneumonia symptoms.

For relief, I am doing one of the horror tales that I outlined some time ago—the one about the piecemeal resurrection of a dismembered corpse.[3] I have thought up a lot of improvements for this, and hope to achieve the limit in sheer gruesomeness. Thanks for your suggestion about magical affiliations on the part of the deceased—I am making both the murderer and the victim practitioners of the Black Arts, and am also taking the liberty of introducing the *Necronomicon*—in its original Arabic text.

Revising a story with inherent merit must be a vastly different job from trying to put life and literary form into something essentially formless and lifeless [. . . .]

I'll send you a batch of magazines the very first time I am able to get out in person. There is quite an accumulation, which you might as well have. I seem to read a lot of this junk, for lack of anything better to read. Even at their worst, the scientifictional magazines are vastly preferable to the other types of newsstand productions, and I don't think they would appeal to the most moronic types of readers. And, once in a while, there is a story with some degree of merit, such as "The Forgotten Planet" in *Astounding*, "The City of the Living Dead" in *Wonder Stories*, and "Anachronism" in *Amazing*. There were two yarns in the last *Oriental*, "Golden Rosebud" and "The Green Jade God," that struck me as being superior to the rest.[4] I certainly can't "see" Frank Owen, though, and I must have missed his finer contributions to *W.T.*, since I am unable to find anything of his that strikes me as being out of the ordinary. The short, jerky sentences "kill" his work as far as I am concerned. One or two tales in the current *Ghost Stories*, notably the one by Hugh B. Cave,[5] seem to mark a certain departure from the McFadden standard of plot. But some of the others are certainly "fierce."

Later—

I have given the whole of a cloudy Sabbath to finish my dismembered corpse story—"The Return of Helman Carnby." I shall enclose the carbon with this; and I hope you will like it. The thing became a sizeable yarn, with all the details that I worked out . . . It goes to *Ghost Stories*, then to *W. T.*,—both of which will doubtless reject it. But I think myself that the tale is a pretty fair literary beginning for the New Year. I like to picture it in the sunny and lightsome pages of the *Ladies' Home Journal*.

I have also done another little Orientale—"The Justice of the Elephant"—for Wright to turn down. It is grim and gruesome;

but he *might* take it, since it doesn't involve the supernatural and is not at all poetic. The plot idea is quite similar to that of a tale which I sold to *The Black Cat* back in my boyhood.[6]

Well, I must put a scientific—or at least a pseudo-scientific—curb on my fancy, if I am to sell anything. There is a tentative tale of this kind which I may call "Prisoners of the Black Dimension"—dealing with some people who disappear while in full view on the street, through the machinations of beings in another sort of space than ours.[7] This might have possibilities.

I wish you would do another story—even if it's only a "short." May I have the ms. of your "Shunned House" to re-read?[8] I shall look forward to the James books when Dwyer is through with them.[9]

> As ever, with all best New Yr. wishes,
> Klarkash-Ton. [. . .]

1. *Strange Tales,* intended to be a direct competitor of *WT,* published only seven issues between September 1931 and January 1933.
2. "An Adventure in Futurity" (*Wonder Stories,* April 1931; *OD*).
3. "The Return of Helman Carnby," eventually titled "The Return of the Sorcerer."
4. S. Peaslee Wright (1897–1970), "The Forgotten Planet" (*Astounding Stories,* July 1930); Laurence Manning (1899–1972) and Fletcher Pratt, "The City of the Living Dead" (*Science Wonder Stories,* May 1930); Charles Cloukey [Charles Cloutier], "Anachronism" (*Amazing Stories,* December 1930); Dorothy Flatau, "Golden Rosebud," and John Briggs, "The Green Jade God" (*Oriental Stories,* December 1930–January 1931).
5. Hugh B. Cave, "The Strange Case of No. 7" (*Ghost Stories,* January 1931).
6. "The Justice of the Elephant" (*Oriental Stories,* Autumn 1931; *OD*). CAS refers to "The Mahout" (*Black Cat,* August 1911).
7. See *SS,* p. 155.
8. HPL's "The Shunned House" was not printed in his lifetime. See letter 181 n.1.
9. HPL had lent his James books to Bernard Austin Dwyer (1897–1943), a correspondent in West Shokan, New York.

---

[116]   To H. P. Lovecraft [ALS, JHL]   [c. 27 January 1931]
> At the apex of the Singing Flame, in the Titan city
> beyond the trans-dimensional columns.

Dear Éch-Pi-El:

Your letter and the copy of "The Shunned House," which came in the same mail with a letter from Dwyer, were more than welcome.[1]

I have re-read "The Shunned House" with the same *increased* appreciation which has attended my re-perusal of your other stories. Like Dwyer, I am often rather slow in absorbing the full import of a work of art; and all the books which have meant anything in my mental life are those in which I have steeped myself by repeated reading. Others I have tended to forget, since my memory is not naturally retentive. I have no intention whatever of flattering you when I say that a story such as "The Shunned House" makes Bulwer's "The House and the Brain" look like the proverbial thirty cents. The thing you have conjured up is incomparably more impressive and terrifying than any traditional, classified "spook."

I was greatly pleased and gratified by your reaction to "Carnby"—a tale to which I devoted much thought. The more veiled ending you suggest as possible was my original intention— certainly it would have been the safest and most surely successful method. I think what tempted me to the bolder and more hazardous revelation, was the visualizing of the actual *collapse* of that hellishly vitalized abnormality. If the tale is rejected as too gruesome, I can try the other ending, and have the secretary unable to enter the room till all is over, and there are merely *two* heaps of human segments on the floor.[2]

Wright's rejection of your "In the Vault" was certainly on a par with his other capricious decisions and "trick" valuations. The tale is neither more nor less "gruesome" than many others of your best, such as "The Rats in the Walls."[3] By the way, why don't you try this yarn on *Ghost Stories?* The stuff I have sent in, such as "Medusa" and "The Ghoul," has evidently been read carefully, and has drawn personal letters. I even submitted "The Willow Landscape," though with no idea that it would have any real chance;—and drew the only editorial compliment ("very charming and poetic") which this tale has yet received. As to their present rate of payment, I am unable to speak with authority; but I don't think that the general rates of the Hersey magazines are more than one cent, or, at most, 1½ cents per word. Hersey paid me seven dollars apiece for two or three sonnets when he was editing *The Thrill Book;* but this was double the regular verse rate. One can readily figure out the corresponding regular rate for prose.

I am enclosing a new trans-dimensional story, "The City of the Singing Flame," in which I have utilized Crater Ridge (the place where I found the innominable Eikon) as a spring-board.[4] Some day, I must look for those two boulders "with a vague resemblance to broken-down columns." If you and other correspondents cease to hear from me thereafter, you can surmise what has happened!

The description of the Ridge, by the way, has been praised for its realism by people who know the place.

I have idled for a few days, but won't be able to keep it up much longer. As to my appalling prolificality, there are doubtless several reasons and explanations. About eighteen months ago, I was taken to task for idleness by a woman-friend,[5] and *pledged* myself to industry. Once started, the pledge has not been hard to keep. Other reasons are, that it is necessary for me to make a little money; also, that I need an imaginative escape from the human aquarium—and, moreover, a "safety-valve" to keep from blowing up and disrupting the whole countryside. And, beyond all this, I am finding a pleasure in fiction-writing, and deriving a mental "kick" from it which I seldom got from poetry. Painting I always enjoyed greatly; and I have merely postponed—not relinquished—my ambitions in that regard; but I am more certain of technical competence in literature. Another, and by no means negligible factor, is my desire to increase the rather limited supply of fiction which suits my own personal taste. There are so many good tales that have never been written.

By this time, you may have heard the welcome news that W.T. is planning to return to a monthly basis after three issues as a b. m. (Derleth says two) I was sorry to learn from Wright's last column-mention that he may have to spend two months in the hospital for treatment. He said that he would continue, however, to oversee the magazine. "The Justice of the Elephant" was taken for O.S.; so, as you suggest, the Senfian jumbo can be utilized again, minus the pedestal.[6] I am inclined to agree with Derleth that W.T. has been sacrificed to O.S. I don't think that hard times have made so much difference when it comes to paying two-bits for an established magazine. But O.S., being a new proposition, has doubtless made a hole in the W.T. exchequer. Let's hope that it (O.S.) soon attains a paying-basis. It is certainly above the usual level of adventure story magazines.

I shall certainly welcome the consignment of James from Dwyer, and will send him *The House of Souls* in a few days. This latter I have just been re-reading. Certainly Machen's prose-style is exquisite in its degree of perfection. I think "The White People" is my favorite now; though I was more impressed by "The Great God Pan" at first reading. "Pan," by the way, has suggested to me an idea so hellish that I am almost afraid to work it out in story-form. It involves a cataleptic woman who was placed alive in the family vaults. Days later, a scream was heard within the family vaults, the door was unlocked, and the woman was found sitting up in her *open* coffin, babbling deliriously of some terrible demoniac face whose vision had awakened her from her death-like sleep. Eight or nine months afterwards, she gives birth to a child and dies. The child is so monstrous that no one is permitted to see it. It is kept in a locked room; but many years later, *after* the death of the woman's husband, it escapes; and co-incidentally the corpse of the deceased is found in a condition not to be described. Also, there are monstrous footprints leading toward the vaults, but not away from them.[7] If I do this tale, I shall head it with a text from the *Necronomicon,* which certainly did great service in "Carnby." The "atmosphere" wouldn't have been half so good without it . . . But of course, it is not likely that the Arabic version was left undisturbed in that awful mansion *after* the death of *both* wizards. There are too many persons and powers that covet its possession. We can only hope that it has fallen into the hands of those who do not design *immediate* evil toward the world, but whose plans involve a respite of years or cycles. This, I fear, is the best that can be hoped [. . . .]

Yes, that red fog in Belgium had a sinister air. And what of that other fog, "the white death," or "pogonip"[8] which has long been feared by certain tribes of American Indians? Can it be that such things are used to cover up the actions and designs of beings from Yuggoth or beyond?

Later—

I'll send you "An Adventure in Futurity," and perhaps some other stuff, presently. But honestly, "Carnby" and the present enclosure are the only late tales of mine worth considering.

I am going to adopt your suggestion about "Carnby" if it comes back from *Ghost Stories.* Here is the way it can be worked: the secretary finds himself physically unable to enter the room till *all* is over; but standing at the threshold, he hears the head as it breaks from the cupboard, and *sees* for a few moments the shadow of that headless monstrosity, and the singular disintegration of the shadows, followed by a sound that is not that of a *single* body falling, but of many. Then, entering, he flees from the inenarrable vision of that *confused heap* of human segments, some flesh and some putrefying, which are lying on the floor, with the surgeon's saw still clutched in a half-decayed hand.

Keep the enclosed drawings; and take your time with the tale (and also with answering this letter) if you are busy. "The City" can also be returned via Derleth and Wandrei.

In the name of the black *shoggothrasn,*
Klarkash-Ton.

1. HPL had lent CAS the sheets for the abortive Recluse Press edition of the story, printed in 1928.

2. CAS in fact adopted the "more veiled ending" before this letter was mailed. For the original conclusion to the tale, see *Klarkash-Ton* No. 1 (June 1988).

3. "In the Vault" was rejected when first submitted in October 1925; "The Rats in the Walls" (*WT*, March 1924; rpt. June 1930).

4. "The City of the Singing Flame," *Wonder Stories* (July 1931); *OST* and *RA*.

5. Genevieve K. Sully; see her letter in Donald Sidney-Fryer, *Emperor of Dreams: A Clark Ashton Smith Bibliography* (West Kingston, RI: Donald M. Grant, 1978), p. 190.

6. Senf inappropriately had depicted the terrible Chaugnar Faugn of Long's *Horror from the Hills* as a circus elephant.

7. CAS developed this idea into "The Nameless Offspring" (*Strange Tales*, June 1932; *AY*).

8. Pogonip (from the Paiute word *pogonah*, meaning "white death") is a dense winter ice fog that comes in late December and early January.

---

[117]   To H. P. Lovecraft [ALS, JHL]   [c. 15–23 February 1931]
         From the vault of Tomeron,[1] catacombs of Ptolemides.

Dear Éch-Pi-El:

"Manifold and multiform are the horrors that infest the visible ways and the ways unseen. They sleep beneath the unturned stone; they rise with the tree from its root; they move beneath the sea and in subterranean places; they dwell unchallenged in the inmost adyta; they emerge betimes from the shutten sepulcher of haughty bronze and the low grave that is sealed with earth. There be some that are long known to man, and others as yet unknown that abide the terrible future days of their revealing. Those which are the most dreadful and the loathliest of all, are haply still to be declared. But among those that have revealed themselves aforetime and have made manifest their veritable presence, there is one which may not openly be named for its exceeding foulness. It is that spawn which the hidden dweller in the vaults has begotten upon mortality."

This dreadful passage from the *Necronomicon* (which one fears to ponder overlong) is the one that I shall use to preface "The Nameless Offspring."[2] Personally, I think that some of Alhazred's appalling hints are beyond anything that I can hope to write, in their endless reverberations of cryptic horror. Is nothing safe, or indesecrate—when *"They sleep beneath the unturned stone, and rise with the tree from its root?"* Are the fountains all polluted, is the very soil pervaded with their poison? Do they veil their obscene entity with the mist, and mask themselves in the cloud of alabastrine whiteness?

I forwarded *The House of Souls* to Dwyer, and received from him some time ago the two volumes by M. R. James. *Mille remerciments!* I think my reaction to James is very much like your own. His tales are about perfect in their way, and some of them—particularly "A View from a Hill," "The Treasure of Abbot Thomas," "The Ash-Tree," and the one about the specter "with the crumpled linen face" (can't remember its title at the moment)[3] are hideously powerful. *All* of them, indeed, are extremely good. No one ever thought up anything more original, and more graphically *realized*, in the way of phantoms and demons. Like you, I would place him a little below Poe and Machen; though he is fully as good as Bierce, and really more sustained and satisfying than B. The latter, somehow, hasn't worn any too well with me since my last re-reading. Even so great a story as "The Death of Halpin Frayser" has begun to reveal flaws. Like Machen's "The Great God Pan," it might have been a better piece of work if the "long arm of coincidence" hadn't been stretched so egregiously. You certainly put your finger on the weakness of "Pan." Another thing which I don't greatly care for is the helter-skelter way in which this latter tale is developed and told from so many different view-points.

It is good to know that "The City of the Singing Flame" was so much to your taste; also that you approved the idea of the ghoul story, which I hope to write before long. This tale will be, as much as possible, a series of implications.

A fresh cold has taken the pep out of me for the past two weeks, with the result that I haven't done much sustained work. However, I re-wrote the ending of "Carnby" and sent it back to G.S. again. Also, here is my attempt at the embalmer story which I outlined some time ago. I know next to nothing about the subject; so you might warn me if I have "pulled any boners." Anyway, it didn't seem necessary or advisable to dwell on the technical side. I hope the yarn will afford *"un frisson nouveau."*[4]

I have lately received a delightful communication from Dr. Whitehead through his secretary. Whitehead, I was sorry to learn, has been very ill. [. . .]

If I really had the energy you credit me with I would try to do something with my translations, poems, etc. But with the market conditions as they are at present, I imagine it would be doubly difficult to interest anyone. However, poetry is still published—I have recently had requests for contributions from the publishers of two projected anthologies. One, called *California Poets,* to be brought out by Henry Harrison of N.Y., will contain five of my best short poems ("Symbols," "Nyctalops," "The Nereid," "Palms," and "Sepulture").[5] The other (I forget its name) is being fostered by a London firm, the Mitre Press. I sent them "Interrogation."[6]

I hope most fervently that your programme will soon admit of some new original tales. Damme, but Brother Wright's rejection of "The Shunned House" (somehow, I had the impression that it *had* been printed in *W.T.*) is certainly a record-breaker. It goes to show that editors and their preferences simply can't be taken seriously. I have become absolutely case-hardened, and refuse to be depressed by anybody's rejection of anything.

It will do no harm for you to try *Ghost Stories*. I intend to go on submitting stuff till something lands. The magazine *does* pay 2 cents per word, as I have lately learned from an item in *The Writer's Digest*. If one were a multimillionaire, it would be huge fun to start a really good magazine devoted to the weird and fantastic, and do it all in style, and print the best obtainable regardless of the yowling public . . . *Nom de Tsathoggua!* what a pipe-dream! . . .

Later—

It is a week or more since I wrote the above. In the interim I have drafted a tale from the Commoriom myth-cycle—"The Testament of Athammaus,"[7]—which I have probably mentioned to you as being among my tentatives. I guess you won't wonder that Commoriom was deserted, when you read this explanation of the *raison d'être*. In my more civic moods, I sometimes think of the clean-up which an entity like Knygathin Zhaum would make in a modern town. I really think he (or it) is about my best monster to date. It would be nice (if ever I get to the book-cover stage) to publish a separate volume of tales under some such title as "The Book of Hyperborea." This primal continent seems to have been particularly subject to incursions of "outsideness"—more so, in fact, than any of the other continents and terrene realms that lie behind us in the time stream. But I have heard it hinted in certain obscure and arcane prophecies that the far-future continent called Gnydron by some and Zothique by others, which is to rise millions of years hence in what is now the South Atlantic, will surpass even Hyperborea in this regard and will witness the intrusion of Things from galaxies not yet visible; and, worse than this, a hideously chaotic *breaking-down* of dimensional barriers which will leave *parts* of our world in other dimensions, and vice versa. When things get to that stage, there will be no telling where even the briefest journey or morning stroll might end. The conditions will shift, too; so there will be no possibility of charting them and thus knowing when or where one might step off into the unknown.

I made an extra carbon of "Athammaus"; so you can keep the one enclosed. But the new ending of "Carnby" and "A Good Embalmer" can be returned at leisure.

I'll return your "Shunned House" anon, in the same package with the James books. Thanking you again for the loan of these,
    Yrs, in the service of the Old Ones,
        Klarkash-Ton

1. Refers to "The Epiphany of Death" (*Fantasy Fan,* July 1934; rpt. *WT,* September 1942 as "Who Are the Living?"; *AY*).
2. The passage given here differs somewhat from the published version.
3. "'Oh, Whistle, and I'll Come to You, My Lad'."
4. "A Good Embalmer," in *SS.*
5. *California Poets: An Anthology of 244 Contemporaries* (New York: Henry Harrison, 1932).
6. *Principal Poets of the World,* volume I (London: The Mitre Press, 1930–1931), p. 182
7. "The Testament of Athammaus" (*WT,* October 1932; *OST*).

---

[118]   To August Derleth [ALS, SHSW]   April 9th, 1931.

Dear August:
    [. . .] I feel the way you do about O'Brien.[1] I once tackled one of his anthologies, but was unable to get very far with it. The tales chosen were damnably arid and dry-as-dusty—which in my opinion is the general characteristic of fiction in the supposedly "better" magazines. I have come to the unconventional conclusion that the despised "pulps" are almost the only ones that ever print anything with any freshness and vitality. The middle-class "smooth-paper" magazines are full of a tame and padded romanticism, and the "quality" publications seem to want nothing but social satire and a sort of dead-sea-apples realism. I'd rather read *W.T.* at its worst—or even *Adventure.*
    I'll certainly look forward to H. P.'s new story.[2] I hope he'll write a lot of them.
    I suppose you've heard of the new weird magazine (not yet named) for which Harry Bates of *Astounding Stories* is now accepting contributions.[3] I fear it will bank pretty strongly on popular plot-appeal, like the other Clayton publications. But 2¢ per word and up on acceptance is certainly tempting. Mystery, terror, and even horror will be stressed, according to Bates.
    Wright seems to have lost what little nerve he ever had. He has returned my two best horror tales, on the plea that they would be too strong for his readers. I think, though, that he will take "The

Testament of Athammaus" later on—it seems to have impressed him greatly. But "Helman Carnby" is quite beyond the pale. This latter tale really seems to be something of a goat-getter.

Through financial necessity, I have written nothing lately but scientifiction. The Gernsback outfit has taken a long novelette which will appear in an early issue under the title of "The Amazing Planet." "The City of the Singing Flame" may come out under an alias too—God knows why. They seem to have a mania for changing titles.

Our premature spring is merging into an even more premature summer—everything is dry as a fish-bone already. There are all the indications of a serious condition of drouth.

I'll send you "The Testament of Athammaus" to read before long.

> As ever
> C A S

1. Edward J. O'Brien (1890–1941), editor of *The Best Short Stories . . . and the Yearbook of the American Short Story.* O'Brien from time to time gave brief notice to various of the contributors to *WT.*
2. *At the Mountains of Madness.*
3. This is the short-lived *Strange Tales of Mystery and Terror* (September 1931–January 1933).

---

[119]   To William Whittingham Lyman [ALS, BL]

May 4th, 1931

Dear Jack Lyman:

The substitutions that you suggest will be perfectly all right, as far as I am concerned, if Harrison will permit them, and if they will fit into the allotted space.[1] Personally, I prefer "Symbols" to "The Secret"; the latter never seemed anything more to me than an experiment in form. But other people seem to like it.

I am glad that you and Helen Hoyt liked the new poems. I agree with you about the unrhymed ones. Such things, with me, are notations rather than completed work.

"Mystery" has been submitted to several magazines, but has never sold.[2] The solemn tense is practically taboo among editors, isn't it? Helen Hoyt is very kind to offer trying to place the poem. Naturally, if this could be done, I should be very grateful to her. But I think almost any other market would be likelier than *Poetry.* I have the impression that Miss Monroe regards me as an incorrigible reactionary, who shouldn't be encouraged in his recalcitrance toward contemporary standards!

Have you been writing any poems lately? I hope to see a volume of your work sometime.

Thanks for suggesting those scientific books. I haven't read Jeans, but am familiar with his main theories and premises.[3] He seems entirely too dogmatic to me, with his ideas about the final dissipation of energy. Millikan's theory of renewal strikes me as being more reasonable.[4] But science is only a guessing-game, anyway. And when it comes to fictional inspiration, I find more in the writings of Charles Fort, author of *The Book of the Damned,* than in any of the orthodox crew. Fort has spent his life in amassing a gorgeous collection of data rejected or disregarded by professional scientists because it didn't fit with their preconceived theories. I admire Einstein, too—as an imaginative speculator, probably with a good-sized element of wagging in some of his speculations.

As to fantastic-scientific fiction: Wells started out with a fine imagination, but succumbed to the sting of the sociological bee. I like his earlier tales, though there was no great distinction or refinement of style. Poe, the originator of the genre, still remains its best exponent, at least from a literary standpoint. Verne was a good *farceur;* but I never cared much for his style.

Here are copies of the poems suggested as substitutes—also, another copy of "Mystery."

With many thanks for your kindness and interest, and with all best regards to yourself and Helen Hoyt,

Cordially yours,
Clark Ashton Smith

1. Helen Hoyt wrote the introduction for *California Poets.* CAS's contributions were "Symbols," "Sepulture," "The Nereid," "Autumn Orchards," and "Consolation."
2. "Mystery" first appeared in *SP.*
3. James Jeans (1877–1946), English astronomer and mathematician.
4. Robert Millikan (1868–1953), American physicist.

---

[120]   To August Derleth [TLS, SHSW]   May 8th, 1931.

Dear August:

Thanks for sending me the picture. You must be psychic—I was about to ask you for one. I like it very much. If I can find one of myself, I will enclose it with this; but I doubt if there is anything on hand. I am thin and wiry—five feet ten in height, and weight somewhere around 135 or 140.

I am certainly eager to see *At the Mountains of Madness* when my turn comes. Also your stories when they are available. In the meanwhile here is "The Hunters from Beyond,"[1] which can be forwarded to Donald and H.P. as per notations. I would include Dwyer too, but imagine he would be the least likely to care for it. The yarn is probably junk anyhow. It was suggested by "Pickman's Model," which I have always admired greatly.

6000 words in one day certainly argues facility! I guess 3000 is the most I have ever done. Usually I consider 1000 or 1500 a good day's work. Latterly I have been pretty lazy; and "Azéderac" is still unfinished. I have also begun a new interplanetary yarn.[2]

Good luck with the Clayton outfit. I think I mentioned their rejection of "Athammaus." "Helman Carnby," however, is still being held, and Bates says that things "look good" for it. A whole raft of my stuff is being held by various editors—one novelette has been with *Amazing* for four months! I suppose they are still trying to decide whether or not it contains "enough science." "The Willow Landscape," by the way, has just been placed with *The Philippine Magazine,* in Manila. The rates are nothing very gaudy; but the editor seems to be appreciative. I have also submitted "An Offering to the Moon," but fear it will prove too long for them. Wright has a weird-scientific under consideration; and I am also tackling an assortment of other markets, ranging from *Gay Paree* to *This Quarter.* The latter I sent some of my Baudelaires; and the former is considering a little Averoigne tale, "The Satyr," which, for some unknown reason, seems to be looked on as risqué by magazines.

> As ever,
> Klarkash-Ton

P.S. The enclosed "snaps" are my only copies, so I'll have to ask their return. The one in the swing-seat looks like the 1890's—something queer about the eyes, too. The lady is Mrs Sully, who admired your "Early Years" so much.

1. "The Hunters from Beyond" (*Strange Tales,* October 1932; *LW*).
2. "The Holiness of Azéderac" (*WT,* November 1933; *LW* and *RA*). CAS did not complete any new interplanetary tales between 9 April ("The Letter from Mohaun Los") and 30 June 1931 ("Beyond the Singing Flame"), so it is not known to which story he refers.

---

[121]   To August Derleth [TLS, SHSW]   June 15th, 1931.

Dear August:

You and your collaborator certainly must have energy![1] Five stories per week makes me dizzy to even think about. Your titles are good—I'm a great believer in titles[2]—and I hope to read some of these tales sooner or later. Remember me when you have any loose copies on hand. And in the meanwhile, I trust that Bates or Wright will view some of them with favor.

I haven't heard from anything lately, though at least a dozen of my tales are out with various editors. Wright is holding "Azédarac," and the "Embalmer" is still with Bates and "The Hunters from Beyond" with *Ghost Stories*. I have erupted rather extensively into print, since, apart from "The Venus of Azombeii" and "The Satyr," two other tales have recently appeared: "The City of the Singing Flame" in the July *Wonder Stories,* with a gaudy cover-design purporting to illustrate it, and "The Willow Landscape" in the *Philippine Magazine,* with a very charming illustration by a native artist.

I agree with you about "Azédarac," which is more piquant than weird. But I like to do something in lighter vein occasionally. "The Satyr" was written more than a year ago, and has had nine or ten rejections, most magazines, for some unknown reason, appearing to regard it as overly risqué. If I were only famous, I might have sold it to the *Cosmopolitan* for a thousand or two! I agree with you also in giving "The Venus of Azombeii" third place in the current *W.T.* The tale is an odd mixture of poetry and melodrama, and may (I'm not sure) prove quite popular with Wright's clientele. It was one of my earliest, and has had to wait about eighteen months for publication. But I wish Wright would hurry up with the publication of "The Monster of the Prophecy." This tale is one of my own favorites, and is quite sizable, too—14000 words.

"The Maker of Gargoyles" has been drafted,[3] but I am deferring the revision and final typing till after the completion of one or two scientifics. It ought to be a real terror when it is polished up. Of course, you shall see it.

The weather is certainly funny—coolness, and a heavy soaking rain, at a time of year when the climate is ordinarily hotter than Satan's Turkish bath and dryer than the brick-yards of Gehenna.

Good luck to yourself and Mark Schorer.

As ever,
Clark Ashton

1. AWD contributed numerous weird shorts to *WT* written with his collaborator Mark Schorer (1908–1977).
2. Numerous evocative titles for prospective stories are reprinted in *SS* and *BB*.
3. "The Maker of Gargoyles" (*WT,* August 1932; *TSS*).

[122]   To Genevieve K. Sully [ALS, private collection]
July 9th, 1931

Dear Genevieve:

I was very glad to get your two letters, which left me with a sort of warm feeling around the cockles of the heart.

For many reasons, I have had no time to write letters, but this morning I shall take the time—for one at least.

The fire was a horrible experience—and a surprisingly exciting one also. I'll give you a few details, since so much about it was dramatic.[1] Not the least dramatic part for me was the fact that I had been writing another story about the Singing Flame; and, at the moment when I was interrupted, had just reached that part of the tale which describes the destruction of the city of Ydmos by the force-bolts of the Outer Lords, the melting of ramparts and buildings like lava, and the blackening of the Inner Dimension like a burnt paper. Then my mother came out to tell me that there was a fire—and I left my work to find that the whole neighboring pasture between Swinburne's and the Shirland Tract road was in flames.

I have not heard that the Indians were responsible for the fire; but I did talk with eyewitnesses who saw it start from a lighted cigarette that was tossed into the wayside grass by a passing auto, in which were four boys (unfortunately, not identified).

Since so many people were out of town over the week-end, it was hard to obtain adequate help. We were short-handed at all times, and some of those pressed into service (Indians, passing vagrants, etc.) were slip-shod and inefficient, so that the blaze broke out again time after time when supposedly extinguished. I do not know yet how it managed to cross certain roads where there was little on either side but short grass; but the fact remains that it did. After the thing was under control in the Swinburne pasture, I went on to find that it had invaded Sutton's, and had crept across the hill into the pine-woods. Here a number of men had gathered; and we started to make a fire-break down the fence between the Sutton and Manning pastures, but were driven out when the flames began to leap in the tall pines. A break was then made through Manning's to the little P. G. & E. ditch, and I and one or two others broke the ditch-bank with shovels and turned part of the water down the ravine. Yet even this, and the concomitant backfiring, would not have saved Manning's house and out buildings, if it had not been for the presence of a fire-wagon. I hope I'll never again see such an inferno as those woods, with fire being sown everywhere from the pines.

I entered the fray about 10 A.M. and did not stop till three in the afternoon, when I went home for a little while to eat. In the meanwhile, the fire continued toward the river over a wide area, endangering the De Gomez house, etc. When I came back, the blaze had broken out again on the hill-top in Sutton with no one in attendance but an Indian or two, since all the others had gone down into the canyon. I tried hard to head this fire off before it could approach the pines by the fence, and could have succeeded if I had even one competent helper; and in this way could probably have averted the recrudescence on the following day, which apparently started in this quarter of the woods from mouldering needles or leaf-mould.

The blaze was finally controlled—but not till it had gotten into dangerous territory. I watched till evening and arose a number of times during the night sleeping only by cat-naps. At day-break, when a strong east wind had arisen, I saw fresh smoke, and went out to find that the fire was approaching the lane between our property and Manning's. I knew it would leap this lane, with the brush trees, and grass on both sides, and just had time to run across the county road to some neighbors and ask them to turn in an alarm. Then I went back and made preparations for defense.

It was difficult to get help, since all the available "regulars" were out fighting the other fire above Auburn. The flames closed in on us in a sort of arc, and I was compelled to sacrifice our spring-house in order to protect the cabin and other outbuildings. Our neighbor Mr. Lane came over and helped immensely, and the two Waddle boys appeared in time to keep the fire from reaching the more heavily wooded portions of the ranch. But the heat was terrific, and some of the foliage on our big live oak was seared in spite of a fire break.

Five or six acres of our land were burnt over, including a narrow strip of woodland down the Swinburne fence. Here I had to watch the mouldering leaves and mould all day—a terrific task— and spade them back and cover them with earth to deaden the fire.

The devastation has been terrific, since practically the whole canyon was gutted on both sides from the dam and Devil's Canyon almost to Rattlesnake bridge. The fire even spread out on Boulder Ridge, past the Indian reservation, toward Newcastle. I believe it crossed the county road on streaks of molten tar or oil.

I haven't been out yet to see the Bowman-Aeolia-Forest-Hill Divide ravages; but they must have been terrific, to judge from the black cumuli of smoke. This fire was still burning yesterday, around Butcher Ranch or beyond; and there was another big blaze behind Pilot Hill.

Crackers were popping merrily in Auburn all day and all night on the Fourth, and also on Sunday. And when I went in Sunday evening, the streets were a torrent of autos. After what I had been through, the reckless idiocy of the merry-making public simply made me boil. I fear that such conditions, and all their accompanying hazards, are going to get worse instead of better.

My mother has been quite ill as an aftermath of the whole damnable business, and apart from nursing her, I have had the job of emptying the spring and improvising a new shelter. The water was like lye at first, and will need another emptying, since it is still unpleasantly alkaline. I don't think I'll ever be able to smell wood-smoke again, without feeling sick.

It wasn't so hot to-day, but still warm enough. I saw the papers —read of the terrific heat in S. F.—also the Mt. Diablo fire. Hope it is cooler now, and will stay cool.

Among the books you mention, I have read only *Confessions of a Young Man,* which I have. *Sister Teresa* ought to be worth having.[2] I can't pronounce on the merit of those various volumes of letters. My general impression is that most letters, even by men of genius, are interesting mainly to their writers and recipients.

No, I wasn't especially flattered by the alleged Tibbett resemblance. Speaking of photos, reminds me that Pablo Polson has started a studio in Auburn, according to the local papers.

I'll try to write you again soon. Aff., as ever,
    Clark

1. This incident possibly contributed to CAS's development of his tale, "The Vaults of Yoh-Vombis" (*WT,* May 1932; *OST* and *RA*). See the Foreword to *The Vaults of Yoh-Vombis,* ed. Steve Behrends (West Warwick, RI: Necronomicon Press, 1988).
2. George Moore (1852–1933), *Confessions of a Young Man* (1888); *Sister Teresa* (1901).

———— • ————

[123]   To August Derleth [ALS, SHSW]   July 20th, 1931.

Dear August:

The whole world, at least in these parts, is enshrouded by a hell-blue pall of smoke, and the air is hot as the hinges of Tophet, and the sky is dark and dingy as the burnt-out sky of the planet Mars. More fires, ad infinitum, though, luckily none are so near that I have to fight them. Some dirty work going on, I imagine.

Better luck with Wright next time. . . . He refused a good short of mine not long ago ("A Tale of Sir John Maundeville") as being "almost without plot." No, he hasn't many fillers of mine on hand—just one more, I believe; the other accepted tales all running upwards of 4500 words.

Bates was willing to buy "A Good Embalmer," but the publisher, Clayton, seems to have disapproved. Evidently C. keeps a close check on his editors. [. . .]

I liked "Old Roses" quite well; but I agree with you that the current Hamilton yarn is undiluted bilge.[1] How does he get by with it? Wright has turned down some of my best work as "unconvincing"; but I don't see how anything could seem unconvincing after such ridiculous tripe as Hamilton's.

Yours, as ever,
Clark Ashton

Bates said that "Helman Canby" would appear under my new title for it, "The Return of the Sorcerer."

1. Stella G. S. Perry, "Old Roses"; Edmond Hamilton, "The Earth-Owners" (*WT*, August 1931).

---

[124]   To H. P. Lovecraft [TLS, JHL]   [c. early August 1931]
At the opening, on Eros, of the time-vault that conducts upon
former aeons when Eros was part of the major planet,
Antanoth, which revolved between Mars and Jupiter.

Dear Éch-Pi-El:

Your letter came just as I was on the point of writing you to express my appreciation of *At the Mountains of Madness*. The Ms. came from Wandrei per schedule, and has now been forwarded to Dwyer. I read the story twice—parts of it three or four times—and think it is one of your masterpieces. For my taste, anyway, it is vastly superior to Poe's Antarctic opus, "Arthur Gordon Pym." I'll never forget your descriptions of that tremendous non-human architecture, and the on-rushing *shoggoth* in an underworld cavern! Wright's rejection was certainly a piece of triple-dyed and quadruple-plated lunacy.

You must have had a superb vacation-tour! But I can understand your gladness to be back on natal soil: one is more or less rootless and uptorn anywhere else. I wouldn't mind getting away from Auburn for a brief trip, but see no chance of it this year. The fire-hazard still exists, for one thing.

Thanks for the picture. Something about it—I don't know what—reminds me a little of Sam Loveman; but probably there is no real resemblance. I am very glad to have it, and will remember you the next time I have anything passable of myself on hand. I certainly should have something taken to counteract the cock-eyed Rogue's gallery effect in *Wonder Stories.*

Last month was certainly a busy one for me, with the forest fire, et al. Then, along about the 15th, I received a letter from the *Wonder Stories* editor, enclosing a plot that had taken second prize in the *Quarterly's* plot contest (you may have noticed the details in the issue I sent you) asking me to make a story out of it. The plot, called "The Martian," by one E. M. Johnston of Ontario, was pretty good, so the job wasn't so disagreeable as it sounds. They wanted the story for the Fall *Quarterly,* out Sept. 15th, so I had to write and retype the whole yarn—about 16,000 words—in a little more than a week, so that it could reach N.Y. by the end of July. I hope it will pass muster—it ought to be a pretty fair scientifictional opus.[1] "Beyond the Singing Flame" has not yet been reported on. I'll send it to Wandrei. "The Maker of Gargoyles" will reach you presently via Dwyer.

No great news—nothing worthy of scare-heads, at any rate. I had the same sort of communication from Bates that you received, and sent in several stories. One, "The Door to Saturn," seems to have found favor with Bates, who is holding it for Clayton's inspection. C. vetoed the purchase of "A Good Embalmer," which Bates was willing to buy; so the chances of ultimate landing are problematic. I note the new mag. *Strange Tales,* will appear on the stands Aug. 14th. Bates said that the first issue would contain my "Helman Carnby," re-titled "The Return of the Sorcerer." I hope it won't sink.

I'd certainly urge you to try *At the Mountains of Madness* on the scientific quarterlies, beginning with *Amazing.* They ought to like it, with the geological details and speculations. There is a new pseudo-scientific mag, *Miracle, Science and Fantasy Stories,* published by Harold Hersey, but I haven't seen it yet.[2] Doubtless it has the same popular action requirements as the other Hersey periodicals. I was apparently wrong about *Ghost Stories* going back to McFadden—they must have run out of stationery, and were using some old McFadden letter-heads. [. . .]

I've started three new tales, but haven't gone very far with any of them yet. One, "The Master of Destruction,"[3] will bring in my time-vault idea, and will take the hero into the lost world of which the asteroids are the problematic fragments. Archaeology on the asteroids will prove somewhat mischancy! The hero starts out by finding a beautiful mummy, wearing an amulet which contains a scroll in his own handwriting! The tale will run to 25,000 words or more, and might be utilized as a two-part serial by Wright if it fails to land as a novelette with *Astounding* or *Strange Tales.* Another projected tale is "The Cairn," which brings in the idea of a sort of tread-mill property in space, rendering unapproachable an object which is seemingly near at hand.[4]

Write soon. Yrs, in the dark evangelism of Azathoth,
Klarkash-Ton

P.S. I'll try to send you a *Wonder Stories* containing "The City of the Singing Flame."

1. "The Planet-Entity" (alternate title, "The Martian") (*Wonder Stories Quarterly*, Fall 1931; *TSS*, as "Seedling of Mars").
2. *Miracle Science and Fantasy Stories* (ed. Elliot Dold) survived only for two issues.
3. Nonextant, although *SS* contains a story synopsis and an incomplete draft of the story.
4. "The Cairn" was CAS's first title for "The Secret of the Cairn" (*Wonder Stories*, April 1933; as "The Light from Beyond"; *LW*).

---

[125]   To August Derleth [TLS, SHSW]   Aug. 18th, 1931.

Dear August:
    [. . .] I hope that Wright will return from his vacation with an improved sense of values. I never made an issue of his rejections of my own stuff; but it might not do any harm if I were to mention your work and Lovecraft's *At the Mountains of Madness*. Could you loan me carbons of some of the best things he has turned down? I'd like very much to read them. Wright is readily influenced by other people's opinions, as I happen to know. I believe he reconsidered "Satampra Zeiros" and "Athammaus" partly or mainly through Lovecraft's recommendation of these tales. Another rejected tale that he afterwards took, probably for the same reason, was Wandrei's "The Red Brain."[1]
    Your suggestion anent "The Maker of Gargoyles" is damn good, and I shall adopt it if the tale comes back from Bates, who is evidently holding it for the publisher's reaction, since it hasn't been returned according to the usual schedule. Funny—I seem to have more trouble with the endings of stories than anything else. God knows how many I have had to re-write. I have a dud on hand now—"Jim Knox and the Giantess"—which will have to be given a brand-new wind-up if it is ever to sell.[2] The same applies to my 10,000 word pseudo-scientific, "The Letter from Mohaun Los." I have recently re-touched "The Hunters from Beyond," leaving it more in doubt as to what is actually going on in the studio up to the last moment, and adding at the end, for contrast to the mindless girl who is beyond "even the memory of horror," a last vision

of the ghoul-infested gulf, "the ravening faces, the hunger-contorted forms that swirled toward us from their ultra-dimensional limbo like a devil-laden hurricane from Malebolge." [. . .]

As ever,

Clark Ashton

1. *WT* (October 1927).
2. Published as "The Root of Ampoi" (*Arkham Sampler*, Spring 1949; *TSS*).

---

[126]   To August Derleth [TLS, SHSW]   Aug. 28th, 1931.

Dear August:

[. . .] Bates has accepted "The Door to Saturn"—the somewhat wicked humor of this tale having evidently tickled the publisher, Clayton, as well as B. himself. "Gargoyles" came back, though, and I have given it a fresh ending, utilizing your suggestions, preliminary to sending it on to Wright. I don't think there would be any use returning it to Bates at present: with his limited space, he won't want to stock very heavily on my stuff for awhile. I certainly hope the mag. does become a monthly, and see no reason why it shouldn't succeed. Thanks for your offer of a copy. But the local stands finally got in a supply (all of which have been cleaned out) and I have also ordered some extras from the publishers. I agree with you about the tales—"The Place of the Pythons" and "The Awful Injustice" were pretty good. The vampire yarn, "The Dark Castle," was about the bummest, I thought.[1]

Too bad that *Ghost Stories* will have to retire—especially since they were going to buy something of yours. The Hersey periodicals seem to be short-lived anyhow. I predict that there will be one or two new ventures in the same field before long—not that I have heard anything definite to that effect. But the wind seems to be slanting a little toward the supernatural and the fantastic.

Here is my new ending for "The Hunters from Beyond"—the only real change being the final vision of the devil-ridden gulf. The tale doesn't please me very well—the integral mood seems a little second-rate, probably because the treatment of modern atmosphere is rather uncongenial for me. I am also enclosing the new end for "Gargoyles." "Jim Knox" isn't worth bothering you with. I have re-written the last part and have sent it to another new Clayton venture, *Jungle Stories*. The tale is semi-humorous, and is told by a circus giant, in explanation of how he came to be a giant. [. . .]

I haven't finished any new work, but will send you "The Vaults of Yoh-Vombis," a Martian horror-tale, when I have completed it. I planned an ambitious 25,000 word novelette, "The Master of Destruction," which might be worked off as scientifiction, since it brings in a new device for time-travelling in the form of a temple-vault that encloses a sort of fourth-dimensional vortex.

I'll look for "People"—also anything else you feel like sending.
    As ever,
        Clark Ashton

1. Arthur J. Burks, "The Place of Pythons"; A. B. H. Hurst, "The Awful Injustice"; and Marion Brandon, "The Dark Castle" (*Strange Tales*, September 1931).

———————•———————

[127]   To August Derleth [TLS, SHSW]   Sept. 6th, 1931.

Dear August:
    [. . .] Bates is apparently still on the job, so the holding of "Red Hands" augurs well.[1] I do hope he'll take it, and also the others. I had a letter from him a day or so ago, returning "The Epiphany of Death" (which he liked) on account of its brevity and the previous acceptance of "The Door to Saturn," and the possibility that he would also buy the revised "Hunters from Beyond." He says that he finds it hard to get atmospheric stuff.
    I'm glad you liked the new endings. Your suggestion about Reynard's motivation is excellent.[2] If Wright takes the tale, I can tell him to change one of the phrases, or both. "The Hunters" looked pretty good when I read it over the other day, and I think I prefer it to the Helman Carnby thing now, though I didn't at first. [. . .]
    I'll have "The Vaults of Yoh-Vombis" ready for circulation soon. It's a rather ambitious hunk of extra-planetary weirdness. I want to clean up some other unfinished things, "The Cairn," etc, and will then begin on "The Master of Destruction." In this last, a human archaeologist, exploring some ruins on the asteroid Eros, penetrates a sealed vault or adytum enclosing a fourth-dimensional vortex which carries him back in time to the period when the asteroids all formed a single major planet. There will be some feminine interest in the tale, and a grand conflict between the human or semi-human race of the planet and a terrible metal-feathered bird-people, the Arcroi, which ends in the blowing-up of the planet by the

Master to keep it from being entirely subjugated by the Arcroi. This explosion theory would explain the present wide dispersion of the asteroids. I am planning one terrific chapter in which the archaeologist, the Antanothian princess, and some other humans, having been captured by the bird-people, are turned loose in a desert region, to be hunted down by Arcroi fledglings out for their first taste of blood, like young hawks. It ought to make a thriller. [. . .]
    As ever,
      Clark Ashton

    1. AWD, "Red Hands" (*WT*, October 1932).
    2. In "The Maker of Gargoyles." In a letter dated 14 August (ms., JHL), AWD wrote "Why not have [Reynard] go up and destroy the gargoyles, and in their destruction, himself be killed?"

---

[128]   To August Derleth [TLS, SHSW]   Sept. 26th, 1931.

Dear August:
    [. . .] I guess Wright is swamped with accumulated mss. I haven't had a word from him either. He has "Gargoyles" and "Yoh-Vombis" under consideration. The editorial mills are certainly slow—I've had no communications, checks, acceptances or rejections for ages. Even the money for "The Door to Saturn" hasn't arrived yet, owing to the annual period of house-cleaning in the Clayton book-keeping dept. [. . .]
    The story I am doing is the toughest job I have ever attempted.[1] Also, in spite of a rough road and other safe-guards, the villagers have been busting in on my time more than usual. To-morrow I am going off in the woods all day with pencil and drafting-paper, to avoid another gang that has been threatening to come. I suppose this sounds unsociable, etc; but with me it takes long, grueling, sweaty hours to get anything done even half-way satisfactorily. I'm always glad to see intelligent people—but I've certainly had a surfeit of fools.
    H.P. is an enigma to me. Surely I should think he would prefer doing his own stuff to revising people's junk. He'd make more money too, even if he didn't sell more than half or a third. If I, an unknown, can sell two-thirds of my work (the present proportion) there's no doubt whatever as to the success achievable by H.P. with his prestige and popularity. I agree with you that Wright ought to take "In the Vaults." I believe he rejected it once, on the

silly grounds of over-gruesomeness. But that doesn't mean a thing, as we all know.

I guess I'll quit before I come to another ragged rent in this ribbon.

As ever,
Clark Ashton

1. "The Eternal World" (*Wonder Stories,* March 1932; *GL*).

———————◆———————

[129]   To August Derleth [TLS, SHSW]   Nov. 3rd. 1931.

Dear August:

[. . .] Our weather, too, has been extremely balmy and summer-like, following a heavy rain. Lots of mushrooms in the adjacent fields—I gather a panful every morning.

My new stories have been delayed, since I did a lot of re-typing and revising on old ones. Wright has already accepted "The Vaults of Yoh-Vombis," but I mulcted myself out of 17 dollars on the price by the surgical excisions which I performed. I re-wrote some others, but he still refused to bite at "An Offering to the Moon." However he did take "The Kiss of Zoraida," a short Orientale, for *Oriental Stories.*[1] He thought it wasn't "distinctively Oriental" when I sent it in last year. The insertion of a few thees and thous in the dialogue, and the omission of one or two ironic touches that were more universal than Eastern, seem to have changed his opinion. I've also cut down "The Eternal World" for the Jew out-fit. Too many peeg voids und nod enuf ection. So I went to work and demolished some of my battlements of purple prose.

Bates is certainly slow,—not a word from him about anything. I'll have "The Nameless Offspring" ready to ship to him in a few days, and will also start the carbon on its travels. I doubt if this story will ever get between magazine covers on account of its horrific plot and monstrous subject-matter. It deals with the off-spring of a ghoul and a cataleptic woman who was interred alive by mistake.

On the whole, I agree with you about scientifiction—the less science the better the story, as a rule. But I like such tales when they induce a sense of cosmic mystery, terror, beauty, strangeness or sublimity. Mere machinery, by itself, gives me a pain. Also, a lot of the late scientifiction tales are mere gangster or crime stories with a futuristic or ultra-terrestrial setting. Hardly any of the new stuff comes within shouting-distance of Wells at his best. Stanton Coblentz, who has an ironic, Swiftian turn, is about as good as any of the current crew, and vastly better than most.[2] . . . Incidentally, my forthcoming novelette in *W.T.* is packed with all kinds of open or hidden satire. It even satirizes scientifiction, in the outrageous "space-annihilator."[3] But I don't think any of the fans would have enough humor in their make-ups to see this.

Yes, I can vizualize the coming cover. Judas Priest!

As ever,

Clark Ashton

1. "The Kiss of Zoraida" (*Magic Carpet Magazine* [formerly *Oriental Stories*], July 1933; *OD*).
2. Stanton A. Coblentz (1896–1982), science fiction writer and traditionalist poet, like CAS. He published much of CAS's later work in his little magazine, *Wings*.
3. I.e., "The Monster of the Prophecy."

---

[130]   To H. P. Lovecraft [TLS, JHL]   [c. early November 1931]
From the ghoul-haunted vaults of Tremoth, after
the breaking of the iron chain and lock.

Dear Éch-Pi-El:

[. . .] I was interested in Shea's[1] clippings, which seem very significant as indicating the progress (?) of modern art. I think there is undoubtedly a certain gruesome power in the first-prize winner, though it impressed me very disagreeably at first sight. I'd like to see it in color, before pronouncing a final judgement. The other pictures I didn't care for at all, as reproduced in the newspaper cuts. My frank opinion of the new stuff is that nine-tenths of it is plain, colossal humbug, which the critics and public have been hypnotized or bulldozed into thinking, or pretending, that they like. Of course, there is a residuum of honest and worthy effort. But I simply can't swallow most of the post-Cezannean garbage.

I *would* have told Wright to go chase himself in regard to "The Vaults of Yoh-Vombis," if I didn't have the support of my parents, and debts to pay off. For this reason it's important for me to place as many stories as possible and have them coming out at a tolerably early date. However, I did not reduce the tale by as much as Wright suggested, and I refused to sacrifice the essential details and incidents of the preliminary section. What I did do, mainly, was to condense the descriptive matter, some of which had a slight suspicion of prolixity anyhow. But I shall restore most of it, if the tale is ever brought out in book form.[2] W. accepted the revised version by return mail.

My late work, it would seem, has been mostly revision, though I have now drafted "The Nameless Offspring," and am typing it for circulation. I re-wrote "The Devotee of Evil" (which you may remember) among others, with a view to ridding it of certain vague verbosities; and I also cut down on the pseudo-scientific element. Young Shea, to whom I have showed the revised carbon, thinks it my best weird tale, somewhat to my surprise. [. . .] I also did some cutting on "The Eternal World" for Gernsback. The tale really needed it in places, since there were genuine redundancies of thought and image.

You may have seen "The Demon of the Flower"[3] by now. Bates is still holding it, along with "The Hunters from Beyond" and "The Maker of Gargoyles." It will be hard luck if he doesn't take at least one of the lot, after all his hesitation and delay. I shall send him "The Nameless Offspring," too, though I imagine its commercial chances will be somewhat less than nil. The plot is a terror, though of course I may have botched it hopelessly in the actual writing. Properly done, it would wring the nerves of a hardened mortician. You should have written it, by all rights.

Creeps by Night doesn't sound any too "hot," apart from the contributions by yourself, and Long, Wandrei and Suter.[4] I suppose the conte cruel is the average person's idea of a weird tale; but it seems a distinct and vastly inferior form to me, as it doubtless does to you. I saw *The Omnibus of Crime* some time ago; and the alleged weirds in this were mostly tales of physical gruesomeness and cruelty; one of the few exceptions being "The Novel of the Black Seal."[5] I'd like some time to edit a collection of first-class weird fiction, and would exclude from it anything that lacked the authentic note of supernatural and cosmic terror. A lot of my own stuff, such as "The Venus of Azombeii," would scarcely be eligible!

I'm glad you have some revisory work that is more to your taste than the overhauling of amateur efforts.[6] I've done enough of the latter myself to know what it is like. As to remunerative fiction, I really think there is room for considerable literary art even within the limitations imposed by editors—notwithstanding the lack of it in the usual magazine story. Of course, the problem is to develop adequate atmosphere in connection with fairly rapid action. It *can* be done; and infinite skill can be lavished on it. Of course, the average writer wouldn't take the trouble, even if he had the capacity. I think you are mistaken about yourself in this regard, and believe that you could readily write stuff that would be both excellent and salable.

Give my profound obeisances to the unknown eidolon. I am curious to know if there were some fresh alterations in its periphery, following the October Sabbat. I am not surprised by what you tell me about Walpurgis-Night. These festivals are undoubtedly of pre-anthropologic origin, and were celebrated amid the primal fires and mists of Earth, by beings coeval with, or older than, the nebula of our solar system.

Yours in the Dark Faith,
Klarkash-Ton

1. J. Vernon Shea (1912–1981), youthful correspondent of HPL, CAS, and AWD, and aspiring writer.
2. CAS never restored the 1,500 words of excised descriptive text for the story's appearance in *OST*. See *The Vaults of Yoh-Vombis* (West Warwick, RI: Necronomicon Press, 1988) for the complete and restored text.
3. "The Demon of the Flower" (*Astounding Stories*, December 1933; LW).
4. Dashiell Hammett (1894–1961), *Creeps by Night: Chills and Thrills* (New York: John Day Co., 1931). Contains: HPL, "The Music of Erich Zann"; Frank Belknap Long, "A Visitor from Egypt"; DAW, "The Red Brain"; and Paul Suter, "Beyond the Door."
5. Dorothy L. Sayers (1893–1957) ed., *The Omnibus of Crime* (1928; rpt. Garden City, NY: Garden City Publishing Co., 1931). "The Novel of the Black Seal" is from Machen's *The Three Impostors* (1895).
6. At the time, HPL was editing *History of Dartmouth College* by Leon Burr Richardson (1878–1951) (Hanover, NH, 1932; 2 vols.) for the Stephen Daye Press, managed by HPL's friend Vrest Orton.

---

[131]   To August Derleth [TLS, SHSW]   Dec. 31st, 1931.

Dear August:

California—the mountain region at least—seems to have been having a double or triple allowance of snow, since I hear that there are over 200 inches of it in the high Sierras. Here in Auburn we have been having heavy rains—more than in any season for the past 15 or 20 years.

The holidays have been rather demoralizing for me—too much festivity and too little work. But I'll get back into harness after New Year's. I've been having a touch of muscular rheumatism —back and shoulders—and am now fighting off an incipient cold. [. . .]

I was surprised to get my check three days ago for "The Nameless Offspring," just as I was mailing some slight alterations for the story to Bates. I subtilized the passage about the gnawed corpse, and added one or two paragraphs at the story's end, describing a futile search of the vaults by Chaldane and Harper and including a hint by Harper that he and Sir John had made a similarly useless search many years before. This last touch (suggested by Bates) seems to me a definite improvement, since it lifts the whole business more into the realm of the supernatural to have the monster vanish utterly.

Wright has just accepted "Avoosl Wuthoqquam"[1] but has not yet reported on "The Demon of the Flower." I have given three of my unsold and apparently unsalable shorts—"The Epiphany of Death," "A Tale of Sir John Maundeville," and "The Devotee of Evil"—to one Carl Swanson of Washburn, North Dakota, who plans to bring out weird and weird-scientific fiction in booklet form and may also start a magazine of the same type.[2] I don't expect to reap any great amount of mazuma from the venture, but will be glad to have these tales in print. Wright is scheduling my "The Planet of the Dead" for the March issue, and "The Eternal World" will appear in the March issue of *Wonder Stories*. Maybe "The Hunters from Beyond" will come out in the March *Strange Tales*—Bates spoke quite a while back of buying it for use in the fourth number. [. . .]

I've been reading *The Omnibus of Crime*, which has some excellent weird stories in the latter section (I can't read detective tales, to which the major part of the book is given.) Le Fanu's "Green Tea," Hichens' "How Love Came to Professor Guildea," "The Novel of the Black Seal," Metcalf's "Bad Lands," White's "Lukundoo," and one or two others were enough to give me my money's worth and more. I can't see though why Bierce and M. R. James were so wretchedly represented in this collection. "Moxon's Master" by the former is so obviously mediocre in comparison to real stuff such as "The Death of Halpin Frayser"; and almost anything of James that I remember reading would have been preferable to the somewhat tedious "Martin's Close." [. . .]

> As ever,
> Clark Ashton

1. "The Weird of Avoosl Wuthoqquan" (*WT,* June 1932; *OST* and *RA*).
2. Carl Swanson proposed to publish a weird fiction magazine, *Galaxy.* It never appeared.

---

[132]   To August Derleth [TLS, SHSW]   Feb. 16th, 1932.

Dear August:

I received the ms. of H.P.'s "The Shadow over Innsmouth," and will send it on to Wandrei in a day or two. I liked it greatly, especially in its rendering of a decadent atmosphere, and of course urged H.P. to submit it to Wright. I did, however, make what seemed to me a rather obvious suggestion about the addition of a new chapter, which could be worked in next to the last with very little verbal alteration of the story as it stands. This chapter would be made of the narrator's broken, nightmare-like memories of being captured by the rout of monsters, who take him back to Innsmouth, but do him no vulgar harm, since they recognize his latent kinship to themselves. Without his guessing the reason at the time, they subject him to some horrible rite that is calculated to accelerate the development of the alien strain in his blood, and then let him go. I fear, though, that he won't care for the suggestion.[1]

I am sending you one of the *Overlands* you inquired about, under separate cover, together with a catalogue that lists all of them. I couldn't find the other copies. You are welcome to keep this one, and also the catalogue.

Bates wouldn't bite on my scientific stuff—says it lacks human interest, which is doubtless true. He hasn't reported on the last weirds as yet. I have done a brief fantasy, "Ubbo-Sathla," for submission to Wright.[2] I don't know whether it's any good or not, since I am a bit fagged mentally, and everything seems more or less rotten to me. Confinement indoors gets my goat, and I'll welcome some open weather, when I can work out in the fresh air.

I'll be glad to have Don's novel and your own mss., whenever you get around to sending them.

As ever,
Clark Ashton

1. As CAS surmised, HPL would make no changes to the story. Neither did HPL submit the story to *WT* (although AWD did; see letter 159) and it remained unpublished until brought out as a small booklet in 1936.
2. "Ubbo-Sathla" (*WT*, July 1933; *OST*).

---

[133]   To Donald Wandrei [TLS, MHS]   Feb. 17th, 1932.

Dear Donald:

Herewith is the ms. of H.P.L.'s "The Shadow over Innsmouth," which I have enjoyed greatly. It is a consummate piece of shudder-evoking atmosphere; and my only criticism is that even more could readily be made of the story.

I am also sending a new fantasy of my own, "Ubbo-Sathla," whose ideation may remind you a little of your own tale, "Alfred Kramer."[1] The main object of "Ubbo-Sathla" was to achieve a profound and manifold dissolution of what is known as reality—which, come to think of it, is the animus of nearly all my tales, more or less.

Your novel ought to come any day. I'll read and "report" promptly when it does come. I hope the European trip will materialize.

As ever,
Clark

1. "The Lives of Alfred Kramer" (*WT,* December 1932). See Steve Behrends, "The Birth of Ubbo-Sathla," *Crypt of Cthulhu* No. 45 (Candlemas 1987): 10–13.

---

[134]   To Donald Wandrei [TLS, MHS]   March 1st, 1932.

Dear Donald:

Your novel came o.k., and I have read it with immense pleasure. The plot seems all right to me, and I do not see that it calls for any structural modifications. My only suggestion is, that the wording might be touched up in places, in the earlier chapters. The later chapters are superior in style, it seems to me—especially where they are written in the first person. The tale is full of imaginative ideas; and some of the descriptions of strange phenomena—the changeability of the pitted image, etc.—might stand considerable amplification. I'll send the ms. on in a few days, but would like to re-read portions of it first.

I'm glad you liked Lovecraft's new story and my recent Mss. "The Shadow over Innsmouth" certainly has a most pervasive atmosphere—I can still feel and smell it! I certainly wish H.P. would pitch in and do a lot of new work—he couldn't write enough to suit me!

I'm pegging away at some scientific junk. I think I mentioned writing a horror tale dealing with premature burial. This yarn has been definitely accepted for *Strange Tales;* and Bates has also given me a favorable report on "The Seed from the Sepulcher," which seems to stand a good chance of being taken.[1] I am trying to unload a scientifictional novelette on Wright.

Here's to the placing of your novel. Have you thought of trying it on Wright for a four-part serial? I see no reason at all why he wouldn't take it.

As ever,
Clark

1. "The Seed from the Sepulchre" (*WT,* October 1933; *TSS*).

————————◆————————

[135]   To H. P. Lovecraft [TLS, JHL]   [c. March 1932]
                 The marble, demon-haunted house of Avyctes,
                   on the northernmost promontory of Poseidonis,
                        at the epiphany of the double shadow.

Dear Éch-Pi-El:

Our open spring weather still holds, but it seems impossible that it can last much longer. I wouldn't be surprised if there were another snow-storm before the equinox. The snow in the mountains is melting pretty fast, I hear; and the spring buds are all a-burgeoning.

Yes, "Innsmouth" has an atmosphere that one can't shake off in a hurry. I can still smell and taste it! I think that you will find that Melmoth's[1] opinion is no less favorable than mine. I am indeed rejoiced to hear that you have written another tale, which begins to sound like old times. I shall certainly look forward to it with great and shuddersome expectations when you get around to typing it. I hope it will be followed very shortly by others—you couldn't write enough to suit me.

I guess I wrote you that "Uther Magbane"[2] had been definitely accepted by the Clayton Co. "The Seed from the Sepulcher" pleased Bates, too, but he wanted me to make some slight alterations before showing it to Clayton. He seemed to think there was an inconsistency in the development of the devil-plant; but, as I pointed out to him, the plant merely propagated itself through spores, *after death,* but had the power of extending its *individual life-term* through an extension of the root-system from one victim to another. However, I made several minor changes, adding some horrific details, and mentioning a *second skull* in the lattice-work of bones, roots, etc, in the burial-pit. Derleth's suggestions were very good, but I rather like the thing as it stands. It might have been worked out more gradually, at greater length, as Wandrei suggests; but the present development, as far as I am concerned, has, through its very acceleration, a strong connotation of the unnatural, the diabolic, the supernatural.

You will have seen "Ubbo-Sathla" by now. Wright returned it, to my disgust, seeming to think that it would be over the heads of his clientele. Wright, it seems to me, is more than likely to fire back anything that is genuinely original, or so unusual that he can't align it with something he has previously published and found satisfactory from a reader standpoint.

I gave Swanson another of my short weirds, "The Ghoul," which seems to have made a great impression on him. I haven't sent him anything that I consider really poor. My rejected tales, on examination, seem to fall mainly into two classes—the highly odd, unusual and novel, and the definitely mediocre and hackneyed. There is a third class, mainly scientifiction, consisting of several items that could be greatly improved by revision. However, out of 62 finished yarns, I have succeeded in working off 44 or so, and will probably be able to dispose of several others that are hanging fire at present. If there were only one or two more editors in the market for that sort of thing, I believe I could sell nearly all my weirds: individual taste differs more in regard to horror and fantasy, as Dorothy Sayers observes, than in regard to anything else. Bates, Wright and Swanson all seem to differ markedly in their perceptions.

Have you seen the Modern Library anthology of *Best Ghost Stories*, edited by Arthur B. Reeve?[3] I bought it recently. It contains some old favorites, as well as several things that I had previously missed. On reading them all over, I decided that, for my taste, "Canon Alberic's Scrap-Book," was about the best thing in the collection. Next to it, I liked "The Man Who Went Too Far" by Benson, and the Bulwer and Bierce standbys, "The Haunted and the Haunters," and "The Damned Thing." The Blackwood item, "The Woman's Ghost Story," though good in technique, was too professionally occultistic to please me greatly. The idea of an able-bodied male specter having to hang around and beg strangers to love him struck me as little less than puerile. It's just the sort of thing which makes me feel that spiritualism is about on a par with fetishism—"human, all too human . . ." But there is a magnificent chance for tales dealing with a future state of life—tales that would break utterly with the mere extension of mundane emotions and morals beyond the grave. Sometime I'm going to write a yarn dealing with some moribund who promises a friend, wife or sweetheart that he will return after death . . . but, when he does return, it is in the form of a typhoid bacillus, with no other consciousness or proclivities than would be proper to a bug of that species.

I haven't finished anything lately—too much spring fever. Probably "The Double Shadow," a weird fantasy, will be the first of my several current experiments to achieve completion.[4] Yours, in eager anticipation of "The Dreams of Walter Gilman,"[5]

 Klarkash-Ton

P.S. Your "In the Vault" certainly stands out in the current *W.T.*, though the Whitehead, Sandeson and Kadra Maysi items are pretty fair. Hamilton, consarn him, has ruined an idea somewhat similar to one that I had in mind, for a tale to be called "The Lunar Brain," based on the notion that there is a vast living brain in the center of the Moon.[6]

 1. Melmoth is DAW, the name being a pun on Charle's Maturin's novel, *Melmoth the Wanderer.*
 2. "The Second Interment of Uther Magbane," published as "The Second Interment" (*Strange Tales,* January 1933; *OST*).
 3. Arthur B. Reeve (1880–1936), ed. *The Best Ghost Stories* (New York: Carlton House, 1919; rpt. Modern Library, n.d.).
 4. "The Double Shadow" (*DS* and *OST*).
 5. An early title for HPL's "The Dreams in the Witch House."
 6. HPL, "In the Vault"; Robert C. Sandison, "The Vrykolakas"; Kadra Maysi, "Conjure Bag"; Edmond Hamilton, "The Earth-Brain" (*WT,* April 1932).

---

[136] To August Derleth [TLS, SHSW] March 15th, 1932.

Dear August:

 [. . .] Wright has just accepted "The Maker of Gargoyles," which I sent back to him after re-revising the ending so as to make the fight between Reynard and the gargoyles a little more plausible. Two paragraphs of re-writing caused him to say that the tale "was now much better." I certainly admire your perseverance in sending in stuff as much as ten or twelve times—so far, I haven't had the nerve to go beyond a third submission.

 Here is a new carbon of mine, "The Double Shadow," which you can ship along at leisure to H.P. I like it a little better than "Ubbo-Sathla." The original has gone to Wright, since this type of tale seems a little recherché [*sic*] at present for Clayton. I shall do something of a more modernistic nature before long, for submission to *S.T.* Gernsback has taken a hunk of tripe, "The Invisible City," which is scheduled for appearance in the June *Wonder Stories.*[1] They certainly take the palm for promptness in printing accepted matter—but they make up for it on the payment end.

Senf ought to have been shot before sunrise for his last cover. I liked the illustration for "Mrs. Lorriquer"—also the one for "In the Vault." Wright has sent me the proof of "The Vaults of Yoh-Vombis," illustrated by Nelson;[2] but the drawing is a disappointment as far as I am concerned. For one thing, the mummy looks too much like a living figure—there's no sign of the "incredibly desiccated" appearance that I described in the tale.

My project for a magazine is so remote and nebulous that I've never mentioned it to anyone before. If I ever did publish anything of the sort, its most frequent appearance would be as an annual. I'd try to get together a few choice and first-class items denied publication by commercial magazines. The main slant would be weird and fantastic (no science fiction, unless of extraordinary merit) with a few items dealing with rare moods or incidents of what is known as "reality." A story such as "Five Alone"[3] would be eligible for inclusion. Thanks for your offer—certainly I'll call on you if I am ever in a position to start the venture.

As ever,
Clark Ashton

1. "The Invisible City" (*Wonder Stories,* June 1932; *OD*).
2. "In the Vault" and "Mrs. Lorriquer" (by Henry S. Whitehead) were illustrated by James Napoli; "The Vaults of Yoh-Vombis" by T. Wyatt Nelson.
3. AWD, "Five Alone" (*Pagany,* Summer 1932), a non-weird short story.

———————— • ————————

[137]   To H. P. Lovecraft [TLS, JHL]   [c. early April 1932]
Mohaun Los, after the battle of the ultra-stellar
Robot and the alien time-machine.

Dear Éch-Pi-El:

Yes, it's a confounded shame that Swanson's *Galaxy* should have gone glimmering. There ought to be someone to publish stuff on other than a purely venal and popularity-seeking basis. Sometime—if I ever get out of the financial woods—I may have a shot at some sort of annual or bi-annual. But I won't do it unless I can pay the contributors at least a nominal sum.

I was rejoiced to learn your opinion of "The Double Shadow." Wright, you will be interested to hear, has rejected it on the same plea as "Ubbo-Sathla"—that his readers wouldn't like it. I have sent it to Bates, though of course with little hope that it will pass the rigorous Claytonian scrutiny.

Re the phrase *volumes and books* in "The Double Shadow." This was a deliberate Latinism, since I used volumes in the very special sense of *rolls or scrolls.*

I hope you will go ahead with your writing, regardless of editors and their more or less stereotyped requirements. I have a notion that a large proportion of the resulting tales will prove salable anyway. And I trust that the Vanguard Press proposition may come to something.[1] You have certainly sent them a strong selection. Thousands of *W.T.* fans would buy the book, so I fail to see how they could lose on its publication.

I read Blackwood's *The Wave* not long ago (a friend wanted my opinion of it) and I certainly feel inclined to second your judgement.[2] Of all the goshawful goo and guff! I must get the Blackwood books you mentioned in your monograph, as soon as possible.

Here is "The Plutonian Drug," which you can return direct to me, at your leisure.[3] I am sending it to *Amazing,* in the hope that it might have "enough science" for that medium. It was certainly tough writing, and I am still a little groggy.

> Yrs for the reversement of all terrene cycles,
> Klarkash-Ton

1. Vanguard had asked HPL to see his stories for book publication, but ultimately rejected them.
2. Algernon Blackwood, *The Wave: An Egyptian Aftermath* (1916).
3. "The Plutonian Drug" (*Amazing Stories,* September 1934; *LW*).

---

[138]   To Lester Anderson[1] [TLS, private collection]
May 4th, 1932

My dear Mr. Anderson:

I received *The Horrid Mysteries,*[2] the copy of *W.T.* and your letter last week, but have delayed acknowledging them until I had time to read the books. The *Mysteries* are quite a treasure, I think, and I am glad to have them. I had never read much in the way of Gothic romance but Grosse's book has started me on *The Mysteries of Udolpho,* which promises to be delightful. [. . .]

> With many thanks for your various kindnesses, I am,
> cordially yrs.,
> Clark Ashton Smith

1. Lester Anderson (1910–1980), Bay area science fiction fan and friend of CAS.
2. Karl Grosse (1768–1847), *Horrid Mysteries* (1796; rpt. London:

R. Holden, 1927). Robert E. Howard referred to this title in "The Children of the Night" (*WT,* April–May 1931).

———◆———

[139]   To Lester Anderson [ALS, private collection]
May 14th, 1932

Dear Mr. Anderson:
    [. . .] You are quite right to defend Burroughs if you enjoy his books. All literary criticism narrows down to a matter of personal taste. I have long ceased to have any vestige of respect for "authority" in such matters, and read only what I please. Not long ago, I had occassion to defend *Dracula,* also, "The Moon Pool," against the scorn of a high-brow friend. [. . .]
        Cordially,
        Clark Ashton Smith

———◆———

[140]   To August Derleth [TLS, SHSW]   May 15th, 1932.

Dear August:
    I am glad my suggestions anent "The Menace" were not too impossible. I have a notion you will make a good and also salable story from it. There are vast possibilities in the science fiction tale, but most of the work published under that classification is too trite and ill-written. From a literary standpoint, *Amazing Stories* and *Wonder Stories,* taking them tale by tale, compare very wretchedly indeed with *W.T.*
    I hadn't bothered writing to Swanson, since I was confident that his venture would blow up anyway; and yesterday, in the same mail with yours, I got a letter from him saying that he had decided to abandon all his publishing projects, and was returning my tales by express with a copy of a book by Flammarion[1] which I ordered some time ago. I'd feel like printing the stories myself, in booklet form, if money were coming in as it should; but checks are too shy and tardy these days. Anyway, I guess it's just as well that the Swanson business blew up. Evidently he's one of these birds, all too familiar in America, who are always trying to start something on a basis of hot air.

I wish the Holt Co. would publish something of yours. It is utterly incomprehensible to me why publishers and readers are all bughouse on the novel form, to the detriment of the more artistic short story and novelette. I have about decided that most novels, even those of high literary reputation, are hopelessly tedious from their very length. I'd buy a book of short stories any time, in preference to a novel, all other things being equal.

No word from Bates about my various stories. He sent me yesterday, however, a terrific communication from one G. P. Olsen of Sheldon, Iowa, which had been addressed to me in care of *S.T.* I've had letters from madmen before, but this one really took the gilt-edged angel-cake. Twelve single-spaced pages, much of it phrased with a lucidity almost equal to that of Gertrude Stein or Hegel. Among other things, as well as I could make it out, the fellow seemed to be desirous of correcting certain erroneous ideas about demons and vampires which he had discovered in "The Nameless Offspring." Also, he wanted to point out the errors of Abdul Alhazred! Some of the stuff about vampires was really weird: "You never thought of a Vampire in your life but he appeared like an Emperor or an Archangel." Then he exhorts me to refrain from putting vampires in a bad light, since, by virtue of a little blood-sucking, they really confer immortality on those they have chosen! Later, apropos of godknowswhat, he told me that "you must realize it will never be stood for if you act in any other way than that befitting a Spanish Don." The letter is the damdest mixture of paranoia, delusions of grandeur and mystic delirium that ever went through the U.S. mails. The fellow writes of Ammon-Ra and Ahriman—a regular hash of Oriental mysticism— in the language of an illiterate Swede. He ends with something to the effect that his letter is the most momentous intellectual pro- mulgation of the age. I'm not in the habit of ignoring letters; but there's nothing else to be done in this case.

I hope your tales will land with Wright; also, that B.&C. will approve *The Tree near the Window.*

As ever,
Clark Ashton

I've finished one new tale, "The Mandrakes"—short, sweet & medieval. It's about a sorcerer who murdered his wife and buried her in the field where he got the mandrakes for the love-philters in which he specialized. Later, something happened to the mandrake- crop. . . .[2]

1. Camille Flammarion (1842–1925), French astronomer and author, who served at the Paris Observatory and the Bureau of Longitudes. Noted chiefly as the author of popular books on astronomy. His later studies

included many works on psychical research, among them *Death and Its Mystery* (3 vols., 1920–21; trans. 1921–23).

2. "The Mandrakes" (*WT,* February 1933; *OD*).

———————— ♦ ————————

[141]   To Lester Anderson [ALS, private collection]
June 22nd, 1932

Dear Mr. Anderson:

[. . .] Devolution is a grand theme. I rather suspect that Darwin inadvertently dropped a *d* when he promulgated his famous theory. The sort of evolution that is going on is hardly upward.

I should think Burroughs would get quite a lot of fun out of critics. A peep at current book reviews, no matter what their theme, moves me to ribald rabelaisian laughter. As to the popular condemnation of the weird by readers and reviewers, it seems to me that this can be simply and solely accounted for as lack of imagination. The nearer people are to the animal, the feebler their powers of imagination and abstraction. That's why realism is so popular to-day. If a dog were to develop any taste for art, his idea of a good picture would be a still-life of a nice meaty bone or juicy sirloin.

Thank you again for the books,
Cordially yours,
Clark Ashton Smith

———————— ♦ ————————

[142]   To Lester Anderson [ALS, private collection]
June 4th, 1932

My dear Mr. Anderson:

Again I am your debtor—you were very good to hunt up that copy of *Seven Footprints to Satan* for me.

I'll return *The Ship of Ishtar* early next week. Needless to say I enjoyed the rare and original fantasy of this tale, and have kept it longer than I should otherwise, for the sake of re-reading certain passages that were highly poetic and imaginative. Merritt has an authentic magic, as well as an inexhaustible imagination.[1]

I read portions of "The Snake Mother" in the *Argosy,* but somehow did not become greatly interested in the tale. It might be better, though, in reduced form. I am curious about *The Face in the Abyss,* and of course would be glad to read it.

As to magazines of fantasy, I have a notion that *Weird Tales* and *Amazing Stories,* being the oldest, are the most firmly entrenched, having built up for themselves a solid clientele. Gernsback, too, is clever and adaptable, and his magazines may weather the storm. I hope that *Strange Tales* will survive, since it is a badly needed alternative medium to *W.T.* Clayton's expenses are heavier, I imagine, than those of the others because of the larger number of magazines that he publishes, and the higher rate of payment. *W.T.* is the only magazine of fantasy which is paying as promptly for stories as it did a year ago: all the others seem to be in arrears. Which reminds me that I'm afraid to lay out any more money on buying books (much as I should like to) till I receive payment for some more of my stories. No less than eight yarns (for which I should have had the money ere this under normal conditions) are still unpaid for.
    [. . .]
        Cordially,
            Clark Ashton Smith

1. Abraham Merritt (1882–1943), American fantasy writer, author of *Seven Footprints to Satan* (1927); *The Ship of Ishtar* (1924); "The Snake Mother" (1930); "The Face in the Abyss" (1923).

---

[143]   To Lester Anderson [ALS, private collection]
                                                July 4th, 1932

Dear Mr. Anderson:
    I had meant to write before, but have been absorbed in my usual summer round of fiction-writing.
    Yes, I saw most of the fantastic motion pictures that you mention—all but *Dracula* and *Tarzan.* I agree substantially with your estimates—*Jekyll and Hyde* was by far the best, and was a truly artistic performance. *The Murders in the Rue Morgue* was terrific balderdash—even worse, if possible, than the grossly melodramatic perversion of Mrs. Shelley's *Frankenstein.* Yes—strange to say—the producers of *Jekyll and Hyde* actually did improve on the story—a most unique happening! [. . .]
    Apropos of the invented name in my stories: these aren't so hard to pronounce—most of them can be sounded with the accent on the next-to-last syllable: Sata´mpra, Wutho´qquan, Mmatmu´or, Hestai´yon, etc. The main exceptions to this rule are the names purporting to be of French origin, which would be pronounced

according to French rules, with the stress on the last syllable, as in Sodaguï. [. . .]

Write when the spirit moves.

Cordially,
Clark Ashton Smith

———————————◆———————————

[144]   To August Derleth [TLS, SHSW]   July 10th, 1932.

Dear August:

[. . .] Wright returned "The Beast of Averoigne," with no specific criticism, merely saying that he didn't like it as well as my other medieval stories. I am going to send you the carbon in a day or two, and ask you to look it over with an idea to structural or other flaws. Personally, I don't quite see why it was rejected, unless the documentary mode of presentation may have led me into more archaism than was palatable to Wright. The abbot's letter to Thérèse might be cut out, thus deepening the mystery; but I can't quite make up my mind in this.[1] Anyway, I'd like to know your reactions.

I finished "A Star-Change," which is high-grade scientific fiction, and am trying it on Wright out of curiosity, though I think its ultimate destination—if any—will be *Wonder Stories* or *Amazing*.[2] I have also sent Wright a newly finished medieval, "The Disinterment of Venus," dealing with the demoralization brought on a Benedictine abbey by the Roman Venus that was dug up in the garden.[3] It's a rather wicked story. [. . .]

Probably *Pagany* won't be interested in anything of mine; but occasionally I take a long shot in submissions. I have even sent a story, "The Devotee of Evil," to *Illustrated Detective Magazine,* which is said to favor the psychic and the subtle rather than what is usually known as a detective story. But now that postage has gone up, I shan't fool away any great amount of ammunition.

Good luck with the summer's writing. I'm doubling up on quantity myself—there are no female distractions at present!

As ever,
Clark Ashton

1. "The Beast of Averoigne" (*WT,* May 1933; *LW*). CAS heavily edited the story for publication. Among other changes, the Abbot's letter was indeed removed. See *SS* for the text of the rejected version, and Stefan Dziemianowicz's essay "Into the Woods" (*Dark Eidolon* No. 3, Winter 1993) for an insightful discussion of the revisions.

2. "A Star-Change" (*Wonder Stories*, May 1933, as "The Visitors from Mlok"; *GL*).

3. "The Disinterment of Venus" (*WT*, July 1934; *GL*).

———————————◆———————————

[145]   To Genevieve K. Sully [ALS, private collection]

Monday morning
July 18th, 1932

Dear Genevieve:

I am starting the day with this missive, and trust that you approve of my method of matutinal procedure.

Your latest was delightful reading: and of course I stand properly rebuked for the former. However, I had always been reminded of the fashion of referring mysteriously to people by their initials in old Gothic novels. So my intentions, at least, were not those of modern haste and vulgarity.

Re the electrical storm: I must have forgotten to mention that there were a few flashes the other evening, far away in the northwest—also a few spattering drops of rain that pitted the dust. It did not amount to much, as far as this part of the country was concerned. Yesterday, after threatening to become rather torrid, turned cloudy and cool; and the same regime is in effect today, with the addition of a brisk breeze from the south-west.

As to the garden: I consider the care of it a privilege, and always find refreshment in its multifarious growing beauties. Together with the wealth of endearing memories about the place, what more could one ask?

Sphinx Creek and Roaring River are magnificent names, and I shall be eager to hear Marion's reports. The very names carry the idea of something wild, mysterious, remote, tremendous.

I fear education can do nothing for the multitude, the net result is to turn simple ignorance into addled mediocrity. I suppose the vicious results would be especially magnified and glaring in an art so delicate and complex as music.

It has become so chilly as I write, that I have had to drape a blanket over my shoulders—July in Auburn!

Here is a letter that came in the mail with your last. You might return it some time. I don't feel equal to answering it as present. The ideation in it seems to be rather "steep," and I wonder how much meaning is in some of the philosophic jargon. Hawkins, too, seems to be confusing the issue a little. In my letter in *Wonder Stories*,[1] I merely argued that it was more salutary and diverting to turn the imagination *outward* to use it perpetually in contemplating people's gizzards, like the modern novelists. But in speaking of the effects of such imaginative adventuring, Hawkins seems to get off on the actual results of a bodily precipitation into the outward universe: which is a horse of another color entirely. It's an interesting letter, however, and I like what he says about science.

I haven't gone on with *Under the Greenwood Tree* yet, but have read the major portion of *The Woodlanders*,[2] and will probably finish it to-night. The tale is marvellous in its consummate simplicity, and the *understanding,* the all-inclusive implications of chapter such as the one where Grace and Mrs. Charmond get lost in the wood, really made me gasp. And the arboreal setting pervades and shadows the tale with an indescribable charm.

As to "contacts"—I haven't made any that would sweep me off my feet. The fetish of "importance" in such matters is quite funny. Amusingly enough, my recent *recontres*—or encounters—have been mostly with foreigners. Laforge's guests, Prof. Morandini and Madame Dubois and daughter Suzanne, were here a few days ago. Morandini wanted to type a line to a magazine editor on my "machine," and since neither he nor Mlle. Suzanne seemed to be familiar with the idiosyncrasies of a Remington, I ended by writing it for him myself from dictation. The Dubois, both *mere et fille,* may be summed up for your pictorial imagination by saying that they are substantial testimonials to French cooking.

The other foreigners were Miss Trent's Danish friends, the Uldahls, who seem to be rather nice. They are young—about 25—and the young man has been sent out by the American Consulate of Learned Society (or some such name) to collect information about the language and folklore of the California Indians. He told me some rather interesting things about their beliefs. He and his wife are no doubt significant examples of the post-war generation in Europe: quiet, intelligent, but terribly sad and disillusioned.

This seems to be something of an "extra" for me—and I hope it isn't too tedious.

As to your father, I am sure that his idea about happiness is what might be termed a "notion," and would not materialize if put to the test. He would be happy only if there is a household that he could rule with a fist of iron. At least, that is my surmise.

I hope for some news of Marion in your next.

Affectionately,
Clark

1. CAS had a letter in "The Reader Speaks" department of *Wonder Stories* for August 1932, collected in *PD* under the title "On Garbage-Mongering."
2. Thomas Hardy, *Under the Greenwood Tree* (1872); *The Woodlanders* (1887)

[146]   To Genevieve K. Sully [ALS, private collection]

Saturday morning
July 23rd, 1932

Dear Genevieve:

[. . .] That Beethoven quartet must have been tremendous—I like your description of it—and of the effect. The sensation you describe must have been unique; but I see no reason why nervous and emotional reactions should be standardized. Why shouldn't one experience a few—or a good many—individual phenomena? [. . .]

I don't quite know what I will write next, though many tales have been more or less fully plotted. The idea of a super-scientific satire, farcical but devastating, has been buzzing in my head. It would be called, I think, "The Third Hemisphere," and would deal with a fourth-dimensional extension of the globe—an unknown limbo into which, around the year 1950, atavistic undesirables, such as poets who wrote in rhyme and meter, and musicians who employed harmony, were banished by means of a super-electric projector! This world, however, had a population of its own—and here the satire would come in, in the ghastly reproduction of terrene conditions. For instance, the people went hurtling around externally in private projectiles, killing and maiming their fellows with the carnage taken for granted. The place was a bedlam of evil noises, and advertising was even carried so far that the belles of the region, for a consideration, would permit ads to be tattooed on their epidermis; the rate, of course, being graduated to the individual degree of S.A. The earth-heroes, projected into this revolting milieu with its ghastly and insufferable parallelism, invented a space-ship in which to escape to other planets of the fourth-dimensional universe. There they got in to another but more original mess.

Adieu for the present—will write again shortly. Much love—
Yr. faithful & obedient servt,
Park [sic] Smith, Esquire

———————— ◆ ————————

[147]   To Genevieve K. Sully [ALS, private collection]

Aug. 5th, 1932

Dear Genevieve:

[. . .] I must say that I disapprove most strenuously, cordially, and emphatically of that ungodly idea of your remaining in

Berkeley. Separations are n.g., to put the matter in its feeblest terms. As to Marion's angle, it seems to me that the question of college or no college is for her to decide—and I have an idea that the academic prospect doesn't appeal. Why break up a happy foursome—not to mention the *twosome,* and Marion? I never heard of anything so heinously impractical; and as for myself, I can only testify to the abominable desolation of having you at such a cruel distance, for any length of time. The past month, and the present, are bad enough and entirely too long for my liking. So you see that any advice I can offer is likely to take the form of special and perhaps sophistical pleading! [. . .]

Where do you get those ideas about my predilection for the abstract? It seems to me that I have a notable preference for things that can be rendered in terms of the five senses—and I always think of the "abstract" as being that which cannot be rendered in such imagery. But perhaps you have a different definition of it! The letter that I got from Mr. Hawkins treats of abstractions, I should say; and I must confess that I haven't much of a head for such things. (The letter is still unanswered.)

More meteors last night—perfectly gorgeous ones, which should have punctuated a philosophical conversation between us twain, rather than the voidness of the air. A beautiful meteor would emphasize the point that one was making, would it not? And would afford a sufficiently brilliant illumination for things not meant to endure the garish glare of day. Well, I hope there will be some suitable evenings for astronomical study when you return. I'd like to be out by the reservoir—or under the magnolia with you to-night—and can at least indulge the luxury of picturing to myself what it would be like, with the young crescent passing early from the sky, and leaving the great arch of the galaxy and all the stars above us in a balmy heaven. Does the picture appeal to thee, by any chance?

Those quotations from "The Lake" are beautiful indeed—the first one a perfect picture of the feverish desolation of a hopeless longing. I like, too, the imagery about the lake that every man must cross.

The Blackwood book, *Incredible Adventures,* turned out to be uneven, as far as my taste is concerned. Two of the stories, "A Descent into Egypt" and "The Damned," I liked very well; the others I did not care so much for, chiefly, perhaps, because of the heavy moralistic streak. One of these was about a listless youth who became a regular demon of energy after taking part in certain primitive rites of fire-worship. He applied the energy to British politics, and became a worthy son of his imperialistic father—which seemed a peculiarly flat and unpicturesque manner of wasting such primordial force. If he had to go to the devil, he might at least have done so in a way that would have made a good story. The very title—"The Regeneration of Lord Ernie"—set my teeth on edge to start with. But the book is worth having for the Egyptian tale alone. I believe *John Silence* and *The Listener* will arrive to-day; and I hope they will contain more of A. B. at his best rather than his worst.[1] [. . .]

If dreams should descend to you from the horned moon, you can know that I have sent them. Their mission is ineffable and not to be told in anything cruder or less subtle than the interlinear hieroglyphics of Isis or the unwritten cuneiform characters of Ishtar . . . Selah!

Lovingly,
Clark

1. Algernon Blackwood (1869–1951), British fantasist, author of *The Listener and Other Stories* (1907), *John Silence—Physician Extraordinary* (1908), and *Incredible Adventures* (1914) .

---

[148]   To August Derleth [TLS, SHSW]   Aug. 11th, 1932.

Dear August:

Your energy and prolificality are enough to floor *me!* 50,000 words in three weeks would be unimaginable, at my rate of production. I average about 150,000 per year, which is no great amount for a "pulp" writer. The only compensation for my slowness is that most of it sells, somewhere or sometime. Out of the twenty yarns that I wrote in 1931, only three now remain on my hands. [. . .]

I've been pottering away at science fiction, and don't expect to do anything else before Sept. Lovecraft and James E. [*sic*] Morton have recently suggested that I might devise an ending for Beckford's unfinished "Third Episode of Vathek," and get Wright to publish the composite whole. It sounds promising; and if I can get hold of the *Episodes* (which I have yet to read) I may try it. A fourth and even a fifth Episode might be cooked up also; since, if I remember rightly, there were five princes in the Halls of Eblis who had started to tell Vathek the particulars of how they went to hell; and whose tales were to form these Episodes.[1]

Am I wrong in imagining that there has been an unusual amount of crap in the last two or three issues of *W. T.?* It looks as if a special bid for the morons were being made, with so many mediocre and uninspired rehashings of stock plots and superstitions. I agree with you, though, that "The Eye of Truth" wasn't so bad. Eadie is quite respectable and capable, and would be even noteworthy with a little more fire and originality and daring. As to "The Death Mist," I guess the idea is one of the first that would occur to a dabbler in the weird.[2] I thought of it many years ago, before I began to write weird stories; but dismissed it as being too trite long before I started to do any serious work.

Wright has not yet reported on my last stories. I hope he won't pass up "The Isle of the Torturers."[3]

Speaking of books, I have recently acquired several bargains— Machen's *The Secret Glory,* and Blackwood's *Incredible Adventures, John Silence,* and *The Listener.*[4] The first I got for 15¢, the other three at 50¢ apiece. All were in prime condition. I doubt if books will ever be any cheaper than they are now.

Good wishes for your various *oeuvres.*

As ever,
Clark Ashton

That's fine news, about Machen receiving a pension.[5] British Govt. does have its lucid intervals. Too bad the U.S.A. never does.

1. HPL had lent CAS his copy of *The Episodes of Vathek* by William Beckford (1759–1844), trans. Sir Frank T. Marzials (Boston: Small, Maynard & Co., 1922). RHB published CAS's "Third Episode of Vathek" in *Leaves* (Summer 1937, as "The Story of the Princess Zulkais and the Prince Kalilah"; AY).
2. Arlton Eadie, "The Eye of Truth"; Capt. George H. Daugherty, Jr., "The Death Mist" (*WT,* September 1932).
3. "The Isle of the Torturers" (*WT,* March 1933; *LW* and *RA*).
4. Arthur Machen, *The Secret Glory* (1922).
5. Machen received a Civil List pension of £100 a year.

[149]   To Genevieve K. Sully [ALS, private collection]
Friday morning—
Aug. 12th, 1932
Dear Genevieve:
[. . .] I got up at three a.m. to-day, when the Perseids were supposed to appear in force, but failed to see anything very spectacular. They came singly, about one per minute, many of them very faint and remote. The watching was cold, lonely work, so I went back to bed very prosaically after counting about fifteen. But with a nice, comfortable hay-stack, and blankets—à deux, of course, *m'amie,*—I'd have been happy to stay out and count any number. No doubt I missed the real display. [. . .]

Do you think of our nights by the Foubay? That glimmering, star-reddened cirque of hill-tops, with you at my side and the dark, magical waters not far away often returns to haunt my reveries with its warm and summer-fragrant enchantments. How incommunicable and ineffable—except to one who shared the memory—the perfume and *nuance* of such things would be. And how clearly it all comes back to me, with a sense of wizard isolation, of lofty, eternal *separateness* from the dark and muddled stream of time.

The stars were wonderful last night, even if the Perseids failed to perform very brilliantly during my brief vigil. Orion was shouldering his way above the hill, and Venus was enormous—a great splash of pale and liquid gold on the Egyptian blue of the heavens.

I hope all this is not too prosaic, mathematical, commercial, clerical, chronological, and non-Parnassian. In other words, I trust you can find a little gold in the rifts—or in the riffles.

Affectionately,
Clark

———————————◆———————————

[150]   To Lester Anderson [ALS, private collection]
Sept. 1st, 1932
Dear Lester Anderson:

[. . .] Thanks for the tip about Dorsey's book on Civilization.[1] I'll look it up when I have the leisure for some "serious" reading. Summers,[2] I gather, *does* believe in the supernatural, the demoniac, etc. Probably he, in his turn, would be somewhat amused at the materialistic dogmatism of Dorsey. No, I haven't read *Why We Behave Like Human Beings*.[3] I have conceived a profound distrust of modern psychology, and think that if human beings ever really learn anything about themselves, it will not be through direct introspection, but through the healthier and sounder channels of an extroversion, mental and imaginative as well as physical. This may enable them to get a glimpse of the *real* forces and motives beneath the apparent, instead of being, like the modern psychologists, spiders caught in their own fantastic webs—or kittens balled up in twine. [. . .]

Clark Ashton Smith

1. George A. Dorsey (1868–1931), *Man's Own Show: Civilization* (New York: Harper, 1931).
2. Montague Summers (1880–1948), British editor, ecclessiastic, and occult scholar.
3. Dorsey, *Why We Behave Like Human Beings* (New York: Chautauqua, 1926).

[151]   To August Derleth [TLS, SHSW]   Sept. 11th, 1932.

Dear August:

No, my check for the "Empire"[1] has not arrived, and I had concluded from this that it would probably be delayed for another month. Too bad that W.T. has to slow up on payments when all the other magazines of fantasy are in arrears. I understand that the Clayton checks aren't coming on the dot with publication either. As to W.T., I suspect that Wright's readers aren't as dumb as he seems to think them, and therefore the sale may have fallen off a little with the late punk issues. I agree with you that the Oct. number is one of the worst. I told Wright in a letter yesterday that the stories in it were disappointing, and commented expressly on the Quinn yarn as being a mere detective story rather than a weird.[2] I might have said quite a mouthful about some of the other tales, but refrained. If there are many more issues like this, I shall indulge in some rather frank criticism. Either Wright's judgement is growing altogether stale and undependable, or else he is making an express bid for the patronage of Moronia. You pays your money and you takes your choice as to which is what. Maybe it's both.

I too had a card from H.P., and am glad that he could make the Canadian trip.[3] Wish I could get away, somewhere, somehow. But for various and sundry reasons, I am pretty well tethered at present. Also there's the money problem: with all the stuff that I have sold, payment has come in lately with painful slowness. There must be a thousand dollars overdue, counting the stuff that Bates holds. I had been planning to build on a much needed workroom and store-room to our shack, but am hesitating now to lay out the money. I hope you can come to satisfactory terms with Wright. Under the circumstances, he ought to loosen up the small sums that are due.

Nothing very sensational to relate. Wonder Stories has announced a short tale of mine, "The God of the Asteroid," for their Oct. issue, to precede "The Dimension of Chance" in Nov. Wright, I believe, is running a filler of mine, "The Supernumerary Corpse," in Nov. Bates has not yet returned "The Ice-Demon," and Wright has not reported on "The Eidolon of the Blind." I have how sent him "The Maze of Mool Dweb," which is ultra-fantastic, full-hued and ingenious, with an extra twist or two in the tail for luck.[4] Probably, however, he will think the style too involved for the semi-illiterates to whom he is catering.

H.P. has loaned me The Episodes of Vathek. The unfinished one is particularly good, and certainly merits an ending. I hope I can do something that won't fall too far short. The development that Beckford had intended is obvious enough. I don't feel at all sure, though, that Wright will be receptive: the length of the tale will militate against it—also, perhaps, the slight hint of perversity in the affection of Zulkais and Kalilah.

> Happy landings!
> As ever,
> Clark Ashton

1. "The Empire of the Necromancers" (*WT*, September 1932; *LW* and *RA*).
2. Seabury Quinn, "The Heart of Siva" (*WT*, October 1932).
3. HPL's second visit to Quebec.
4. "The Master of the Asteroid" (*Wonder Stories*, October 1932 [originally "The God of the Asteroid"]; *TSS* and *RA*); "The Dimension of Chance" (*Wonder Stories*, November 1932; *OD*); "The Supernumerary Corpse" (*WT*, November 1932; *OD*); "The Ice-Demon" (*WT*, April 1933; *AY*); "The Dweller in the Gulf" (*Wonder Stories*, March 1933, as "Dweller in Martian Depths" [originally "The Eidolon of the Blind"]; *AY* and *RA*); "The Maze of Maal Dweb" (*DS*, as "The Maze of the Enchanter"; *LW* and *RA*).

---

[152]   To H. P. Lovecraft [ALS, JHL]   [c. 15 September 1932]
> Written in the treasury of Omoultakos, by the
illumination shed from the eternally burning Tail of the Baboon.

Dear Éch-Pi-El:

As a result of your instigation I have striven, with all due necromantic rites, and the burning of Arabian gums in censers well greened with verdigris, to invoke the spirit of William Beckford. Our ghostly collaboration has eventuated in the continuation and conclusion of Zulkais and Kalilah enclosed herewith. It is, of course, tentative, and may require sundry revisions ere the aforementioned revenant will fully approve it. In the meanwhile, I should greatly appreciate your opinion, before submitting the composite whole to Tyrant Pharnabeezer.[1] My feeling is, that the arbiter of *W.T.* will find it too poisonous, perverse, fantastickal, et al., for his select circle of Babbitts and Polyannas. He has, by the way, returned "The Eidolon of the Blind," with the plea that it was too terrible and horrific, and would be sure "to sicken" many of his readers. Accustomed though I am to W. and his little whimsies, the decision really amazes me.

You will note that my continuation of Z. & K. starts with the last sentence on the first page (44) of the carbon I am sending you—which is an extra one, made for you to keep. I hope it won't disappoint you too much. Anyway, I enjoyed writing it.

    Yours, in the service of the Lord of
      the fiery globe and the shadow caverns
        Klarkash-Ton

1. This and similar epithets, based on HPL's "Satrap Pharnabazus," all refer to FW.

---

[153]   To August Derleth [TLS, SHSW]   Sept. 20th, 1932.

Dear August:

    I enjoyed your epistle to Tyrant Pharnabeezer, which I am returning herewith. I agree with it in toto. His nibs has just rejected my "The Eidolon of the Blind" on the plea that it was too horrific for his select circle of Babbits and Polyannas, and "The Maze of Mool Dweb" because it was too poetic and finely phrased. These rejections of two of my best tales, combined with the cheapness of the recent issues, make me feel that the chances for fine literature in that direction are growing decidedly slimmer. [. . .]

    Here is the carbon of "Mool Dweb," which you can send along to H.P.L. at leisure. I enclose Pharnabosco's letter with it. This can also go to H.P., but I want it back some time, with the idea of framing it in good old-fashioned gilt. I am now sending "Mool Dweb," with some minor verbal substitutions, such as throats for gorges, intrepid for temerarious, etc, to *Argosy*, though I fear it is like offering yellow rubies to people who want only plain yellow corn. Bates might like it, if he had room; but I am sending him "The Eidolon of the Blind," which he ought to like even better. This tale has a magnificent Dantesque ending, where three earthmen, trying to escape from a terrible lightless gulf under the surface of Mars, are overtaken by an eyeless creature from the depths that proceeds to extract their eyes with the suction-cups of its proboscdides [*sic*], and then herd them back on "their second descent of the road that went down forever to a night-bound Avernus." The tale is a first rate interplanetary horror, sans the hokum of pseudo-explanation.

    I had a lot of fun finishing Beckford's "Third Episode," to which I have added about four thousand words. I have sent Zulkais and Kalilah on their hellward way with much arabesque pomp and ironic circumstance, but am waiting for H.P.'s opinion before I send the composite whole to the arbiter of *W.T.* It will certainly be an agreeable surprise if he accepts it. Whatever the merit or demerit of my ending, Beckford's part of the tale is absolutely fascinating. It set me to re-reading *Vathek* with new appreciation. This tale suits me to a t.

Here's hoping your luck will be better than mine has been lately.

Yours for the opening of the subterranean palace of Eblis,
Clark Ashton

---

[154]   To August Derleth [TLS, SHSW]   Sept. 28th, 1932.

Dear August:

I hope earnestly that the depression will lighten for you ere long. Luck—either good or bad—seems to run in cycles; so there is always the hope that the bad kind will exhaust itself, if one holds on. But it really is a cardinal shame that editors are such a time-serving lot. I wish to Hades that some millionaire would endow a magazine for weird and arabesque literature, and have it edited regardless of anything but a genuine standard of literary merit. I have a notion that the results might be surprising—though I don't think it would ever rival the *Post,* or even the he-male adventure magazines, in circulation. Of course, I may be all wet. On the other hand, an anxiety to please the plebs, and offend as few as possible—such as Pharnabizzes is showing—can result in nothing but crap and mediocrity. I certainly think he could afford to run a few high-class tales, if only to keep up any literary reputation that the mag may have acquired. Connoisseurs, I feel morally certain, arc not going to exult over the recent avalanche of tripe.

I haven't heard anything lately, beyond a return of "The Ice-Demon," which Clayton vetoed. Funny—the old rhino seems to be horning in and reading the weird items before Bates gets a chance at them himself. His ideas of the disgusting must indeed be peculiar. I'd certainly like to see your tale, "Death Holds the Post,"[1] if you feel like shipping me the carbon some time. I can't figure out why so much of my stuff has gotten by with C. Bates wrote "that in some mysterious manner, both 'The Double Shadow' and 'The Colossus of Ylourgne'[2] have passed successfully through Mr. Clayton's critical craw. I expect to buy both!" Well—I can only thank Allah and Eblis for my luck. If, by some fluke, he also takes "The Eidolon of the Blind," I'll offer the blood of a gamecock to Demogorgon himself. [. . .]

I have done another tale since writing you, to round out my third year of professional fictioneering. The story, "Genius Loci," is rather an experiment for me—and I hardly know what to do with it.[3] The idea is that of a landscape with an evil and vampiric personality, which both terrifies and allures people and finally "gets" them in some intangible, mysterious way. An old rustic, who owned the place, is found dead there, apparently of heart-failure. Years later, a landscape painter senses the quality of the place, starts doing pictures of it, and undergoes a repellent change of temperament under the influence. His host, who tells the story, calls in the painter's fiancée to counteract this influence, but the girl is too weak, too much under the domination of her lover, to help. Finally, one night, the narrator finds the pair lying drowned in a swimming pool that is part of the evil meadow-bottom. The indications are, that the artist has committed suicide, and has dragged the girl with him against her will. Coincidentally with this shocking discovery, the narrator sees a strange emanation that surrounds all the features of the place like a sort of mist, forming a phantom and "hungrily wavering" projection of the whole vampirish scene. From certain curdlings in this restless, ghostly exhalation, the faces of the old man,—the first victim—and of the newly dead painter and girl—emerge as if "spewed forth by that lethal deadfall," and are decomposed and reabsorbed. There is a hint in the tale that the painter had previously been very much frightened by something that came out of the place at night; and the presence of the old man, as an elusive figure of the scene, was also suggested. At the end, there is a hint that the narrator may eventually make a fourth victim. It was all damnably hard to do, and I am not certain of my success. I am even less certain of being able to sell it to any editor— it will be too subtle for the pulps, and the highbrows won't like the supernatural element. Oh, hell. . . .

Good luck. We'll have to try a little invultuation on some of these editors.

As ever,
Clark Ashton

I'm glad that the Mool Dweb fantasy was enjoyable. I shall make a few minor changes, when *Argosy* returns it. "The Enchanter's Maze" would be a better title, I feel. Also, the wizard's name isn't so good. Māal Dweb—two syllables,—would be preferable, perhaps, for tone-color, etc. The few rare (?) words, with the exception of *valence, Termini,* and possibly one or two others, can be replaced with less exotic terms without an actual sacrifice of meaning. But beyond this, I won't touch the story for anyone, if I never sell it.

1. AWD and Mark Schorer, "Death Holds the Post" (*WT*, August–September 1936).

2. "The Colossus of Ylourgne" (*WT*, June 1934; *GL* and *RA*).

3. "Genius Loci" (*WT*, June 1932; *GL* and *RA*).

------------•------------

[155]   To Lester Anderson [ALS, private collection]
                                                Oct. 6th, 1932
Dear Lester Anderson:

[. . .] I am sending you a recent story herewith. You can keep it. The ms. became so overcrawled with alterations that I had to make a clean copy to send out. But maybe the variant readings will interest you. Wright objected to the "unfamiliar" exotic diction of the tale, so I tried to eliminate almost everything that might bother a fifth-grade grammar student. My sole reason for using words not usually employed by "pulp" writers have been to achieve precision, variety and richness. The words are never plugged in for their own sake, but simply because they expressed a fine shade of meaning or gave the tone-color that I wanted. I am forced to infer, though, that all this is lost on the average reader. And yet the A. R., formally speaking, has probably received more education than I have had. [. . .]

           As ever,
           Clark Ashton Smith

------------•------------

[156]   To August Derleth [TLS, SHSW]   Oct. 8th, 1932.
Dear August:

I am glad that Wright took "The Carven Image," and shall look forward to seeing it in print. His ideas of deadwood must be peculiar, considering the amount of it that he admits to the magazine. In the current issue, Howard's "Worms of the Earth" seems to be the one real first-rater.[1]

I sent W. the story I outlined to you, "Genius Loci," and was agreeably surprised to have him accept it almost by return mail. He has also taken "A Vintage from Atlantis," following my third revision of the ending.[2] He has not yet reported on "The Third Episode"; and if it comes back, I shall loan you presently the carbon of my continuation. The postage rates are a holy terror, and I have never been able to see why one should have to pay first-class rates on typescripts. "The Third Episode" cost me thirty-six cents each way. I think that in mailing any quantity of carbons around to friends, it is a great saving to ship by express, where the first-class nonsense doesn't apply. If I remember right, it doesn't cost any more than printed matter.

Now for the bad news—which you may have heard already. Close on the heels of his acceptance of "The Double Shadow" and "The Colossus," Bates writes me that Clayton has instructed him to discontinue *Strange Tales*. A tough break! I didn't quite understand whether there would be one more issue or two, but Bates said that my "The Second Interment" would appear in the last number to go out to the stands. He said nothing about "The Seed from the Sepulcher," which he has not returned to me with the last two accepted stories. I am now offering "The Colossus" to Wright, but shall hold "The Double Shadow" awhile before re-submitting it to him. The failure of *S.T.* certainly sends my financial prospects glimmering. Also, it leaves Wright the monarch of all he surveys, as far as weird fiction is concerned. It's bad all around.

The Ape, the Idiot and Other People is a fine book, and I congratulate you on obtaining a copy of it. Morrow was a sort of pupil of Ambrose Bierce; and the tales, if I remember rightly, are not unworthy of Bierce.

There was no hurry at all about sending "The Maze" to H.P. I have renamed, revised and retyped the tale, anyway, and have made a clean carbon, so I don't really need that copy. Of course, you can take your time with "The Episode," too, and loan it to Schorer. But if the tale sells, probably you would rather wait and see it all in print. I really think the ending is one of the best pieces of work I have done lately.

I'll be very glad to see your tales when you get around to shipping them. If I am not mistaken, you will find it far cheaper to send them by express.

Good luck to you—and a dash of vitriol in the face of Old Man Depression.

As ever,
Clark Ashton

1. AWD and Mark Schorer, "The Carven Image" (*WT*, May 1933); Robert E. Howard, "Worms of the Earth" (*WT*, November 1933).
2. "A Vintage from Atlantis" (*WT*, September 1933; *AY*).

[157]   To Donald Wandrei [TLS, MHS]   Nov. 10th, 1932.

Dear Donald:

It is not at all surprising that you find seclusion favorable to work. All other things being equal, concentration is far more easily achieved and maintained if there are no interruptions. I know how easily the chain is broken in my case. I am glad to hear that you have succeeded in finishing so much new work, and hope sincerely that a moiety of it can be placed to advantage. Your "Alfred Kramer" certainly held its place in the last *W.T.*

Thanks for your favorable opinion of "The Last Interment." I doubt if much more could have been done with the subject, and feel that the method employed was the only feasible one. The tale was written to order, as I may have told you, and it is almost the only instance where I have done anything good under such conditions.[1]

The failure of *S.T.* sent much of my prospective income glimmering, since Bates had three tales of mine on hand for use, with prices totaling five hundred dollars, and would probably have accepted some new stuff shortly. I have resold one of the unutilized tales, "The Colossus of Ylourgne," to Wright at $150.00, but cannot persuade him that "The Double Shadow," my best weird, would appeal substantially to his readers. He has, however, accepted a fair amount of stuff lately: "A Vintage from Atlantis," "The Ice-Demon," and "Genius Loci," in addition to the medieval novelette above mentioned. He is also holding my continuation of Beckford's unfinished "Third Episode of Vathek" (written at Lovecraft's suggestion) and may print the whole yarn as a sort of necromantic collaboration. I hope so at any rate.

I have recently had my first acceptance from *Amazing Stories*— "The Plutonian Drug." Unluckily, they are overstocked, and won't be able to print it for quite a while. As to *Wonder Stories*, I am somewhat in a quandary. I can recommend the mag. for ultra-prompt publication of material; but they seem to make up for it on the payment end. They have, so far, paid for seven of my stories at ¾ of a cent per word, but are in arrears on the last five or six, and protest their inability to pay at present together with their anxiety to do so. I don't know whether to gamble any more stuff on them or not, since I more than suspect that they are capable of sharp dealing. My worst apprehension is that old Hugo may pull another bankruptcy stunt, as he did with *Amazing Stories* several years back. Undoubtedly the magazine—*Wonder Stories*—is having a hard time just at present. Their treatment of Belknap is pretty raw,

I'd say. The chief reason that I've had anything to do with with them is, that Gernsback has had the perspicacity to print some of my more out-of-the-way stuff which no one else would touch. And I have had, after all, about five hundred bucks out of the old high-binder.

I, too, can't remember just how you came to hear of *Ebony and Crystal* and write me for a copy. But your first letter is somewhere in the depths of my gargantuan litter of papers and epistles; and if I come across it some day, I'll let you know.

As ever,
Clark

P.S. I haven't any plans except work, work and more work. The financial crimps outlined in my letter have to [be] straightened out if possible, or as much as possible. I am trying to do some stuff for *Astounding,* but find the adventure twist peculiarly difficult and unsympathetic.

C.

1. I.e., "The Second Interment." Editor Harry Bates wrote CAS on 22 January 1932 (ms., JHL) "Mr. Clayton recently suggested to me that he would like to see a story recounting the horror a man might feel at being buried alive. His sensations, all the awful things—the states of mind—he would go through. He might prolong his agony by shallow breathing à la Houdini. It would add to the horror of things if he had for years been afraid of being buried alive, and had an obsession that he would. [. . .] Perhaps he has had one unfortunate experience from which he was rescued in time, which would give far more point and tension to a repetition of it for a climax."

---

[158]   To August Derleth [TLS, SHSW]   Nov. 24th, 1932.

Dear August:

A.S. was not my favorite magazine, but I am certainly sorry that it has gone up the flume. The policy of the magazine was taking a slight turn for the better, and away from the usual Clayton melodrama.

The financial angle is certainly a problem these days. I'm sorry to hear that things are no better for you, and hope that Underworld will come through with a check for some of the tales that you are submitting. Congratulations on the new honorary sales, and the starring in O'Brien's anthology. All that should help—and you never know when the "break" will come. It looks to me as if you had a good foothold on the literary ladder.

Clark Ashton Smith, bottom row right, at Long Valley School, 1903.

Earliest Known Photo

Clark Ashton Smith (age 16) with parents, Timeus Smith and Fannie Smith.

1899 Photo Courtesy by Terence A. McVicker

George Sterling (far left) with an ill-at-ease
Clark Ashton Smith (second from left) at a
garden party in Carmel, California.

*Photo Courtesy of the Bancroft Library,
University of California, Berkeley.*

George Sterling from the November 1927
issue of *Overland Monthly*.

Samuel Loveman, October 1935.

**Albert N. Bender, businessman.
Patron of Clark Ashton Smith.**

Donald Wandrei, 1928, at his graduation from University of Minnesota.

H.P. Lovecraft and Frank Belknap Long,
in Brooklyn early 1930s.

August Derleth, early 1940s

Photo by Harold Gauer

Clark Ashton Smith with Genevieve K. Sully, November 11, 1941

Clark Ashton Smith on picnic with
Helen Sully (left) and Marian Sully (center)
at Boulder Ridge, California, Spring 1938.

Clark Ashton Smith and Carol Dorman honeymoon at the Smith cabin in 1954.

Since finishing "The Charnel God," I have done nothing but retype and re-revise unsold stuff.[1] "The Seed from the Sepulchre," reduced to 4500 words, has gone back to Wright, together with "The Beast of Averoigne," also reduced and with a new twist to the climax, and the similarly treated "The White Sybil."[2] Now I am trying to fix up "The Dweller in the Gulf" (formerly "The Eidolon of the Blind") for *Wonder Stories*. The alterations involve the introduction of a new character, who is in a position to offer some kind of semi-scientific explanation of the phenomena in the story. I shan't change the climax to any extent. And the general atmosphere of mystery and horror is not markedly affected.[3] [. . .]

H.P.L. tells me that my yarn, "The Gorgon," got mentioned in the O. Henry Memorial volume.[4] Personally, I think it's a long way from being my best. But there you are. Judges, editors, critics, all of them are more or less bughouse. And I suppose that any kind of a weird tale is lucky to receive official mention in an age tyrannized over by realism.

Have you ever read *The Worm Ouroboros,* by E.R. Eddison?[5] It is listed at 79¢ in a catalogue that I have, and I am tempted to invest, though I have had to cut out book-buying for reasons of economy.

> Good luck!
> As ever,
> Clark Ashton

1. "The Charnel God" (*WT,* March 1934; *GL* and *RA*).
2. CAS and David H. Keller, *The White Sybil* [CAS] and *Men of Avalon* [Keller] (Everett, PA: Fantasy Publications, 1934); *AY.*
3. See *The Dweller in the Gulf* (West Warwick, RI: Necronomicon Press, 1987) for CAS's original text.
4. *O'Henry Memorial Award Prize Stories of 1932,* ed. Blanche Colton Williams (New York: Doubleday, 1932), gave CAS third ranking for "The Venus of Azombeii" and "The Gorgon."
5. E. R. Eddison (1882–1945), *The Worm Ouroboros: A Romance* (New York: A. & C. Boni, 1926).

---

[159]   To August Derleth [TLS, SHSW]   Dec. 24th, 1932.

Dear August:

Thanks for your article on "The Cult of Incoherence,"[1] which touches off the subject very neatly and competently. To me, the tenets of the stream-of-consciousness school have always seemed the absolute negation of art. One can't have even the rudiments of art without selection and coherent order of some kind. The amazing thing is, that people can be found to swallow such ballyrot as Stein and Joyce and Cummings have perpetrated. Abysmal, indeed, are the sinks of human folly and gullibility.

I am sorry to hear of Wright's continued ill health. Damn it all, he deserves a better fate. I agree with you that the line-up for the Feb. W.T. is promising, and I hope that "The Chadbourne Episode" will not be the last of Whitehead's tales to appear.[2] H.P. says that he had written a series centering about the town of Chadbourne.

Wright shouldn't go wrong on "The Shadow Over Innsmouth." And the acceptance of the tale should help Lovecraft's morale.[3] I note, by the way, a story in the Oct. *Wonder Stories* (which featured my "God of the Asteroid") which I am willing to gamble was revised and partly "ghost-written" by H.P. The tale was called "The Man of Stone," and was signed by one Hazel Heald.[4] It contains reference to Tsathoggua, the *Book of Eibon,* The Goat with a Thousand Young, etc.

I haven't tried to do anything yet about my projected pamphlet of stories, which, of course, may not materialize at all.[5] My idea is to put out something that could be sold at about 50¢. Of course, you shall have some copies if the book is ever actually printed. Thanks.

I have finished "The Dark Eidolon," which ran upwards of 10,000 words, and have shipped it to Wright.[6] It's a devil of a story, and if Wright knows his mandrakes, he certainly ought to take it on. If the thing could ever be filmed—and no doubt it could with a lot of trick photography—it might be a winner for diabolic drama and splendid infernal spectacles. There is one scene where a wizard calls up macrocosmic monsters in the form of stallions that trample houses and cities under their hooves like eggshells. The tale ends with the wizard gone stark mad and fighting his own image in a diamond mirror under the delusion that the image was the enemy on whom he had sought to inflict all manner of hellish revenges. A girl, on whose bosom he has trodden in the borrowed body of her own lover united to the legs of a demon horse with white hot-hooves, laughs at him amid her dying agonies, and over all, there is the stormy thunder of the cosmic stallions returning, no longer checked by the wizard's spells, to trample down his own mansion.

The Worm Ouroboros was certainly a grand bargain. I like it better than anything I have read in seven epochs. There isn't much likeness to Cabell,[7] apart from the flavor of archaism. Cabell always gives the impression that he doesn't believe in anything; but

Eddison's book left me with a tremendous impression of imaginative fervor and reality.

As ever, Clark Ashton

1. AWD, "The Case for the Intelligentsia" [I. "The Cult of Incoherence"] (*Midwestern Conference*, April 1931; rpt. *Modern Thinkers and Authors Review*, December 1932, as "The Cult of Incoherence").

2. Henry S. Whitehead, "The Chadbourne Episode" (*WT*, February 1933).

3. HPL refused to submit the story to *WT*, but AWD did so surreptitiously in January 1933. FW rejected the story not on merit but because the story was too large to publish in a single issue of the magazine.

4. Hazel Heald's "The Man of Stone" (*Wonder Stories*, October 1932) was in fact ghostwritten by HPL.

5. This was *The Double Shadow and Other Fantasies*, published at CAS's expense in June 1933, in an edition of 1000 copies, which contained stories that had been uniformly rejected by the magazines.

6. "The Dark Eidolon" (*WT*, January 1935; *OST* and *RA*).

7. James Branch Cabell (1879–1958), critically acclaimed author of anti-realistic novels set in an imaginary medieval kingdom.

---

[160] To August Derleth [TLS, SHSW]   Feb. 1st, 1933.

Dear August:

[. . .] W. finally sent back "The Third Episode of Vathek," saying that he saw no opportunity of using it at present, but might possibly ask me to re-submit it at some future time. Oh, well. . . . He now has "The Voyage of King Euvoran,"[1] which I have suggested that he might consider for the *M.C.* as well as for *W.T.* I've gone on with several unfinished things, and have begun "The Infernal Star," which is to be a weird-interstellar novelette de luxe.[2] The tale involves a harmless bibliophile in a series of wild mysterious happenings, ending in his translation to Yamil Zacra, a star which is the fountain-head of all the evil and bale and sorcery in the universe. It mixes wizardry and necromancy with the latest scientific theory of "radiogens," or atoms of sun-fire, burning at a temperature of 1500 Centigrade in the human body.[3] I am using the innocuousness of the hero's normal personality as a foil to that which he temporarily assumes beneath the influence of an amulet that stimulates those particles in his body which have come from Yamil Zacra.

The current *W.T.* impresses me as being an excellent issue, apart from the banality of the cover. I like the tales by Howard, Eadie and Ernst, especially the former. Quinn's tale was altogether too hackneyed; and I have not read Level's little story.[4] Level, however, is always good. The line-up for the April number is very promising.

Editorial delays are certainly the bunk. *Amazing Stories* holds the long-time record for that sort of thing, among the magazines to which I have submitted material. The regular period of holding seems to be six months. The Gernsback outfit sometimes neglect to report at all, but this invariably means acceptance with them. [. . .]

Here's wishing you the best, as ever,
    Clark Ashton

P.S. There are some irritating misprints in "The Isle of the Torturers." "He *leaped* on the helm" should have been "he *leaned.*" "Freezing," on the last page, should have been *"freeing."*

1. "The Voyage of King Euvoran" (*DS* and *AY*). FW would not accept it for either *WT* or *Magic Carpet,* though the story was later reprinted in *WT* (September 1947, as "Quest of the Gazolba").
2. "The Infernal Star" was never completed; see *SS* for the fragmentary text.
3. In November 1932, Dr. George W. Crile announced the discovery in the protoplasm of cells of "hot points" ranging in temperature up to 6000 degrees. The *New York Times* wrote on 25 November 1932 that "Without exaggeration the concept may be taken to mean . . . that within the very flesh of man burns the fierce fire of the sun, and that within man's body glow infinitely small counterparts of the stars."
4. Robert E. Howard, "The Tower of the Elephant"; Arlton Eadie, "The Devil's Tower"; Paul Ernst, "Akkar's Moth"; Seabury Quinn, "The Thing in the Fog"; and Maurice Level, "The Look" (*WT,* March 1933). The cover was by Margaret Brundage.

---

[161]   To August Derleth [TLS, SHSW]   Feb. 9th, 1933.

Dear August:

I like the conception of "In Far Places," and agree with you that the idea needs a roomier development than is possible in the scope of a short. Thanks for your permission to use the idea. There ought to be some huge possibilities in having a space-ship carried off into some ultra-cosmic Brobdingnag, and I may avail myself of the notion presently. There was something faintly akin to this in my opus, "The Eternal World," where an explorer who had shot himself clean out of the time-space continuum into eternity, was finally returned to Earth through the benignant whim of a macro-cosmic giant, who toted him, time-sphere and all, through gulfs and galaxies.

You are to be congratulated on all your magazine appearances. I think I noticed something in *Ten Story Book,* too, and mean to read it presently.[1] *Bonne fortune* with your various submissions. I am very much interested in "The Return of Hastur,"[2] and hope to see it eventually, whether or not it lands with Wright. W. sent back "King Euvoran," saying he had enjoyed it greatly himself, but feared that it would not have enough plot and suspense for many of his readers. I agree, in a way—it's hardly a magazine story, but is more like a narrative poem in prose. If I print a pamphlet, I may include it for variety. I have an appointment next week with the printer who brought out two of my volumes of verse, and will learn what—if anything—can be done. [. . .]

My triply unfortunate tale, "The Dweller in the Gulf," is printed in the current *Wonder Stories* under the title of "Dweller in Martian Depths," and has been utterly ruined by a crude attempt on the part of someone—presumably the office-boy—to rewrite the ending. Apart from this, paragraph after paragraph of imaginative description and atmosphere has been hewn bodily from the story. I have written to tell the editor what I thought of such Hunnish barbarity, and have also told him that I do not care to have my work printed at all unless it can appear verbatim or have the desired alterations made by my own hand.[3] It shows what fine literature means to the Gernsback crew of hog-butchers. I have clipped out the tale, and am enclosing it with the typescript of the original ending appended, and the interpolated matter crossed out. It would be impossible, for lack of space, to write in the omissions on the margins, so I haven't tried, apart from one or two phrases to give an idea of what they considered objectionable. But I have indicated some of the lacunae with pencil marks. However, I think I'll quote a sample from the part where the men were trying to escape from the gulf: "Looking over the verge at intervals, Bellman saw the gradual fading of the phosphorescence in the depths. Fantastic images rose in his mind: it was like the last glimmering of hell-fire in some extinct inferno; like the drowning of nebulae in voids beneath the universe. He felt the giddiness of one who looks down upon infinite space. . . . Anon there was only blackness; and he knew by this token the awful distance they had climbed." You can send the clipping on to H.P.L. I'm sorry Wright couldn't see the tale. It would certainly have been better than the interplanetary crap he publishes. [. . .]

My new opus, "The Infernal Star," is threatening to assume

serial proportions, since the terrestrial part of the tale has run to 10,000 or 11,000 words in the drafting, and when retyped and polished up, will make an instalment by itself. I have written to query Wright as the length of serial most desirable at present. I understand he is pretty well-stocked. Maybe I'll make a book out of the yarn yet! In the Foreword, the hero, a respectable book-collector, is arrested in *puris naturabilis* by a patrolman while trying to reach his suburban residence at dawn via a main avenue of his home city. He tells the subsequent story to the friend who rescues him from his plight, as an explanation of how he found himself in public in that condition of "Adamic starkness."

My best, as always,
Clark Ashton

1. "Death Is Too Kind" (*Ten Story Book*, February 1933).
2. AWD, "The Return of Hastur" (*WT*, March 1939), a tale employing some of HPL's conceptions, completed only after HPL's death; see letters 209 and 211.
3. As a result of this episode, CAS submitted no further tales to Gernsback's *Wonder Stories*. The closure of this significant market to him contributed to his eventual withdrawal from fiction in the late 1930s.

———————————————————— ◆ ————————————————————

[162]   To H. P. Lovecraft [TLS, JHL]   [1 March 1933]
Vaults of Chaon Gacca—
Hour of the Weaving in the sepulcher of King Tnepreez.

Dear Éch-Pi-El:

I am glad you are going to let Wright use "The Dreams in the Witch House,"[1] and I look forward tremendously to the tale's appearance in print. I wish you would write about a hundred more. It is utterly beyond me why you should be dampened in the least by the criticism of time-serving termites, such as Putnams. Personally (such is my confidence, conceit or what you will) I wouldn't permit a thousand rejections to make me think that my own best tales are anything but first-rate. Contemporary judgement, in 49,999 cases out of 50,000 is almost wholly meaningless. As I told Derleth in a letter to-day, I doubt if any of the popular josses of the present will be heard of at all in fifty years. But I am willing to gamble that you and your work will be known: perhaps not to a very large audience, but certainly to a select and faithful one.

What you tell me (via Bates) about Whitehead's end[2] is very affecting and makes one feel like echoing some of the sentiments about human fate in *The City of Dreadful Night*. I am sorry indeed to hear of his father's condition. . . . "Our life's a cheat, our death a black abyss."[3] But no doubt, Whitehead died in another faith than that—which is just as well.

I think I wrote about my projected pamphlet of tales. It looks as if there are going to be the usual delays with the *Auburn Journal* crowd, who are slower than government mules. But I guess it will be ready before next Yulemas.

I am doing some more short tales at present—"The Weaver in the Vault" and "The Flower-Women."[4] "The Infernal Star" will have to wait, since there is no prospect of landing it as a serial even if completed. Wright is so heavily loaded down with long tales (all of them tripe, I dare say) that he can't even consider anything over 15,000 words till next year.

You can keep "The Dweller in the Gulf." I have had a letter of apology from David Lasser, managing editor of *W.S.*, saying that he made the alterations only at Gernsback's express order. Gernsback must be loco to have a story spoiled in that fashion. I judge that the idiotic revision has cooked it with readers who might have liked it otherwise. Oh, phooey . . . . . .

The Book of Dzyan[5] is new to me—I haven't read any great amount of theosophical literature. I'll be vastly interested in any dope you or Price can pass on to me. Theosophy, as far as I can gather, is a version of esoteric Yoga prepared for western consumption, so I dare say its legendry must have some sort of basis in ancient Oriental records. One can disregard the theosophy, and make good use of the stuff about elder continents, etc. I got my own ideas about Hyperborea, Poseidonis, etc., from such sources, and then turned my imagination loose.

Too bad about your client. I read her story in *W.S.*, and rather liked it, mainly, perhaps, because I detected your revisory touch. Lasser said he would try to get some action on my arrears from the accounting dept. But I fear that the whole outfit has developed a well-organized system of "passing the buck." I have, by the way, just recently received my check for "The Second Interment," which appeared last October in the concluding issue of *Strange Tales*. And I got it only in response to a polite note to Clayton, asking if the matter had been overlooked. I must say that the depression is "the biggest and best" of its kind—if you'll pardon a lapse into the lingo of American promoters.

I saw the *Episodes of Vathek* listed at 50¢ in a catalogue (Gotham Book Mart) that came the other day, and am sending for a copy. I am, by the way, submitting "The Third Episode" to *The*

Golden Book, which has published some mildly fantastic material of late; but, of course, I am thoroughly cynical about the chances of acceptance. I know too much about the gutless emmets and pismires who edit magazines—particularly of the "quality(?)" type.

The weather is clear and balmy—first intimation of spring that we've had. If it keeps up, I'll take some of my scribbling out of doors.

> Yours, under the sign of the Black Seal, or Sixtystone,[6]
> Klarkash-Ton

P.S. Dwyer's tale came, and I am passing it on to Price as per instructions. It is quite good—would be vastly better if the sentiment at the end were left to the reader's inference rather than expressed.

1. "Let" because HPL had refused to submit his work for publication following the rejection of *At the Mountains of Madness.* AWD had submitted the story, and so when *WT* offered to publish it, HPL acquiesed, lest he seem ungrateful to AWD.

2. Whitehead had died on 23 November 1932.

3. *The City of the Dreadful Night,* XVI.41.

4. "The Weaver in the Vault" (*WT,* January 1934; *GL*); "The Flower-Women" (*WT,* May 1935 [originally "Maal Dweb and the Flower-Women"]; *LW*).

5. H[elena] P[etrovna] Blavatsky (1831–1891), founder of Theosophy and author of *The Secret Doctrine* (1888) and *The Stanzas of Dzyan* (1908). The pulp writer E. Hoffmann Price (1898–1988) had suggested that HPL read various Theosophical works as inspiration for fiction writing.

6. CAS alludes to Ixaxar, the Sixtystone of Arthur Machen's "Novel of the Black Seal."

[163]   To August Derleth [TLS, SHSW]   May 12th, 1933.

Dear August:

This is my first letter on my new portable Underwood. One of the thingumajigs in my ancient Remington broke loose a week ago, disconnecting one of the letters, and I decided that it was time to invest in a new machine. I have, however, mended the Remington with liquid solder. But it had grown so temperamental, and the type was so worn, that the purchase of another machine had become really imperative.

I like very much the poem, "Hawks in April," which you quote in your letter. Hope "Colonel Markesan" will land with new revisions—it probably will.[1]

The housecleaning has been one hell of a chore—I've moved

out several truckloads of old newspapers and magazines, to mention nothing else. Dusting and re-arranging my books required days, and I have spent several evenings in mending broken bindings and devising covers for volumes that were clad only in their fly-leaves—and not always that much. Bookbinding is fascinating, and I believe I could work out some very effective ideas with the time and means. Commercial book-cover designs are almost invariably dull and mediocre. My masterpiece, so far, is the binding of a battered pulp copy of Sir John Maundeville's *Voyages and Travels.* The materials used are insubstantial—merely cardboard and colored paper, but the effect, with the aid of gold paint and water color, is very rich and ornate. The second best job is an old *History of the Inquisition,* for which I devised a design in leathery black, parchment white and blood-red, the center being a black cross on a red field, with sharp black points impinging on the field from the sides and corners, and the lettering cut out from the same black and pasted on like the other embellishments. A series of black hasps around the back contribute much to the effect.

Yes, "The Dreams in the Witch House" will doubtless be the leading story of the year in *W.T.* I hope to God you can knock a little sense into Wright, and induce him to print "The Shadow over Innsmouth."

May has been quite rainy so far—an innovation for this part of the country. It will defer the drying of the grass, so I won't need to hurry so much with the making of my fire-breaks.

Bad news from Clayton, who is retiring because of ill-health, and is deferring the resumption of *Astounding.* I think he would have taken "The Double Shadow" and the other tales that I submitted. "The Death of Malygris" goes now to Wright.[2]

I am sorry to hear from Fredericks that *The Midland* is to be suspended. Let's hope that better times—if such ever eventuate—will permit its continuation.

Bonne fortune.

 As ever,
  Clark Ashton

1. AWD and Mark Schorer, "Colonel Markesan" (*WT,* June 1934).
2. "The Death of Malygris" (*WT,* April 1934; *LW* and *RA*).

---

[164] To August Derleth [TLS, SHSW]   May 23rd, 1933.

Dear August:

Yes, the new machine is a great acquisition. The last three years have been pretty hard on my old Remington, which I bought second hand more than two decades ago. A machine with fresh type had become an absolute necessity, since I intend to prepare some of my work, both stories and poems, for submission to book publishers next fall. And not the least advantage is, that my carbons will no longer tax the eyesight of my friends!

The job of housecleaning has been herculean, since my mother and I have simply let things accumulate for years. Literally speaking, I have moved out whole truck-loads of papers and magazines. Also, I have gone through a gargantuan accumulation of letters and have collected together the hundreds that were written me by the late George Sterling.

Wright returned "The Death of Malygris," somewhat to my surprise and much to my disgust, and on the usual plea that it was too poetic for his precious readers. A fine opinion he must have of them. The tale is a sort of companion to "The Double Shadow."

I haven't written anything new, but hope to be back in harness next month. A brief lay-off from fiction may be a good thing. I have been making a selection of poems from my various volumes at the instigation of an admirer who thinks he can exert some influence with British publishers, and have typed part of the selection, making some minor revisions as I went along.[1] It would be funny if the poems should win some sort of recognition in England, after the way in which they have been passed over by American critics. I am too cynical to cherish any high hopes, but feel sure that the treatment they will receive abroad could be, at the worst, no lousier than their reception here. The admirer I have mentioned is George Work, whose novel, *White Man's Burden* [*sic*], published by Heath Cranton, has elicited some high praise from reviewers. He maintains that I belong in the highest rank of English poets, with Keats, Shelley and Swinburne.[2] I fear that few will agree with him in this present age, with its ghastly perversion and confusion of values. As Sterling once wrote: "Bedlam's loose and the bars are down."

Good luck with your poems and stories. "Wild Hawks" was indeed charming. Too bad Wright docked you on the price of "Colonel Markesan." It seems to be a habit with him. Through some inadvertence, I gave the length of "Genius Loci" as 6300 words, when it reality, it was 6500. The result is, that I will be five dollars short on the price, receiving only $60.00.

Glad you liked "The Secret of the Cairn." "A Star-Change" (misnamed "The Visitors from Mlok") is more realistic, but, in my estimation, equally good. As far as I know, it is almost the only attempt to convey the profound disturbance of function and sensation that would inevitably be experienced by a human being on an alien world.

Good luck!

Clark Ashton

1. Provisionally titled *One Hundred Poems*. CAS still pursued the notion years later (see letter 216).

2. George Work, *White Man's Harvest* (London: Heath, Cranton, Ltd., 1932). Work's comments are quoted in "Local Poet Praised by Noted Author. Clark Ashton Smith Declared Greatest American Poet," *AJ* (27 April 1933): 1.

---

[165]   To Margaret and Ray St. Clair[1] [TLS, private collection]
May 23rd, 1933.

My dear Margaret and Ray:

Your letter was indeed interesting, and I had meant to write before this, but have been swamped by housecleaning and various other duties.

I have never read Thorndyke's book on magic,[2] but am listing it as a future purchase if I should ever have any more money to spend for books. In reality, I have read very little dealing with the occult sciences, and, in writing about such things, have merely turned my imagination loose. One of my most prized possessions is Montague Summers' erudite and curious monograph on *The Vampire*,[3] which contains much that is récherché. [*sic*] Summers actually seems to believe in the existence of vampires.

I know very little about The Rosicrucians, who, from your account, must be pretty closely allied to the theosophists. I do remember seeing some articles by Manly P. Hall in the *Overland,* but assumed him to be a theosophist.[4] I am vastly inveigled by what you tell me concerning that shack at Oceanside, which is supposed to be the home office of black magicians and the antechamber of some infernal edifice. If you can give me any more details about it, I'd certainly be indebted to you. I'd like to write a story on the subject at some future time, locating the shack, for the sake of a thoroughly realistic basis, in some locale that I know personally.[5]

Thanks for your praise of my little drawing. I have done far better things, but, during the last three years, have practically abandoned any attempt at pictorial art. If leisure should ever fall to my lot, I hope to return to it, as well as to poetry. As to illustrating my pamphlet, I fear that the cost of reproduction would be prohibitive. Even as it is, I shall make little enough from the venture, since I am planning to sell the pamphlet at 25¢ per copy. The printing, done in a shorthanded country office, has been endlessly delayed, but I shall be glad to send you a copy when it is ready. I enclose a prospectus.[6] As to an omnibus, I fear that the printing of anything so ambitious would be utterly beyond my means. But I am going to prepare a selection of my best tales for submission to book publishers in the fall, and may possibly be able to interest someone in it. Selwyn and Blount, London publishers, who bring out a yearly anthology of weird tales under the title of *Not at Night,* have recently selected "The Isle of the Torturers" for inclusion in their next collection.[7]

I hope you will like "Genius Loci" in the next *W.T.* Thanks for your praise of my recent stories. *Wonder Stories* has nothing more of mine at present, and they have been so dilatory in payment that I hesitate to submit anything more. Since I have given Gernsback some of my finest work, I really think he could make an effort to pay at least a small part of his indebtedness. I have placed some work with *Amazing Stories,* but do not know when it will appear, since this magazine is overstocked with contributions.

At the instigation of an admirer, I am making a selection of my poems for submission to British publishers in the fall. It would be funny if they should win some sort of recognition abroad, after decades of neglect in the U.S. But this, after all, would be merely the usual procedure. Poe and Bierce and Whitman had to be lauded in Europe before America would take them seriously.

I think you are wise to purchase your own house, particularly at a time when monetary values and realty are down to rock-bottom. I know the Cragmont district well, and congratulate you on your selection. My best thanks for the invitation which, sooner or later, I hope to accept.

Yours,

Clark Ashton

1. Margaret St. Clair (1911–1995), also known as "Idris Seabright," writer of fantasy and science fiction. She and her husband met CAS while they were students at the University of California at Berkeley.

2. Lynn Thorndyke, *History of Magic and Experimental Sciences* (1923).

3. Montague Summers, *The Vampire: His Kith and Kin* (1928). Summers also wrote *The Vampire in Europe* (1929).

4. Manly Palmer Hall (1901–1990), author of numerous books on Freemasonry and founder of the Philosophical Research Society.

5. CAS attempted to develop a story around this suggestion. The synopsis to this story, "The House of Haon Dor," appears in *BB,* and an aborted draft can be found in *SS.*

6. CAS's prospectus for *The Double Shadow* is reprinted in *Dark Eidolon* No. 2 (July 1989).

7. Christine Campbell Thomson (1897–1985), ed., *Keep On the Light* (London: Selwyn & Blount, 1933).

---

[166]   To Albert M. Bender [ALS, MCL]   June 11th, 1933.

Dear Albert:

I thank you for the welcome check and order, and will mail you 20 copies of *The Double Shadow* tomorrow. A copy, inscribed to you, went forward yesterday.

I am glad to hear your favourable opinion of my tales, and hope that the items in the pamphlet may please you. The title story and "The Voyage of King Euvoran" are my own favourites.

As to the O. Henry Memorial committee, I suspect that their standards are, more or less, of an ephemeral and time-serving type. They have ignored the best of my published tales, selecting only second-rate ones for mention. There is, unfortunately, among certain classes of intellectuals, a sort of prejudice against weird, occult or fantastic subject-matter.

I am sorry indeed to hear that you are unwell. May Aesculapius restore you speedily to the full enjoyment of health!

My parents join me in the best of cordial good wishes and remembrances,

Yours,
Clark

---

[167]   To August Derleth [TLS, SHSW]   June 18th, 1933.

Dear August:

[. . .] The pamphlet, with extra copies, should have reached you some days ago. Apart from the inevitable misprints, it is, I feel, a good job. I like the decoration on the cover, which I selected at the last minute from amongst a lot of do-jiggers in the *Journal* office. It goes well with the classic touch in *The Double Shadow* itself.

We have sold quite a few of the pamphlets locally, and I have received a sprinkling of orders in response to circulars which I am sending out to addresses procured from magazine letter columns. Counting 35 presentations, I have distributed 110 copies of the book in the first week following publication. My little ad in *W.T.*

will appear in the July no., and I am also advertising in the fan magazine, *Science Fiction Digest*. A one-man job of publication like this means more work than you might imagine; and I can only pray that I will at least get my money back out of [it] and be able to pay the printer. The delayed checks from *W.T.* have been driving me to the boneyard, with the prospect of being busted by the summer's end if conditions don't improve.

I rather agree with you that H.P.L. should not collaborate with anyone, no matter how good he may be.[1] But anything in which he has a hand will be of great interest.

A new "Fan" magazine is being started by Charles D. Hornig of Elizabeth, N.J.[2] It will be devoted more to weird fiction than to science fiction. I enclose one of a bunch of rainbow-colored circulars which Hornig has just sent me.

There are rumours that Clayton is bankrupt, but hopes to reorganize. Let's hope for the best. [. . .]

After a week of torrid weather, with temperatures around and above 95°, the thermometer has dropped suddenly, with a cool and brisk sea-wind blowing steadily from the south-west. When I got up at 7 this morning, the mercury stood at 49°; and now, three hours later, writing this at my out-door table, I am actually freezing. I'll have to move in-doors again, if this brumal regime continues.

Yours,
Clark Ashton

1. CAS refers to "Through the Gates of the Silver Key" (*WT*, July 1934), written with E. Hoffmann Price (at the latter's instigation). The story had been circulating in ms. and was soon to be submitted to *WT*.
2. The *Fantasy Fan* was published from September 1933 to February 1935.

---

[168]   To Lester Anderson [ALS, private collection]
June 20th, 1933

My dear Lester:
[. . .] I saw *Kong*, which came to Auburn a few nights ago.[1] A first-rate primeval nightmare! The island part appealed to me very much, and I wish there had been more of it. As far as the human actors went, the island chieftain was by far the best. But Kong himself was magnificent—I don't see how the effect was obtained! I was sorry when the airplanes got him in the end. [. . .]

Incidently, it might be remarked that Forrest J. Ackerman has been pretty badly bitten by the superstition of science and realism.[2] He wants me to refrain from publishing such work as "The Visitors from Mlok" in *Wonder Stories*! The funny part of it is, that this tale is about a hundred times closer to genuine reality in conveying the problematic sensations of an interplanetary traveler than the usual tales dealing with such themes. Oh, well . . . what's the use? [. . .]

Cordially,
     Clark Ashton Smith

1. *King Kong* (RKO, 1933), produced and directed by Merian C. Cooper and Ernest B. Schoedsack; starring Fay Wray, Robert Armstrong, and Bruce Cabot.
2. See letter 171, n.2.

---

[169]   To August Derleth [TLS, SHSW]   July 12th, 1933.

Dear August:

Your new poem titles sound interesting, and I hope you will find placement for all of them, as well as for the new stories.

The Summer issue of *Wings,* containing my "Lichens," has just arrived. The work in it really isn't anything very tremendous. I like Coblentz's enthusiasm for neglected poets of high merit, such as O'Shaughnessy and the latter James Thomson. I hope he will include Beddoes, who is a favourite of mine.

I'll look forward to your stories in forthcoming issues of *W.T.* Yes, I noticed the reference to the Tcho-Tcho people in "The Horror in the Museum."[1] There is no doubt that H.P.L. was largely instrumental in the shaping of that tale—it shows his hand on every page. I have, by the way, recently received a letter from some reader who was struck by the numerous references to *The Book of Eibon* in that issue, and wanted to know where he could procure this rare work![2]

Wright has accepted "The Flower-Women," which he rejected on its first submission a month or two ago. Later, I'll try him again with "The Death of Malygris," a better tale than "The F.W." There is no excuse for his not accepting it. I have given three stories to *The Fantasy Fan,* and have promised the editor some brief articles dealing with the technique and philosophy of weird fiction, later on. The stories were "A Tale of Sir John Maundeville" (retitled "The Kingdom of the Worm"), "The Ghoul," and "The Epiphany

of Death." No payment, except in extra copies of the magazine—
four copies for each page of text contributed. The editor has also
offered to advertise my pamphlet free of charge.

We are having a few warm days—temperature in the nineties.
But, on the whole, the summer has been phenomenally cool.

Snakes seem uncommonly plentiful this year. I found a young
king-snake devouring a mouse in one of our outbuildings (feed-
house) the other morning. Needless to say, I did not molest him—
a fellow like that would be a great improvement on our two lousy,
loafing cats, if he cared to stay. But the next day, my father caught
and killed a less desirable visitor—a yearling rattlesnake, with a
spike on his tail, in one of our chicken-yards. The snake had bitten
a young broiler, which died. Rattlers are rare in this immediate
vicinity, though common enough in the nearby canyon of the
American River. I have heard that a large one, two inches thick,
has been seen in the creek-bottom on the neighboring ranch, and
went gunning for him this morning with a shotgun loaded with
buck. There was no sign of him, however. Much of that creek-
bottom is absolutely impenetrable, being a tangle of poplars, wil-
lows, alders, blackberry and Himalaya-berry vines, wormwood,
mullein, cat-tails, tules, wire-grass, wild oats and other vegetation.
A perfect hangout for snakes.

Kingsnakes, as you may know, are death on rattlers—they kill
them by constriction. I can testify to the muscular power of a
kingsnake, since I have handled several of them. I'd like to see a
fight between one of them and a rattler!

My best, as ever,
Clark Ashton

1. HPL had used AWD's Tcho-Tcho people in "The Horror in the
Museum" (*WT,* July 1933), another story he ghostwrote for Hazel
Heald.

2. Besides CAS's mention in "Ubbo-Sathla," the July 1933 issue of
WT referred to *The Book of Eibon* in HPL's "Dreams in the Witch-
House" and Hazel Heald's "The Horror in the Museum." CAS explained
the situation in a letter to editor Charles D. Hornig, published as "Star-
tling Fact" (*Fantasy Fan,* November 1933; in *PD*).

[170]   To August Derleth [TLS, SHSW]   July 22nd, 1933.

Dear August:

[. . .] "Through the Gates of the Silver Key" is an extremely interesting piece of work in my opinion; though I agree with you that the Cthulhu-myth-cycle has not fused very well with eastern occultism. But there is really a tremendous speculative idea in the story, albeit one that is supremely difficult to work out in graphic detail that the reader can envision clearly. I think one source of the trouble lies in this, that portions of the tale, together with much of the phraseology, are still too abstract. And if I were doing it myself, I confess I would chuck the swami. In picking a facial mask for himself, Carter might well have chosen as a model one of his own ancestors, such as the wizard Edmund Carter; and the resemblance, coupled with a *strange name*, would have been noticed and puzzled over by at least one other of the group—Ward Phillips. At any rate, C. would probably have taken the part of some Occidental mystic.

A paucity of news here. I have sent "The Tomb in the Desert" to Wright,[1] and am working desultorily on "The House of Haon-Dor," a fantastic horror which used the old hydraulic mining country above Auburn for a base of departure into submundane and infra-spatial depths of nightmare. It is partially based on a yarn retailed to me by a correspondent, concerning a shack supposed to be the home office of black magicians and the vestibule of an immense immaterial edifice haunted by fiends. The actual locale of this shack is Oceanside, with which I am not familiar at first hand; but I thought the old hydraulic diggings would serve equally well; and I have the advantage of knowing them thoroughly.

I had a rather unpleasant thrill two hours ago, when I happened to look up from my writing (pencil drafting) and saw a rattlesnake coiled only a yard from my table at the foot of the big live oak under which I work at this season. The fellow had crawled under an old screen, in a position where I could not reach him with a cudgel; so I went for the shotgun in a hurry. The snake had four rattles. It seemed to be sluggish, probably from the heat, for it must have crossed an open area of ground to reach the shelter of the oak.[2] [. . .]

    Clark Ashton

1. "The Tomb-Spawn" (*WT,* May 1934; *TSS*).

2. In CAS's synopsis to "The House of Haon Dor" (*BB*), Haon Dor assumes the shape of a 15-foot-long rattlesnake. The incident described in this letter inspired the story in part.

[171] To August Derleth [TLS, SHSW]   Aug. 4th, 1933.

Dear August:

[. . .] No more rattlesnakes in our immediate neighborhood; but I have been hearing all manner of tales about their prevalence around Auburn. One friend, living on the other side of town, says that a rattler has taken up its abode in his barn. The critters are certainly sociable: I hear of their being found on porches and town streets and pavements.

Wright has finally accepted "The Death of Malygris." He is using "A Vintage from Atlantis" in the Sept. *W.T.*, "The Seed from the Sepulcher" in Oct., and "The Holiness of Azéderac" in November. I liked your little story in the current issue, and look forward to "The Return of Andrew Bentley." I have not found time to read the whole of the Aug. number, but feel that it is not an especially good one. Suter's "The Superior Judge" is quite good, but "The Owl" is rather punk, and the serial is just one more adventure yarn. I thought the reprint from Whitehead one of the poorest of his that I have seen.[1] The idea is about the first that occurs to an amateur writer of weird tales.

One Forrest J. Ackerman, writer of letters to magazines, has been assailing some of my *Wonder Story* contributions quite extensively, claiming that they are too weird and horrific and fantastic for the soberly realistic pages of that medium. The joke is, that he has lauded and taken seriously an even more outrageous, impossible yarn of mine, which was written as a burlesque! He has a vehement attack on "Dweller in Martian Depths" and "The Light from Beyond" in the first issue of *The Fantasy Fan;* and sometime ago I received a personal letter from him urging me to refrain from contributing this type of material to *W.S.!* Since the editor of *The Fantasy Fan* wanted me to answer the published attack, I have written a brief letter pointing out the inconsistencies and flaws of logic that A. has committed.[2] Some of these kids certainly take their science pretty seriously. Science and the State, it is plain, are going to be the principal Mumbo Jumbos of the near future.

Yours ever,
Clark Ashton

1. AWD, "An Elegy for Mr. Danielson"; J. Paul Suter, "The Superior Judge"; F. A. M. Webster, "The Owl"; and Henry S. Whitehead, "The Door" (*WT*, August 1933); AWD and Mark Schorer, "The Return of Andrew Bentley" (*WT*, September 1933).

2. *The Boiling Point* (West Warwick, RI: Necronomicon Press, 1985)

documents the published exchanges between CAS, Ackerman, and their respective supporters. *PD* reprints CAS's comments.

———————◆———————

[172]   To R. H. Barlow[1] [TLS, JHL]   Aug. 6th, 1933.

Dear Mr. Barlow:

I had been meaning to answer your letter for some time past; also, to mail you, in a flat package, another copy of *The Double Shadow* to indemnify you for the one that got crushed in transit. I'll try to get the book off in a day or two. If you like, you can remit the postage on it sometime.

I have not yet located any more Whitehead letters.[2] There are such vast quantities of correspondence lying around here in an unassorted condition, that it means no end of research to locate anything that is more than a few months old. Let's hope you will be able to carry out your plan for printing the letters you have. No, I don't think that I shall print a Sterling collection. So many of the letters are complimentary to my work, that it would seem like a self-advertising stunt if I were to bring them out. Also, I have not, at present, either the means or the time to embark on another publishing venture. *The Double Shadow* has brought me enough grief in the form of work, worry and expense.

A friend once read me some enjoyable chapters from A. A. Milne;[3] but apart from that, I am not familiar with his books.

I rather enjoyed *King Kong*, which came to Auburn some time ago. But I seldom attend movies, and, as a rule, am disappointed in the few that I do see.

The last three months have been pretty slack with me, as far as writing is concerned. A multitude of other things, mainly flat and unprofitable, seem to have intervened. Also, my father has been unwell. I have, however, recently sold two new stories to Wright: "The Flower-Women" and "The Death of Malygris."

Have you seen *The Fantasy Fan*? I enclose a circular describing it. Lovecraft and I are both contributing some stories to future numbers.

Too bad that conditions are so inharmonious for you. The only defense is to make up your mind that you won't take anything seriously. Also, make an effort to concentrate on something abstract, and to view the irritating conditions in a sort of cosmic perspective that will cause them to dwindle into triviality. Well, I can see that you don't think much of the practicality of my advice; but believe me, the mere endeavor to see things in this way will help if you keep it up.

The spirit photograph is good—I am sure Conan Doyle would have accepted it as proof of an authentic materialization! I return it herewith.

Here is a note from Sterling that you might like to add to your collection.[4] I can well afford to spare it. [. . .]

All best wishes, and hopes that this will find you in a less depressed mood.

> Yours cordially,
> Clark Ashton Smith

Sorry I can't identify the quotation about the moonbeam that turned to worms.

1. R[obert] H[ayward] Barlow (1918–1951), author, publisher, and collector. In the 1940s he went to Mexico and became a distinguished anthropologist.

2. RHB intended to publish extracts of Whitehead's letters in a small volume entitled *Caneviniana*. Some letters were set in type, but the book was never published (although Paul Freehafer printed some of the letters in a 1943 mailing of the Fantasy Amateur Press Association as *The Letters of Henry S. Whitehead*).

3. A[lan] A[lexander] Milne (1882–1956), prolific author of plays, novels, stories, poems, and essays, but best known for his children's books.

4. A postcard from GS to CAS, postmarked 18 June 1912; ms., JHL.

---

[173]   To Donald Wandrei [TLS, MHS]   Aug. 6th, 1933.

Dear Donald:

I felt sure you would like Helen, and think that you did wonders in helping to make her N.Y. sojourn a success.[1] Your epic letter is certainly eloquent of a good time enjoyed by every one. Helen's progress, as I foresaw, has been a triumphal one; and I only wish I could have been present. Her mother, sister and I speak often of your marvellous goodness and kindness. I don't see how you did it, under the circumstances. You seem to have beaten my record for going without sleep!

Your job sounds interesting, and I hope that it has been worth while. Don't worry about returning the paltry enclosure that I sent you. I am not yet bankrupt, and can always dig up a little dough somewhere if necessary. [. . .]

I am glad to hear your good opinion of *The Double Shadow* collection, and await your further comments with great interest. "The D.S." is my own favourite; then, in order, "The Maze of the Enchanter" and "A Night in Malnéant." The pamphlet continues to sell slowly, and I have now worked off close to 250 copies. I have, however, given up any hope of making a little money on it. The cost of advertising, etc, added to the expense of printing, is too great. Also, it has involved me in considerable correspondence—which means time and postage-stamps.

I hope that you will soon receive a check from Wright for "Spawn of the Sea."[2] My story, "The Ice-Demon," in the preceding number, was paid for some time ago, but I have not yet received payment for "The Beast of Averoigne," in the same issue with your story. Wright has ten of my yarns on hand for publication, and will use "A Vintage from Atlantis" in September, "The Seed from the Sepulcher" in Oct., and "The Holiness of Azéderac" in Nov.

I have several partly written tales on hand, and others that will have to be re-written before I can sell them. "The House of Haon-Dor" and "The Witchcraft of Ulua"[3] are two that I hope to finish ere long. The last-named is an erotic nightmare, and deals with a youth who had spurned a young witch and was bedevilled by her with various disagreeable sendings. He found amorous corpses in his bed, and was persecuted by peculiar succubi. [. . .]

I wrote a poem some time ago—the first in three years!—and will hunt up a copy to enclose with this. The composition of the poem, by the way, was interrupted by the arrival of a rattlesnake that had crawled close to my outdoor writing-table before I perceived it! I had to kill the snake, though it seemed a pity to snub his social inclinations in a manner so decided. This year has been a phenomenal one for rattlers, since my father had killed one not long before in one of his chicken-yards, after it had struck down a broiler; and the whole neighborhood is full of yarns about their incursions. Previous to this, we had not seen one on the ranch for many years.

I hope you can make, sooner or later, that promised trip to California. I can offer you a bed, and food, for as long as you care to stay with us, and anything that I can do will be yours to command.

It is a high honour to have *Ebony and Crystal* bracketed with *The Hill of Dreams* and *Urn-Burial*.[4] The former I read many years ago (unfortunately I do not own it) and liked greatly. The *Urn Burial* is one of my favourite pieces of prose—or poetry. In regard to Machen, my present preference is for some of his shorter stories, such as "The White People," "The Novel of the Black Seal," and "The Novel of the White Powder," which I consider unexcelled in literature. But perhaps, if I were to re-read *The Hill of Dreams* now, I might prefer it to these.

Yours ever,
Clark

My thanks to Belknap and his family also, for their kindnesses to Helen.

Yes, I have heard that Gernsback has a doubtful reputation in matters of payment. Though I disapprove strongly of the Hitler regime, I think that it might be administered, not unjustifiably, on a Jewish gyp and literary sweat-shop keeper such as H. G. I have a suspicion that he may try another of his bankruptcy stunts before long. I have the address of a lawyer in N.Y. who is said to be good at collecting money from backward publishers and shall at least try holding the threat of legal action over Gernsback.

1. Helen Sully visited the East Coast in the summer of 1933, stopping in Providence to meet HPL and New York City, where she met DAW, Frank Belknap Long, and others.

2. DAW, "The Spawn of the Sea" (*WT,* May 1933).

3. "The Witchcraft of Ulua" (*WT,* February 1934; *AY*).

4. Sir Thomas Browne (1605–1682), *Hydriotaphia; or, Urne-Burial* (1658).

———————◆———————

[174]   To August Derleth [TLS, SHSW]   Aug. 29th, 1933.

Dear August:

I shall forward the ms. of *Evening in Spring* to Helen Theile as soon as I have re-read certain portions of it. It is strong and beautiful work, and it grew upon me as the general plan unfolded. You have conveyed very pervasively the feeling of a whole arc of nature and human life. I might single out for praise some of the particular vignettes (those I had read before seemed even better on re-perusal) but all of them take their place in the enrichment of the general scheme. I like, too, the flexibility of the style: the prose-poetry of the landscape pieces is well supplemented by the more succinct phrasing and rhythms of the human vignettes. If I were to cavil at anything—which seems ungracious—it would be at certain wordings such as "bring alive," which I have never cared for. Also, I dislike the making of a separate sentence from a clause, and would sometimes use colons where you use periods. But this is a matter of idiosyncrasy and no doubt you and others will disagree with me. At any rate, it is very little to set against the force and beauty of your book, and if I mention such matters at all, it is only because I think that the book is *worthy* of perfection.

Your autumn letterhead is very nice—it makes a well-balanced drawing. Autumn, it would seem, is upon us here: the sky has become grey with a mixture of smoke and sea-fog, and the sun burns dimly at noon, with the mercury dropping to 54° or 56° at sunrise.

Howard is a rather surprising person, and I think he is more complex, and is also possessed of more literary ability, than I had thought from many of his stories. The Conan tales, in my opinion, are quite in a class by themselves. H. seemed very appreciative of my book of poems, *Ebony and Crystal,* and evidently understood it as few people have done.

I am anxious to see "The Snow-Thing":[1] that class of theme has a marked fascination for me. I am, by the way, writing an Arctic fantasy, "The Temptation of Evagh," which purports to be a translation of Chapter IX from the celebrated *Book of Eibon.*[2] It is hard to do, like most of my tales, because of the peculiar and carefully maintained style and tone-colour, which involves rejection of many words, images and locutions that might ordinarily be employed in writing. The story takes its text from a saying of the prophet Lith: "There is one that inhabits the place of utter cold, and One that respireth where none other may draw breath. In the days to come He shall issue forth among the isles and cities of men, and shall bring with Him as a white doom the wind that slumbereth in His dwelling."

Wright has fired back "The Witchcraft of Ulua," saying that it is a sex story and therefore unsuitable for *W.T.* Perhaps he is right; though erotic imagery was employed in the tale merely to achieve a more varied sensation of weirdness. The net result is surely macabre rather than risqué. I am enclosing the ms. and would appreciate your opinion. Also, if you can think of any possible market you might mention it. I can think of none, and will no doubt have to lay the story aside for inclusion in my volume, *Tales of Zothique* when, and if, I should procure a publisher for that opus. With the completion of two more tales, "Xeethra," and "The Madness of Chronomage," I will have a series totalling about 60,000 words, all dealing with the future continent of Zothique.[3] These could be collected with a brief note as to suppositional geography and chronology. My Averoigne series also lacks about two more tales to bring it to book-size; and the Hyperborean and Atlantean suites are perhaps half-finished. Printed on good paper and decently bound, I think that all of these tales would show up as fine literature, in no wise inferior to Dunsany or Cabell.

I have bought *The Collected Ghost Stories of M. R. James*—his four volumes all in one—from Dauber & Pine.[4] It was a bargain at $2.00 cash. I wonder if you saw the catalogue: Sam Loveman gave H.P. a fine send-off in his blurb on James.

Well, I must adjourn and go back to Eibon.

Yours,

Clark Ashton

I'll look forward to seeing your thesis on the weird tale in *TFF*.[5] I may write a critical note on the stories of M. R. James for Hornig to use. In the meanwhile, he has three of my stories and one poem ("Revenant") and also a reply to that offensive simp, Ackerman.

1. Published as "Ithaqua" (*Strange Stories,* February 1941).

2. Published as "The Coming of the White Worm" (*Stirring Science Stories,* April 1941; *LW* and *RA*).

3. "Xeethra" (*WT,* December 1934; *LW* and *RA*). For "The Madness of Chronomage,"see *BB* item 9: "A king who beholds a vision not shared by others, and passes into the vision in his hour of need." *Tales of Zothique* as CAS invisioned it was never published.

4. *The Collected Ghost Stories of M. R. James* (London: Edward Arnold, 1931).

5. AWD, "The Weird Tale in English Since 1890," *Ghost,* No. 3 (1945): 5–32.

———————— ◆ ————————

[175]   To August Derleth [TLS, SHSW]   Sept. 14th, 1933.

Dear August:

[. . .] I agree pretty much with your opinion of "The Witchcraft of Ulua," and shall not bother to attempt re-writing the yarn for *W.T.* As to the so-called sexiness, it would not interest me to write a story dealing with anything so banal, hackneyed and limited as this type of theme is likely to be. Too many writers are doing it to death at the present time; and I have ended by revolting literarily against the whole business, and am prepared to maintain that a little Victorian reticence, combined with Puritan restraint, would harm nobody.

I have not yet finished the Eibon story to my satisfaction, but feel pretty sure that it has "the makings." I found occasion to re-title it as "The Coming of the White Worm." You will, I think, find it altogether different from "The Thing that Walked on the Wind"; nor do I imagine that it has any real likeness to Blackwood's "Wendigo," which I know only by Lovecraft's mention in his monograph on Supernatural Horror.

I took time off to write my note on James—about 1100 words.[1] Nothing very original about it, I fear; but I tried to summarize the special qualities of James, in regard to style, development, themes, milieus, motifs, etc; and, in particular, to give an idea of what I think is his greatest gift: the evocation, through appeal to sense-images, of weird, malign, hyperphysical phenomena. I did not, however, give synopses of particular stories, as H.P. does in his monograph, but instanced a number of James' most diabolic specters and empusae.

Later, I may do a brief article on The Philosophy of the Weird Tale.[2] This will not touch on the aesthetics of weirdness, but will emphasize the implicative (though not didactic) bearing of the w.t. on human destiny, and, in particular, its relationship to man's spiritual evolution and his position in regard to the unknown and the infinite. I shall frankly outline my own stand, which is that of one who keeps an open mind and is willing to admit that all things are possible, but accepts neither the dogmatism of material science nor that of any "revealed" religion or system of theosophy. I shall, too, point out that the only road to an understanding of the basic mysteries is through the *possible* development in man of those higher faculties of perception which mystics and adepts *claim* to develop. There is no reason at all why powers transcending our present range of sense-perception may not be developed in the course of future evolution; and such powers may have been attained by individuals in the past. The point I want to make is, that a psychological interest in the weird, unknown and preternatural is not merely a "hangover" from the age of superstition, but is perhaps a sign-post on the road of man's future development.

Good luck with your current stories. The letter from Scribners is certainly encouraging, and I predict that you will hit the mark sooner or later. I shall look forward to seeing "The Snow-Thing."

As ever,
Clark Ashton

1. "The Weird Works of M. R. James" (*Fantasy Fan*, February 1934; PD).
2. "The Philosophy of the Weird Tale" (*Acolyte*, Fall 1944; PD). See also *BB*, item 19.

[176] To R. H. Barlow [TLS, JHL]   Sept 19th, 1933.

Dear Ar-Éch-Bei:

I have exhumed the unanswered letters of the past month or six weeks (filed in a peach-box on my outdoor table) and am answering them all in one fell swoop. Yours comes early in the list.

Glad my advice was not so remiss and remote from the point. Even major annoyances are not so important if one can see them in a sort of macrocosmic perspective—which is the only way to regard them. Anyway, I hope that your father is better.[1]

So you too have been dumping off some specimens of the crotalus horridus! I admire your resolution in skinning one of them and tanning the hide, but I lack the fervor to emulate you.

As to book-collecting, I have some first and old editions, but doubtless lack the true bibliophilic ardour, since I buy books mainly for their contents, and am now specializing wholly on items of the weird and fantastic. And with the present financial outlook, I am buying very few indeed even of those. My last purchase was *The Collected Ghost Stories of M. R. James,* all in one volume. James is a growing favourite with me, and I admire his tales more as I re-read and analyze them. I have recently written a brief article on him, which will be published in *The Fantasy Fan.* I saw Eliphas Levi's *History of Magic*[2] listed at $5.00 in a catalogue which came recently, and would like to buy it, but hesitate over the expenditure. One highly prized item which I possess is Montague Summers' monograph on *The Vampire.* I wonder if Quinn hadn't been reading that when he cooked up his yarn about the penang-galan in the last *W.T.*[3] Confound Quinn—he has botched something on which I had an eye myself.

Re Cabell: I esteem him as a remarkable stylist, but do not admire and relish his type of fantasy nearly as much as I did ten years ago. Too many allegories and double meanings; and since I have lost most of my interest in mundane sophistication, I am easily bored by such obvious though inverted didacticisms. Satire, in my opinion, contrary to that of my friend Benj. De Casseres, is far from being the highest form of art. As Lovecraft once remarked in a letter, if one laughs too persistently at things, it might come to seem that they were worth laughing at.[4]

No, I never met Bierce—he passed out of the American (and, no doubt, the mundane) scene not long after the beginning of my acquaintance with Sterling. I could have met him, one occasion, and have often kicked myself since that I did not stretch my leave and do so.[5]

If I ever visit S.F. again, I may be able to pick up a copy of *Odes and Sonnets* for you. A friend of mine procured one there last summer. [. . .]

I'll see what I can dig up in the way of enclosures. Thanks for the interesting cut of your house.

Yours, under the black onyx seal of Azathoth,
Klarkash-Ton

You might like the enclosed card from De Casseres (acknowledging *The Double Shadow*) for your autographic collection.[6]

1. E. D. Barlow, a lieutenant-colonel of the army, had retired because of poor health. Before making his trip to De Land in 1934 to visit RHB, HPL was concerned that his presence "might disturb him [RHB's father] & increase his depression to have a stranger—& a far from breezy & exuberant stranger at that—butting in on him" (HPL to RHB, 10 April 1934; ms., JHL).

2. "Eliphas Lévi" (Alphonse Louis Constant; 1810–1875), *Histoire de la magie* (1860); trans. by Arthur Edward Waite (1857–1942) as *The History of Magic* (1913).

3. Seabury Quinn, "The Malay Horror" (*WT*, September 1933).

4. HPL to CAS, 9 August 1926: "Nothing in the universe matters very much, & to laugh habitually at any one set of things seems almost to imply that they are worth laughing at" (*SL* 2.62).

5. See letter 6, n. 6.

6. Benjamin De Casseres to CAS, 16 June 1933; ms. JHL.

[177]   To August Derleth [TLS, SHSW]   Sept. 26th, 1933.

Dear August:

[. . .] Things are slack enough here. No news from editors. Wright has "The Coming of the White Worm" under advisement; and the new S. & S. *Astounding* has three of my tales, none of which has been reported on. These tales are: "The Tomb-Spawn" (revised), "The Demon of the Flower" (slightly abbreviated and simplified) and "The Witchcraft of Ulua," in which I decided to revise one or two pages—not including, however, the temptation scene.[1]

I bought the October *Astounding* and perused it with interest. It seems a slight improvement on the Clayton magazine of that name, but I found it inferior to the average issue of *Strange Tales*—mainly, I think, because of the absence of any really outstanding and memorable story. Some of the entries, like Donald's, were pretty fair; but others struck me as being terribly trite and flat. The editors profess to want fine writing—the finer the better; and I hope that the general quality of this issue is not a genuine reflection of their tastes. I also invested in the current *Dime Mystery,* which is certainly going strong for gruesomeness and physical horror.

One William Crawford, of 122 Water St., Everett, Pa., is projecting a magazine of weird and pseudo-scientific tales, under the title *Unusual Stories.* No payment. I sent him "The White Sybil" in response to a request for material, and he seemed immensely pleased with it. I have a lurking fear that the venture may fizzle like Swanson's *Galaxy;* but hope that I am wrong. If you have some unsalable weirds that you want to give away, Crawford would doubtless be a grateful recipient. I took the liberty of suggesting that he might write you.

I too am anxious to see "The Thing on the Door-Step."[2] I do hope that the Knopf outfit will have enough acumen and gumption to bring out a volume for H.P. It would have immense therapeutic benefit for him if they did.

I am writing another of my Hyperborean series—"The Seven Geases."[3] The demon of irony insists on having a hand in it.

Bonne fortune.

As ever,
Clark Ashton

1. See *The Witchcraft of Ulua* (West Warwick, RI: Necronomicon Press, 1988) for the complete, unexpurgated text. CAS did in fact revise the tempation scene somewhat.
2. HPL, "The Thing on the Doorstep" (*WT,* January 1937). HPL had completed the story only recently.
3. "The Seven Geases" (*WT,* October 1934; *LW* and *RA*).

[178]   To H. P. Lovecraft [TLS, JHL]   [c. late September 1933]
Obsidian block before the hut of Ezdagor
on Mt. Voormithadreth.

Dear Éch-Pi-El:

Thanks for the picture of the Carlsbad subterranea! It certainly looks like an adytum of that Hyperborean underworld through which the Commoriom magistrate and mighty hunter of Voormis, Ralibar Vooz, hero of my latest yarn,[1] was conducted on an extensive tour by a wizard's familiar in the shape of a night-flying archaeopteryx!

I read with vast enjoyment and envy your account of the

Quebec visit. I can well imagine the likeness to Vyones and Ximes, and wouldn't be surprised to meet the bishop Azéderac or the abbot Hilaire in that Place d'Armes of which you enclosed so inveigling a view.[2] I am sure that werewolves might howl at certain times of the moon in the environs of such a city. The sunset that you describe must indeed have been impressive. The only effect of a remotely cognate sort which I ever saw occurred a year or two ago, and I don't remember mentioning it in my letters to you. In this case, the rose and salmon hues of a vivid sunset were reflected in the east, toward the Sierras, on the upper domes and battlements of a huge mass of blue-black thunder-cumulus, which, from time to time, was riven with forked lightning-bolts. It was magnificent and unforgettable; but there was no accompanying rainbow as in the effect that you saw.

Your visits to Winthrop and to Salem and Marblehead must have been a re-saturation in weird centurial atmosphere, too. Even from the coloured cards, I get an impression of something eerie and ghostly that is inherent in these old houses and landscapes. [. . .]

So far I have failed to get a line on the Jay Pub. Co., mentioned by M. le Comte D'Erlette. I bought the current issue of *Dime Mystery,* which is no less lurid in appearance than the title would intimate. It is certainly going strong for gruesomeness, coupled with melodrama; and our friend Hugh B. Cave is evidently a star contributor. Though the general style of the mag is staccato and rapid-fire, it is possible that they might consider something on the lines of "Helman Carnby." Certainly they ought not to cavil on the grounds of too much horror, after printing Cave's yarn about the zombi and the vat of hydrochloric acid!

I hope you will decide to give your friends a peep at "The Thing on the Doorstep."[3] I am very anxious to see it, or anything else that you may write. I fail to see anything wrong with your handling of plot and incident, which seems always in keeping with the atmosphere and basic substance. It is an interesting feat of analysis, however, to take the work of others apart and note the mechanics of effect. I feel highly honoured that you should include *The Double Shadow* among those indubitable classics which you are analyzing![4] Of those that you mention, I think I care least for Walter de la Mare; but perhaps I have not read enough of his work. My only criticism, however, is that most of his tales are not weird enough, and that the element of character analysis is too obtrusive for artistic balance. James, on the other hand, I should say, has just enough characterization, and does not let it detract from the main effect. But, no doubt, de la Mare is more interested in human idiosyncrasies than in weirdness.

James certainly repays careful study; and I find myself appreciating him even more than I did when you loaned me *A Warning to the Curious* and *Ghost Stories of an Antiquary*. Also, I am very much taken with certain of the more inferential tales, such as "Mr. Humphreys and his Inheritance," which seem full of unfathomably baleful suggestion. Tour de forces like "The Treasure of Abbot Thomas" knock one out at the first reading; and, of course, always retain their power; but the less overt yarns certainly grow on the reader. It is an object lesson in what can be done by skilful adumbration and by veiling more or less the main horror.[5]

The enthusiasm roused by *The Double Shadow* in select readers is certainly encouraging. Two more of your correspondents, R. F. Searight and Lee White Jr., have recently ordered copies. Lumley[6] is certainly a rara avis, and I wish sincerely that there were more like him in this world of servile conformity to twentieth century skepticism and materialism! More power to such glorious heresy as that which he avows. I, for one, would hardly want the task of disproving his beliefs—even if I could disprove them. I must write him again before long. [. . .]

Wright has not yet returned "The Coming of the White Worm." I'll look over the carbon; and, unless I decide to hold it for revision, will mail it to you for reading before long. You, in turn, might forward it to Lumley, who can return it to me.

I am now midway in "The Seven Geases," another of the Hyperborean series. The demon of irony wants to have a hand in this yarn; but I am trying to achieve horror in some of the episodes even if not in the tout ensemble. It brings in the Voormis, those subhuman anthropophagi who figured in Athammaus; and also the mountain Voormithadreth, an extinct four-coned volcano under which is the abode of Tsathoggua and of many other primordial entities. Ralibar Vooz, hunting Voormis (a popular Commorian sport) upon Voormithadreth, intrudes unwittingly on certain private business of the wizard Ezdagor; and Ezdagor, furious at the interruption, puts a geas[7] on Ralibar Vooz; the geas being that he shall go bare-handed into the caves of the Voormis, and fight his way to the subterranean dwelling of Tsathoggua; where, presenting himself before that sleepy and sluggish deity ("Who rises not from his place even in the ravening of hunger") he was to announce himself as "the blood-offering sent by the sorcerer Ezdagor." This geas was duly accomplished; but Tsathoggua, having dined amply a little previous, merely put another geas on the hero and sent him off to the spider-god, Atlach-Nacha, who was weaving his webs across a Cimmerian gulf which had no other bridges . . . And so it went . . . . till he (Ralibar) came to that

blind and formless Thing which dwelt in the lowest depths . . . .
    I am glad to know that your aunt's improvement is so marked.
        Yours for the resurgence of R'lyeh,
        Klarkash-Ton

    1. "The Seven Geases."
    2. Vyones and Ximes are cities mentioned in stories set in Averoigne; Azéderac appears in "The Holiness of Azéderac" (*LW*) and Hilare in "The End of the Story" (*OST*).
    3. CAS acknowledges that HPL refused to submit any work in the wake of the rejection of *At the Mountains of Madness*.
    4. At the time, HPL was systematically rereading the classic works of weird fiction, in an attempt to determine what made them successful as a means of improving his own writing, with which he had grown profoundly dissatisfied.
    5. *A Warning to the Curious* (1925); *Ghost-Stories of an Antiquary* (1904).
    6. William Lumley (1880–1960), correspondent and revision client of HPL.
    7. See letter 181 re the meaning of *geas*.

[179]   To H. P. Lovecraft [TLS, JHL]   [c. mid-October 1933]
        From the room embossed and paved with demon faces,
                in the subterranean palace of Haon-Dor.
Dear Éch-Pi-El:
    I return the Ullman-Knopf communication herewith. Knopf should remove the Borzoi from his imprint, and substitute either a Golden Calf or a jackass with brazen posteriors. I wish Herr Hitler had him, along with Gernsback. If I were a practising wizard, like Namirrha or Malygris or Nathaire,[1] I'd devise a behemothian Sending and dispatch it to his office. The Sending would include a brace of penanggalans, and about a dozen rokurokubis with jaws elastic as their necks, and a regiment of poltergeists equipped with sledge-hammers. Callicantzaris and vrykolakes and barguests and Himalayan Snow-Men and Eskimo tupileks and the more unpleasant Aztec gods would form the main body; and a mass formation of shoggoths would bring up the rearguard. After their passing, the Knopf headquarters would be one with the middens of Nineveh.[2]
    In return, here is the epistle from Pharnabozus anent "The White Worm." Please do not lose it. Of course, I realize that he has to sell the magazine; and readers who would appreciate Eibon are not to be found in every Methodist chapel, synagogue, packing-

house or retail grocery.[3] In fact, I fear that they would form a mathematically insignificant portion of the census-list. I am glad you enjoyed the ms., and trust that Lumley will not be disappointed in its revelations.

That picture of the werewolves—even though a cartoon—is infernally good. Here, by the way, is a recent portrait—sketch of our Lord Tsathoggua, which I made for you the other day. My Indian wood-cutter saw it (as I think I mentioned on a card) and said instantly: "That's one of the Old Boys." He then proceeded to narrate a tribal legend about a young squaw who was carried away by some prehuman entity into a cavern. Nearly a year later, the squaw emerged to the light, bringing with her an infant that was half human and half something else.

The Oct. issue of *Astounding* was pretty tepid to say the least. I hope that succeeding numbers will be put through more of a delousing process. I guess I told you on the card that they had accepted "The Demon of the Flower." "The Tomb-Spawn" was held by them for over a month, but finally came back, together with "The Witchcraft of Ulua."

Dime Mystery seems to be going in for what the British would call "shockers." More action and even less atmosphere than in the other magazines. Cave must be running a regular factory, to judge from the amount that he turns out. Crawford's proposed *Unusual Stories* will be more pseudo-scientific than weird, to judge from his last letter.

The dream you relate was certainly extraordinary, and it will be interesting to see the story that young Bloch makes of it. With a preliminary notion about the depredations of the rubbery bat-thing, and the *uncommon zeal* shown by the young horseman at all times in trying to hunt it down, the dream really needs no alteration or addition to form the skeleton of a weird short. My own recent dreams have been pretty tame; but in the past I have had some that were memorable. One that comes to mind was fraught with all the supernatural horror of antique myth: I was standing somewhere on a bleak, terrible plain, while past me and over me, with appalling demonic speed and paces and voices of thunder, there swept a vast array of cloudy, titanic Shapes. One of these, as it went by, pealed out the sonorous words "Eiton euclarion," which I somehow took to be the name of the cloudy entity or one of its fellows.[4]

One of my most diabolic dreams, however, was of being somewhere in a high tower room with sloping small-paned windows, above a weird exotic city. At first I was alone in this room—and then, with frightful instantaneousness, it was full of malformed children with bloated and distorted faces, who swam upward around me in the air, beating me over the head with the large, curious brazen pans which they carried. Another dream, repeated many times at one period, was that of being breathed upon by a cold wind which swept me before it with all the irresistible force of a solid body, pressing me down into gulfs of ineffably deranged and confused sensation and entity. Still another, much more recent, was of wandering through a strange city together with other people, under a sense of urgent haste and portentous compulsion. It seemed that we must reach a certain goal before an unnamed doom should overtake us in the open streets. But as I went on, I became aware that the atmosphere was thickening slowly but steadily and was taking on the character of a liquid. [. . .]

No, you hadn't told me about Lumley's travels. Perhaps he is an adept and does it via the fourth dimension. Rocket-ships and stratosphere traffic will never improve on *that* mode for getting you somewhere and back without waste time or motion. Seriously, I am tremendously interested and prepossessed in his favour. I hope he will write me at length when he is through with the Eibon Chapter. The two letters I have had from him certainly contained some fascinating hints. I too would be the last person to make fun of any of his ideas. Anyhow, the bare truth about the nature of things may be more fantastic than anything that any of us have yet cooked up. I, for one, find it as hard to swallow the dogmas of the physicists as it is to down those of the ecclesiasts. Mind, for all that I know, may exist as readily without matter as matter seems to exist without mind; or the two may exist together in a million undetected forms. Five senses and three dimensions hardly scratch the hither surface of infinitude. Which doesn't mean that one should emulate the gullibility of Sir Arthur Conan Doyle.

I hope to peruse "The Thing on the Door-Step" when you get around to typing it. In spite of your disparagement, "The Festival" holds its place in my affections, and has an imaginative quality that puts it above the new stories in the current *W.T.* Howard has some fine romantic fantasy in "The Pool of the Black Ones"; and Long's tale has the makings of more than a pot-boiler. With more concentration on development and detail, it would have been first-rate. I must re-read the story by Merle Prout. I liked the idea and some of the incidents; but certain crudities rather jarred upon me in the hasty perusal which I gave it. My own tale was chiefly conspicuous for certain scientific horror-touches, carefully accumulated; and if the idea of flesh-eating plants weren't so hackneyed it would deserve a higher place.[5]

*   *   *

Later. This triply blasted Underwood seems to have gone blooey all at once, so I am continuing the letter on the old Reliable Remington.

I hope F. Lee Baldwin will carry out his plan of printing "The Colour out of Space" as a pamphlet. If he does, put me down for at least four copies. I have, by the way, just received a letter from him asking me the cost per copy of *The Double Shadow* and the cost of the paper used, etc. He was one of the early purchasers of the pamphlet. The net cost of the *D.S.* to me was $125.00 for a thousand copies, linotyping being the heaviest item of expense on a small edition. It shouldn't cost nearly so much to print a single story like "The Colour out of Space."

Wright has accepted "The Tomb-Spawn," and has sprung a genuine surprise on me by suggesting that I do an illustration for "The Weaver in the Vault," which is scheduled for the Jan. issue! Well, I can try at any rate. Someone has evidently been extolling my drawings around the *W.T.* office.

I'll loan you "The Seven Geases" if both *Astounding* and *W.T.* should reject it. I have gone on a little with "The Chain of Aforgomon,"[6] which I began last spring, and plan to finish this and also "The House of Haon-Dor" before I attempt any new tales. Haon-Dor, by the way, figures in "The Seven Geases," and the description of his subterrene palace, with its entrance guarded by a giant rattlesnake, is one of the weirdest passages in that tale. The thing in the ultimate gulf was Abhoth, "father and mother of all cosmic uncleanness," to whom the Archetypes had sent Ralibar Vooz in the gentle hope that Abhoth would mistake him for one of its own progeny and "devour him according to that custom which it followed." Even Abhoth, however, was suspicious of anything so foreign and outlandish as a surface-dweller; and the doom that finally overtook Ralibar Vooz was more or less accidental.

I agree with you that "Seaton's Aunt" is a fine weird tale—the best in the volume (*The Riddle*) by de la Mare that I have read. I have never seen the others that you mention—"All-Hallows' Eve," "Mr. Kempe," and "A Recluse." I liked "The Tree" pretty well as a fantasy, too.[7]

I wondered about that letter from Ostrow in the Eyrie—the Shakespearean portion of it, since I couldn't recall seeing or hearing of anything by you on the immortal William.[8] Of course, he must have confused you with Sam Loveman, who seems to have a remarkable feeling for the Elizabethan. I must confess—probably to my shame—that I haven't looked into any of the old dramatists for ages.

*   *   *

plus tard. This letter was interrupted the other day by a damnable accident that happened to my mother: the overturning of a pot of hot tea, which scalded her left foot badly. I fear she will be laid up for weeks or months. It is most unfortunate and provoking, though I hope less serious than the effects of your aunt's fall.

Your last card received. Yes, there has been an attempt to revive the old gold-mining industry hereabouts. Any number of amateur placer miners on the local streams; and many old quartz ledges and gravel mines have been re-opened. Also, there has been some hydraulicking in the Sierra foothills above Auburn.

The weather continues phenomenally warm and dry. I am writing this in my shirt-sleeves. Have about finished the drawing for "The Weaver in the Vault," and hope that Wright will like it. I'll enclose a rough pencil sketch which gives the idea. The pen-drawing, however, has much more detail, as well as a different arrangement.

Yrs for the exaltation of the gods of Zothique,
Klarkash-Ton

1. Namirrha appears in "The Dark Eidolon" (*OST*), Malygris in "The Death of Malygris" (*LW*), Nathaire in "The Colossus of Ylourgne" (*GL*).

2. CAS refers to the rejection by Allen G. Ullmann of Alfred Knopf of a collection of HPL's short stories.

3. FW rejected this story on 29 September 1933 (ms., JHL), stating "It would occupy 11 or 12 pages in *Weird Tales,* and many of our readers, I fear, would object strongly to reading a prose poem as long as this."

4. CAS fictionalized the dream in "The Primal City" (*Fantasy Fan,* November 1934; *GL*).

5. "The Festival" (orig. January 1925); Robert E. Howard, "The Pool of the Black One"; Frank Belknap Long, "The Black, Dead Thing"; Mearle Prout, "The House of the Worm"; CAS, "The Seed of the Sepulcher" (*WT,* October 1933).

6. "The Chain of Aforgomon" (WT, December 1935; *OST*).

7. "Seaton's Aunt" and "The Tree" appear in *The Riddle and Other Stories* (New York: Knopf, 1923). "All-Hallow's Eve" and "Mr. Kempe" are collected in *The Connoisseur and Other Stories* (New York: Alfred A. Knopf, 1926). "A Recluse" first appeared in Lady Cynthia Asquith's *The Ghost Book* (London: Hutchinson, 1926) and is collected in de la Mare's *Over the Edge* (London: Faber and Faber, 1930)

8. Alexander Ostrow's letter in the October 1933 issue of *WT* stated: "Your readers might be interested in knowing that not only is Lovecraft a master of weird fiction, but that he is also an authority on Shakespeare" (*H. P. Lovecraft in "The Eyrie"* [West Warwick, RI: Necronomicon Press, 1979], p. 36). He appears to have confused HPL with Samuel Loveman who, though no expert, had written his own scenes for several of Shakespeare's plays.

[180]   To August Derleth [TLS, SHSW]   Oct. 19th, 1933.

Dear August:

[. . .] As to Crawford, I should judge that his prejudice against weirdness applies largely to stuff dealing with stock superstitions. He seems to class work such as mine and Lovecraft's as "pure fantasy." However, I could wish that he didn't have so much of the scientific bias.

The *Astounding Stories* crew certainly don't seem to go in much for letter-writing amenities. My "The Witchcraft of Ulua" and "The Tomb-Spawn" were returned with printed slips, and even the check for "The Demon of the Flower" was unaccompanied by any other intimation of acceptance. However, if they'll buy a few of my yarns for spot cash, I'll overlook their epistolary short-comings.

Wright finally took "The Tomb-Spawn." Also, he sprang a genuine surprise on me by asking me to do an illustration for "The Weaver in the Vault," which appears in January. Evidently someone had been extolling my pictorial abilities around the *W.T.* office. I have done the illustration, taking much care with it, and hope that Pharnabosus will like the result. It will mean seven dollars extra on the story. [. . .]

Hope you will be able to land some stuff with *Astounding*. The second issue, just out, is not much of an improvement on the first; though one or two of the stories are at least a step in the right direction. The others might have gone unchallenged in the Clayton *Astounding*—same old heroes, girls, villyans and complications. As a correspondent of mine (R. H. Barlow) says, "the mag is pretty low in the literary scale."

Good luck with your stories and poems.

The spacing gadgets on my Underwood have gone blooey, so I'm back with the Old Reliable Remington, which I have mended with liquid solder. Let's hope the solder will hold.

            As ever,
            Clark Ashton

[181]   To R. H. Barlow [TLS, JHL]   Oct. 25th, 1933.

Ar-Éch-Bei,
Phlegethonian Envoy to Phlo-Ri-Dah:
Esteemed confrere:

I was pleased to learn that "Ulua" was neither too pediculous nor pudendal for your taste. As to Wright and his taboos, well, I give it up. I have re-submitted the tale to him with a slightly sub-tilized version of the temptation scene; and if he returns it this time, shall not bother to do anything further with the tale for commercial purposes.

A Southern Recluse Press[1] would be a grand idea, and of course I'll contribute something—either "Ulua" or some better tale. Hornig only uses very short stories in *The Fantasy Fan;* and my best things usually run upwards of 3000 words. As to Cook's arrangement, that, I believe, was "completely amateur." My advice to you, in regard to this printing project, is to publish a small edition that you can dispose of within a reasonable length of time, and to take any financial profit—if such should accrue—as an agreeable surprise. If I had published only 300 or 400 copies of *The Double Shadow,* I might at least have broken even on it by this time; but 1000 seems to have been a serious over-estimate of the possible demand. Cash sales to date number somewhere around 250 or less; and new sales, even with my ad in *W.T.,* are not drift-ing in very fast.

As to Flagg, I am not sure that he is seriously ill—merely con-jectured this as a possible explanation of his non-appearance in magazines. The current *Science Fiction Digest* contains an article by him.[2] Some of his tales are quite passable, and far less stereo-typed than the usual scientifiction. "The Dancer in the Crystal" and "The Picture"[3] were really fine.

Yes, "The Seven Geases" is the title; geases being the plural of geas, a Celtic word meaning a magical compulsion that is laid upon someone to do something. Cabell uses it several times in *Figures of Earth.*[4] *Astounding* still holds "The S.G."; and I hope they will have the guts to publish it. They have also held "The Coming of the White Worm," which Wright rejected pro tem as being too poetic, with the proviso that he would use it if times ever got better. Wright, by the way, has bought "The Tomb-Spawn," a monstrous item belonging to my Zothique series; and he has also sprung a complete surprise by asking me to do an illus-tration for "The Weaver in the Vault," which appears in January.

I have finished and mailed the drawing, and hope it will pass the art board of *WT*.

My mother is laid up with a bad burn—result of pouring hot tea on her foot—and this unfortunate accident has thrown another monkey wrench into my literary programme. I am doctor, nurse, chief dish-washer and god knows what. Apropos of all this, I wonder if your offer about typing still holds? If it does, I wish you'd make me a typed copy of "The Maze of the Enchanter" from my booklet. It is possible that I can sell the serial rights of this tale to *Astounding Stories;* and at any rate there is no harm in trying. You needn't bother about a carbon. Though I cannot give you a ms. copy of this tale (I don't believe there ever was one) I'll see that you don't lack for other Mss., autographic items, etc.

I note that a copy of my *Odes and Sonnets* is listed at $4.00 in the catalogue of the Holmes Book Co of Oakland, Cal. Do you want to pay this much for the item? If you do, let me know and I'll buy and autograph it for you. If I could get down to the Bay region in person, it is probable, or at least possible, that I could find a copy at $3.00. But, with present indications, it looks as if I were nailed to the mast.

Here are some drawings which I have made at night as exercises in pen-and-ink technique. I assure you that I was not thinking any invidious thoughts about the Hon. Franklin D. Roosevelt when I did the one of the gentleman with the choker of Kohinoors.[5]

Yrs, under the night-black seal of Thasaidon,[6]
Klarkash-Ton

1. W. Paul Cook of Athol, MA, published HPL's "Supernatural Horror in Literature" in a one-shot magazine called *The Recluse,* as well as books by various of HPL's friends and colleagues under the imprint of The Recluse Press. Barlow's few publications ultimately came out under the imprint of the Dragon-Fly Press.

2. Francis Flagg, "Tyrants of Saturn" [Chapter 5] (*Science-Fiction Digest,* October 1933).

3. Francis Flagg, "The Dancer in Crystal" (*WT,* December 1929) and "The Picture" (*WT,* February–March 1931).

4. James Branch Cabell (1879–1958), *Figures of Earth* (1921).

5. The Koh-i-noor ("Mountain of Light") is a very large rose-colored diamond obtained in India, now part of the Royal Family's crown jewels residing in the Tower of London.

6. Thasaidon is "lord of evil" in CAS's stories of Zothique.

[182]   To H. P. Lovecraft [TLS, JHL] [c. early November 1933]
                            Tower of black jade in lost Carcosa.[1]
                      Hour when the twin suns are both at nadir.

Dear Éch-Pi-El:
    This letter would have been written sometime ago if it were
not for my program of nursing, doctoring, general housework, etc.
My mother's burn is healing slowly, and she is still in bed. On the
whole, I suspect that the enforced rest will be beneficial to her; but
otherwise it is all pretty tedious and exasperating; and with my
time so broken up, it is hard to concentrate on story-writing, or
even letters.
    I await "The Thing on the Doorstep" with tremendous eager-
ness. Hope you received "The Witchcraft of Ulua" from Ar-Éch-
Bei, Phlegethonian Envoy to Phlo-Ri-Dah. Wright, by the way, has
finally taken this tale. I submitted a version in which the temptation scene was a little less flamboyant and more subtle.
    Thanks for the fine views of 66 College St. The fan carving
certainly does remind me of your bookplate. I'd like to keep these
pictures and shall prize them highly. I return the newspaper cut-
tings. That sunset effect with the rainbow must indeed have been
striking. Rainbows are frequent here in the winter and spring, and
I have seen immense double arches of the most extraordinary
brilliance and perfection. Our weather has been clear again since
the storm I mentioned on my card; but stray clouds and fog-banks
over the Sacramento valley have given us gorgeous sunsets of gold,
orange, crimson and salmon. "The moon-tints of purple and
pearl"[2] have been noticeable on several evenings, too. The heavy
rain (over four inches) was of great benefit; and a velvety green is
now visible amid the dry windlestrae of yesteryear. The nights and
mornings are pretty sharp, though without frost as yet. I looked
for a fine crop of mushrooms after the rain; but none have
appeared. Perhaps it is too early—late November and December is
their usual time; or perhaps it is an "off" year. They were very
plentiful last winter.
    Your drawing of the Lincoln woods region conveys a genuine
charm, with its leisurely winding road and foreground of trees and
background of steepled roofs. Together with your descriptions, it
increases and confirms my desire to visit New England at some
date not too far in the future.
    Glad you liked the portrait of Lord Tsathoggua.[3] Of course,
I could only depict an aspect that was renderable in terms of

terrestrial form and dimension. Wright hasn't returned my drawing for "The Weaver"; so I suppose he will use it. Thanks for your
advocacy of my pictures. Bloch, I believe, had also mentioned them
to Pharnabosus.

Yes, I noticed W's plural mention of The Black Book &
Unaussprechlichen Kulten. Shades of Von Junzt!⁴ ****** In his
last letter he apologized for misquoting one of my sonnets several
years back in the Eyrie. Since I can't remember seeing the quotation I would have remained in ignorance till doomsday if he
hadn't told me. I am glad that Crawford took "Sarnath" and
"Celephaïs" and look forward with pleasure to having printed
copies of them. Howard writes me that he has sent Crawford some
material. *Unusual Stories,* at this rate, will be something of a family affair for us, in spite of its avowed scientifictional bent.

What you tell me about the *Astounding* editors merely confirms my intuitions. Why in hell couldn't the publishers have
picked someone who at least knew the ropes and was interested in
the game? They fired back "The Seven Geases" after keeping it for
a month; but have not yet returned "The White Worm."

I didn't imagine that the plot Robot would be of much use to
you.⁵ I've never seen the contraption, but have read accounts of it,
and judge that it works by a sort of lottery combination and
recombination of certain stock elements. Few of my stories, I fear,
exhibit what is known in pulpdom as a "plot." Perhaps my current
W.T. yarn, "The Holiness of Azéderac," comes as near to it as any.

Lumley's hints are certainly inveigling as well as portentous.
Apparently he was delighted with the Eibon chapter. The idea of a
primeval serpent-race seems to be a favourite one with him, since
he refers to it in his last letter as well as in one or two previous
epistles. Granting that he may be a little mad—well, such madness
is infinitely preferable to the sort of thing that commonly passes for
sanity. Olsen, as you wisely say, is a totally different matter; mega-
lomania, dementia, mystic delirium and whatnot were all scram-
bled together in the one interminable screed he wrote me.

Of course, it would seem that the arguments of material science
are pretty cogent. Perhaps it is only my innate romanticism that
makes me at least hopeful that the Jeans and Einsteins have overlooked something. If ever I have the leisure and opportunity,
I intend some first-hand investigation of obscure phenomena.
Enough inexplicable things have happened in my own experience
to make me wonder. I am pretty sure that I saw apparitions in my
childhood; one instance remaining especially vivid in memory. The
phantasm was that of a bowed and muffled woman, weeping or at
least sorrow-stricken, which appeared one night in a corner of my
bedroom in an old house which my parents had rented for several

months. It certainly left an eerie impression. Another queer happening, of a totally different kind, occurred four or five years ago. A woman-friend and I were out walking one night in a lane near Auburn, when a dark, lightless and silent object passed over us against the stars with projectile-like speed. The thing was too large and swift for any bird, and gave precisely the effect of a *black* meteor. I have often wondered what it was.[6] Charles Fort, no doubt, would have made a substantial item out of it for one of his volumes.

Montague Summers is certainly a mine of rare erudition; and I will admit that he interests me greatly. Have you seen his *The Geography of Witchcraft*?[7] I found this book listed at $1.50 in a recent catalogue and have ordered it. Am also ordering (from a firm in Glasgow, Scotland) Lewis Spence's *History of Atlantis* and a volume on magic by C. J. S. Thompson which sounded very interesting.[8] These volumes were also priced very cheaply. Summers' translation of the *Malleus Maleficarum* was listed at one pound five shillings. I coveted this, but did not feel equal to the extravagance.[9]

Re levitation (as allegedly performed by yogis) I have seen it explained as a matter of controlled breathing. A certain rhythmic mode of respiration is supposed to fill the body with *positive* electricity, which temporarily counteracts the negative electric force of gravity. It sounds interesting, even if pseudo-scientific.

The modern explanation of the growth of myths and superstitions is certainly well worked out. Yet, after all, it is possible that brand new psychological theories may in time supersede much that is now regarded as self-evident. Also, there is the fascinating possibility that human beings may in time develop new senses or faculties that will take them a little further into the cosmic penetralia; though, of course, never approaching ultimates or near-ultimates. It may then be suspected that the sources of human thought lie deeper and remoter than has been supposed. We are *not insulated* from the myriad unknown forces of the cosmos that play upon us; and, after all who knows what the *real* effect of these forces may be? Lacking the effect of some unconsidered radiation, the whole trend of human mentation might be totally different from what it is.

I shall be very glad to avail myself of your offer to loan me *The Connoisseur*. The book is unobtainable locally. In return, let me remind you that any of my books, or all, are at your disposal.

The enclosed clippings may be of interest. I have accumulated a vast mass of oddities by watching the daily papers.

Yours for the resurgence of the Old Ones,
Klarkash-Ton

1. Carcosa was invented by Ambrose Bierce, and mentioned later (in a different context) by Robert W. Chambers; HPL mentions Carcosa in "The Whisperer in Darkness."

2. Poe, "Eulalie," l. 11.

3. Published as an illustration for "The Seven Geases."

4. Robert E. Howard invented *Unaussprechlichen Kulten* (also known as The Black Book) and its author, Von Junzt.

5. HPL had purchased "Robo—The New Game for Writers—The Game that writes a Million Story Plots," a device for plotting stories as a means of helping him to write material more readily salable to pulp magazines. See HPL to CAS (22 October 1933; ms. private collection): "I sent for that 'plot Robot', but find it is nothing at all I could use in my own work. All it concerns is the purely conventional hack junk—with hero, heroine, obstacle, crisis, & all that. But it may come in handy in revising commercial tripe for dumb clients—certainly, it gives a very forceful idea of the artificial hokum called 'plot' & considered an indispensable factor in pulp fiction."

6. One of the stories outlined in *BB* is titled "The Dark Meteor" (see item 64, p. 28).

7. Montague Summers, *The Geography of Witchcraft* (New York: Knopf, 1927).

8. Lewis Spence (1874–1955), *The History of Atlantis* (London: Rider & Co., 1926); Charles John Samuel Thompson (1862–1943), *The Mysteries and Secrets of Magic* (London: John Lane, The Bodley Head Ltd., 1927).

9. Heinrich Kramer and James Sprenger, *Malleus Maleficarum*, trans. with introduction, bibliography, and notes by the Rev. Montague Summers ([London]: J. Rodker, 1928).

---

[183]   To H. P. Lovecraft [TLS, JHL]   [c. 4 December 1933]
From the black desert of Zoir,
beneath the seven ultra-spectral suns.

Dear Éch-Pi-El:

I have just finished reading "The Thing on the Doorstep" for the second time, and am re-impressed by its power. The theme is carefully developed (needless to say) and the climax comes like a thunderclap. In all frankness, I must disagree with Dwyer or anyone else who criticises any portion of the tale as being below par. I hope you will submit the tale to Pharnabosus. Unless I am grievously mistaken, he will grab it with exceeding promptless. Allah! what a contrast between your handling of this theme and a hunk of melodramatic hooey such as "Abd Dhulma, Lord of Fire," in the Dec. *W.T.!* I instance the Pendarves opus because it deals with a magician who lives on from age to age by absorbing the souls of others: a theme slightly congenerate with yours, but infinitely less impressive and effective in the actual treatment.[1]

Edward Derby's character is well realized. I have one very minor suggestion to make, and this I offer with much doubt and hesitation. I wonder if it would be better to add a hint (perhaps no more than a sentence or phrase) to the effect that Derby's abnormal ability to animate the corpse of Asenath was due to his own far from negligible achievements in dark magic. However, this is perhaps implicit in the tale as it stands.

I trust that Conan and most of the others on the circulation list fully appreciate the treat in store for them. The ms. goes forward to the Cimmerian monarch today.[2]

One of my cards will have informed you of my pleasure in hearing that "Through the Gates of the Silver Key" has finally received the satrapic approval. Any of the ultramundane scenes in this story would be well adapted to my style of pictorial treatment. I have heard nothing further from Wright about the pictorialization of "The Charnel God." Evidently there is no hurry: the tale will not appear till March; and at last hearing W. had not decided whether to favour "The C.G." with a cover design or to take the March cover from one of Cave's melodramas.

Speaking of covers, the current *W.T.* design, though pleasing enough in color, is curiously suggestive of a Christmas card! I don't wish to be ungallant: Mrs. Brundage (between you and me and the asymmetric eikon from Crater Ridge) has about as much genuine feeling for the weird as a Jersey cow is likely to possess. The best angles in this picture (the hands of the Chinaman, etc) seem to have been swiped by unconscious cerebration from Utpatel's drawing for "The Star-Spawn" by Derleth and Schorer.[3]

To touch upon certain points in your last letter: You have certainly pointed up my vagueness and ignorance in regard to Gallic history! Of course, if I had stopped to reflect, I ought to have known that the Romans were still strong in Gaul about the time of Moriamis, and that French, as a language was not yet born from the Latin womb. I suppose that the fact that I was dealing with a realm no less mythical than Cabell's Poictesme made me doubly careless about correlating its chronology with that of historic Europe. If ever there is any prospect of issuing Azéderac and the other Averoigne tales in book form, I shall certainly correct the anachronistic reference to the "obsolete variant" of French spoken by Moriamis. I think, though, that the Druids can well stand: Averoigne was no doubt even more of a stronghold for the cult than Brittany; and the Roman occupation (though I have spoken of it in another tale, "The Disinterment of Venus") was quite nominal, especially in its religious effect on the Averoignians.[4]

Indeed, the long decadence of the Roman Empire is a fascinating study; and evidently you are thoroughly posted on its details. I agree with you that a fine and poignant story could be drawn from the sensations of a Gallo-Roman who had outlived his own time and had seen about him the gradual crystallization of wholly alien medieval France. The linguistic specimens you quote, showing the transition of Latin into old French, are highly interesting. I wonder if a study (theoretic, at least) could not be made of the obscure racial, mental and palatal peculiarities that led (or contributed) to this phonetic devolution and clipping of the stately Latin. The study could cover also the development of the other Romance languages.

I have greatly enjoyed the de la Mare volume. "Mr. Kempe" is a fine tale, and one is not likely to forget either the setting or the central character. However, it seems to me that a stronger suggestive element could easily have been worked in. "All Hallows," on the other hand, is beyond improvement and beyond praise. To me, it is even more satisfactory than "Seaton's Aunt." The powerfully hinted idea of demoniac reconstruction is about as good as anything in weird fiction and is wholly original.

No, I have not read *The Dark Chamber,*[5] and would be vastly indebted to you for a sight of the volume. *The Geography of Witchcraft* and *The Lady who Came to Stay*[6] are both awaiting your summons. I regret that I cannot altogether share the enthusiasm of Derleth and Shea in regard to the latter. However, it is far from bad, albeit, in the main, a second-rate reminiscence of Henry James. *The Geography* is a veritable mine of evidence bearing on the witch-cult; and the dark identity of details in numberless cases far scattered in time and place is surely proof of the under-lying reality. No doubt the prevalence of the cult in medieval times was partly due to intolerable social misery: this flight into Satanism, supernaturalism and carnal orgy was an avenue of escape for the more neurotic or unfortunate. Also—granting the existence of supernatural powers and their influence on human life—the belief in evil forces and the impulse to propitiate them and form alliances with them was certainly far from irrational. Manichaeism is a practical inference when one considers the world as it is, and tries to explain the world as a creation or playground of superhuman forces.

Other theories than those of Summers and Miss Murray have been advanced anent sorcery. Some time ago, there was a series of articles by one Prof. Rene Thevenin,[7] which appeared in the Sunday supplement of Hearst's *Examiner.* Possibly you saw a syndication of these articles, in which Thenevin maintained the existence of prehistoric supermen, a little of whose science survived the foundering of former continents and was preserved by ancient priests and medieval witches. From this viewpoint, the witches and warlocks were the only enlightened people in ages of darkness and gross superstition, and their Sabbats were merely secret educational conclaves or class-meetings! If you haven't seen these articles, I'll enclose the ones I have with *The Geography.* Unluckily, I only procured three or four out of the seven chapters of the series. I know nothing about Thevenin's claims to scholarship; but at any rate his contentions and data are abundantly stimulative to the imagination. In one chapter, he brings forward a theory that the African negroes are a degenerate remnant of the Lemurians, and supports this by instancing the progressive decadence, through historic times, of certain African civilizations. This is pretty much in line with theosophic theories; though, as far as I can gather, Thevenin is not familiar with occultism, or at least has not considered it in forming his own theorem.

Of course, I do not think for a moment that there is any doubt about the true character of the Sabbats and those who participated in them. But Thevenin's ideas anent the survival of the elder lore are not so remote from our own fictional speculations!

I'm glad the newspaper clippings were of interest. Thanks for your suggestion about the Boer witch-woman: she might well have gone to Zimbabwe and imbibed certain vaporous or shadowy outside influences from those unholy ruins. I may yet use her in a story; she certainly looks the part assigned to her.

The pictures by Biegas[8] are certainly powerful. Many years ago, I saw a magazine article giving reproductions of some of his sculptures which, if my memory does not fail me, were even stronger and more striking than this pictorial work. Many of them symbolized music or the work of particular musicians; and the sense of fluent, surging rhythm imparted to the static medium was indeed extraordinary. Some were like sea-billows towering and breaking in a foam of eerie faces. There was one remarkable piece, entitled Beethoven: the torso and head of an austere Titan, with separate faces in the eyeballs! Another, called Chopin, whose details I cannot remember, has left an impression of macabre fury and madness.

Morse sent me a list of his collection of weird literature and art; and it seemed to me that he had a quite respectable beginning.[9] The field of weird art is an immense one however; and no doubt one could spend several fortunes and lifetimes in covering it throughly. I imagine some of the most potent examples would come from the Orient, particularly from China and Japan. All peoples and ages would contribute, more or less. By the way, apropos of this subject, did you know that John Barrymore did some quite powerful eerie drawings in his younger days? I have, or did have, an article from the *Cosmopolitan* (dated somewhere around the early 1900s) in which some specimens were reproduced.

Thanks for that news photo of the Ashton house! I knew there were some Ashtons in the South (Virginia, I believe) but had not seen the name before in connection with New England. Most of my family (the old direct line, anyway) were Catholics. One sometimes sees the name spelt Assheton; and there are evidently a lot of Assheton-Smiths or Smithes in England.

Thanks too for the offer to loan me some of your choice clippings. Don't go to any extra trouble in this matter, but you might slip in a few with your letters. I'll read and return them carefully.

My writing is still held up, and I have not finished anything. I hope my mother will be able to get around a little before long.

I enclose a recent letter from Desmond Hall. . . . "Play around with psychoanalysis . . . . suggest that nothing in the universe is inexplicable," etc. Grrrr! I'm afraid I'll have a hard time in suiting the requirements of that crew. Psychoanalysis is not my favorite superstition or form of pseudo-science. However, there is no doubt that some excellent weird or semi-weird tales could be written dealing with obscure physical and mental phenomena, without actual recourse to anything supernatural; and I infer that this is what Hall wants. Anyway, he evidently feels that *Astounding* needs some variety to raise it out of the ruck; and in this I heartily agree with him. In my own letter, I had expressed polite regret over the narrowing of policy, and had suggested that the magazine could well afford to run at least one tale of non-technical fantasy per issue. Also, I pointed out the glaring inconsistency of science fiction readers, who will swallow any sort of outrageous fairy tale if it is served up with an accompaniment of ray-guns, ether-ships, time-machines, etc.

The Olsen letter, which I return, is most illuminating. Some one, I forget whom, has fathered a book on the sort of cosmogony at which O. is apparently driving. Of course, if you accept the idea that the earth's surface is really the *inside* of a sphere surrounding the negligible remainder of the cosmos, then the space-conceptions implied in your Witchhouse story are most egregiously fallacious. This letter is really a marvel of lucidity compared to the 10 or twelve page monograph on the nobility of ghouls, vampires et al which I received from Olsen in correction of my "Nameless Off-spring" and the errors of Abdul Alhazred. It would seem that the bats in Olsen's belfry—or the spirochetæ in his spinal column—are less gyrationally active than of yore. However, it is plain that he has not relinquished his position of mentor-in-chief to the *Weird Tales* contributors! His offer to instruct you in person for 25 paltry pazoors[10] is truly magnanimous not to say magnific.

Winter seems to have arrived, and the mercury hugs the freezing-point around sunrise. I envy your steam-heat!

Yours, in the name of Kamog,[11]

Klarkash-Ton

1. G. G. Pendarves, "Abd Dhulma, Lord of Fire" (*WT*, December 1933).

2. I.e., Robert E. Howard, creator of the fictional Conan the Barbarian.

3. Margaret Brundage (1900–1976), cover artist for *WT*. Her early experience included fashion design. As noted, her design borrowed from that of Frank Utpatel's illustration of "The Lair of the Star-Spawn" (*WT*, August 1932).

4. On the envelope of this letter HPL laid out some historical details of Averoigne in Roman times, and composed a poem or incantation to Tsathoggua: "Black and unshap'd, as pestilent a Clod / As Black Sadoqua, Averonia's God" (*SL* 4.332).

5. Leonard Cline (1893–1929), *The Dark Chamber* (New York: Viking Press, 1927).

6. R[obin] E[dgerton] Spencer (1896–1956) *The Lady Who Came to Stay* (New York: Book League of America, 1931).

7. René Thévenin (1877–1967), author of science fiction under the pseudonym Martial Cendres.

8. Boleslas Biegas (1877–1954), Polish sculptor and painter of weird themes.

9. HPL's correspondent, Richard Ely Morse, who was interested in weird art. His sonnet "Dark Garden," *Californian* (Fall 1936), was dedicated to CAS.

10. Monetary unit used in Hyperborea.

11. An allusion to an entity in HPL's "The Thing on the Doorstep."

---

[184]   To Lester Anderson [TLS, private collection]

Dec. 31st, 1933

My dear Lester:

[. . .] *The Invisible Man* came to Auburn some time ago.[1] I liked it, but thought that even more—much more—could have been done with the idea. Fantasy should be an ideal medium for the films; and I believe the producers will do better with experience. The first part of *Deluge* was good—I enjoyed the innudation of New York.[2] [. . .]

I haven't seen *Elysia*,[3] but am not at all shocked by the idea of nudity. However, I think the modern fad for it is, at bottom, a sign of decadence rather than health. It is not new, either: Montague Summers, in his *Geography of Witchcraft*, mentions a sect called the Adamites, who held nude parades, etc., in the Middle Ages in Germany, till the authorities put the lid on them. Nudism seems too artificial under present-day conditions of life; and it sounds damned uncomfortable, outside of a steam-heated apartment. I fear the real motive, with most of those who undertake it, is a sort of exhibitionism. On the other hand, however, it should be a corrective to imaginations overheated by the secrecy of clothes. [. . .]

Best New Year wishes.

  Cordially,
  Clark Ashton Smith

 1. *The Invisible Man* (Universal, 1933), directed by James Whale, produced by Carl Laemmle, Jr., starring Claude Rains.
 2. *Deluge* (RKO, 1933), directed by Felix E. Feist, produced by Carl Laemmle, Jr., starring Sidney Blackmer, Peggy Shannon, and Lois Wilson; based on the novel *Deluge* (1928) by S. Fowler Wright.
 3. *Elysia: Valley of the Nude* (1933/4), a documentary filmed at California's Elysian Valley nudist colony, directed by Bryan Foy, starring Betty De Salle.

---

[185] To H. P. Lovecraft [TLS, JHL] [c. late January 1934]
        Hour of the dawning luminosity in the
           sunless gulf of Aforgomon.

Dear Éch-Pi-El:

Your New York visit seems to have been signalized by a number and variety of "contacts!" I was vastly interested by your account of the divers notables, A. Merritt, Hall, Koenig, Howard Wandrei, Harré, and the editors of *SFD*. Merritt's new projected story about the city of Ys certainly sounds like a humdinger. I had surmised that he was largely responsible for the moiety of outré and scientific articles in the Hearst supplements. Harré must have been interesting—I like very much his anthology, *Beware after Dark*, with its enthusiastic preface. This collection, to my way of thinking, is much better than the Hammett volume, *Creeps by*

Night, which I have recently acquired. Your "Erich Zann" was almost the only genuinely atmospheric tale in Hammett's selection, most of the others being pretty mundane and sophisticated.[1]

I'd certainly like to see H. Wandrei's batiks and drawings, and hope that Donald will send me the photographs which he has taken or intends to take. By the way, Melmoth gave me some interesting mementoes of your visit, in the shape of snapshots including Long, you and himself. These seemed very life-like indeed.

Returning to Merritt, if you will give me his address, I'll be very glad to send him a copy of *The Double Shadow* gratis. I am glad to know that the Averoigne stories appealed to him. Harré's expressed admiration of my work is very gratifying, since I think that H. has shown remarkably sound taste in his anthology, and therefore his opinion would be significant.

The Loveman museum must indeed be a choice and rare collection! The *ushabti,* Mayan idol and Balinese monkey-carving sound ineffably fascinating, and such generosity was truly apropos, if you know what I mean. I'd like to see these—and also the Greek maiden's head that you describe.

Congratulations on the improved ductility of flow in your fountain-pen! It would certainly make an immense difference, particularly to one who does a large amount of writing. Personally, I've almost given up the use of pens, and employ a common steel dip on the occasions when one is really requisite.

I am glad the drawing for "The Weaver" appealed to you. The reproduction was not all bad, to judge from the copies on local news-stands. Wright seems to have been pleased with my design for "The Charnel God," and has now ordered one for "The Death of Malygris" (April). "The Witchcraft of Ulua," for which I *could* have done something especially good, will appear as a filler, sans illustration, in the Feb. *W.T.* I hope W. will give me a chance at the "Silver Key" sequel—probably he won't want a drawing for it till two months before the publication date.

Howard Wandrei's tale in the last *W.T.* was quite good and original, I thought. Conan, as usual, put on a very entertaining and imaginative show. Merritt's "Woman of the Wood," though excellent, impressed me as being somewhat overrated. The other tales in the issue were hardly noteworthy.[2]

I imagine Koenig's library must be very much the same sort that I myself would accumulate with ample money and facilities. I envy him with all my heart, since volumes of outre and fantastic literature are among the few desiderata of my existence; and my own collection is painfully limited.

I forwarded *The Dark Chamber* to Koenig several days ago, as per instructions. As you will have gathered from a former letter, I enjoyed the book greatly. The theme of mnemonic delving is a tremendous one, and the story certainly suggests a lot. From the standpoint of pure weirdness, it seems to me that the story would have been better with a minimizing of the erotic element, which, for my taste, does not add to the atmosphere. But no doubt the author was not trying for pure weirdness. Re the treatment of music in this tale, I think that it is inferior to your mode of treatment in "Erich Zann." Cline, it seems to me, tries to be too definite; and one cannot be definite about music. Thanks again for the loan of *The Dark Chamber*. I am certainly glad to have read it; though you will perhaps infer that my estimate of the book is not quite so high as yours and Long's. I believe—coming down to comparisons—that you and Long have both done sounder work than the *D.C.*

Later. Yr. card and the books came, and I hasten to thank you for the Wakefield loan and the gift, jointly with Es-El, of the book on Beddoes.[3] I read one of the Wakefield stories last night—" 'He Cometh and He Passeth By' " — and found it excellent, especially in the suggestion of the diabolic Shadow.[4] Crowley is surely a picturesque character, to have inspired anything like Clinton! I know little about Crowley myself, but wouldn't be surprised if many of the more baleful elements in his reputation were akin to those in the Baudelaire legend . . . that is to say, largely self-manufactured or foisted upon him by the credulous bourgeoisie.

Beddoes is indeed an old favourite, and I consider *Death's Jest Book* as good as anything in Elizabethan literature, with a super-added subtlety and atmosphere which none of the old dramatists seem to have had. I shall read this book by Royall Snow with immense avidity. [. . .]

Re the scarab discovery, I too doubt if it ever came from Egypt. But to me this does not necessarily mean that it is a fake. After all, there is no reason why one of the prehistoric American peoples shouldn't have used an insect symbol. The Egyptians surely had no copyright on beetles. Coincidental art-development seems the likely explanation of the matter.

I hope you have found time and inclination for some new work. Surely you need feel no uncertainty about "The Thing on the Doorstep." Malik's[5] card, which I return, sounds pretty enthusiastic to me, and I do not imagine that his criticisms involved anything very radical.

I finished, after a fashion, the long-deferred "Chain of Aforgomon," and have already had it turned down by Pharnabosus, on the plea that "it sagged as a tale toward the end," whatever that means. Pharnabosus ordered a drawing for "The Death of Malygris." This I have just finished, and am inclined to think it is the best of my *W.T.* illustrations so far. [. . .]

Congratulations on the Weigall purchase.[6] I certainly like the theory about the Britanno-Roman blood in modern English veins. Forty-five generations isn't such a great remove after all; and it sounds credible enough. I rather think that my own inheritance is predominantly Celtic; but it wouldn't be so surprising if there were a drop of Roman blood somewhere in the line.

If you have not before seen pictures of Prorok's excavations, you might be interested in his book, *Digging for Lost African Gods,*[7] which I possess. This I'd gladly send you for a long-term loan. Lewis Spence's *The History of Atlantis,* which came not long ago, also might interest you, if you have not already seen it.

I fear that the chances are none too good for *Unusual Stories,* particularly in view of the recently announced deficit of *The Fantasy Fan.* This tallies with my own experience in printing a one-shot like *The Double Shadow.* I am discontinuing my ad in *W.T.,* since returns are not enough to justify the expense. And I still owe the printer a sizable sum.

Science Fiction Digest wants only weird tales with a rationalistic explanation, I understand. I don't think I have anything that would quite fill the bill at present. I have, however, sent them a recently revised copy of my translation of Baudelaire's "Rêve Parisien"[8]—a poem which might be of interest to scientifictionists as well as fantaisists.

The new shipment of books from Koenig certainly sounds like rare meat! I've never seen any of the items you list. I have, by the way, ordered a new Machen book, *The Green Round,* which Derleth recommended; also, the Edith Thomson anthology, *Keep on the Light,* which contains my yarn, "The Isle of the Torturers."[9] These have not yet arrived. I hope Machen's volume won't be too much of a disillusionment.

As to Hoffmann, I guess my reaction would be similar to yours. The three or four tales of his that I have seen were distinctly disappointing.

Yes, I shall assuredly endeavor to collate the texts of Valerius Trevisus and Carnamagos when I write that tale of Regio Averonum.[10] Regarding Kranaos of Alexandria, there are those who maintain, if I mistake not, that his somewhat ambiguous though terrible suggestions referred to the inhabitants of primal Thule rather than to the Averones; but since the Averones were tainted with a dark strain of Hyperborean ancestry, it is possible that he included them by implication in his black shadowings of the unmentionable. . . .

I'll return *The Connoisseur* and your miscellaneous clippings before long. The Thevenin articles were certainly stimulating, whatever their scientific background. I shall comment specifically on some of the other clippings in my next letter. Needless to say, I found them all of great interest.

Have you heard from Lumley of late? I wrote him around New Year's, and received a letter later in the month, expressing apprehension as to the possible non-delivery of a letter from me, through the blundering of a mail-carrier. It seems he has had considerable trouble with his mail. I wrote again promptly, but have heard nothing since.

I thought you would like that page of felines! All of them were beauties! I don't think I have ever mentioned my two cats—the black and sinister witch-cat, Simaetha, and the roistering Maltese, General Tabasco. Simaetha, in her wanderings, must have lapped up an alchemist's elixir—I have really lost track of her age. Her somewhat baleful aspect is heightened by a permanent oblique list of head and neck, acquired many years ago in a most heroic and protracted vigil at the mouth of a rat-hole. The devoted animal stayed there for days without moving!

The weather continues mild, though with fog once more in the offing. I believe you would enjoy it thoroughly. // Malik Taus has sent me a card, announcing that his safari has reached the wilds of Oklahoma without mishap or ambuscade; so it seems likely that he will appear in Auburn during the not far distant future.

Keep the enclosures. You might, however, send the lizard article to Lumley—I think he would prize it. The implications of that steady rapid growth of iguanas, etc, through recent generations are simply terrific!

Yrs for the pilgrimage to Chorazin,[11]

Klarkash-Ton.

1. T. Everett Harré (1884–1948), ed., *Beware After Dark! The World's Most Stupendous Tales of Mystery, Horror, Thrills and Terror* (New York: Macauley, 1929), containing HPL's "The Call of Cthulhu"; Dashiell Hammett (1894–1961), ed., *Creeps by Night: Chills and Thrills* (New York: John Day Co., 1931), containing "The Music of Erich Zann."

2. *WT* for January 1934 contained Howard Wandrei, "In the Triangle"; Robert E. Howard, "Rogues in the House"; and A. Merritt, "The Woman of the Wood" (a reprint).

3. Royall Henderson Snow (1898–?), *Thomas Lovell Beddoes, Eccentric and Poet* (New York: Covici, Friede, 1928). The book was a gift of HPL and Samuel Loveman.

4. H. Russell Wakefield (1890–1964), *Others Who Returned: Fifteen Disturbing Tales* (New York: D. Appleton & Co., 1929), contains "He Cometh and He Passeth By,'" the subject of which was the mystic and Satanist Aleister Crowley (1875–1947).

5. HPL's epithet for E. Hoffmann Price was "Malik Taus, the Peacock Sultan."

6. Arthur Weigall (1880–1934), *Wanderings in Roman Britain* (London: T. Butterworth, [1926]).

7. Byron Khun de Prorok (1896–?), *Digging for Lost African Gods: the Record of Five Years Archaeological Excavation in North Africa* with notes and translations by Edgar Fletcher Allen (New York; London: G. P. Putnam's Sons, 1926).

8. In *S* and *SP* as "A Parisian Dream."

9. Arthur Machen, *The Green Round* (London: Ernest Benn, 1933); Christine Campbell Thomson, ed., *Keep on the Light: Tales of Thrill and Horror* (London : Selwyn & Blount, 1933).

10. Possibly "The Oracle of Sadoqua," outlined in *BB* (item 48, p. 21).

11. Khorazin (or Chorazin) is one of the places mentioned in the Bible as the birthplace of the Antichrist. It is cited in M. R. James's "Count Magnus."

---

[186]   To Donald Wandrei [TLS, MHS]   Jan. 23rd, 1934.

Dear Donald:

[. . .] That early yarn in *Black Cat* (it must have been either "The Mahout" or "The Rajah and the Tiger"—the only ones that I landed with this magazine) was nothing much to crow about. It does evince, however, the enormous interest which I felt in things Oriental during my teens.[1] I wrote ream after ream of such stuff (most of it, luckily, unpublished) between the ages of thirteen and sixteen, under a mélange of influences ranging from the *Arabian Nights* to Kipling, with *Lallah Rookh*[2] and Beckford's *Vathek* included. Two or three of the shorter yarns appeared in the *Overland Monthly.*[3] Then, for some unfathomable reason, I switched suddenly and entirely to verse, and did not think seriously again of fiction-writing till the summer of 1929.

I didn't know that Schachner was a lawyer. Thanks for suggesting him as a legal intermediary in the Gernsback matter.[4] Not being in actual dire need of the money, and disliking the unpleasantness of legal action, I have deferred doing anything about it. Hornig, the editor, seemed to think I had a good chance of getting some of the arrears this Christmas; but said arrears have not yet materialized. Some time, if you can do so conveniently, I wish you'd get me the low-down on Gernsback; that is to say, whether he is paying any of his authors voluntarily, and is in a position to loosen up without feeling the pinch. If he is really in straits it would make a difference in my attitude. If he is not, then assuredly the blighter ought to pay. [. . .]

Best wishes for 1934! As ever,
Clark

1. "The Mahout" (*Black Cat,* August 1911); "The Rajah and the Tiger" (February 1912); both in *OD.* See also CAS's juvenile novel, *The Black Diamonds* (New York: Hippocampus Press, 2002).

2. Thomas Moore (1779–1852), *Lalla Rookh: An Oriental Romance* (1817).

3. "The Malay Krise" (*Overland Monthly,* October 1910); "The Ghost of Mohammed Din" (*Overland Monthly,* November 1910); both in *OD.*

4. Nat Schachner (1895–1955), chemist, lawyer, and writer. Like CAS his work had appeared in *Wonder Stories.* CAS ultimately hired Ione Weber as his attorney to secure $769 in back payment from *Wonder Stories.* See Mike Ashley, "The Perils of Wonder: Clark Ashton Smith's Experiences with *Wonder Stories*" (*Dark Eidolon* No. 2, July 1989): 2–8.

---

[187]   To H. P. Lovecraft [TLS, JHL]
[c. late February–early March 1934]
In deep Dendo—hour of the spiral dawning.

Dear Éch-Pi-El:

Your last would have had an answer ere this; but I managed to catch a severe cold—the first of the season, and, I hope, the last—which has disinclined me even toward letter-writing, for the past week.

The card came today—thanks for the imposing picture of the John Hay Memorial Library. Hope that Prorok and the returned volumes will arrive safely. I am awaiting A. Vigalis[1] and *Others Who Returned* with immense expectations. My advance thanks for the much appreciated loan.

I am glad you liked my note on James—the title given it was Hornig's. It was at least a clear summing up of James' special and salient qualities. Lumley's "The Dweller" is a fine thing, and I was pleased to see it in print. I wrote again to Lumley the other day, having received a line from him. Evidently some of his previous letters, or mine, must have been sunk without trace in the mails. I return herewith the letter from him enclosed in your last.[2]

Before I forget it, let me thank you for Merritt's address. I mailed him an inscribed copy of *The Double Shadow* some time ago, and hope he will enjoy the contents.[3]

Koenig wrote, acknowledging *The Dark Chamber,* and offering to loan me a catalogue of his library. Needless to say, I accepted the offer, and shall be vastly interested to look it over. Like you, I fail to comprehend the mania for first editions—any correctly printed edition with good clear type will fill the bill as far as I am concerned.

Your reaction to "The Weaver in the Vault" is gratifying. I rather like this tale myself. I must re-read "The Woman in the Wood": I went over it rather hastily, and may like it much better on a second perusal. I admired the idea tremendously, but received the impression of choppiness in some of the writing. Merritt, it seems to me, sometimes sounds like a gifted and imaginative newspaper man who has set out to do some fine writing. If he could transcend his journalistic and pulp magazine experience, he would be a world-beater.

Dunsany's The *Curse of the Wise Woman* sounds rather inviting.[4] I have, by the way, received the new Machen book, *The Green Round,* and have read it with mixed reactions. It is well written, and the mystery and suggestion are well handled. It does not, however, have the powerful climax of his earlier horror tales; and conventional poltergeist phenomena, smashing of windows, crockery, etc., by an unknown force, are repeated overmuch in the latter part. I received also the new Not at Night anthology, *Keep on the Light,* and was struck by the immense superiority of the items taken from *Weird Tales,* over others which, I presume, are by British authors. Howard's "Worms of the Earth" and Whitehead's "The Chadbourne Episode" were the leaders.

Wright found my drawing for "The Death of Malygris" satisfactory, and has ordered one for "The Colossus of Ylourgne" (June issue.) In my last epistle to Pharnabosus, I conveyed an intimation that I should regard it as an honour if he were to delegate to me the illustrating of "The Silver Key" sequel. If it does not fall to me, I fervently hope that Rankin will be the artist selected for the job. Howard Wandrei would be a great addition to the W.T. pictorial staff, to judge from the photographs of some of his pictures which Donald has recently sent me. I was particularly impressed by a thing called "The Sorcerer's Workshop"—a mélange of ingenious and provocative abominations.

Truly, matters don't look very hopeful for Crawford's venture. He seems to be having worse luck with the printing than I did with my disastrous and ill-omened one-shot, *The Double Shadow.* I still owe the printer fifty pazoors, and have been stalling him off because of the continued delay in magazine payments. I am, by the way, giving the Gernsback outfit a broad hint that some legal action will be forthcoming unless they pay up a good installment of their arrears at an early date. Wandrei recommends Nat Schachner, one of the star scientifictionists, as a capable lawyer for such collections. Schachner must have had some experience with old Hugo, since he contributed a number of stories to *W.S.* some time back. I must admit that the idea of setting a Jew to catch a Jew is one that appeals to me. But, on the whole, I'd prefer to collect something without legal bother and expense, if I can.

So Sultan Malik has gone into the garage business! Shades of the Silver Peacock and the Hashishins! Well, perhaps he is displaying a modicum of wisdom at that. No matter how serious the depression becomes, the U.S. population will go on running its chariots till the last tire blows out and the ultimate half-pint of gas is exhausted.

However, I am sorry that the Malik's Occidental progress will be delayed. I hope he can hit Auburn either in the late spring or early autumn—the best seasons here. The winters are too wet and the summers are not only hot but arid. We continue to have heavy, soaking showers; and the Sierran snowfall has deepened considerably during the past week. Spring flowers are appearing in quantity, the season being a good two weeks earlier than usual. So far, we have not had any snow in Auburn this year. I certainly commiserate you on the run of blizzards that have afflicted New England. Truly, you are fortunate to have such comfortable housing-conditions, to offset the outdoor rigours.

Judging from Harré's reactions, it would appear that Aleister Crowley is a pretty hard specimen. I had discounted the legends on general principles, knowing nothing whatever about the mysterious magus.

I am fascinated by your account of Roman Britain. The period has been passed over so briefly by most historians, that I hadn't realized the length and thoroughness of Roman tenure. Indeed, I am most eager to read the Weigall book. I'd certainly like to think that I have a little of the old Latin blood. Certainly some of my forbears, on the paternal side, must have been in Lancashire at the time of the occupation, when Lancaster, Ribchester and other places were Roman camps. My father remembers the Roman roads, and the walls at Chester in Cheshire; but either he had not seen, or did not recall, a tower built in the time of Hadrian which forms part of the castle at Lancaster. I believe I'd get a tremendous thrill out of visiting the English and Welsh counties and seeing such antiquities.

When one comes to realize it, the power and shadow of Rome

survives in myriad ways; and there are many trains of association which, if one follows them, connect us with the Latin past. For instance, the California sherry that I drink (my favorite kind of wine) is a legitimate descendant of the wines of Xeres that were imported to Rome in the days when Andalusia was part of Hispania Ulterior. I imagine that the process of making is similar, apart from the modern practice of fortifying the wine with more or less distilled grape-spirit. Distillation, which seems to have originated with the Chinese, was brought into Europe by the Arabs and was little known before the 13th century. At least, this is my impression.

I enjoyed your account of the K.A.T. fraternity in Providence.[5] Simaetha and Tabasco are certainly full of feline originality and character. Simaetha, I notice, still keeps her Maltese offspring in order by an occasional razor-keen and lightning-swift slash of her ivory claws. She has all the look of an enraged witch's familiar on such occasions; and her slitted yellow eyes are demoniacal enough at times. However, she will purr amiably, like any harmless house-cat, if stroked. Tabasco, in spite of his burliness, is really very good-natured, though he has a habit of querulous and persistent miauling acquired in his somewhat puny kittenhood. Unluckily, I have no pictures of my companions; but I shall make some drawings of them at the first suitable opportunity, and will send you these if they are successful. I really think that Simaetha must be connected with the guardian felines of the fane of Sadoqua: her incredible age and undiminished vigour are more than suggestive of such lineage. Count Magnus and Peter Randall certainly sound like aristocrats capable of maintaining the highest traditions of noblesse oblige. And I can easily picture that rascal of an Alfred Galpin.

I hope you can find a suitable elephant image to replace the one lost by Lumley. *One should make sure, however, that the selected eikon has nothing to do with Chaugnar Faugn.* Many lost secrets must be exchanged in the night by your Mayan image and *ushabti* . . . and those uttered by the Nameless Entity are, it is to be hoped, *forever lost* in the black oubliettes of bygone cycles.

Thanks for the clippings and for your kind permission to keep them. I am particularly taken by that account of the lost city of the lizard people. The theory that planets are formed by accretions of cosmic atoms is certainly plausible, and would multiply the likelihood of alien systems similar to ours throughout the universe.

The Loch Monster, it would seem, is beginning to shrink from the glare of publicity; at least, there have been fewer accounts of it in recent papers. Apart from the creature reported in Sweden, I have seen a rumour of one in an Irish Lough; also, of one in a Nevada lake! I'll return the Thévenin articles in my next. Your mixed assortment of clippings went back with the books. Among these, I was especially taken with the drawings of the London artist, Spare. The man certainly must have had a vision of paganry and demonry![6] His drawings made me think of Machen's "The Great God Pan." He'd certainly be an ideal illustrator for that story, and also for "The White People." There is grand literary material in those ruins. I think too that you will find much that is provocative in Prorok's account of the antiquities of North Africa. The number and magnitude of Phoenician, Roman and prehistoric remnants is simply staggering. Note that picture of the rutted pavement at Timgad—at least, I think it was at Timgad (I have an inaccurate memory for names, dates, etc.)

I hope to finish my new Zothique story, "Xeethra," before long. This infernal cold has knocked me out lately. I believe I must have caught it by a three days' abstinence from anything vinous. (This isn't altogether a joke, since I believe that wine has a distinct prophylactic value.)

Yours for the Cauldron of Abundance,
Klarkash-Ton

1. A latinized form of Arthur Weigall.

2. *Fantasy Fan* (February 1934) contained William Lumley's poem, "The Dweller."

3. Merritt was writing *Creep, Shadow!* (1934) when he received *DS* and found that the title story anticipated certain plot elements, necessitating rewriting. See Sam Moskowitz, ed., *A. Merritt: Reflections in the Moon Pool* (Philadelphia: Oswald Train, 1985), p. 112.

4. Lord Dunsany, *The Curse of the Wise Woman* (London: William Heinemann; New York: Longmans, Green, 1933).

5. HPL dubbed the group of cats that frequented the area adjoining his home in Providence the Kappa Alpha Tau, which stands for Compson Ailuron Taxis (i.e., band of elegant [or well-dressed] cats).

6. The English artist Austin Osman Spare (1886–1956), the youngest artist of his time to exhibit at the Royal Academy, was known for his "automatic" and "psychic" drawings. He was a friend of Aleister Crowley.

---

[188]   To R. H. Barlow [TLS, JHL]   May 21st, 1934.

Dear Ar-Éch-Bei:

By this time, you should have received my cards, the painting, and mss. I hope you will like the exotic landscape, "Beyond Cathay," which has been singled out for admiration by most of the people who have seen it. The mss. may be of interest to you, as illustrating my rather toilsome method of working. If you compare "The Devotee of Evil" typescript with the printed story, you will find material alterations. Also, the first version of "The Vaults of Yoh-Vombis" is longer by about 1700 words, mainly descriptive, than the tale as it appeared in *W.T.* Wright demanded the excisions, which are all in the first part.

Thanks for the loan of *The Metal Monster.* I shall look forward to it, since I missed several instalments of the story as published in magazine form.[1] It contains magnificent stuff.

I hope that Éch-Pi-El is still with you, and am writing him in your care. Wish I could look in on some of your sessions, via Brazen Horse or Arabian Nights carpet. Price's visit here was all too brief; but since he is staying indefinitely in Oakland, little more than a hundred miles away, he will probably be able to come again before long. We nearly talked the clock around and paid visits to several of the gold mines in the neighbourhood apart from consuming a certain amount of liquid gold. (Our sessions however, were not nearly as alcoholic as you might have inferred from the joint card. We drank only a little of the Muscat brandy, having decided that said beverage was not all that it purported to be; and Price consumed the lion's share of the sherry without visible effect.)[2]

I'm glad you liked "Vergama."[3] I think I told you that I had amplified and embroidered the tale somewhat. It will form the concluding item of my Zothique series, if this series should ever appear between book-covers.

I hope that you and Theobaldus have gone ahead with the phonograph records.[4] Some friends of mine here in Auburn will gladly play them for me. I like the idea tremendously, and hope that you have chanted the rituals of R'lyeh[5] in antiphon as well as chorus.

My copy of *The Overland* containing Wandrei's article seems to have mislaid itself; but I think it was either November or December 1926. My article on Sterling, along with many other appreciations of S., was in *Overland* for March 1927. As to weird material, the *Overland* has never gone in for it much: my fantasy "The Abominations of Yondo," which I believe you have, being the only example that I can recall in its pages. I heard that this tale evoked many loud, lugubrious and indignant howls from the readers.

Certain sounds, sights and odours—particularly odours—

intruded themselves hereabouts on Walpurgis Eve; but it would seem there were no influences that could not be fended and driven away by the Medal of St. Benedict. As least, so far. I am still alive and with no marks of invultuation, no obsessions or possessions other than those of my wonted devils.

Thanks for the likable snapshot. I'm damned sorry about your eyes, and hope the trouble will somehow ameliorate itself. Mine give me the deuce on occasion. Each of my line drawings for *W.T.* has given me a severe headache in consequence of the strain involved; and moving pictures are also a sure-fire cause of such headaches. I've about given up going to movies—which isn't a very serious deprivation.

Your drawing of Nushain and the salamander is quite spirited. In my new version, the salamander whacks Nushain into the flames with "flailings of his dragon-like tail," when Nushain tries to escape. There are some nice new episodes in the catacomb portion; the astrologer, passing with his guide through a vault where tapers of black pitch burn about an immense unlegended sarcophagus, steals one of the tapers and tries to return to the upper world. His exit, however, is barred in certain curious manners.

If certain editors persist in rejecting my stories, I shall perform to their detriment the fearful and dreaded Mass of St. Secaire.[6]

Yrs. by the inkhorn of Eibon,
Klarkash-Ton

1. A novel by A. Merritt serialized in *Argosy All-Story Weekly*, 7 August–25 September 1920.
2. See E. Hoffmann Price, "Clark Ashton Smith: A Memoir," *TSS* 3–17; also in Price's *Book of the Dead: Friends of Yesteryear* (Sauk City, WI: Arkham House, 2001), 94–125.
3. See letter 190, n.1. "In the Book of Vergama" was the first title of "The Last Hieroglyph."
4. RHB had hoped to make recordings of himself and HPL.
5. The undersea city where's HPL's Cthulhu was imprisoned.
6. The Mass of Saint-Secaire, which is said to have originated in the Middle Ages in Gascony, is a famous form of the Black Mass. Its purpose was to curse an enemy to death by slow illness. Montague Summers describes it in *The History of Witchcraft and Demonology*.

[189]   To R. H. Barlow [TLS, JHL][1]   June 16th, 1934.

Dear Ar-Éch-Bei:

I have made up a package of drawings to loan you and will

mail it the first of the week. I might have done this before—in fact, I *should* have sent you a number so that you could make your own choice. Perhaps you would have preferred something else to "Beyond Cathay." If you wish, you can make another selection. I am not setting prices on any of the drawings, since, in one sense, they are priceless; and, in selling them to a connoisseur, the tariff must be determined by what the aforesaid c. feels able to pay.

Your praise of "The Colossus of Ylourgne" is heartening. Others have commended the tale, so I begin to think that perhaps I have under-estimated it. So far, I haven't found any ms. of this story and I am inclined to think that I burned the preliminary scraps and notes from which I worked it up on the machine. I have, however, the first carbon of "The Passing of Aphrodite" (a prose poem) and shall send it on shortly. Also, I have located an item which you will like to have—the holograph of my continuation of "The 3rd Episode of Vathek." I'll take another look for the H.E. holograph. As to "The Disinterment of Venus," the copy held by Wright is the third or fourth revision of that pesky little opus. The cabin is littered with discarded versions of the damned thing. I'll see if I can find the original one. If there is an express office at De Land, I'll ship you a huge consignment of typescripts and holographs. First-rate postage is too much of an extortion, in my opinion. I resent such robbery more, if possible, than the U.S. tax on liquors! Express rates, on the other hand, are reasonable enough. [. . .]

Re my drawings: Loveman, I would say, has by far the largest collection of them. God knows how many I gave him. He used to present me with whole shelves of books, and the drawings were the only return I could make. Wandrei purchased three or four of my landscapes. I don't believe that Long has anything, except, perhaps, a few of the grotesques. George Kirk, another of the "gang," bought 2 or 3 pictures when he visited me in 1920. Other purchasers include Bio de Casseres and a New York Russian Jew (friend of De Casseres) whose name temporarily eludes me. This Jew has several of the best landscapes, done about the same time as "Beyond Cathay." [. . .]

      Yrs, in the faith of Hzioulquoigmnzhah,
      Klarkash-Ton

1. Portions of this letter (not included here) were published as "The Family Tree of the Gods" (*Acolyte*, Summer 1944; in *PD*). CAS's mock genealogy was meant to reconcile certain facts about Tsathoggua mentioned by HPL in his ghost-written tale, "The Mound"; see letters 190 and 241.

[190]   To H. P. Lovecraft [TLS, JHL]   [c. 16 June 1934]
                    Salt-pale desert of Dhir, at the hour of the
                    multisonous beating of invisible drums.

Dear Éch-Pi-El:

I hope that this will find you still domiciled at the Barlovian
manor. Your prolonged visit there is certainly enviable from all
angles. The pictures of yourself that you sent, under a strong read-
ing-glass, appear to prove the salubriousness of the Florida
climate. Incidentally, I am glad to note that Ulthar is well represented, and have studied with interest the picture showing the
kitten and Doodlebug.

I wish I could see that famous bas-relief of Cthulhu! I have
done what I could toward elucidating the genealogy of Tsathoggua, and am sending Ar-Éch-Bei the result of my delvings into the
Parchments of Pnom, the chief Hyperborean authority on such
matters. Pnom has much more to say about Tsathoggua than
about Cthulhu, Yog-Sothoth and Azathoth; but no doubt you have
access to other records, mainly concerning these entities; and I'd be
glad of more specific information about them. As I am pointing out
to Ar-Éch-Bei, Pnom's account of Ts. can be reconciled with the
legendry told to Zamacona in "The Mound." The myth, through
aeons, was varied in the usual mythopoeic fashion by the cavern-
dwellers, who came at last to believe that merely the images of
Tsathoggua, and *not* the god himself, had emerged in former cycles
from the inner gulf. Ts., travelling fourthdimensionally from
Saturn, *first entered the Earth* through the lightless abyss of N'kai;
and, not unnaturally, the Yothians regarded N'kai as his place of
origin. Undoubtedly the god now resides in N'kai, to which he
returned when the ice overwhelmed Hyperborea.

I was glad to know that "Beyond Cathay" proved satisfactory
to Ar-Éch-Bei, and am now loaning him a large consignment of my
more exotic pictures. Glad to hear also that "The Colossus" was
up to sample. My drawing for it was pretty lousy, apart from the
demons. Wright, by the way, is planning to use a pen-drawing of
Tsathoggua (which I gave him some time ago) as an illustration for
"The Seven Geases." I may or may not have told you that he accepted my new version of "The Last Hieroglyph."[1] No, I am not
taking Malik's suggestions too literally. But in this case, I really
saw a chance to improve the story. I couldn't adopt his suggestions
about "Xeethra"; and my revision of this tale (which I'll send you
if Wright still rejects it) is merely a slight abridgement of the first
version.

By all means don't forget me, if you have photographs taken of the two clay deities! I can imagine Lumley's rapture when he receives the Ganesha-Chaugnar.[2] I look forward also to those phonograph records.

Glad to hear that the missing Jack had returned. I certainly hope that his weakness and lack of coordination were not due to snake-bite. If they were, the local reptilia are certainly due for a cleaning-out. So far, I have not encountered any rattlers this summer, but have already killed three of the deadly Black Widow spiders, which seem to have established themselves quite numerously in this neighbourhood. The females (who carry the venom) are small, shiny, and marked on the thorax with orange red.

Yes, Auburn is quite in the center of the old mining district. I am glad that you and Ar-Éch-Bei found the pamphlet of interest. Thanks exceedingly for the postcards and alluring folder!

I'd write at greater length, but want to mail this as soon as possible. Will enclose a few clippings from Ulthar which I have saved for you.

Yrs, under the civic seal of Yoth,
Klarkash-Ton

1. "The Last Hieroglyph" (*WT*, April 1935; *LW* and *RA*).
2. RHB had made clay sculptures of HPL's Cthulhu and Frank Belknap Long's Chaugnar Faugn (which, like the Indian god Ganesha, resembled an elephant).

———— ◆ ————

[191]   To Lester Anderson [TLS, private collection]
July 31st, 1934

Dear Lester Anderson:

It certainly looks as if my answer to your letter were a somewhat delayed "quarterly." In the meanwhile, history has been adding a few glosses to one or two of the points we were discussing! If there are many more general strikes, it looks as if the descent of the Iron Heel in the U. S. would be accelerated.

Yes, I have read Sinclair's EPIC plan and am much inclined to doubt its workability.[1] I fear it would break down in operation through the inevitable conflict between private and public enterprise. Sinclair too obviously intends it as an entering wedge for socialization; and he will have all the forces of the present system against him. Personally, I do not believe that socialism will ever work in the U. S.; and I shouldn't be surprised if it were to fail even in Russia. The human instincts of aggrandization are against it.

I've never read *The World Below*. As to Chambers, I fear one would get stung on almost anything of his, except *The King in Yellow,* which I believe you already know. Lovecraft has mentioned a volume of fantasies by C., entitled *The Maker of Moons;* but I have not seen this. *Slayer of Souls* (I saw one or two magazine instalments years ago) was inexpressibly pediculous.[2] [. . .]

Astounding Stories is certainly the leader now among the scientifiction magazines. *Dime Mystery* is wretched stuff—the crudest kind of physical horror, written in a style so cheap and staccato as to be simply ridiculous. It seems to have gone over so well that another magazine of the same type, *Terror Tales,* is being put out by the publishers. The success of such luridities, after the failure of *Strange Tales,* is certainly full of a comment on public taste. [. . .]

Cordially,
       Clark Ashton Smith

1. During the economic crisis of the 1930s, the muckraker novelist Upton Sinclair (1878–1968) organized the EPIC (End Poverty in California) socialist reform movement; in 1934 he was defeated as Democratic candidate for governor.
2. S. Fowler Wright (1875–1965), *The World Below* (New York: Longmans, 1930); Robert W. Chambers (1865–1933), *The King in Yellow* (1895), *The Maker of Moons* (1896), and *The Slayer of Souls* (1920).

———————————◆———————————

[192]   To Lester Anderson [TLS, private collection]
                                         Sept. 20th, 1934

Dear Lester:
       [. . .] As to sociology, et al., I guess about all one can do is to watch the monkey-show. Maybe the whole damned shooting-match will end by liquidating itself. Have you ever read Ambrose Bierce's book of essays, *The Shadow on the Dial?*[1] This book was certainly prophetic of the present situation; and Bierce puts the blame where it belongs—on the shoulders of *both* labor and capital. He also suggested a solution****which neither plutocrat nor proletariat is likely to follow. The solution wasn't a New Deal or a 5 yr plan or an EPIC—in fact, it would need neither land colonies, bureaus nor soviets. Without it, however, all the Utopian schemes ever fathered, from Plato to Carl [*sic*] Marx, will prove worse than unworkable. That solution was—the application of the Golden Rule of Jesus Christ . . . . Well—do you wonder that Bierce is disregarded by the Moderns? Do you wonder that liberty is

being bartered for a pot of fascistic beans or a mess of communistic cabbage soup? Do you wonder that every cockeyed social panacea can find adherents? Following which queries, I hope you will not suspect me of being a Nazi or a Vigilante in disguise. But I simply can't see the collectivistic idea as anything but a new and particularly odious form of tyranny. If you put everything—property, resources, etc., in the hands of the State, you give the state omnipotent power over the lives and liberties of individuals—and that power will be exercised. Your dictatorship of the proletariat is nothing but a proletariat fascism. Me for the Himalayas—or a rocket trip to Mars—if the U. S. is going German or Russian. Make sure there will be no place for non-propagandistic authors under either system.

  Yours cordially,
  Clark Ashton Smith

 1. Ambrose Bierce, *The Shadow on the Dial and Other Essays*, ed. S. O. Howes (1909).

---

[193] To Donald Wandrei [TLS, MHS] Feb. 28th, 1935

Dear Donald:

  My unconscionable delay in writing must be laid to a number of causes, chief of which has been the difficulty of snatching enough leisure for a really adequate letter. I have been grinding away steadily at some new stories, and, with my slowness of composition and frequent recasting, it has been hard to make any headway without putting in from four to six hours per day on the labor. This, in addition to a multitude of chores, etc., has made anything else almost impossible. Letters have piled up to a most appalling extent: but yours can simply not be neglected any longer.

  I am glad indeed that your California trip has proved so fruitful in pleasant memories. Certainly it was a most memorable and agreeable occasion, or series of occasions, for me. I shall never forget the charm of our evenings at the Sullys, and your visits to the cabin. Here's hoping that it will all be repeated at some early date—the earlier the better. Perhaps, when you come again, I shall have better accomodations to offer, since I am hoping to build a sort of workshop for myself this spring, and if the building materializes, shall equip it with a couch, etc., for the use of guests.

  The New Year sessions at Long's and Loveman's apartments must have been great! I enjoyed prodigiously the imposing round robin from the gang. I can imagine the diversity of erudite conversations or dissertations that must have been going on, with so many specialists present! Sometime—I don't know just when—I may be able to join in on one of those conclaves.

I'll be glad of any fresh tips about Tremaine's policy anent *Astounding*.[1] So far I haven't done any new science fiction, but will start some new items this month. I have turned out several weirds, including "The Treader of the Dust," "Necromancy in Naat" and "The Black Abbot of Puthuum." The two last-named items are longish additions to my Zothique series. Wright surprised me by taking "The Treader of the Dust" offhand, without revision or resubmission. The last quarter of "Necromancy in Naat," however, will have to be rewritten according to the specifications of the satrap (Damn!!....******)[2] I have also done a few poems, and may enclose one of them with this. You would laugh, I dare say, at my methods of story-composition: my usual procedure is to scribble a rough draft of several paragraphs in pencil, and then work these up with more detail and literary finish on the machine. Then I draft a few more paragraphs, etc. The typed pages, I might add, are often recast two or three times. I don't imagine that many writers for the pulps pursue such methods. 1000 or 1200 words is a big day's work for me.

Have you done anything with your play? From Helen's account of your letters to her, I judge you have been caught in an increasingly hectic round of work.

My copy of the De Givry[3] volume came a day or two after your departure. It is certainly a valuable acquisition; though one needs a magnifying glass to get the full beauty of some of the illustrations! I have recently purchased M. Summer's anthology, *Best Ghost Stories*,[4] which you have probably seen. If you haven't, I can certainly recommend it, since it contains much material that is not commonly met with. I do very little reading, however, but have gone through the late issues of *W.T.*, which seem rather pediculous not to say downright lousy. I wish that Miss Moore[5] would write a new story (hope this observation doesn't stamp me as a member of the feline tribe!)

The aspect of Auburn and the surrounding hills is quite vernal now, since fruit blossoms, acacias, japanese quince, and numerous wild flowers are all in evidence. We have had much rain, but comparatively little cold weather, and no snow whatever. There were heavy snows in the Sierras, but these seem to be melting away prematurely.

How about poetry? I hope your resolution will change. Anyway, I'd like to see a large collection of your poems in print. That last evening, when you read a number of them to us, was perhaps the best and most memorable occasion of all!

My parents join me in the kindest of regards and good wishes. I hope you'll overlook my apparent remissness, and write me when the leisure offers and the spirit moves.

Yours ever, Clark.

My regards to your brother, to Long, Loveman, and others of the gang.

Blast this pen!***!!

1. F. Orlin Tremaine (1899–1956), American writer and editor of the revived *Astounding Stories*.

2. "The Treader of the Dust" (*WT*, August 1935; *LW*); "Necromancy in Naat" (*WT*, July 1936; *LW* and *RA*); and "The Black Abbot of Puthuum" (*WT*, March 1936; *GL*).

3. Grillot de Givry (1870–1929), *Witchcraft, Magic & Alchemy*, trans. J. Courtenay Locke; with 10 plates in colour and 366 illustrations in the text (London: G. G. Harrap, [1931]).

4. Montague Summers, ed., *Victorian Ghost Stories* (1933), a collection of fourteen stories with 35-page introduction by Summers.

5. C[atherine] L[ucille] Moore (1911–1987), American pulp writer who achieved instant fame upon publication of her story "Shambleau" (*WT*, November 1933).

---

[194]   To August Derleth [TLS, SHSW]   May 28th, 1935.

Dear August:

Your card administered a salutary prick to my conscience; though, God knows, that conscience has long been sore enough. Really, it has been so long since I wrote you that I had grown ashamed to write. For several months, owing to the double illness of my parents, letter-writing was a physical impossibility, since I had all the house-work, nursing, chores, etc. Both, however, are now improved; and the improvement seems particularly surprising in my mother's case, since her advanced arterial degeneration had brought on premonitory symptoms of paralysis. [. . .]

Please write and tell me all the news. I am terribly out of touch with everyone. Have not written to H.P. for months—or, in fact, to any of our group.

I suppose you have done, and sold, a lot of new material. Some tales that I wrote early in the year were all placed with Wright; and I also landed a revision of the several-times-rejected "Chain of Aforgomon." Then came my mother's breakdown; and I've had to defer a number of projected things. My own health seems to have held up pretty well, in spite of all the worry, strain, etc., plus some private emotional unhappiness. Financially, I've been able to keep going because of the more or less regular payment of the Gernsback arrears, which will be cleaned up in two more instalments. After that—well, I guess I'll have to go in for harlotry and "make" some of the cheap horror magazines. *W.T.* seems to be more and more laggard in payment, and I fear the sales are being cut by the competition of the aforementioned c.h. ms. Also, I fear, from recent issues, that Wright is making some damnable concessions to such competition. I simply couldn't read some of the stuff in the April number.

By the way, I have developed a new art, which serves admirably to occupy any spare moments too brief and broken for writing. This art is the carving of small figurines and heads with a penknife; the chief material so far used being a mottled soapstone or steatite, which is very easily worked and lends itself to my sort of grotesquery. I am also experimenting with dinosaur bone! truly, an appropriate medium for the limning of certain Hyperborean entities!

My best to you, as ever,
Clark Ashton

———————— • ————————

[195]   To H. P. Lovecraft [TLS, JHL]   [c. June 1935]
Hour of the ninefold sounding of the green brazen gong
in Mho-Lhun, citadel of the primal gods of doom.

Dear Éch-Pi-El:

I was doubly rejoiced to receive your letter and to learn that you are again domiciled in the temple of Krang, amid the sub-equatorial flora.[1]

I should have written you several cycles ago, but, apart from the time-consuming domestic conditions, a sort of slump or doldrums appears to have overtaken me, and I've lacked the energy for letters even when I could have found the time. It's a damnable condition, no doubt partly due to the prolonged monotony, with small recreational escape or relief. You are certainly fortunate to be able to get away on trips and visits.

Thanks for the enclosures. Searight's quotation from the Eltdown Shards is a valuable contribution to the somewhat limited list of renderings of prehistoric lore.[2] However, it is to be discreetly hoped that not *too much* of that lore will find translation into living languages. The clippings are interesting too. I must confess that I had never heard of the elusive Gillis Land,[3] which could afford a very fertile theme for imaginative fiction.

Sorry to learn the bad news from Ulthar, anent Crom. Let's hope that there are no vengeful poulterers in his hunting-grounds beyond the black River. As to Tabasco, it's plainly a case of exeunt in mysterium, and no faintest rumor of his fate has ever reached me. Simaetha still flourishes, as does the redoubtable Son. I did some caretaking for the latter personage, while his mistresses were away recently in the Yosemite; and I can testify that his appetite, though sufficiently robust, is not equal to the capacity of Dame Simaetha. Some day, if I ever come into a fortune, I'm going to find out just how much liver she would consume at a sitting! No, I hadn't heard about Nimrod's six day absence. He must have been out for big game![4] [. . .]

Thanks for Ar-Ech-Bei's offer of *The Golem*.[5] However, I read the book several years ago, when it was loaned to me, by a young friend in the Bay region. I agree with you that it is a most consummate and eerily haunting study in strange atmosphere; probably one of the best things of the kind ever written.

My parents are a little better, and I am trying to settle down to some writing. My mother's condition, however, is one of settled feebleness, with seriously impaired eyesight; and no great or permanent improvement can be hoped for. My father, too, has a condition of high-blood pressure and "pipestem" arteries, and has to guard against much exertion. It all puts me "in a spot," since there is no one to whom I can delegate the job of housekeeping, etc. There are no near neighbors, and none at all whom I'd care to ask for any favors.

By the way, I have taken up carving as a spare-time diversion; though of course the spare time is none too abundant. The materials used so far, are a sort of talc or steatite from the Kilaga mine where Price got some specimens for Morton; and bits of mineralized dinosaur bone (of which I once sent you some exemplars) from Clifford Gap. Also I've used a yellowish claylike material which I rather suspect was originally dinosaur steak, since it occurs in combination with the aforesaid bone. Under separate cover I am sending you a little carving of Cthulhu in d.b., also, a cameo depicting one of the hyperborean wizards (Om Omris, perhaps) in d.s. The latter is for Ar-Éch-Bei. The top shelf of my bookcase of weird fiction is now guarded by sundry teraphim, including The Archetype (pale grey rhyolite), The Blue Goddess (pale blue talc), The Ghoul (light purplish talc), St. Anthony, Eumolpas, The Satyr, The One-Eyed Simulachre (mottled reddish-brown and red and white talc) and The Hippocentaur (dinosaur bone). Also, there is a tiny head of Eibon in d.b., and a mask of Tsathoggua in cherry-gum, and several still unnamed entities, two of which I have painted in gold and black. The mottled talc, in especial, lends itself to grotesquery. Some day if I ever have the time and the tools, I'd like to try working some of the local igneous rocks, which are very hard and close-grained, and would probably take a high polish, like porphyry. The rhyolite pebble with which I experimented was partly decomposed, and not so difficult to work; but the center was hard as hell, and I had to do the finishing touches with a file! Granite would be easy compared to some of this stuff on Indian Hill; but any sculpture wrought from it certainly should be permanent, relatively speaking. I've no ambition to make life-size sculptures. Large sculpture, in my opinion, has no proper place except as an architectural adjunct.

I'm enclosing a line for Ar-Éch-Bei.

Yours, by the Shemhamphoresh,[6] the ineffable Name,
Klarkash-Ton

1. HPL was again in Florida visiting RHB.
2. Richard F. Searight (1902–1975), *WT* author. Om-Omris is a character in his story, "The Sealed Casket" (*WT,* March 1935).
3. A mysterious Arctic island, sighted and named in 1707 by the Dutch captain Cornelius Gillis.
4. Crom was RHB's cat; Nimrod was E. Hoffmann Price's.
5. Gustav Meyrink (1868–1932), *The Golem,* trans. Madge Pemberton (London: Gollancz; Boston: Houghton Mifflin, 1928).
6. According to kabalistic lore, this was the secret name by which God Himself could be subjugated. See CAS's last poem, "Cycles" (*BB* and *LO*).

---

[196]   To Donald Wandrei [TLS, MHS]   June 24th, 1935.

Dear Donald:

I was glad to hear from you again, but sorry to learn of your recent illness. Here's hoping that your health and other circumstances will permit of whatever work—plays, fiction or anything else—that you wish to do.

I seem to have lost all track of my own correspondence, and don't know whether or not I have written you since my mother's breakdown in March. Her condition is one of settled feebleness, together with seriously impaired eyesight. My father hasn't been so very much better than she; and for months I ran a hospital, cooking, nursing, serving meals in bed, etc. Writing of any sort has been difficult under the circumstances; and to make matters worse, my nerves are now beginning to wear ragged from the strain and from certain superadded infelicities. To quote the vulgar adage, it's a great life if you don't weaken.

Your "The Destroying Horde" in *W.T.* certainly shone by contrast with most of the other work in that issue.[1] Wright, either through impaired judgement or a mistaken idea of what his readers want, seems to have undertaken the ruining of the magazine. Everyone that I know, almost, has severely criticized the recent numbers. Most of the stuff he runs is plain mediocre, and lacks even the crude kick that an occasional yarn in *Dime Mystery* or *Horror Stories* attains.

Lovecraft has just written me from Florida, where he is again visiting young Barlow. The milieu seems to agree with him. I have also heard lately from Derleth and Jacobi.[2] The latter wanted your new address, and I shall give it to him when I write.

Some day, when we meet again, I may be able to throw some light on certain matters that have mystified and perhaps wounded you. The Study of Woman is certainly a fearful and wonderful branch of biologic science. However, it is only fair to say—and well to know—that women don't all fall under the same classification. As Lafcadio Hearn says somewhere, they differ amazingly and diabolically. Also—contrary to the common idea—they are often too damned easy to understand. Where men, especially artists, make the mistake, is in crediting them with all sorts of things that simply aren't there as a rule. Most of them are hard-boiled and practical at bottom, as few men, even the most commercial, ever are. Also, they are more prone to petty snobbery, and are swayed to an unbelievable degree by such details as the cut of a man's hair, the way in which he tips the waiter, or helps them out of a car. They are worshippers of success, who fling themselves in regiments and cohorts at the head of the recognized genius but scorn the one who has still to make his way through obloquy and hardship.

Of course, all this is generalization, and shouldn't be taken as bearing on a particular case. The girl in question is remarkable, and undoubtedly superior to most of her sex. She has been brought up with standards which, I sometimes think, no man will ever be able to meet. The one who could meet them would have to possess a combination of old-time chivalry with modern savoir faire. He would speak and write little of himself, much of the girl and her interests, and *would never show offense or hurt* under any circumstances. His attitude would be *cheerful, patient, modest,* what is called *"manly"* at all times and under all conditions. He would assume that all misunderstandings were his fault; that he was to blame in some way for any coldness or unfavorable reactions toward him. He would demand nothing, would make her feel that he was devoted without dramatizing his emotions or using language too high-flown and exaggerated. Here, as in all cases where more than mere gallantry is the object, the advice of Stendhal might well be followed, when he says that the art of love consists in expressing precisely the emotion felt, at the time it is felt, without abuse of superlatives or of any falsifying locution. . . . But of course, I don't know what your feelings are. If your affections are seriously engaged, it would do no harm to write a letter along the general lines indicated. But if you do this, for Christ's sake don't ever hint that *I* gave you any tips or advice. Avoid, above all things, either the complaining or the supplicative attitudes. I have been through the mill and know whereof I speak—even though I'm not always able to put my Lotharian wisdom into operation. But maybe you could profit by it. Anyway, I believe the attempt would strengthen you. Giving up the battle in love at the first reverse is bad psychology; and many an apparent defeat has been turned into a victory at the end by good generalship. A woman's disfavor isn't necessarily final. To become personal, I've had my face slapped, and have been loved to death an hour afterward by the slapper. Little things like that shouldn't be taken seriously in regard to such elemental perversities as the phenomena of sex. Hate and love, disgust and desire,* belong to the same spectrum and shade into each other through a thousand semitones.

Well, I hope that all this doesn't bore you. I've had it on my mind for a long time.

To return to literary matters, I fear that I have little news. I'm trying to cook up some fiction that will sell for cash, and have had to take time out for vomiting between periods, thus slowing my progress nearly to a standstill.

Apart from that, I've experimented recently with carving, and have done some small heads and figures, mostly grotesque, in such materials as steatite and dinosaur bone. I should have lived in the Middle Ages and carved gargoyles; or else have made the idols of some barbaric tribe! In either role, I might have had the success that seems to elude me under present conditions.

Yours for the Grail of blood and Malmsey,[3] and the black debaucheries of the Sabbat,
        Clark

*It's a nice art to turn the first into the second. "Can do," as the Chinese say.

1. "The Destroying Horde" (*WT*, June 1935).
2. Carl Jacobi (1908–1997), American pulp writer.
3. A strong, sweet wine chiefly from Madeira.

[197]   To Ethel Heipel[1] [ALS, private collection]

Sept. 13th, 1935

Dear Ethel:

I appreciated your letter greatly, and had hoped to answer it before this. But it has been hard for me to write letters under the circumstances. However, I want you to know that I thought yours very charming, and enjoyed its newsiness.

I fear I shan't have anything very good to write in return. My mother passed away suddenly last Monday evening. Services were held yesterday. The only consolation is that the end came quickly and, I like to think, with little or brief pain. Only five mintues before, she was still able to talk and move about. When one thinks of the prolonged suffering that some undergo, one can be thankful for such comparative mercies. But the loss is great and irreparable, since no one could ever take the place of one so beloved and so saintly.

My father is bearing up pretty well. A sister of my mother's, Mrs. Ferrell[2] from Chicago, is with us and will remain for a week or two. She has taken over the cooking and housekeeping, and I shall avail myself of the partial leisure to rest up a little and attack my pile of unanswered correspondence.

I am glad that you are staying within easy distance of the big trees. Their majesty and peace, their age-long permanence amid the brief generations of men, should help one to forget sorrow. Between those mighty columns, as through some titanic gateway, one can pass into a serener and diviner sphere.

I shall look forward to seeing or hearing from you again,

Sincerely, Clark

1. Ethel Heiple (1899–1980) was a friend and neighbor of CAS living in Auburn.
2. Emily Ferrell of Chicago, Mrs. Smith's sister and Clark's aunt.

---

[198]   To R. H. Barlow [TLS, JHL]   [c. November 1935]

Dear Ar-Éch-Bei: I had meant to write, aeons ago, and thank you for your expression of condolence and offer of assistance in preparing typescripts; also to answer your letter at proper length.

I hope you will not think me ungrateful because of the delay, which has been due to nervous demoralization plus a piling up of unfinished (and, alack, unattempted!) tasks.

I appreciated greatly, as a card may have hinted, the gift of *The Goblin Tower* and *The Shunned House*.[1] These certainly form a promising beginning for the Dragon-Fly Press and bindery! I liked the first issue of your magazine greatly, too, and hope that you will continue the venture. It would certainly raise the standard of amateur publications. Edkins' article[2] would have done honor to any of the professional reviews, to mention nothing else.

I hope you received the consignment of mss, etc, which I expressed to you some time ago. Lately, I have been going over the possible material for *Incantations,* which you have so generously offered to print. A *large* volume seems to me no less impossible than inadvisable, since I have turned out no great body of verse since the publication of *Sandalwood;* and much of what I have done is in the form of trifling madrigals written for the semi-utilitarian purpose of pleasing the lady or ladies to whom they were addressed. At a rough guess, I'd say the venture will hardly run to more than 60 or 70 compactly printed pages. Very few of my Baudelaire translations are in shape for issue; but perhaps half a dozen items would be worthy of inclusion. I have also racked up some metrical experiments in French, which I was so rash as to attempt several years ago, and may possibly add one or two of these by way of variety. I enclose a specimen, with literal English translation appended. Before long, I'll mail or express you a first selection of items for the volume, to which a few others, held back for revision, might be added later. I admire and applaud your program of Art for Art's sake, and I certainly don't want you to spend time and money on anything unworthy of the labor.

Your binding of *The Star-Treader* certainly sounds like a de luxe production! I have, by the way, an *S.T.* bound by hand in *olive*-green morocco by a Canadian admirer; a fine piece of work.

Ech-Pi-El will relay to you a carving which seems to depict one of the prehuman serpent-eating people of Hyperborea. This carving was found in a much-shattered condition amid the jungle-matted columns of lost Commoriom; and the ingenuity of the finder was taxed in piecing it together . . . Incidentally, Commoriom seems to be a fruitful field for archaeologic labour: I have retrieved therefrom various graven entities, including what is undoubtedly a representation, in some sort of prehistoric bone or ivory, of the woman-breasted cat-goddess, Phauz, whom the Hyperboreans worshipped aeons before Bast was set up in Khem. Also, I have found a strange cameo with edges oddly worn and rounded, bearing the head of that Black Dog who warded the east-

ern gate of Commoriom against intruders neither brute nor human. . . . Also, there is a bust of the Inquisitor Morghi,[3] who so rashly followed Eibon through the ultra-terrene panel giving on a singular landscape in Saturn; moreover, the head of a dinornis, some cameos depicting obviously unnamable entities, and the head of a creature which is part bird, part insect and part reptile. So much for Commoriom: my researches in Mu and Poseidonis (with the aid of a future-scientific diving-bell) I leave for a later bulletin. Some curious eidola have been retrieved; and, emboldened by such success, I may yet venture amid the dreadful purlieus of abysmally sunken R'lyeh!

Yours, by the black pentagram with *two* angles in ascendance,
Klarkash-Ton.

1. RHB bound only a few presentation copies of HPL's *The Shunned House,* which had been printed in 1928 by W. Paul Cook but never bound. Arkham House eventually bound and distributed the booklet. *The Goblin Tower* was a book of Frank Belknap Long's poetry, published by RHB. HPL had assisted in the typesetting during his visit to Florida in 1935.

2. E. A. Edkins, "Fragment of a Letter to a Young Poet" (*Dragon-Fly,* 15 October 1935). Edkins (1867–1945) was an old-time amateur journalist with whom HPL had recently come into contact.

3. A character in "The Door to Saturn."

[199]   To Albert M. Bender [TLS, MCL]   Dec. 4th, 1935.

Dear Albert:

I am sending you herewith a number of poems and translations which you have probably not seen before. Some of the poems, such as "Alienation," "Dominion," "The Phoenix," and "In Thessaly" have been written during the past year. So, you will see, I have not deserted the lyric Muse entirely!

I had meant to write and send the poems long before this; but various circumstance have almost put me out of commission as a correspondent during the past 9 or 10 months. My mother suffered the premonitory symptoms of paralysis in March, and was very feeble and half-blind henceforward, necessitating constant care on my part. She died on the 9th of September, very suddenly, and, I think, with little or no suffering. Her death has been, as you may surmise, a terrible blow for me, and I cannot accustom myself to the loss. My father, who is very feeble and in wretched health, is still with me. The various duties and chores of cooking, nursing, housekeeping, etc, etc, have occupied the major part of my time, leaving little for art or literature. Our isolation has thrown everything upon me, and my nerves are pretty well exhausted with the strain, worry, grief and suspense. I have been able to write and sell only four short stories during the year—and stories, alas, are my one source of income. [. . .]

 As ever, your friend,
  Clark.

---

[200] To R. H. Barlow [TLS, JHL]   [c. January 1936]
          Hour of the Opening of the Sub-
            marine portals, in R'lyeh

Dear Ar-Éch-Bei:

 Many thanks for *The Cats of Ulthar*.[1] You have done a good job for a good story.

 The typescript of *Incantations* goes forward to you by express. It includes 65 titles: 49 more or less lyric poems, 18 of which are grouped under the subtitle of The Jasmine Girdle; 3 renderings from Paul Verlaine, 9 from Baudelaire; and 4 of my prose pastels at the end.[2] Many pieces have appeared in magazines, and I have made a note of this on the mss. for your private information. I have submitted two other pieces, "Ennui" and "The Sick Muse," to Wright;[3] but if he accepts them, they will no doubt appear in *W.T.* before the completion of your job on the book.

 I hesitated a long time over the inclusions, and spent many hours revising some of them; hence, partly, the delay in sending you the collection. These verses, I feel, are only shards and wraiths of the poems I had once planned to write under the title of *Incantations*. As to my Baudelaires, most of these were done only in rough, literal prose; and they still need a world of polishing.

 I hope that you received, and liked, my little carving of the Hyperborean Snake-Eater. For some time, I have had it in mind to circulate a few of my smaller heads and figurines, as a sort of private loan exhibit, and am wondering if you would care to see them. I don't believe the expressage will amount to much on a small wooden box holding ten or a dozen of these miniature eidola. They would be well worth your while, since they resemble nothing that has been done in sculpture since the founding of Poseidonis.

 Yrs for the descent into Annwyn,
  Klarkash-Ton

1. RHB published *The Cats of Ulthar* (Cassia, FL: Dragon-Fly Press, 1935) as his 1935 "Christmas card" in an edition of forty-two copies.

2. No typescript of *Incantations* is known to exist, although there is an unlabeled table of contents for it among CAS's papers. CAS had long planned a book entitled *Incantations,* and its contents, before it was finally published as a section of *SP,* undoubtedly changed considerably over time.

3. "Ennui" (*AJ,* 25 June 1925; *WT,* May 1936; *SP* and *LO*); Charles Baudelaire (trans. CAS), "The Sick Muse" (*WT,* April 1936; *SP*).

---

[201]   To Donald Wandrei [TLS, MHS]   Nov. 17th, 1936.

Dear Donald:

As usual, I seem to be damnably and hopelessly in arrears on correspondence, and am sorry that I have not answered your last before this.

I note your story in the current *Esquire,*[1] and shall buy a copy the next time I visit the newsstand. I read the opening, which is fine.

I am glad that "Song of the Necromancer"[2] pleased you so well, since I too felt that it is one of my best things. It is, however, the only lyric that I have written in an indigo moon. Wright accepted it by return mail.

Yes, I heard from Lovecraft, some time ago, and received the sculptures back from him. He seems, by the way, to have been as badly swamped as I am with various and multitudinous accumulations but is apparently having better luck at digging out from under. I was delighted to read "The Haunter of the Dark"[3] in print, and found it, as one often does, even better than in ms.

Ina Coolbrith, concerning whom you inquire, died some years ago after a long life. Her poetic career began back in the Bret Harte period; and during her latter years she was poet laureate of California. I had the pleasure of meeting her in 1927, a year or two before her death: a lovable soul, still bright and unquenched by the infirmities that had then gathered upon her.

I hope you were able to get a satisfactory photograph of Winchell's portrait.[4] I'd appreciate seeing the photo, if you have a copy to lend.

I haven't any news that is really worthy of headlines but have received some sort of local encouragement regarding the sculptures. My friend Harry Noyes Pratt, poet, and director of the

Crocker Art Gallery in Sacramento,[5] came up to see them a couple of days ago and was evidently much impressed. He will give me a showing at the gallery after the first of the year—which, at least, can do no harm. He also expressed the opinion that they could be sold through high-class novelty stores but advised me that my best way of making money would be to turn them out in plaster or terra cotta casts that could be sold cheaply. I am going to experiment a little with mould-making and hope that I can get satisfactory reproductions of some of the pieces best adapted to this purpose. Incidentally, I have done some new things that you would like, including a grotesque "armless Venus" and a sizable statuette (11 inches high) showing a hoofed monstrosity with two serpent-like tentacles issuing between eyes and mouth. One tentacle is looped on the creature's body, its four-fingered hand clasping the swollen side of a pendulous and asymmetrical belly; the other tentacle droops down with its hand reposing on the right hoof. I have christened it Cthulhu's Child and am sure that Lovecraft would be delighted with the conception. Pratt, to my surprise, admired it greatly and took several snapshots of the thing.

I'll send you something presently, as a gift. Yours, for sales unlimited,

Clark

1. "The Eye and the Finger" (*Esquire,* December 1936).
2. "Song of the Necromancer" (*WT,* February 1937; *SP* and *LO*).
3. "The Haunter of the Dark" (*WT,* December 1936).
4. Paul M. Winchell painted DAW's portait, titled *The Voice,* in September. In the painting, DAW holds a sculpture made by CAS.
5. Harry Noyes Pratt (1879–1944), *Hill Trails and Open Sky: A Book of California Verse* (San Francisco: H. Wagner Pub. Co., 1919).

---

[202]   To R. H. Barlow [TLS, JHL]   Nov. 23rd, 1936.

Dear Ar-Éch-Bei:

It would seem that I have been owing you (and nearly everyone else) a letter ever since the fall of Uzuldaroum.[1] To detail the obstacles and impediments, the harassments and bedevilments that have occasioned and prolonged this epistolary lapse, would require the minor part of a new kalpa; and I shan't exhaust my paper or your patience with the execrable catalogue. Suffice it to say that the lapse has been involuntary.

I hope that I at least thanked you by card for the last *Dragon-Fly*. I am damnably sorry to learn, both from your letter of last June and Éch-Pi-El's more recent letters, the troubles and difficulties that you have been having. Such matters are beyond our control, and it would seem that misfortunes have a way of "ganging up" on the victim: at least, that has been my own experience. I have had enough grief, the past two years, to founder a dreadnought and am beginning to wonder if sea-bottom has yet been reached!

Don't worry about *Incantations*. There's no hurry about presenting it to a world that hasn't yet exhausted the edition of *Ebony and Crystal* printed nearly 14 years ago, and which has left me about 600 copies of *The Double Shadow* parked under my bed along with the empty wine-jugs et cetera. In the meanwhile, here's a new poem which you can add to the mss. Wright is using it in W.T. and will no doubt print it before long.[2] Which reminds me, before I pass to other matters, that I greatly liked your sonnet-tribute to R.E.H. in the pages of our old standby.[3]

In answer to certain queries in your June letter: The projected play, *The Fugitives,* ran only to 2½ pages of blank verse and several songs that I planned to intercalate in the dialogue. I had these pages laid aside somewhere to send you but seem to have mislaid them again (or *did* I send them?).[4] The plot was a simple and quite romantic one: it began with the mutual dawning of love in an Atlantean boy and girl, soon to be separated. Later, they were to meet again: the boy a wandering poet of recognized genius, the girl a king's concubine. Their old love reawakens, they flee from the Atlantean court and capital, to perish in the wilderness after several days and nights of mad happiness. On this framework, much lyric beauty and romantic imagery could have been strung. But somehow, the impetus failed and I never went on with it. I doubt very much if I shall ever write a play.[5] Possibly I shall yet do some imaginative romances of book length; but the dialogue form doesn't appeal to me greatly for personal use.

Éch-Pi-El said that you planned a mimeographed magazine and had expressed a desire to use my ending to "3rd Episode of Vathek" in it.[6] By all means go ahead, if you can utilize the thing.

I am glad that the poems of *Incantations* pleased you so well. Probably any future verse that I write will mark more of a return to, or development of, my older and less lyrically emotional style. I feel in myself an urge and ability to fare even further afield in the cosmic dreamlands that I have yet gone. Also, I believe I could do better paintings of these regions. At present, my new art of sculpture engrosses me immensely. I believe it will be quite possible to make a little money by casting some of my milder grotesques in a hard and durable plaster. The replicas could be sold at fifty cents upward if placed in novelty stores. My originals, if they had been dug up in Guatemala or Cambodia, would be fetching handsome prices from art-collectors! Also, if exhibited in some European capital, they might cause a revolution among the modernists! At present, the only prospect of art-exhibition is at the Crocker Gallery in Sacramento. The director, a personal friend, says that he can give me a showing some time after the first of the year.

I have started to make moulds for five carvings, and if I get some good replicas, will be glad to send you a specimen when I hear from you again and verify your address.

Yrs, by the pipings of Nyarlathotep,
Klarkash-ton

P.S. You might like to see the enclosed article by a San Francisco admirer,[7] which appeared a couple of years ago in some Carmel magazine. I was quite touched at reading what G.S. had said about me not long before his end. You can forward the article to Éch-Pi-El, with instructions to return it to me at his leisure.

1. A city in Hyperborea.
2. "The Song of the Necromancer"; see letter 201.
3. "R. E. H." (WT, October 1936).
4. The songs for The Fugitives appeared in Sandalwood ("The Song of Aviol," "The Song of Cartha," "The Love-Potion," and "Song"). A fragment of The Fugitives appears in SS (pp. 225–26). The "blank verse" portion does not appear to survive.
5. CAS did write one play, The Dead Will Cuckold You (1951; SS).
6. I.e., Leaves; see letter 214.
7. David Warren Ryder, "The Price of Poetry," Controversy 1, No. 7 (December 1934): 86; rpt. by the Futile Press in June 1937 and laid in CAS's Nero.

---

[203]   To H. P. Lovecraft [TLS, JHL]   [27 November 1936]
Palace of the Mithridates, at the serving of the
strychnine-seasoned supper.

Dear Éch-Pi-El:
I might have written before this, but have been stayed by the realization that your press of correspondence is no doubt far heavier than mine. Anyway, you should have had a couple of cards from me; the first one acknowledging the return of the sculptures.

I am pleased that you and Ar-Éch-Bei found the collection of teraphim so much to your liking. I infer, though, that my list of titles, which corresponded to the numbers on the bases, was not passed along. The names were really a good part of the fun. No. 1, the little cameo that you mentioned, was The Black Dog of Commoriom; no. 13, the unicornous female monster with claws and carapace, was The Harpy; no. 8, the slim black thing with rows of ciphers on its body, was The Reptile-Man. And the one you referred to ⅄A must have been The Entity from Algol. The number (9) was erased from its base. ⅄A is merely a signature—my first two initials in old Etruscan.

Dagon, which Donald bought, was really the masterpiece of the whole lot.[1] He sent me some excellent photos of it and the others. If you haven't seen copies of these photos, I'll ship them along to you presently. Don't worry about not feeling able to buy anything: you will, in time, become the recipient of more than one gift. At present I am experimenting with the making of moulds for five pieces and hope to make some more accurate casts in the hardest plaster obtainable. These, I believe, might sell as "novelties," if offered at prices running from 50¢ upward. Certainly this seems the best way to make money from the stuff, if any is to be made. Few people, especially in this neck of the woods, will pay more for an original sculpture than they would for a cast of some cheap abomination from the 5 & 10. That being the case, I see no reason why I should waste any more of my originals upon them. Incidentally, I can have an exhibition of sculptures at the Crocker Art Gallery in Sacramento after the first of the year. According to the director, who came to see my stuff some time ago, prices should range from $5.00 for the smallest originals up to $50.00 for my largest piece, an eleven-inch statuette. The last-named would please you, since it represents a monster somewhat akin to Cthulhu—in fact, so much so that I have christened it Cthulhu's Child.

I hope that your routine is less overburdened now and that weather and health conditions are at least tolerable. Here, things are pretty much the same, though my father seems slightly improved for the present. We have had a long dry fall, with only the veriest sprinkling of rain; and at present indications such weather may continue indefinitely. The nights, though, are getting colder, and have sometimes been little above the freezing-point. As for my own condition—well, I pretty nearly succumbed to various worries, griefs and bedevilments a little while back. But a round scolding from Mrs. S.,[2] in addition to even more self-beratement and ridicule, is getting me out of it. I think I shall soon become like that old Persian king who thrived upon upas and aconite.

I re-read "The Haunter of the Dark" with immense pleasure, and look forward to a like experience with "The Thing on the Doorstep." It would have surprised me prodigiously if Wright had not accepted these tales. I believe he would accept anything of yours that didn't violate his cast-iron prejudices about length and "plot." As to the proposed English collection of your tales, I must say that it sounds like a damn good idea. For some reason, British publishers seem more receptive to weird collections than their American congeners. Our old friend Doc. Keller, I notice, has had some of his stuff published in France.

I have writen to Ar-Éch-Bei, and feel more concerned over his general hard luck than over such trivial details as the delay of *Incantations*. As I told him, there's no hurry in presenting the book to a world that has not yet exhausted the edition of *E.&C.* printed 14 years ago.

Thanks for clippings and acrostics.[4] I return the latter, as per request. Yours and Barlow's strike me as being much the best ones. Such things must be damnably hard to write, and I have never attempted them. But if I could have joined that group in the old churchyard, I am sure that I should have felt a similar inspiration and impulse toward emulation.

The crop of Fan magazines is even more amazing and astounding and weird and wondrous[5] than most of the stuff to which they devote their attention, enthusiasm and criticism. Surely two or three of such things, with interests divided between pure fantasy and its more or less scientific corival, would be enough. I rather agree with your estimate of *Science-Fantasy Correspondent*. *Science Fiction Critic*, issued by Claire P. Beck of Lakeport, Cal., is refreshingly sound and genuinely critical, from what I have seen of it. Young Beck came to visit me some months ago and impressed me by his intelligence. But I confess I don't see how these magazines can survive: they are getting thicker than wood-mushrooms after a warm rain.

Howard's death startled and shocked me as it must have shocked everyone else. It is understandable but infinitely tragic and regrettable . . . Sometimes, though, the anticipation of an event is more unbearable than the event itself; and I wonder if Howard might not have pulled through if the nurse had been less frank.

I admired Barlow's memorial sonnet greatly. Your prose tribute, and that of Price, were fine.[6]

I enclose a recent poem. Wright accepted it and will no doubt print it before long.

> Yours for the resurgence of R'lyeh and the
> melting of the ice-cap from utmost Lomar.
> Klarkash-Ton

1. Pictured on the spine of *AY.*
2. Genevieve K. Sully.
3. David H. Keller (1880–1966), American physician and pulp writer.
4. HPL and his visitors RHB and Adolphe de Castro had written acrostic poems on the name of Edgar Allan Poe.
5. Each adjective used to describe the fan magazines corresponds to the title of a pulp magazine.
6. Robert E. Howard had committed suicide on 11 June. HPL's tribute was "In Memoriam: Robert Ervin Howard" (*Fantasy Magazine* [September 1936]; a shortened version, "Robert Ervin Howard: 1930–1936," appeared unsigned in *Phantagraph* [August 1936]). E. Hoffmann Price also had a unsigned tribute in the same issue of *Fantasy Magazine* as HPL. Also, both HPL and Price had untitled tributes in "The Eyrie" (*WT*, October 1936).

[204]   To Albert M. Bender [TLS, MCL]   Dec. 12th, 1936

Dear Albert:

My hearty thanks for the Christmas check which you so kindly and thoughtfully sent me. It was doubly welcome this year, since I have been unable to do much writing and have had most of my time consumed by necessary but unprofitable chores.

I hope this finds you in good health. Truly, financial conditions seem to have improved, and the indications are good for an old-time holiday season. I trust that you will be able to enjoy it to the fullest.

I agree with you that it should not be necessary for poets and artists to endure abnormal suffering or privation. Something, from what one hears, is being done to encourage art and literature: but the encouragement, it would seem, is only for such art and literature as deals directly with contemporary and local subject-matter. The imaginative, in fiction, poetry, painting, sculpture, is pretty much overlooked when it comes to the handing out of official honors and emoluments: and yet imaginative art is surely the highest and purest art.

Some of my sculptures, by the way, will be exhibited next year at the Crocker Gallery in Sacramento. On the advice of Harry Noyes Pratt, the director, I am experimenting with the molding and casting of a few pieces. These, if turned out in good plaster reproductions, could be sold at a price within the reach of anyone who might care for the exotic, outré, grotesque and imaginative type of sculpture: a type that seems to be almost non-existent in modern European and American art. So far, through delay in getting proper materials, etc., I have not done much; but I have turned out a few casts in plaster of Paris (a damnably soft and unsatisfactory material) and will send you specimens before long.

My father joins me in all best holiday wishes and remembrances.

As ever,
Clark Ashton Smith

———————————————◆———————————————

[205]   To Ray and Margaret St. Clair [TLS, private collection]
Jan. 20th, 1937.

Dear Ray and Margaret:

I had hoped to write ere this and render my thanks for the foursquare sybilline image (prequickened) that I received around New Year's. It has long since gone the way of such eidola, with additional libations of port or burgundy, and was always partaken of a little before the hour of retiring. I don't remember any kakodaemones as a result of such evocation: but I did have some exceedingly pleasant dreams on those nights. It would seem that my nightmares are mostly evoked (or exorcised) in fiction and sculpture, since I rarely have a good one any more. The nearest approach to one was a rather bothersome recent dream, in which I found myself fighting a large number of swollen rubbery reptiles with a short-handled shovel, and was unable to get any action on the critters except by heaving them over a conveniently adjacent precipice! This dream, as well as some others that were quite vivid and somewhat disagreeable, was apparently stimulated by the excessive cold (12 or 15 degrees below freezing) which had begun to strike through my bedclothes; and, as far as I can figure, it had nothing to do with Freudianism or anything that I had eaten.

I am glad the several casts and carving arrived intact, and trust that you achieved satisfactory results from the New Year's Eve ceremony of interrogation. Perhaps I should have told you that if one drink doesn't draw a reply, the libation should be repeated. Perseverance is invariably rewarded by such words of golden wisdom as may well serve to illustrate the old adage, in *vino veritas*. But no doubt you discovered this.

Re your query as to the order in which the four carvings were done: to the best of my recollection, The Dog of Commoriom was the oldest, the Sorcerer next, and The Mermaid's Butler third, with Tsathoggua the most recent. Tsathoggua was done in a curious fibroid form of serpentine; and the casts, as a consequence, tend to look like wood-carvings if tinted with colors appropriate to wood. You will note the fibrous structure if you look closely.

I hope you can manage a trip to Auburn, and suggest April or May as the best months. March is often cold or stormy, and the summers are likely to be pretty torrid and dusty. If my quarters were more commodious and comfortable, I'd be very glad to offer you some hospitality; but the place is really impossible for guests. You'll find an ungodly condition of congestion and litter, with most of the bookcases doing double duty as shelves for carvings, and hunks of rough rock and mineral parked anywhere, together with piles of magazines, wine-jugs, sacks of plaster, etc, etc.

As to hostelries, I guess the old Freeman Hotel is as good and reasonable as any. But I'll make inquiries before you come.

Your Nazir Indian must have been rather good: not every prophet could shoot around the International Date Line and score a hit!

I hope January has been more profitable and pleasant with you than with me. Evidently I am not designed for Arctic rigors, since the prolonged cold (42° has been the warmest so far this year) has simply petrified me. As a consequence, I haven't done much with my casting or with anything else, and have developed an inordinate appetite and a taste for straight whisky.

No, I haven't tried any San Francisco art stores with my carvings and believe San Francisco, in general, to be too conservative, and disposed to appreciate an artist only after he has found appreciation elsewhere. Perhaps I shall be able to place some work in the southern part of the state—I have the address of at least one dealer who sounds likely. At present, I am sending out a few typed circulars offering the casts I have made to certain hand-picked fantasy lovers. If the casts sell at all they should net me more money than the sale of originals; but so far, I have only seven moulds that are usable, and the stock of casts is very limited—about 45 in all being ready for distribution. The remnant of my mould-making material (a sort of liquid rubber) froze the other night and is consequently useless; and I won't dare to order any more till the present glacial period is over!

   Best wishes and regards, as ever,
   Clark Ashton

P.S. I enclose photos of several carvings. These (my only copies) can be returned at leisure. They were taken by Donald Wandrei, whose stories you may have read in *Weird Tales*. Donald purchased Dagon, which I regard as one of my best pieces. I have made a mould of The Harpy, and am giving the casts a rather lurid tinting: mouth, claws, breasts, and the rock under the Harpy all being dabbed with blood-red. Curiously enough, there was a suggestion of this in the markings of the original mineral!

———◆———

[206]   To August Derleth [TLS, SHSW]   March 23rd, 1937

Dear August:

The news of Lovecraft's death seems incredible and night-marish, and I cannot adjust myself to it.[1] The few meager details in my possession I owe to Harry Brobst, H.P.L.'s Providence friend, who can be addressed at the Charles V. Chapin Hospital, Providence. Late in February, I had mailed Lovecraft some photographs and other matters. These he was too ill to acknowledge directly; but asked Brobst to write me and explain the circumstances. Brobst's letter, written March 1st, said that Lovecraft appeared to be suffering from some gastro-intestinal condition of long standing. He could not lie down, slept very little because of the pain, and could eat very little. He was still at 66 College St.—had not been removed to the hospital. All this sounded pretty serious and depressing, since Brobst did not hesitate to character-ize his condition as "grave." However, I kept hoping that amelio-ration and improvement would occur. Then, on the 20th, came a brief note from Brobst, dated the 15th, saying that Lovecraft had died at 7.30 that morning and would be buried on the 18th. This is all that I know. It saddens me as nothing has done since my mother's death; and, somehow, I can't help feeling that it should have been unnecessary.

In my last letter from H.P.L. (postmarked Feb. 5th) he spoke of feeling "rather on the bum," with a combination of indigestion and general weakness, and some sort of foot-swelling caused by exposure to cold. The letter (12 closely written pages) was, how-ever, full of his usual enthusiasm, erudition, delight in scenic walks, etc., and gave little hint of a coming breakdown in health. It is all too melancholy; and it would be no less futile than needless to expatiate on the loss to us who are left. Perhaps it may hasten the awakening of publishers to the loss incurred by American litera-ture—and also to the Poe-like bequest that it has gained.

I've been meaning to write for ages—will promise to be a better and more frequent correspondent in future. Tell me something about yourself when you write again. There is no special news here. I have definitely settled down to a program of story-writing and have finished a couple of new shorts.

My best, as ever,
Clark Ashton

1. HPL had died on 15 March of intestinal cancer.

[207]   To August Derleth [TLS, SHSW]   March 30th, 1937.

Dear August:

I am very glad to hear of the project for an omnibus volume of HPL's work, and am particularly pleased that the task of arrangement, etc., is in hands so capable and thoroughly qualified as yours and Donald's. The general plan of contents, as outlined, seems all right to me. Certainly HPL's own written selection of titles should be followed as much as possible. Among the poems, I trust that "Nemesis" and the "Fungi" will be included. An appendix containing specimens of revisory work would be interesting. Somehow, I missed "The Curse of Yig," but understand that it was mainly if not entirely Lovecraft. From a close perusal of the Hazel Heald stories, such as "Out of the Eons" and "The Horror in the Museum," I am persuaded that they are about 99½ percent pure Lovecraft. It is really a pity that they can't be included as simon-pure originals. If I can be of the least help at any time, in any way, do not hesitate to call upon me. I have kept all of Lovecraft's letters to me (covering a period of about 17 years) and will try to get them together before long. I'll be happy to type such specimens and passages as Don may want to include in the privately printed volume. Some of the longer letters are marvels of fancy, literary criticism, scenic description, erudition, etc, all mingled in that inimitable epistolary flow which, it is safe to say, will never be duplicated or approached in these latter days. The letters are perfect models of a virtually extinct courtesy, since everything that I had touched upon or mentioned, however briefly, was noted and enlarged upon in the answering letter. His very last letter to me was a particularly fine one, and contained several vivid and highly atmospheric pages describing a totally new region of woodland walks and vistas (in fact, two such regions) which he had only recently discovered in close vicinage to Providence. One thinks of him as still wandering in those beloved woodlands, still accompanied by the familiar felidae, the chance-met members of the Kappa Alpha Tau.

Your elegy is beautiful and touching, and I shall prize the copy you sent me. I too intend to write some memorial verses which will evoke something of his daily life and surroundings together with the imagery and atmosphere of his literary work.[1] It seems better, however, to wait a little for the required energy and inspiration which the Daemon will supply presently. I did write, the other day, a very brief prose In Memoriam at the request of a San Francisco fan magazine (*Tesseract*).[2] It seemed hollow and inadequate—as, indeed, anything that one could say would seem at this time. I am writing a letter of tribute and condolence to Mrs. Gamwell— a letter that would have gone forward some time ago if it had not been for delay in verifying her name. In going through a lot of HP's letters, I couldn't find that he had ever referred to her as anything but "my aunt."[3] I feel sure that she will have received myriads of letters and expressions of sympathy.

I'll mail you a couple of my casts in a day or two. These casts, I must explain, reproduce with perfect exactness the form of the original carvings; but I have tinted them as fancy dictated and have not tried to reproduce the original coloring of minerals. The carvings themselves are purely inspirational, and sometimes, in beginning one, I have not the least idea what form it will take under my hand. I feel as if they were prompted by forces outside myself— forces perhaps identical with those which have inspired archaic and primitive art. It can no doubt be argued that they are the product of a certain "psychology," but perhaps the psychology is merely a channel. Sometimes I wonder if the real motivations of art, as well as of all human thought, emotion, action, etc, are not hidden beyond all fathoming or suspicion of modern psychologists. Anyway, they are beyond Freud, who is hopelessly lopsided. But enough of this—I had no intention of starting a dissertation, or discussion, for which neither of us has the time at present. What I have said is partly prompted by the queer feeling of personal detachment from the sculptures which I have: the feeling that they are not really mine but might as well have been dug up in Yucatan or Cambodia.

As ever,
Clark Ashton

P.S. I'll send one or two recent poems in my next.

By the way, some friends have suggested that Lovecraft's study at 66 College St., with his collection of books, etc, should be maintained permanently just as he left it, as a fitting memorial. This, it seems to me, is a fine idea. I am sure that a lot of people would contribute money toward it, if necessary. Anyway, the suggestion seems worth making if it has not already been made.

1. "Elegy: In Providence the Spring . . ." (*River*, June 1937). CAS composed "To Howard Phillips Lovecraft" on 31 March 1937 (*WT*, July 1937; *SP* and *LO*). AWD included both items in the HPL omnibus, *Marginalia* (Sauk City, WI: Arkham House, 1944).
2. "In Memoriam: H. P. Lovecraft" (*Tesseract*, April 1937; *PD*).

3. HPL was survived by his maternal aunt Annie E. P. Gamwell (1866–1941).

[208]   To Donald Wandrei [TLS, MHS]   Apr. 3rd, 1937.

Dear Donald:

I can readily understand how HPL's death has affected you, since even to me, who knew him only through prolonged correspondence, the loss is a staggering and grievous one. Other deaths in the past have brought sorrow to me (2 women friends, Sterling, my mother) and one can't compare degrees of grief. What one feels in HPL's case is necessarily unique; for the man himself was incomparable and in all ways extraordinary. There never was, and never will be, anyone to take his place either in life or literature.

The irony of your writing to Lovecraft on the day of his death is something that I can almost match with the enclosed poem. In his last letter to me Lovecraft copied a fine complimentary sonnet which he had recently addressed to me.[1] When I received that sonnet, I little dreamed that my answer to it would take the form of an elegaic ode. My poem is poor and meager enough; but perhaps he would have liked some of its lines, which carry on the literary play-spirit that often marked our correspondence.

I am glad the posthumous volume is to be sponsored by you and Derleth. As to the letters, I believe that a collection of them would establish Lovecraft as one of the supreme masters of that latterly neglected art.[2] Many of those that he wrote me (sometimes running to 6, 8 or more sheets) are unique mélanges of erudition, fancy, criticism, humor, personalia, scenic description, etc., and no doubt those to more intimate friends must surpass them. I agree with you heartily that they complement the genius shown in his tales. I am starting to get together in one box the letters I have (the correspondence began about 1920) and if you need any specimens or passages, will be glad to type them. Derleth had already written me when your letter came. [. . .]

Re that theory about an artist's growth being linked with or rooted in his native soil: probably it depends a great deal on the type of mind or temperament possessed by the artist; that is to say, whether he reacts realistically *upon* his environment or romantically against it. However, maybe it could be argued that there is an indirect debt in the latter case as well as a direct one in the former. Poe, who reflected nothing of America in his writings, may have owed to America the reverse impulse that drove him so far into fantasy and sheer creation. Lovecraft is essentially different from Poe, combining as he does both local realism and cosmic fantasy.

I, though not incapable of realism, am plainly more of the Poe
order. Derleth, I would venture to say, is more thoroughly and
positively identified with his native milieu even than Lovecraft, and
feels no need of trans-dimensional dreams or flights into the vasts
of antiquity and cosmic space. Perhaps, too, he draws from the soil
his astounding electric vitality, like Antaeus in the myth.

Write when you have leisure and inclination.

As always, Clark

1. "To Clark Ashton Smith, Esq., upon His Fantastic Tales, Verses,
Pictures, and Sculptures" (*WT*, April 1938; as "To Clark Ashton Smith").
DAW actually had written to HPL on 17 March.

2. The book *The Outsider and Others* (Sauk City, WI: Arkham
House, 1939) was coedited by AWD and DAW. The two founded Arkham
House to publish the book when a commercial publisher could not be
found. Many years later, they published HPL's *Selected Letters* in five
volumes.

[209]   To August Derleth [TLS, SHSW]   April 13th, 1937.

Dear August:

To the best of my knowledge and belief, HPL, in creating the
Cthulhu mythology, can have owed nothing more to Poe, Bierce
and Chambers than the mere hint of a prehistoric and infra-
mnemonic world. This world he peopled according to his own
fancy, with beings originally descended from the stars and referred
to generally as The Old Ones. Hastur, I think, comes from Bierce
through Chambers and is mentioned only casually by HPL. Since
I haven't read "An Inhabitant of Carcosa" for at least twenty
years, I recall little of the story; and I don't remember anything
very *specific* about Hastur in *The King in Yellow*. HPL, I suspect,
gave him his faculty of "stalking the star-spaces." Hastur is mentioned in "The Whisperer in Darkness," in a listing of fabulous
names that includes Bethmoora (from Dunsany) and L'mur-
Kathulos and Bran (partially or wholly from R. E. Howard:
though there is also a Bran in Celtic mythology). The intent here,
it would seem, is to suggest a *common* immemorial background
for mythic beings and places created by *various* modern writers.
Tsathoggua receives his first *published* mention in "The Whisperer
in Darkness" (*W.T.*, Aug. 1931). Tsathoggua, Eibon and *The Book
of Eibon* are, however, my own contributions to the mythos of the
Old Ones and their world; and I first introduced Tsathoggua in
"The Tale of Satampra Zeiros," written in the fall of 1929 but not

printed in *W.T.* till Nov. 1931. Eibon made his debut in "The Door to Saturn" (*Strange Tales,* Jan. 1932), where Tsathoggua was also featured under the variant of Zhothaqqua. Tsathoggua is again mentioned in "The Testament of Athammaus" (*W.T.,* Oct. 1932); and is linked with the Averoigne legendry under the variant Sadagui, in "The Holiness of Azédarac" (Nov. 1933, *W.T.*). I think my only mention of Yog-Sothoth is in "Azédarac," where he is given the Gallicized form, Iog-Sotôt. *The Book of Eibon* is first mentioned and quoted in "Ubbo-Sathla" (*W.T.,* July 1933); and Eibon also enters indirectly another Averoigne tale, "The Beast of Averoigne" (*W.T.,* May 1933). Tsathoggua plays an important part in "The Seven Geases" (*W.T.,* Oct. 1934) and my still unpublished tale, "The Coming of the White Worm," purports to be Chapter IX of *The Book of Eibon.* This summary seems to exhaust my own use of the mythology to date. Yog-Sothoth is purely Lovecraft's creation, and first appears, if my memory serves me right, in "The Dunwich Horror" (*W.T.,* April 1929). As to classifying the Old Ones, I suppose that Cthulhu can be classed both as a survival on earth and a water-dweller; and Tsathoggua is a subterranean survival. Azathoth, referred to somewhere as "the primal nuclear chaos," is the ancestor of the whole crew but still dwells in outer and ultra-dimensional space, together with Yog-Sothoth, and the demon piper Nyarlathotep, who attends the throne of Azathoth. I shouldn't class any of the Old Ones as *evil:* they are plainly beyond all limitary human conceptions of either ill or good. Long's Chaugnar Faugn, the Rhan-Tegoth of Hazel Heald's opus, "The Horror in the Museum," and the Ghatanathoa of her later tale, "Out of the Eons," belong, I should venture to say, among the spawn of Azathoth and the brethren of Cthulhu and Tsathoggua. Rhan-Tegoth and Ghatanathoa, I'd be willing to gamble, were created by HPL in what was practically a job of ghost-writing. The first-named is a survival and earth-dweller, somewhat analogous to Tsathoggua; while Ghatanathoa is a sea-submerged entity more akin to Cthulhu.

I hope all this will be of some use. Bob Barlow, I imagine, can tell you even more about the Old Ones and their affiliations, etc. Personally, I don't think it necessary to enter into quite so much detail in presenting the stories to intelligent readers; but the growth of the whole mythos, the borrowings and contributions by various writers, is certainly an interesting study. No doubt the serious mythologies of primitive peoples sprang up in a manner somewhat analogous, though, of course, non-literary. Every god or demon, somewhere in the dim past, must have had a human creator.

I am terribly curious to see the newly completed "Return of Hastur" and hope you will loan me the carbon if Wright rejects the tale. From what you say, it would seem that some remarkable inspiration, either subliminal or external, is involved. My theory (not favored by scientists!) is that some world, or many worlds, of pure mentation may exist. The individual mind may lapse into this common reservoir at death, just as the atoms of the individual body lapse into grosser elements. Therefore, no idea or image is ever lost from the universe. Living minds, subconsciously, may tap the reservoir according to their own degree and kind of receptivity. HPL would have argued that no mentation could survive the destruction of the physical brain; but against this it might be maintained that energy and matter, brain and ideation, can never quite be destroyed no matter what changes they undergo. The sea of Being persists, though the waves of individual entity rise and fall eternally. The truth about life and death is perhaps simpler and more complex than we dream.

I am glad to know that the little casts pleased you so well. Some day, when I have time to do some more casting, I'll try to send you one of The Harpy, which seems to be the special favorite among purchasers and gift-recipients. Later, I plan to cut some imaginative pieces as models for book-ends, trays, incense-burners, etc., and believe that they may have distinct commercial possibilities. There seems to be a great demand for such objects, generally classed as "novelties."

Genevieve K. Sully, who wrote you, is the mother of Helen Sully. Helen met HPL in 1933, and also met Donald. Donald, in his visit to California, spent much time at the Sully home. HPL's letters to the Sullys, from what I have seen of them, are marvelous and show a slightly different and most lovable angle of his multi-sided personality, together with amazing knowledge of California history and western scenery.

As to my own letters from HPL, I have now recovered nearly 150 of them (not counting numerous closely written postcards) and think that there must be a couple of dozen more about the cabin. The worst gap is in 1935, so there must be a box of recent letters that I have carefully put away and mislaid somewhere. My procedure, a damned sloppy one, has been to clear the answered letters from my desk by bundling them all away in boxes when the accumulation became too unwieldy and topheavy. Few letters have ever been destroyed; but the mixture and confusion make it a herculean task to sort out those from one particular person over a couple of years. My impression is, that you will be forced to limit space given to letters—unless you can publish a ten-volume set! I am starting to read over the ones in my possession, and am making some brief notation as to main contents on envelopes or at top of the most significant and valuable ones. For instance, in one of the earliest, I find an acute summary of H. L. Mencken and his service and detriment to the cause of American letters: this in passing, in a concise paragraph, at a time when few could have had the temerity or acumen to challenge Mencken.

Express will be the best way to ship the letters, I suppose, if it is necessary to ship them; but, like you I hate to think of entrusting anything so irreplaceable to the mercies of modern transportation. Perhaps the best alternative would be for me to type a liberal selection of letters *in toto* (single spacing?) and let you and Donald do your own editing.

I have suggested the memorial preservation of the study to Mrs. Gamwell; admitting, at the same time, that I am in no position to judge the practicality of the plan. Certainly nothing could be more desirable. I have also put the suggestion to Harry Brobst and Barlow. Let's hope that something can be done. I don't see why there should have been any *haste* about the removal of books, etc.

On looking this letter over, I note that the first paragraph doesn't list in strict order my tales referring to the mythos of the Old Ones. Therefore I am typing a separate list to enclose. Of course, the order of publication is not entirely the order in which they were written. HPL certainly got ahead of me when he presented old Tsathoggua to the world before Wright's rejection, vacillation and eventual reconsideration of "Satampra Zeiros" enabled me to present him! The July 1933 *W.T.*, containing "The Horror in the Museum," "The Dreams in the Witch-House" and "Ubbo-Sathla," certainly featured the whole mythos and the fabulous books (*Eibon, Necronomicon*, etc.) more prominently than any one issue before or since. Incidentally, HPL and I received dozens of queries, at one time or another, as to where *The Book of Eibon*, the *Necronomicon*, Von Junzt's *Nameless Cults*, etc., could be obtained! I believe one of HPL's correspondents, a Maine Yankee with leanings towards wizardry, promised not to put any information given him to evil uses! Another, a woman claiming descent from infamous New England witches and also from Lucretia Borgia, offered HPL some inside dope on the witch cult and its practices. As for me, I'll never forget the letters from that paretic Swede, Olsen; one of which letters corrected at great length certain mistaken notions of Abdul Alhazred. But I remember also that you had some experience with Olsen and his patents of infernal and grandiose nobility!

I hope "The Chain of Aforgomon" will pass muster. "Necromancy in Naat" seems the best of my more recently published weirds; though Wright forced me to mutilate the ending.* * * * * * * * * * *1

Well, this is enough. I'll soon be rivalling HPL as to length of letters, even though the quality may fall short!

As ever,
Clark

P.S.: I have *started* to read your novel. Opening is most vivid and impressive.[2]

P.P.S. [on envelope:] In Adolphe de Castro's yarn, *The Electric Executioner* (*W.T.*, Aug. 1930) there are references to Yog-Sothoth and Cthulhu; the names having an Aztec termination—Yog-Sothotl, Cthulhutl. H.P.L. must have had a hand in revising this tale.

Of course, the Old Ones might be considered relatively evil, since the overwhelming horror and hideousness of their aspect, their ravenousness toward man, etc., are always emphasized. These qualities of terror and horror would seem to inhere in their *sheer alienage;* and all things equally akin would have the same or kindred effect on human sentiency.

1. The original conclusion to "Necromancy in Naat" has not been found.
2. AWD, *Still Is the Summer Night* (New York: Scribners, 1937).

———————— ◆ ————————

[210]   To August Derleth [TLS, SHSW]   April 21st, 1937.

Dear August:

I have one or two suggestions to offer anent the contents of the primary Lovecraft collection. If a choice is necessary between "The Tomb" and "In the Vault," I should vote for the latter as the more powerful tale. However, the earlier yarn certainly has its value and interest too. I am inclined to question the grouping of "The Colour out of Space" amid the Mythology tales, since it seems to me that the incursive agency in this tale is merely an unknown cosmic force, hardly to be classed as supernatural or even animate. It should find place perhaps more fitly in the Miscellaneous: New England Tales group. However, I haven't the story at hand to verify my impressions about the "Colour." Incidentally, "The Colour out of Space" should make a fine title for the whole collection, as typifying Lovecraft's contribution to literature. Of course, "The Outsider" would be good too for this purpose.

Re the mythology: my own ideas on the subject are taken almost wholly from the stories themselves, especially "The Call of

Cthulhu." Oddly enough, I can't find and don't recall any letters in which HPL touched on the general system as he did to you and Dean Farnese. (I have, however, a letter giving detailed data about *The Necronomicon* and will transcribe it among the letters and passages I am now starting to type!) A deduction relating the Cthulhu mythos to the Christian mythos would indeed be interesting; and of course the *unconscious* element in such creation is really the all-important one. However, there seems to be no reference to *expulsion* of Cthulhu and his companions in "The Call." According to the testimony given by the cult-member, De Castro,[1] Cthulhu and the other Old Ones "died" or were thrown into a state of suspended animation "when the stars were wrong." When the stars were "right," some outside force would serve to liberate and resurrect them. This would seem to indicate the action of cosmic laws rather than a battle between good and evil deities. However, the passage that you quote from a letter to Farnese would seem to give the problem another complexion.[2] However, if the "expulsion" was accompanied by animate agencies or gods, it is strange that they are not referred to in the stories. On the other hand, a parallel can certainly be drawn between the ultra-dimensional Old Ones and the Satanic or demonian beings invoked by wizards or witches, or called upon during the abominations of the Sabbath.

By the way, I have received a letter from Lovecraft's Providence friend, Harry Brobst, stressing the point that HPL's philosophic convictions, his atheism and disbelief in immortality, should be made plain in anything written about him and his work. Brobst, an atheist and materialist himself, seems almost pathetically anxious concerning the matter! I told him I felt sure you would touch upon it in your study. Certainly any representative selection of letters will leave no doubt as to HPL's conscious convictions. [. . .]

I hope you and Don are in no great hurry for the transcribed letter passages. Things have piled up on me here; and the sudden onset of warm dry weather make it imperative that I should do a lot of outdoor work—brush-burning, firebreak-hoing, extirpation of poison-oak, etc. All of it devolves upon me, since I can't even hire satisfactory help. Also, the financial angle will force me to turn out a few tales as soon as possible. I'll do something on the letters every day, however. The later and meatier ones will certainly present a problem! Possibly I may have to ship on some of them after all—which I shall hate to do, knowing how overburdened you are. As to safety, no doubt they will be safer almost anywhere out of this region during the fire-season. The risk becomes worse hereabouts every year, because of the tindery dryness over a period of six or sometimes even eight months, and the god-damned careless-ness of autoists, hunters and other tobacco addicts—not to men-tion professional incendiaries. This is one reason (not the only one) why I have thought of quitting California. Of course, it is my native state, and I am attached to the scenery. But there is an increasing destruction and pollution of landscape beauties, and a growing influx of undesirable humans bringing with them filth and pestilence. Auburn, for example, has been ravaged this winter by a virulent species of measles sometimes terminating in death and always serious: an epidemic which, I am convinced, can be blamed on the auto-tramps and their "trailers." California, it would seem, must serve as a kind of sink or cess-pool for the whole U.S. . . . Apart from this, the local attitude toward art and literature is dis-couraging. Perhaps, however, when I do go (or if I go) I shall make a clean jump out of the U.S. and perhaps end up in the East Indies. But of course this is all nebulous. Any one of a number of con-tingencies—such as death, marriage or the hoosegow—might forestall my dreamt escape into the exotic! You needn't take it too seriously.

"Hastur," and any other tales you may write continuing the mythology, will present a most unique interest. Those plots in the commonplace book would no doubt be capable of immense devel-opment. I am wondering if the plots of stories he had read aren't the synopses he mentioned making at a time (early in 1934, I think) when he was overhauling his own technique with the idea of strengthening his plot-structures.[3] If they are the same, they will include Poe, Machen, Blackwood and James plots—and per-haps even something from my booklet, *The Double Shadow!*

Here's to your new novel!

Always,

Clark

1. The name of the character in "The Call of Cthulhu" is simply Castro (a confusion with HPL's associate Adolphe de Castro).

2. The passage CAS refers to likely was not by HPL at all, but a botched paraphrase by Harold Farnese. See David E. Schultz, "The Origin of Lovecraft's 'Black Magic' Quote," *Crypt of Cthulhu* No. 13 (Fall 1986).

3. CAS refers to the unpublished manuscript, "Weird Story Plots," not identical to HPL's commonplace book. Actually, HPL compiled the list c. September 1933.

[211]   To August Derleth [TLS, SHSW]   April 28th, 1937

Dear August:

Thanks for the fine photograph of HPL, which I prize immensely. Do you know when it was taken? It seems younger than any other picture of him I have seen.

From what you say, the instructions as to preservation and arrangement of stories must indeed be confusing. Truly, it would seem that he must have grouped the stories in relation to creative period and style development rather than theme.[1] Obviously there is no connection between "Cthulhu" and "The Colour," except that they were written in sequence, if I recall rightly. "Dunwich" came later and seems to mark a growing realism of groundwork which is continued through the longer subsequent tales. It seems to me that the grouping you have decided to follow is about as practical as any.

As to the varying references to the mythos in different tales: I wonder if these weren't designed to suggest the diverse developments and interpretations of old myths and deities that spring up over great periods of time and in variant races and civilizations? I have, intentionally, done something of the sort in my own myth-creation. In "The Tale of Satampra Zeiros," certain vague legends were briefly cited to explain the desertion of the city of Commoriom. Then, in "The Testament of Athammaus," I cooked up, in fullest and most elaborate detail, an explanation of which the earlier tale gave no hint. I believe a similar theory would account for the discrepant characters given to Azathoth, Nyarlathotep, etc., in different stories. "Cthulhu" contains the germ of the mythos; "The Dunwich Horror" introduces Yog-Sothoth; and I am inclined to think the first mention of Azathoth occurs in *Fungi from Yuggoth* and "The Whisperer in Darkness." Evidently HPL developed and varied the mythos as he went on. I believe the theory I have outlined above will afford the best explanation of discrepancies: HPL wished to indicate the natural growth of a myth-pattern through dim ages, in which the same deity or demon might present changing aspects. [. . .]

I have read "The Return of Hastur," twice, with deep interest. Indeed, it is a remarkable production; and yet, as it stands, I do not find the tale very satisfactory. I believe, for one thing, that it suffers (small wonder, under the circumstances!) from too hasty writing; and this is all the more regrettable since it contains the material of a first-rate weird tale. Since you asked me for suggestions, I am going to give you my full reactions—which, of course, may not coincide with those of any other reader. One reaction, confirmed rather than diminished by the second reading, is that you have tried to work in too much of the Lovecraft mythology and have not assimilated it into the natural body of the story. For my taste, the tale would gain in unity and power if the interest were centered wholly about the mysterious and "unspeakable" Hastur. Cthulhu and the sea-things of Innsmouth, though designed to afford an element and interest *of conflict,* impress me rather as a source of confusion. I believe a tremendous effect of vague menacing atmosphere and eerily growing tension could be developed around Hastur, who has the advantage of being a virtually unknown demon. Also, this effect could be deepened by a more prolonged incredulity on the part of Paul Tuttle and Haddon, who should not accept the monstrous implications of the old books and the strange after-clause of Amos Tuttle's bond until the accumulation and linking of weird phenomena leaves them no possible alternative. One of the best things in the tale is the description of those interdimensional footsteps that resound beneath the menaced mansion. These could be related significantly to Hastur alone by having them seem to mount by degrees on the eastern side of the house, reverberate like strange thunder in the heavens above, and descend on the west in a regular rotation, to echo again in the subterrene depths. Eventually it would be forced upon the hearers that this rotation was *coincidental with the progress of Aldebaran and the Hyades through the heavens;* thus heralding the encroachment of Hastur from his ultrastellar lair. More could be made of the part about Amos Tuttle's corpse and its unearthly changes: the coffin should show evidence of having been violently disrupted from *within;* and the footprints in the field, though monstrous in size, could present a vaguely human conformation, like those of some legendary giant; and Tuttle's corpse, when found, would have burst open in numberless places as if through some superhuman inflation of all its tissues; showing that the unknown entity *had* occupied it but had soon found it useless *on account of the increasing corruption.* At the climax, just before the house is dynamited, a colossal figure might rise out of, mingling the features and members of Paul Tuttle with the transcosmic monstrosity of Hastur; and this shape, because of its *mortal* elements, could be shattered and destroyed by the explosion, compelling Hastur to recede invisibly though with soul-shaking footsteps toward the Hyades. Some fragment of the incredibly swollen and gigantic energumen might survive the explosion, to be buried hastily, with shudders and averted glances, by the finders. So much for my suggestions, which you may find worthless, impractical, and too foreign to your own conception. I suggest that you get the opinions of other readers. As it stands, the tale is certainly superior to many that Wright has published; and I agree that the wording is quite unusual for you, and often recalls HPL. [. . .]

April 29th

I started to read over some of HPL's stories last night, with a critical eye to mythologic references. Certainly some of the variations *are* puzzling. In "Cthulhu," the Great Old Ones are clearly specified as the builders and inhabitants of R'lyeh, "preserved by the spells of mighty Cthulhu," and worshipped through the aeons by obscure and evil cultists. Then, in "The Shadow over Innsmouth," Cthulhu and his compeers are referred to as the Deep Ones; and the Old Ones, whose "palaeogean magic" alone could check the sea-dwellers, are evidently something else again. Certainly these latter references would support your theory as to good and evil deities. In the earlier story, it might be argued that Castro was making out a case for his own side and ignoring the true Old Ones or confusing the evil gods with them. In "The Dreams in the Witch House," Nyarlathotep seems clearly identified with the Black Man of Satanism and witchcraft; since, in one of his dreams, Gilman is told that he must meet the Black Man and go with him to the throne of Azathoth.

That paragraph about Galpin occurs in a letter dated Aug-28th, 1925, and is as follows: "Galpin—whose wife passed through here (Brooklyn) last week and stopped with us—has wholly repudiated literature and devoted his life to music; giving up his instructorship in Texas. He is becoming a typical Parisian boulevardier; wearing long hair surmounted by a cap, old sporting clothes and the like, and carrying a stick with the proper air of nonchalance. American tourists point him out as a characteristic Frenchman, whilst small boys mistake him for the cinema comedian Harold Lloyd." This seems to present a rather graphic picture of the mercurial A.G., who was a frequent and enthusiastic correspondent of mine during his weird fiction and poetry period but dropped out abruptly and entirely after he switched to music.

My best as always,
Clark

1. CAS seems to refer to a list—still extant among HPL's papers at JHL —of three possible story collections drawn up by HPL late in life.

[212]   To August Derleth [TLS, SHSW]   May 13th, 1937.

Dear August:

Herewith the draft of your Commentary on HPL, which seems to cover the main points. His modesty about his own work was excessive, to say the least. Personally, I can find no fault with the style of his later tales, except that there is, in places, a slight trend toward verbosity and repetitional statement. Many of his style-traits, perhaps, are not in accord with present-day taste; but, as far as I am concerned, the writing is all the more refreshing for such differences. Things that the average sophisticated reader of today may regard as flaws will not necessarily be regarded as such a generation or two hence. The influence of fashion, always ephemeral, and always changing, must be considered here.

I'd have written before this: but since I knew you were busy with your own deferred work, I thought there was no great urgency. I hope the mystery puzzle book, the poetry anthology, and your new novel, will all reach a satisfactory completion in due time. Your energy and speed of composition never fail to arouse my profoundest envy and wonderment. I, alas, to finish anything at all (that is to say, literature) am condemned to a sort of galley-slaving such as was suffered by Flaubert. Painting and sculpture are child's play in comparison: which may or may not indicate that my natural talents are toward the graphic rather than the scriptural arts. Benjamin De Casseres, in his latest book (*Fantasia Impromptu*),[1] speaks of Flaubert as a "second rater," and this, apparently, because of his lack of spontaneity and his infinite labours. Says De Casseres: "If my books had cost me one-millionth part of the effort that he expended on one chapter alone, I should have said God damn literature! I'm going to be a bartender or a pimp." However, I don't agree with this. Flaubert's hard writing certainly made easy reading; and too much of this facilely written stuff reminds me of the proverbial rocky road to Dublin. [. . .]

Bob Barlow is trying to convert me to Bolshevism! A thankless task, I fear, in view of my natural Yankee hardheadedness together with a bare smattering of historical knowledge. The tenets of Karl Marx are about as practical, and likely to be practised, as the Golden Rule of Jesus Christ. Aside from that, I fail to see any particular point of desirability in a dictatorship of the proletariat, and can't stomach the Soviet materialism, anti-religious bigotry, censorship, regimentation, etc. These things are too much to pay for a mess of cabbage soup. Also, I predict that they will never be established in America, except through a prolonged and bloody internecine warfare that will make the Spanish embroilment look like a Rotarian barbecue by comparison. Admitting—as I am more than willing to admit—the wrong and injustice of present social conditions, I fail to conceive that such conditions can be improved by the bloodshed and bitterness of civil war.

As to the Lovecraft mythos, probably he had no intention or desire of reducing it to a consistent and fully worked out system, but used it according to varying impulse and inspiration. The best way, it seems to me, is to enjoy each tale separately and without trying to link it closely with all the others. This is the way I have always read them: a rather non-analytic and non-critical way, perhaps; but possibly they were written in a similar spirit. However, it will be all the more interesting if you can determine any pre-eminent facts.

My best, as ever,
Clark

P.S. Glad my suggestions about "Hastur" didn't seem too impertinent. I wonder if you didn't depart too radically from your *own* original conception of the story, owing to emotional disturbance and an intensified preoccupation with the Cthulhu mythology.

1. Benjamin De Casseres, *Fantasia Impromptu: The Adventures of an Intellectual Faun* (self-published, 1937).

———————————◆———————————

[213]   To Virgil Finlay[1]   May 15th, 1937.

Dear Virgil Finlay:

I was delighted to receive your letter—doubly so since I have had it in mind to write you for some time past. Ever since the appearance of "The Chain of Aforgomon" with your magnificent and finely interpretative drawing, I have wanted to express my pleasure in your work; and Lovecraft, in his very last letter to me, five or six weeks before his death, suggested that I get in touch with you.

I appreciate deeply the compliments that you pay my stories. It is no compliment at all to say in return that your illustrations are incomparably the best that I have ever had. In fact, I doubt if any living artist could surpass them. Your work, it seems to me, can take its place with that of the best modern illustrators, such as Sime, Rackham, Harry Clarke, Alastair, etc.[2] It is original and finely imaginative and fantastic with a delicacy of technique that rouses my envy as well as my admiration, since I have dabbled a little in India and Chinese white ink myself. The originals of your drawings for "Aforgomon," "The Black Abbot," and "Necromancy in Naat," which Wright was so kind as to give me, are among my prized possessions. I have been greatly impressed, too, by many others of your *W.T.* illustrations, particularly the ones for Bloch's "The Faceless God" and Lovecraft's "The Thing on the Doorstep." The finer the story, the more inspired, it would seem, is your illustration; and yet I must marvel too at the merit of drawings made by you for certain tales of the most inferior caliber.

As for my writing, circumstances have made me very unproductive during the past two years. My mother's illness and death, my father's growing feebleness, and our virtual isolation with everything devolving upon me, are chiefly responsible for my lapse from the pages of *W.T.* One story, however, has recently been completed and sold to Wright, and I am hoping he will soon turn it over to you for illustration. I have some others under way, and trust that many more of my efforts will prove acceptable to Wright and will be embellished by your drawings. If, during my lifetime, any Eastern publisher should bring out a volume for me, or if I sell work to any of the smooth paper magazines, I shall certainly urge the securing of your services as illustrator. Personally I don't feel that a story is hurt by appearing in a pulp magazine: but, for inevitable technical reasons, drawings suffer from that medium. [. . .]

In his last letter, Lovecraft mentioned your sculptures. I hope you will tell me more about them. Though I have always been rather indifferent to conventional sculpture, either classic or modernistic, I have lately become fascinated by the possibilities of three-dimensional bizarrerie. My own experiments in that line have been made during the past 25 months; and I fear that the number of masterpieces is still rather small! Most of my carvings have suffered from hasty execution, and some from the skimpiness of the material used. I haven't had time to work any of the harder substances apart from one or two pieces of roughly chiselled tufa; but, for the most part, have used certain kaolins, soapstones and schists that are readily cut with a knife. Many of these, after cutting, can be hardened more or less by fire. I am enclosing some photographs of carvings, which you can return at leisure. Keep the drawings, however. The one labelled Warden of the Dead is drawn from a sculpture that I made in rhyolite clay, a very hard, heavy and durable kaolinic substance. The other drawings are of entities that I haven't yet tried to render in three-dimensional form.

With all best regards and wishes,
Klarkash-Ton

1. Virgil Warden Finlay (1914–1971), prolific illustrator noted for his painstaking black-and-white stippling technique.

2. Arthur Rackham (1867–1939), illustrator of historical and fantasy subjects; Alastair (1887–1969), pseudonym of Hans Henning, Baron Voigt, poet, dancer, and illustrator.

---

[214]   To R. H. Barlow [TLS, JHL]   Auburn-in-Malebolge,
May 16th, 1937.

My dear Bob:

No doubt you will be astounded to receive so prompt an answer from me. Once in an epoch, I really get the impulse to write a letter; and this time you're the victim.

I received the book on Beddoes which you sent me from HPL's library. Strangely enough, HPL himself sent me a copy of that same book two or three years ago! I believe he bought several of them. Do you want the copy that you mailed me—I hardly need duplicates?! The book has certain merits as a critical and psychologic study; though I hardly feel that the author is temperamentally fitted to do full justice to Beddoes, who was a genuinely great and rare poet. As for my receiving other items from HPL's library, I certainly hope that Mrs. Gamwell will take her time. Though I should be glad to have whatever was left to my choice, there is no urgency whatever. I do little reading—and have less room for storage. My bookshelves are jammed full, with sculptures roosting all over the ledges and on the piled volumes at the top!

The typing of HPL's mss. must certainly keep you busy. I have started to type excerpts from his letters to me for August and Donald, and have found it very slow work. A volume of representative letters certainly should establish him as one of the world's great correspondents. There must be a whole library of material buried in his correspondence. The letters to me in one year (1933) must aggregate forty or fifty thousand words if not more.

As to the Sterling letters, I got them together for safe-keeping rather than anything else. They are now in a strong and supposedly fire-proof iron box. I hadn't thought of printing them, and have no money for such a venture anyway. On the whole, they are more personal than literary, and are in no sense comparable to Lovecraft's letters for general value and interest. One of them contains a far from fortunate criticism of Lovecraft's "Dagon," which I lent to G.S. in manuscript. G.S. thought the tale derivative,* and considered that it lacked sufficient "climax." It was, he complained, "all over in 30 seconds, like a rabbit's amour." He made the melodramatic suggestion that the monolith should fall forward and crush the worshipping monster! When I passed this suggestion on to HPL, the latter protested very gently and justly that it would hardly be in keeping with the atmospheric development he had intended.

What hurts me more than anything else about HPL's death, is the feeling that he might have lived for many more years with proper recognition, financial recompense, and the nourishing food that his condition must have made doubly imperative. Truly, as you suggest, America has killed her finest artists. And when she hasn't killed them, she has driven them into exile, as in the cases of Hearn and Bierce. Personally I am goddamned sick of the killing process (I seem to die hard) and have fully and absolutely made up my mind to quit the hell-bedunged and heaven-bespitted country when my present responsibilities are over. I haven't any definite plans, but will probably gravitate toward the orient. Anyway, I shall remove myself from Auburn, California and the U.S.A, even if I have to stow away on a tramp steamer.

As you surmised, I am not deeply enamored of the Republican system. On the other hand, I have no faith in *any* political or economic isms, schisms, and panaceas. On the other hand, almost any kind of a system might serve well enough, if human beings were not the stupidest and greediest and most cruel of the fauna on this particular planet. No matter what system you have—capitalism, Fascism, Bolshevism—the greed and power-lust of men will produce the same widespread injustice, the same evils and abuses: or, will merely force them to take slightly different forms. The Marxian motto: From each according to his capacity; to each according to his need, is no doubt a beautiful sentiment; but it is about as impractical, and as likely to be practiced, as the Golden Rule of Jesus Christ. From this, you can see that I am not a likely convert to Communism. I doubt if Communism could be established in this country without prolonged internecine warfare that would make the Spanish embroilment look like a Rotarian barbecue in comparison. The immediate result of revolutionary tactics will be to precipitate a dictatorship of the type now prevalent in Germany and Italy. I don't like to think of what will follow. Whatever ensues will hardly be to the advantage of artists and intellectuals: they'll be damned lucky if they even have pulp magazines to write for. In my opinion, the whole fabric of western civilization is nearly due for a grand debacle; and the spreading class-struggle will hasten rather than avert it. After that—well, it is a familiar platitude that the sun rises in the East.

As to conditions in Russia, I'll admit that I know little about them and do not see how it is possible to know much without visiting the country and circulating freely among its people. Writers on the subject, whether for or against, are equally open to a strong suspicion of propagandism. Some of the strongest Communists, like Emma Goldman, seem to have soured on the idea after a sojourn in Russia. Though I have no religious beliefs myself, I must confess to a profound distaste for the anti-religious bigotry that forms an avowed feature of the Soviet program. In the name of Iblis, Satan, Thasaidon and Ialdabaoth, why can't they leave religion alone? In trying to suppress it, I believe they have made a similar error to the one made by the late tsar in suppressing vodka. No wonder the mujiks lent themselves to revolt!

One other observation: communism, as practiced in the insect world, is a poor recommendation for its possible effect on humanity. Nothing sickens me more than to watch the mechanistic activities of ants, who have certainly achieved the ultimate in regimentation and operation. I guess I must be an anarchist myself; and I am sure I would be strictly non-assimilable in any sort of co-operative society, and would speedily end up in a concentration camp.

Don't think, from all this, that I am unsympathetic toward the revolutionary spirit, which is the natural reaction of youth when it awakens to the vision of social injustice. My own nature is that of the rebel: if it weren't, I would hardly write, paint and sculpt in the manners I have chosen. But, in the political sphere, history has convinced me that revolutions are futile: nothing is changed, except the codes and the masters.

Re certain other matters in your letter. Mrs Gamwell sent me *The Californian* with your "Night Ocean," which HPL had put aside in an envelope addressed to me. I liked your story very much, and also enjoyed the one by Edkins.[1]

I look forward to *Leaves,* which has a fine program. Offhand, I can't think of any good literate material to suggest. Weiss might have something. He has written some good tales, such as "The Smell" in *Strange Tales*[2] and "The Dancer in the Crystal" in *W.T.* My stories, "Red World of Polaris" and "Metamorphosis of the World" were passably written, but suffer from triteness of plot: this because I wrote them at a time when I had not read enough science fiction to avoid the more obvious plot-ideas. "Mother of Toads" is a sort of carnal and erotic nightmare and I can't decide on its merits.[3] *Spicy Mystery Stories* rejected it after holding the ms. for nearly two months. I have now shipped it to *Esquire,* which, judging from the two issues I have read, will sometimes print stuff that would hardly make the grade with an honest pulp. Wandrei's tales, and one by Arthur Davison Ficke, are the only good ones that I have found in aforesaid issues.[4] The magazine seems aimed at a rather naive class of readers who like to feel that they are wicked and sophisticated. I believe that a yarn like "Mother of Toads" would arouse considerable Sound and Fury if printed in that quaint periodical (Sound and Fury is the name of the letter department, as you may know. It's [a] good name—one of the best things about *Esquire*—particularly when one recalls the Shakespearian passage from which it is taken. However, I must correct myself here—they no doubt took it from Hemingway.)

I have sold one yarn to *W.T.* recently ("The Death of Ilalotha")[5] and have others under way. "Ilalotha" is quite good, I believe, especially in style and atmosphere. It is unusually poisonous and exotic. Writing is hard for me, since circumstances here are dolorous and terrible. Improvement in my father's condition is more than unlikely, and I am more isolated than ever. Also, I seem to have what psychologists call a "disgust mechanism" to contend with: a disgust at the ineffable stupidity of editors and readers. I think that some of my best recent work is in sculpture: and I find myself confronted with another blank wall of stupidity. Oh well and oh hell: some one will make a "discovery" when I am safely dead or incarcerated in the bughouse or living with a yellow gal in Cambodia.

> Yours for the bombing of Philistia and Boetia
> with Chinese stinkpots
> Clark Ashton

P.S. On glancing over this letter, I note a few asperities of tone, and, in places, a lack of Arnoldian "sweetness and light." In extenuation, I must plead that I have been pretty much at the boiling point lately.

I believe the late R.E. Howard and I would have had a grand time together lambasting civilization; that is, if I have not been misinformed as to his views. Barbarism, barbaric art, barbaric peoples, appeal more and more to me. I could never live in any modern city, and am more of an "outsider" than HPL. His "outsideness" was principally in regard to time-period; mine is one of space, too.

*an exhibition of the common fallacy that *all* weird writing derives from Poe, Bierce, etc. G. wasn't much on *nuances*.

1. E. A. Edkins, "The Affair of the Centaurs" (*Californian*, Winter 1936).

2. Francis Flagg, "The Smell" (*Strange Tales*, January 1932). *Leaves* No. 2 (1938) contains Weiss's poem, "Flower of War."

3. "Mother of Toads" (*WT,* July 1938; *TSS*).

4. DW, "The Painted Mirror" (*Esquire,* May 1937). Arthur Davidson Ficke, "Mrs. Morton Buys a Fish" (*Esquire,* June 1937).

5. "The Death of Ilalotha" (*WT,* September 1937; *OST* and *RA*).

---

[215]   To Donald Wandrei [TLS, MHS]   May 17th, 1937.

Dear Donald:

[. . .] Barlow's delays in turning over mss. must have been provoking. As to HPL's choice of B. for executor, I believe it can very readily be explained. I do not believe it occurred to HPL that there was any prospect of his work being brought out by a professional publishing firm; and from this angle he would have felt that he was imposing a thankless and futile task on Belknap, Loveman, or any of the older friends. On the other hand, he would have felt that Barlow, with ambitions toward the establishment of a fine private press, might some day be in a position to print his work. This sounds logical to me. Certainly the choice shouldn't be taken as a slight to Belknap or others: HPL could only have thought that he was sparing them an embarrassment. [. . .]

August was apparently rather shocked when I spoke of intending to quit California. No doubt he would have been even more shocked if I had told him my full intention—which is to leave the U.S.A. when my present responsibilities are over. I haven't made any definite plans; but such plans are not important, since, varying the title of Baudelaire's prose poem, I shall take as my motto "Anywhere out of America." There are many reasons—too many to list here. One is that I don't wish to be killed by the country that killed Poe, Lovecraft and A. P. Ryder. I'd rather perish at the hands of cannibals, or the fangs of cobras or wild dogs, than be done to death over a course of years by the Boeotians of this republic. I believe that my life-expectation (normally a long one, if heredity means anything) has already been shortened many years by hardship and neglect. The last two years have been terrible ones; and it would seem that the worst is still to come. But I hope to live through it and escape.

The best of fortune with your plays or with anything else you choose to write. I am getting back to my own work after a hiatus due to the brush-burning, etc. I am submitting a recent short to *Esquire,* and intend to keep after them till I land something. Your tale in the last issue was excellent, and it is plain that the magazine is open to well-written fantasy.

I enclose a recent poem that Wright accepted; also, a new Baudelaire version. The Baudelaire is a nice depiction of what the artist or poet often receives at the hands of an idealized female.
Yours ever, Clark.

———————————•———————————

[216]   To Virgil Finlay   June 13th, 1937

My Dear Virgil:

Your letter of last month was extremely welcome and interesting, and I appreciated seeing the enclosures. I should have answered far more promptly, but seem afflicted with a sort of nerve-fatigue or exhaustion which makes me defer even the pleasantest tasks. In fact, this condition has become such a problem that I am being forced to take such therapeutic measures as are practicable under the circumstances.

I anticipate seeing your designs for "Psychopompos" and "The Death of Ilalotha," and feel sure that you will do ample justice to both the poem and the story. It is too bad—too damned bad—that at least a few of your illustrations can't be used in the Lovecraft memorial volumes.[1] However, since Derleth may have to bear a considerable portion of the expense of publication, I suppose we'll have to forgive him for not wanting to increase the cost. It would seem that illustrations are seldom used in first editions of fiction anyway. Personally, I think that this is regrettable. When one considers the high prices at which novels and books of short stories are sold, there seems to be no good reason why a few pictures shouldn't be added to enhance and illuminate the text . . . As to my stuff being put out in book form—well, the chances seem more than meager at present. There is a bare possibility that a selection of my poems (carefully chosen so as to omit stuff that might shock the well-known Mrs. Grundy) may find placement with some British firm: at least, an attempt will be made before long. But if anything of the sort materialized, I fear it will come out minus illustrations. However, if I can place work with some of the smooth paper magazines (I am trying hard for *Esquire*) there might well be an opening for your drawings. I'll blow your horn good and hard when I get the chance!

I am returning your photos and prints herewith. These came out with surprising clarity under a good glass. The still-life "Africa" seems very beautiful in design; and the landscapes are eloquent of sylvan loveliness. The colour prints fascinated me especially. It seems to me that such work should command a ready sale if there are any art-lovers and collectors in your locality. (However, perhaps your Art Lovers and Collectors are like the ones here in California, who, as a San Francisco art-dealer once said, are interested mainly "in buying Big Names at bargain-counter prices.") The two sculptures are interesting too, the half-figure "Aspiration" being especially pleasing.

I have seen quite a number of A. Beardsley's drawings at one time or other. A good selection from his different periods (small-size reproductions, of course) is available in the Modern Library volume, *The Art of Aubrey Beardsley,* with preface and essay by Arthur Symons.[2] I'll be glad to loan you my copy. Beardsley was a great illustrator and original decorative artist—easily the greatest ever born in England. Much of the modern decorative black-and-white is more or less derived from, or influenced by him. Harry Clarke, for the most part, seems to pattern after his most ornate and detailed style of workmanship. Clarke is sometimes very fine—at others, as you justly say, ridiculous. I have recently been studying his designs for Poe (*Tales of Mystery and Imagination*) and note, together with many excellent illustrations, others that are marred with meaningless and inappropriate detail or repetitions of decorative motifs used in his designs for Anderson. In short, there is too much Harry Clarke and too little Poe in the pictures. One of the worst is the design for the "Red Death," where the cerements of the Death, disappearing into the tall clock, recall irresistibly the unwinding of ticker-tape! The second design for "The Pit and the Pendulum" is extremely bad, too, since the bonds of the prisoner suggest velvet bands, and the terrific possibilities of the scene are reduced to trivial patterns.

Jean de Bosschere is one black-and-white artist who seems, as far as I can tell, unaffected by Beardsley. I rather like some of his pictures for *The Golden Ass of Apuleius:* they certainly convey something of the atmosphere of Hellenistic decadence.[3] In a more realistic vein, Norman Lindsay is admirably spirited and effective.[4] But I confess that I have really seen no great amount of illustrative or other pictorial art. Felicien Rops, the Belgian, and the French symbolist painter, Odilon Redon, are among a few to whom I feel instinctively drawn without ever having seen more than two or three specimens of their work. My own paintings and drawings have been compared to those of Redon; though I cannot judge the aptness or justice of the comparison.

I am sorry to learn of your father's death. Truly, the circumstances under which you labour are not of the most encouraging kind; but I hope that you will "stay with it." Talent so remarkable as yours will surely find some sort of recognition. I think it is a good idea to keep on submitting your work to publishers and editors: perseverance may "ring the bell" and secure a good opening somewhere. Incidentally, have you exhibited any of your oil paintings? One can always get something shown at the Independent blow-out in N.Y.; though I am not altogether sure as to the worthwhileness of the Independent shows . . . As to isolation— I guess that is more or less inevitable for anyone whose tastes and ideas run counter to the conventional grooves. No doubt I shouldn't complain of mine; but, on the other hand, should congratulate myself on keeping out of the hoosegow! I'm sure that I wouldn't last long in Germany or Russia: someone would be sure to get the idea that I was against the *status quo!*

I was greatly interested to learn that you have made models in plasticine (a material with which I am not familiar) for the figures in some of your pictures. When you get to doing outré and bizarre sculptures, you will probably put mine in the shade! Glad you found the photos of "Dagon" and "St. Anthony" impressive. My carvings are mostly very small, and the tallest one to date (a 12-inch figurine of Lovecraftian grotesquery entitled "Cthulhu's Child") dwarfs most of the others. "St. Anthony" is barely 2 inches in height, and no doubt should be done on a larger scale for exhibition purposes. As to art-training or other education, I have had none at all—unless a somewhat broken and irregular attendance at grammar-school can be accounted as such.

Like Lovecraft, I began to write at an early age. In my middle twenties, during a period of unusually poor health, I began to dabble with drawing and painting and have kept it up at intervals ever since. Not, however, till April, 1935, did it ever even occur to me that I might experiment with three-dimensional art. The inception of my sculptures really seems to have been an accident: I had brought home, from a mine belonging to my uncle, some specimens of a soft talcose mineral, and found that the stuff was easy and pleasant to cut with a knife. Hence, almost without premeditation, I carved my first grotesque, a head half-reptile and half-animal, which still remains far from being the worst that I have made. These carvings exhibit, I think, considerable variety and range from pieces of rough primordial type to others which, though still non-realistic, are not wholly lacking in refinement of technique. I have even done a few feminine heads to vary the array of monsters and demons and primal gods. Out of the 130 or more carvings that I have done, there are few that suggest the medieval horror spirit of the Notre Dame gargoyles; and though people have found resemblances to Mayan, East Indian and even African art, I believe that such resemblances are more a matter of coincidence than influence. No doubt the two or three drawings that I sent you may have suggested the gargoyles; but the creatures of my pictorial art as well as sculpture are more often unearthly—or, at least, too elaborately synthetic to bear much resemblance to anything else.

As to mechanics, most of this work is done with a knife and then finished with sandpaper. I have, however, sometimes used chisels (or, better still, a strong sharp blade driven chiselwise with a hammer) for blocking out some of the larger pieces. The minerals used vary in hardness; and one which I have discovered—a fibrous species of soapstone—can be burnt almost to the hardness of jade after carving. After being kept at a red heat for a long time (eight or ten hours, not necessarily continuous) the stuff loses its soapy character and has more the look of agate or petrified wood.

Your sonnet-sequence, if appropriately illustrated, might prove eligible for the pages of *Esquire!* "Sonnets of Seduction" is a catchy title, and I confess to being curious anent the outcome of the cycle.

As to books, I've been too poor recently to buy any and can't advise you on anything really new in the way of weird or grotesque literature. There is an abundance of old stuff, however. Have you read the early books of Lafcadio Hearn, the horror tales of Ambrose Bierce, the ghost stories of M. R. James and Algernon Blackwood? These should be part of the nucleus of any weird collection. There are some good anthologies, particularly Everett Harré's *Beware After Dark*. Aside from fiction, I recommend the books of Montague Summers, such as *The Geography of Witchcraft, The History of Demonology and Witchcraft,*[5] etc. Grillot de Givry's *Witchcraft, Magic and Alchemy* would interest you greatly, since it contains more than 350 illustrations, many of which are taken from rare prints and cuts; but the book is rather expensive, costing at least 5 or 6 dollars.

The pictures of yourself suggest a Goya-like robustness. This is all to the good—an artist certainly needs a strong physique.

    Yrs,

      Klarkash-Ton

1. Finlay ultimately did the cover for *The Outsider and Others.*

2. Aubrey Beardsley (1872–1898), *The Art of Aubrey Beardsley* (1918; New York: Modern Library, 1925).

3. Jean de Bosschère (1878–1953), Belgian illustrator, painter, novelist, and poet.

4. Norman Lindsay (1879–1969), Australian painter and illustrator.

5. Montague Summers, *The History of Demonology and Witchcraft* (New York: Knopf, 1926).

[217]   To R. H. Barlow [TLS, JHL]   July 12th, 1937.

Dear Bob:

I was on the point of writing when your last letter came. Glad to hear that the booklet impressed you so favourably. (Mr.) Claire P. Beck, aged nineteen, is the printer; address, Box 27, Lakeport, Cal.[1] It was his own idea to reprint a selection from *The Star-Treader*. I, however, made the selection of titles and revised several of the poems, particularly "Song of a Comet," which now contains some brand-new lines and passages. Beck is one of the higher-grade science fiction enthusiasts, and prints a magazine, *Science Fiction Critic*, which "pans" the popular magazine junk with proper severity. He is very partial to pure fantasy—and, incidentally, has been an enthusiastic customer for several of my carvings. So far, I don't believe he has used any illustrations; but you might get in touch with him. He is desirous of bringing out a book of R. E. Howard's stories, and also a selection of mine. Later on, a reprint of "The Hashish Eater"[2] might be a good idea, especially since I have made a number of alterations in the poem, designed, for the most part, to vary the cadence of the verse.

This brings me to the bound mss. of "The H.E.," which came some time ago with your painting and copies of my grotesques. The viper-skin makes a beautiful back-strip; but you should really have a few contrasting reptile-skins (Gila monster preferably!) to cover the rest of the binding. If you don't mind my keeping the ms. till fall, I may be able to return it with one or two pictorial embellishments. Incidentally, I can add some more viper.

Thanks for the painting, which seems very expressive. The photos and copies of my grotesques were certainly a surprise—I had totally forgotten several of them! You seem to have done a very good job—at first glance I took some of the pictures for the originals!

I look forward to *Leaves,* and hope that the sale will at least partially reimburse you for the outlay. I'll try to write something of a purely artistic type for No. 2, but can't positively promise that anything of magnitude will materialize. "Shapes of Adamant,"[3] which still sticks at about 1000 words, might fill the gap if I can complete it. There is small chance that any professional magazine would care for an opus of such mystical and fantastic nature, involving four avatars in a future continent. . . . "The Letter from Mohaun Los," concerning which you inquire, was published in *Wonder Stories* several years ago under the title "Flight into Super-Time"[4]—a title for which Gernsback was no doubt to blame.

Regarding *Incantations:* there are a couple of changes that you might make in the ms. Please change the title of "Alienation" to "The Outer Land." The first title seems rather inadequate and inexpressive. Also, in "A Fable," the two lines next to the last should read: "And raise from realm-deep ice the boreal cities pale / With towers that man has neither built nor overthrown." As to the placement of new poems: I can't at the moment find my list of titles, but think that "Farewell to Eros" might come at the very end of the verse-items. "Song of the Necromancer" wouldn't be bad as an opening, to set the tone of the whole collection. The poem to HPL should be placed toward the last—perhaps after "Revenant." Did I send you a new Baudelaire—"La Beatrice"? I can't quite remember. This would do well for the parting squirt of Baude-lairian vitriol in *Incantations*. I enclose a sonnet, "Outlanders," which you can place after "The Envoys." This, I think, is the last item I'll try to add to the volume; it should be quite enough for you to wrestle with now. By the way, speaking of lithographs, I wonder if you could make anything out of my pencil drawing for "In Slumber"? I always thought this drawing one of my best.

Not much news at this end either. My writing goes on like the progress of a broken-backed snail. "The Garden of Adompha,"[5] in which some unusual grafting occurs, is partly written. I make an occasional sculpture, and am inclined to think that my growing collection of such opuses is one reason for the falling-off in visitors. "Hideosities" . . . "chamber of horrors." . . . "nightmares" . . . . such are the key-notes of local art-criticism. Evidently the stuff has a kick. If I were in Paris, I might give the surrealists some competition . . . To date I have made about $40.00 from the sale of carvings.

I hadn't thought of sending any copies of *Nero* to reviewers, but may gamble one on the *N.Y. Times*. Thanks for the suggestion. Derleth is giving the booklet some reviews (one in *Voices*) and probably Stanton Coblentz will mention it in *Wings,*[6] since a copy was sent to him by a mutual friend. I have mailed one to Alexander Woollcott,[7] at the instigation of a girl-friend. Beck, in his last letter, said that he had already sold about 50 copies, which is certainly a good beginning. At that rate, he won't lose anything on the venture. He has an ad. in *W. T.*

Your arguments for bolshevism are about the best that can be put up, I imagine; and I must admit that you put them well. Perhaps communism will eventually become universal—perhaps not: I don't feel able to predict. I could never embrace it, since, as far as humanity is concerned, I see little good in anything but development of the exceptional individual, and am unable to think in terms of mass-values and numbers. My feeling is, that communism could not really favour the genius, the "sport," the exception: it would stamp him out as a traitor to the party, since he would inevitably react against it. The present system is bad and cruel enough, but at least one has a fighting-chance, with liberty in speech and press. Such liberty is plainly non-existent under any form of dictatorship, proletariat or otherwise. Any system of government that can't stand honest criticism and opposition is strictly n.g. in my opinion. To hell with it. You may argue that censorship and the other rigors are only temporary, and necessary for the establishment of the new regime; but I'm damned if I can subscribe to any regime that would find them necessary. Russia has been trying it out for nearly a generation, and from the recent wholesale murder of generals and other officials, it doesn't seem that there can really be much "belt-loosening." Russia might well blow up, if she becomes internally divided, and is assailed by Japan on one hand and Germany on the other.

On the other hand, as I admitted before, Communism *may* be the future of the race. The effect on human development will remain to be seen; but my own feeling is, that it will favour the mediocre, the uniform, the materialistic, at the expense of anything rare and exceptional and spiritual. If this is true, it might be better if civilization collapsed in a general Armageddon, leaving the remnants of the race to start again from scratch in complete barbarism. This, from present indications, becomes more and more the most probable of all the possible eventuations. Maugre what I have said above, I confess that I am almost disinterested in regard to the whole business; and, being a sort of spectator from Mars or Yuggoth, I really have little desire to convert you to monarchism. What is to be will be; and no man, unless he were Attila, will weigh much in the sweep of cosmic forces and temporal tides.

Yrs for the epiphany of Satan,
Clark Ashton.

P.S. I enclose a little squib on Communism by Ben De C. Of course, it would surprise the "worker" to find themselves labelled "parasites"; nevertheless, Ben covers the biological aspects with his usual neatness.

1. *Nero and Other Poems* (Lakeport, CA: The Futile Press, May 1937). See letter 220.

2. None of these three projects was ever realized.

3. Nothing by CAS appears in *Leaves* No. 2. "Shapes of Adamant" does not appear to have been completed (see *SS* 131–32).

4. "The Letter from Mohaun Los" (*Wonder Stories*, August 1932, as "Flight into Super-Time"; rpt. as "Flight Through Time," *Tales of Wonder*, Spring 1942; *LW*).

5. "The Garden of Adompha" (*WT*, April 1938; *GL* and *RA*).

6. AWD, "The Poets Sing Frontiers," *Voices* No. 91 (Autumn 1937): 44–46; [Stanton Coblentz], [review of *Nero*], *Wings* 3, No. 6 (Summer 1938): 27–28.

7. Alexander Woollcott (1887–1943), acerbic theater critic for the *New York Times* best remembered as a member of the Algonquin Round Table.

---

[218]   To R. H. Barlow [TLS, JHL]   Sept. 9th, 1937.

Dear Bob:

I was glad to get your letter, enclosing Mrs. Barbauld's fragment (which I had never seen before); also, the much appreciated copies of *Leaves*. I'd have written sooner; but August was a particularly crowded month, since, in addition to homework and writing, I took on the care of the Sullys' extensive flower-garden while they were away. I did the watering mostly at night, and acquired the general habits of a hoot-owl; incidentally avoiding much of the deadly ultra-violet radiation.

That suggestion about The Last Sabbat is a good one, and I may attempt the subject some time. HPL, however, should have written the story himself. I can't hope to compete with him when it comes to New England setting and atmosphere; though perhaps the actual orgies of the Sabbat would be a little more in my line. As to "Sir Bertrand," I must admit that there would be some possibilities in an amplification of the fragment, whose present banal ending seems no more than the deceptive curtain of horrors to come. If you don't mind a delay (possibly of months) I will undertake to extend the piece. The opening is the best piece of Gothic writing that I have seen, and is worthy of the praise given it in the monograph on Supernatural Horror.[1]

Leaves certainly contains a distinguished line-up, and I was especially glad to see the opus on Cats and Dogs and the reprint of Merritt's best story, "The People of the Pit." HPL's article is delighting the Sullys who, like myself, are fervent ailurophiles. "Dead Houses" forms a good foil for the fantastics. If it should get the magazine barred from the mails, *Leaves* will become a precious collectors' item overnight. However, barred or unbarred, it is going to be valuable. . . . . Regarding E. A. Edkins' comments on weird fiction: it seems to me that he doesn't quite get the point in the use of fantastic names; such nomenclature being necessary (if one is to use names at all) when introducing unknown gods and places and people outside of terrene geography or historic time.[2] However, I will readily grant that the nomenclature should be subtilized, with an eye (or ear) to find onomatopoetic values and phonetic or verbal associations. But to cavil at said nomenclature in itself is too much like denying the runner his starting-place. Too many people approach the weird and fantastic—if they approach it at all—with a grudging attitude. However, what can one expect? The modern mind takes the local illusions of Maya with such deadly seriousness; and the writer or artist who prefers to invent his own illusions is, I suspect, regarded as being slightly immoral or, at least, reprehensible.

"The Garden of Adompha," a tale which I am inclined to like, was finished and promptly sold to *W.T.* Wright spoke of a possible cover-design by Finlay to go with the story. He also took "Mother of Toads," from which I had excised the more overt erotic details as being unsuitable for the chaste perusal of the PTA.[3] The tale remains a passable weird, with a sufficiently horrific ending, in which the hero is smothered to death by an army of diabolic toads after he had refused the second dose of aphrodisiac offered him by the witch, La Mère des Crapauds. Wright has also taken a slightly abridged and pruned version of "The Maze of the Enchanter" which I had previously submitted to *Esquire* under the restored original title, "The Maze of Maal Dweb" (I think it should be admitted that some of my nomenclature achieves certain nuances or suggestive and atmospheric associative value.) The *Esquire* editor thought it "reminiscent of both Burroughs and Cabell"; a criticism that amazed and disgusted me. I was not aware that Burroughs had any copyright on jungle hunters, or that Cabell had acquired a monopoly of irony. *******!!******** I fear that Mr. Gingrich is a better judge of garbage than of literature.[4]***********!!

The H.E. ms. will go back to you before long with some additions, including the fragment of *The Fugitives:* a play which I am never likely to continue, having long forfeited the romanticism that is prerequisite for such work.

I am enclosing a copy of "La Béatrice," which can go anywhere among the Baudelaires in *Incantations.* Re edition of this book: I'd suggest a small one, as originally planned. Claire P. Beck (from whom you should have heard ere this) had sold only 75 of *Nero* at last report. *Sandalwood,* of which I printed 250, was the only volume of mine that completely sold out in any reasonable or semireasonable length of time; and I doubt if *Incantations* (though probably a better book) will rival its popularity. The fewer you print, the more the collectors of 1987 will pay for a copy of the volume . . . . and the fewer you'll have to store in the attic or basement. I still have about 600 of *The Double Shadow* parked under my bed with the empty wine-jugs.

The sonnets you quote in your letter seem slightly prosy and didactic; not enough poetic yeast in them. Otherwise, I find it hard to lay my finger on any specific fault. Technically, some of the lines seem too slow in their movement; a phrase such as *"by ceaseless feet worn deep"* being an example. The two spondees and the three long ees make it a bit heavy. However, this wouldn't matter greatly by itself. If I were you, I'd try other forms than the sonnet, and would proceed from the basis that imagery is more valuable than philosophic ideas. As Ambrose Bierce once said, the thought in any poem never really amounts to much.[5] The fallacy that it does amount to something seems to be widespread at the present time: "life," "reality," "psychology" and such like fetiches having taken the place of the moral didacticism of earlier days in America.

I'll look through the Sterling letters some day and see if there is anything suitable for your use.[6] The iron box containing them is at present buried under magazines and old mss.

I wrote three poems in August (counting a burlesque item in vers libre) and will send copies presently. One of them, "The Prophet Speaks," was accepted by Wright. It described the doom and destruction of an unnamed seaport city. The best one, "Desert Dweller," I am submitting to the "quality" magazines, beginning with *Yale Review,* which took one of my poems in the rather remote past.[7]

Glad you liked "Ilalotha," a story in which I seem to have slipped something over on the PTA. The issue containing it, I hear, was removed from the stands in Philadelphia because of the Brundage cover.[8] Query: why does Brundage try to make all her women look like wet-nurses? It's a funny, not to say tiresome, complex.

I was amused by your account of the nudist camp. If I were you, I'd do most of my nuding at night or in shady places: ultra-violet is no good for a white man. I believe that I am finishing the summer in far better shape than usual because of my avoidance of U.V.

Too bad about Robert S. Carr.[9] At present indications, it seems not impossible that we'll all have to take our turn at dodging Fascistic bombs and bullets: that is to say, if Japan and her European allies start a world-war. It will be hard for the U.S. to keep clear. . . . Incidentally, the word "civilization" would make a jackal vomit in view of the general situation.

Since it is now time for the evening chores, I shall bring this rather lengthy screed to a conclusion.

Yrs, in the name of AntiChrist and under the
sign of the Beast 666,
Clark Ashton

P.S. I hope you got the Whitehead mss. and will use them in *Leaves*.[10]

I hope the suggestion for an illustrated edition of the H.E. will materialize. Beck seemed favorably disposed toward it.

1. See HPL, *Supernatural Horror in Literature* (in *Dagon and Other Macabre Tales* [Sauk City, WI: Arkham House, 1986], pp. 375–76), re "Sir Bertrand" by Mrs. Anna Letitia Barbauld (1743–1825), "in which the strings of genuine terror were truly touched with no clumsy hand." "Sir Bertrand" is a section of an essay, "On the Pleasure Derived from Objects of Terror," in *Miscellaneous Pieces in Prose* (London: J. Johnson, 1773) by John and Letitia Aikin (later Mrs. Barbauld).

2. HPL (as "Lewis Theobald, Jun."), "Cats and Dogs"; A. Merritt, "The People of the Pit"; Edith Miniter, "Dead Houses"; E. A. Edkins, quoted in RHB, "Obiter Scriptum; or, Succotash without Seasoning" (*Leaves,* Summer 1937).

3. See *Mother of Toads* (West Warwick, RI: Necronomicon Press, 1987) for the complete text prior to these revisions.

4. Arnold Gingrich (1903–1976), founding editor of *Esquire*.

5. Cf. "Prattle" (*San Francisco Examiner,* 15 December 1895): 6: "It is not often that I get a poem, or, for that matter, see one, of which the excellence is so much in the feeling, so little in the thought."

6. Presumably CAS had sent RHB the typescript of GS's "On Fifth Avenue" (*Munsey's,* February 1915) and the clipping of "The Voice of the Wheat" (*Overland Monthly,* April 1926), which are among the HPL papers at JHL.

7. "The Prophet Speaks" (*WT,* September 1938); "Desert Dweller" (*WT,* July 1943). *Yale Review* (July 1913) had published "The Nereid."

8. Margaret Brundage had done a cover for Seabury Quinn's story, "Satan's Palimpsest" (*WT,* September 1937).

9. Robert S[pencer] Carr, (1909–1994), author of a number of stories for *WT,* went to the Soviet Union in 1932 and was apparently feared dead. In actuality he returned to the U.S. via Finland in late 1937.

10. *Leaves* (Summer 1937) contains only Whitehead's "The Tree-Man" (orig. *WT,* February–March 1930).

---

[219]   To Virgil Finlay   Sept. 27th, 1937.

Dear Virgil:

I'd have written long before this except for an uncommonly strenuous program. During July and August my working day usually extended from 6 in the morning till 10 or later at night; and as a consequence I wrote few letters. Early in the current month I managed to come down with a grippy cold, which still leaves me feeling rather worn out and worthless.

Your drawing for "The Death of Ilalotha" was quite good, I thought, especially in the rendering of the lamia and her monstrous shadow. I liked also the one for "Psychopompos" in the same issue of *W.T.* "The Shunned House" illustration in current *W.T.* is superb.[1] I hope Wright has sent you some more of my stuff to illustrate by this time. During August he accepted two stories, "The Garden of Adompha" and "Mother of Toads"; also, a full page poem, "The Prophet Speaks." More recently he has taken a slightly abridged version of "The Maze of the Enchanter" (which you will have read in my pamphlet, *The Double Shadow*) under the title of "The Maze of Maal Dweb." "Mother of Toads" is probably too short to "rate" an illustration; but the others are of suitable length. I am hoping that the poem will come into your hands for a border design, since Derleth tells me that such designs are to be used again in *W.T.* in connection with full, or nearly full, page verse. Yes, I know that the *W.T.* rates for drawings are low. Wright paid me $7.00 apiece for some that I made in illustration of my own stories several years back.

I am glad that you liked the pamphlet so well. "A Night in Malnéant" is one of my own favorites. For some reason, Wright thought this tale (as well as some of the others in the pamphlet) too plotless and poetic for the general run of *W.T.* readers. Possibly he is correct in this. I doubt if any of my work will ever have a wide public appeal, since the ideation and esthetics of my tales and poems are too remote from the psychology of the average reader. It is reassuring, however, that my work should appeal so strongly to a few.

I was greatly interested in what you said about the attitude and function of the illustrator in dealing with bizarre, exotic and fantastic literature. The points that you make are perfectly clear, and I agree wholeheartedly with them. It seems incontestible that the artist should try to catch and convey the precise atmospheric tone, and should strive for a *realistic* accuracy of setting. Also, you are right in thinking that atmosphere, rather than mere event, is the essence of the weird tale. You lay your finger on the common weakness of magazine fantasies, which fail to convince because of inadequate atmospheric treatment; in other words, there is little or nothing to *prepare* one for the incidents and climax. Such tales must be hard to illustrate, and I do not envy you your task in connection with some of the *W.T.* contributions. I think you define very well the main difference between my tales and those of Lovecraft. HPL, in his most characteristic stories, always built up an elaborate and minutely detailed groundwork of realism, no matter how fantastic the eventual departure. Though I have sometimes written tales with an actual setting, I am more at ease when I can weave the entire web on the loom of fantasy. It is probably idle to speculate as to whether one method is more creative than the other. No doubt my own preference is motivated by a certain amount of distaste for the local and the modern, and a sort of nostalgia for impossible and unattainable dreamlands. Yes, I agree with you that my tales—especially the Zothique stories—would call for an arabesque type of illustration, with much ornamental detail; while drawings for HPL's work should be more austere and bleak. Different types, page sizes, bindings, etc., could be utilized appropriately in publishing books by HPL and myself.

So far, I've had no luck in "hitting the slicks." But I intend to keep on trying. No word yet from the selection of poems that was to be submitted in Britain. I'm hoping, of course; but past experience has inured me to disappointment. Luckily, as I grow older, I seem to care less and less about "fame," "recognition," etc. Under present-day conditions of transit and communication, widespread fame would probably prove a godawful nuisance anyway. Sour grapes? Well, I am not conscious of feeling sour about it.

The isolation that I spoke of is perhaps more physical than spiritual. I live two miles from the village of Auburn, on a rather arid volcanic hilltop. The highway, and the nearest neighbors, are a quarter of a mile distant. Oddly enough, there is less *quiet* than one would expect in such a situation; since airplanes pass at all hours, following the line of the nearby American River canyon; and the noise of auto and railroad traffic rises all too distinctly. The best feature is the wide and elevated view; since, on the west, we see a long stretch of the Sacramento Valley and the Coast Range mountains; and on the east the higher foothills topped by more than a hundred miles of snowy Sierran peaks . . . I have a few friends locally, but never seem to mind being alone. I did suffer from a sense of isolation, though, when I was younger, and am inclined to think that solitude is often harder to bear in youth.

Your admiration for the Preraphaelites is certainly a sound one, and your work has an esthetic background and a fineness of technique not dissimilar to theirs. Truly, there is no sensible reason why art and literature should not be allied, as in the paintings of Rossetti and Burne-Jones. I believe the modern prejudice against literary ideas in art springs from the fact that many modern artists are incapable of ideas of any kind. Incidentally, I think that the work of Gustave Moreau[2] (mentioned by J. K. Huysmans in *Against the Grain*, together with Odilon Redon and other imaginative artists) would interest you. Moreau is little known, and is usually dismissed and damned as a "poet-painter," but, judging from the two or three black-and-white reproductions I have seen, he did some great things. By the way, if you have not yet procured anything of Beardsley's, don't forget to remind me, and I will gladly forward my little volume of his drawings.

Your athletic record is truly an enviable one! You must have the lifting power of a Turkish porter! I fear that I could never have competed, since my own physique, though wiry, is very slight. I might, at one time, have made a good half or quarter mile runner with practise. My height is five feet eleven, and weight is never more than 140 lbs. I have, however, done a considerable amount of hard physical labor, such as woodcutting and fruit-picking.

Perhaps you are wise to refrain from exhibiting till you feel sure that you have reached your fullest development. Anyway, one must admire the attitude, when so many artists of powers vastly inferior to yours are rushing to show their work. I have an idea that your exhibition, when you hold it, will prove eminently successful.

I hope that Derleth will use your drawings of HPL as a frontispiece to one of the Lovecraft volumes. It is admirable, and I can't imagine anything that would be more representative or better calculated to catch the attention of prospective readers . . . I look forward to your *W.T.* cover, and trust that there will be many others. Brundage is a curio, and I can't help wondering how or whence she derives her weird ideas of anatomy. The *W.T.* public should be disabused of such pictorial misinformation!

I haven't done any more drawings, but have sold several small carvings lately for the net sum of $7.50. The sale of a pseudo-science short to *Thrilling Wonder Stories*[3] at $55.00 brings my September income to $62.50! If such sales continue, I shall become a bloated plutocrat! Anyway, I won't need to dig so often or so deeply in the old boneyard.

I believe that you should congratulate yourself on being, as you say, "out of tune with your generation." Undoubtedly a serious condition of unbalance is prevalent at the present time, as indicated by exclusive or excessive preoccupation with drink, amorous orgies, etc. This seems to be part of the intense materialism, "realism," or whatever you want to call it, of the age. Modern science, philosophy and invention are at least partly responsible. Some day there will be a return toward mysticism, a recovery of spiritual values. The question is, will it come before—or after—Armageddon? I am not making any predictions; but the query is more than pertinent.

More power to your brush and drawing-pen!
With cordial best wishes,
Klarkash-Ton

1. *WT* (October 1937). The illustration also appeared on the dust jacket of *Marginalia*.

2. Dante Gabriel Rossetti (1828–1882) and Edward Coley Burne-Jones (1833–1898), two of the most well-known of the Pre-Raphaelite painters.

3. "The Dark Age" (*Thrilling Wonder Stories*, April 1938; *AY*).

---

[220]   To Claire Beck[1] [TLS, JHL]   May 10th, 1938.

Dear Mr. Beck:

I mailed you the inscribed copy of *Nero* yesterday and received at the same time the ms. of "The Hashish-Eater" and proof-sheets of "Semblance."[2] The type used in "Semblance" is very good, I think; and I am your debtor for these copies.

Since I believe you were unable to procure a copy of *Sandalwood* and have typescripts of only a few of the pieces, I am loaning you my own copy, which goes forward today by insured mail. I have marked (with dashes before and after the titles) 33 of the original poems for reprinting. You will note a few slight changes and corrections pencilled on the margins. If 33 is too many for the volume I will suggest other omissions. Re pictures: I am querying Barlow and will be glad to loan him any that he wishes to work on. Drawings with clear-cut lines and rather simple composition, I imagine, would lend themselves most readily to his purpose.

Thanks for the neatly bound *Nero*. I like this: but wish that *Sandalwood* could be bound in something similar to the original binding. The soft green paper was inexpensive, pleasing, and appropriate.

You will notice that my Baudelaires are badly overscrawled with alterations, some of which are perhaps none too legible. Most of them fail to satisfy me; but some day, I hope to have a few tolerable specimens—enough, at least, for a very small volume.

I am glad that *Nero* has had a tolerable sale. Enclosed, by the way, is a typed copy of a review of *N.* by Stanton Coblentz, which I have been forgetting to send you. Perhaps it is in print by this time. You can return the copy at your leisure.

I shall look forward to your visit here. Too bad that the Lakeport locale is uncongenial; but I doubt if it could be much more so than Auburn. However, with old age and its concomitants, I have ceased to worry about such matters.

My exhibition of carvings at Gumps has resulted, so far, in one sale. Incidentally, I have recently done to order a small bust of Tsathoggua for a weird tale enthusiast in Northern Rhodesia!

Cordially yrs,
Clark Ashton Smith

1. Claire Beck (1919–1999) and his brothers Groo and Clyde were fans and amateur publishers. Their Futile Press published CAS's booklet, *Nero and Other Poems* and HPL's *Commonplace Book*.

2. "Semblance" (*AJ*, 12 April 1923; also 19 April 1923; *S* and *SP*).

---

[221]   To R. H. Barlow [TLS, JHL]   May 10th, 1938.

Dear Bob:

I know I should have written you months and months ago. But the death of my father (Dec. 26th) after a long term of single-handed nursing left me pretty much exhausted; and I have been slow to recuperate. Letters have piled up in the manner of Ossa on Pelion;[1] and I fear that many of them never *will* be answered.

I am sorry that the H.E. volume has temporarily fallen through. Perhaps, with recovered energy, and time, I may eventually be able to make some fresh illustrations for the poem. I did not keep any sketches of those presented to Loveman; and have only the vaguest memory of most of them.

Beck seems eager to go on and print something else in the meanwhile; and I am suggesting a selection from *Sandalwood,* the least circulated of my volumes. Beck's idea (I believe he has written you) is to use reproductions of half a dozen of my paintings or drawings in the volume, irrespective of whether or not they illustrate any of the pieces. I wonder how this appeals to you, and whether you could make lithos from pictures of mine that you have on hand or wish me to loan you others. I don't believe I have ever done any pictures based on the lyrics in this volume, which are largely amatory; so the designs used would probably afford contrast rather than complement. . . . Incidentally, the originals that I sent you with the returned H.E. ms. volume are to be retained. I'd gladly go ahead and do some special illustrations now: but from sad experience I am convinced that my drawings are nothing if not inspirational and I must wait upon the mood, which has not visited me in years. Some of my *W.T.* illustrations were a horrible example of what happens when I try to work in cold blood and without definite impetus.

I hope that your optical trouble has been mitigated. Eyestrain is certainly hell: I suffer from more or less of it, though my sight is fairly good. I hope too that your proposed experiments with the cinema will materialize. "The Outsider" should be tremendous if properly filmed.

Some of my carvings are on exhibition at Gumps, in San Francisco; and one piece, at least, has been sold. But I have done little work of any sort recently. Poverty, and the pressure of debts, are conspiring to drive me into literary hackwork. I have just bought and perused a brand new "science fiction" magazine, *Marvel Science Stories*, which fathoms new depths in the mental muck of Moronia. However, I believe it pays on acceptance. . . . This magazine, by the way, exhibits a covert trend toward "spiciness" in one or two of its yarns; brassières and step-ins (ripped from the heroine by some salacious monster) divide the interest with spaceships and ray-guns. The next thing will be a magazine specializing in futuristic or ultra-planetary eroticism, entitled *Spicy Marvel Stories* or *Snappy Wonder Stories*. We will see such titles as "Rape in Utopia" and "The Whorehouse on the Moon." Henry Kuttner, who wrote an opus called "Hollywood on the Moon,"[2] should oblige with the latter subject!

    Yrs for the Red Apocalypse,
        Clark

1. The Titans piled Mount Pelion on Mount Ossa to ease access to heaven in their war with the gods.
2. Henry Kuttner (1914–1958), "Hollywood on the Moon" (*Thrilling Wonder Stories*, April 1938).

———————————◆———————————

[222]   To R. H. Barlow [TLS, JHL]   July 5th, 1938.

Dear Bob:

Finally, though with some doubt as to their suitability for your purpose, I am mailing you a few of my smaller landscape paintings and drawings. Perhaps you have enough anyway, for the illustrating (or should one say illuminating?) of *Sandalwood*. I should have mailed these weeks ago; but, as usual, have suffered from the infernal dilatoriness consequent on several and sundry kinds of exhaustion. The crayon drawings are the most recent, having been done since I began my sculptures; and I am sending them along because they may interest you rather than with any idea to reproduction. I am also including, in a separate envelope, some of the photographs of aquarelles and drawings by John Allan which he has sent to me in folios of typed verse of his own composition. The verse does not quite show the technical mastery and imaginative genius of the pictures, though it is highly interesting, romantic and with many fine lines and phrases. I believe you will agree with me that the Italian monograph in appreciation of Allan's work (typed translation enclosed with the pictures) is thoroughly deserved and even somewhat moderately phrased.[1] I copy hereunder the sonnet in which Allan describes "L'Évocation de Scorphael," which seems to be his supreme pictorial masterpiece:

> The Spirit's profanation who would know:—
> Behold, eclipsed are heaven's last rays, that light
> Its sculptured fane, and in Cimmerian night
> It shall lie desolate, a Mystery of Woe;
> Archdemons of abandonment shall haunt
> Its holiest shrine; nor death nor dread shall daunt
> Their blood-wrought ritual, evoking so
> A strange creation, shaped in Heaven's despite.
>
> Convened by Death, who knows no exorcism,
> Shall come the adepts of Abaddon and Baal,—
> Ecstaticii whose trance unlocks the Abysm;
> Then pale, resplendent, from the accursed travail,
> Shall crawl Hate's sublime, Hell's fairest microcosm,—
> The Scorpion-seraph, demoness Scorphael!

Allan and his nephew, A. Scott[2] (also an artist) were very appreciative of *Leaves,* and I believe you have heard from J.A. before now. I must remember to pay you for those numbers, and shall put aside for that purpose the next paper dollar that falls within reach of my Satampran digits.

I have recently enjoyed a visit from Claire P. Beck, who stopped here overnight on his way to Reno. His brother, as you doubtless know, will continue the printing press in Lakeport. The copy of HPL's notebook, which reached me the other day, seems a worthy job and rather attractively bound.[3] As to *Sandalwood,* it seems to me that we should by all means retain the original title. Add the poem entitled "Sandalwood,"[4] and the fragment of *The Fugitives* if you like. As to *The Jasmine Girdle,* or other material from *Incantations,* it seems to me that there is no hurry whatever. Perhaps, with indefinite delay, I could do some special illustrations for these later and uncollected poems. Horace (or was it Virgil?) said that poetry should be kept for at least 9 years before publication. Personally, I feel like naming an astronomical figure for the period for which most modern verse should be retained in cold storage.

Thanks for the photo of the beautiful Khmer head. This sort of thing makes most modern Occidental sculpture look like the Indian on a 5¢ piece.

I have done a little work (science fiction) but continue to loaf abominably. Thanks for the suggestion about historical fiction. This might offer possibilities but would require research. Egypt has been overworked; but there seem to be many fields of ancient history and archaeology that have been little touched in fiction.

I am glad your eye-trouble has been somewhat mitigated. John Allan, by the way, seems to have quite ruined his eyes by drawing and painting late at night and tells me he has had to give up art work. This is a tragedy. His best pictures, in my opinion deserve a place beside the highest imaginative art of any land or time. Pictures such as "L'Évocation de Scorphael" and "The Sorceress" seem to render (as the art of no other artist quite does) the very essence of black magic and Satanry.

I am hoping to strengthen my own eyes (the left is the weakest) by persistent exercise and massage of the surrounding muscles; this being part of a general plan of physical improvement. I don't expect to become a Sandow or a John L. Sullivan;[5] but I believe that I can correct a few defects and ward off the encroachments of middle age. I spring from a tough and long-lived stock, and therefore should have some material to work on. My height is close to 5 feet eleven; weight at present somewhere around 140 lbs; chest measurement 37 inches; waist 30. I am neither phtysical[6] nor obese by tendency, but should like to gain about 10 lbs of permanent muscle together with renewed nervous vitality and driving-power. The last five years have been hard on me, both emotionally and physically; and much of the time I have consumed habitually an amount of alcohol (some of it of rather poor quality) which most authorities on the subject would consider dangerous. Recently, for a while, I have abstained entirely; but find now that the continuance of a moderate amount of table wine is desirable.

Charles D. Hornig, of *Fantasy Fan* renown, expects to stop in Auburn this month on his way East from a vacation in Hollywood. I certainly look forward to seeing him. E. H. Price and his mother may run up during the summer, and perhaps bring with them a girl friend of mine whom I have corresponded with regularly, but have not seen, for more than twenty years.[7]

As ever,
Clark

1. John Allan (1875–1958), artist of occult and weird images, was born at Westray in the Orkney Islands, but lived and ran a studio in Hamilton, Ontario. The CAS papers at JHL contain copies of Allan's

illustrations. CAS refers to Vittorio Pica (1866–1930) *Pittore dell'oc-cultismo: John Allan* [*The Works of John Allan: Poems, Paintings and Drawings*] [194-?]. The book includes Allan's translations of poems by Baudelaire and other French poets.

2. Adam Sherriff Scott (1887–1980), Canadian painter of landscapes, portraits, and still life.

3. *The Notes & Commonplace Book Employed by the Late H. P. Lovecraft Including His Suggestions for Story-Writing, Analyses of the Weird Story, and a List of Certain Basic Underlying Horrors, &c., &c., Designed to Stimulate the Imagination.* [ed. RHB.] Lakeport, CA: The Futile Press, 1938, printed by Groo Beck; rpt. West Warwick, RI: Necronomicon Press, 1978.

4. "Sandalwood" (*Leaves,* Summer 1937; *LO*). The poem was originally intended as "Proem" to *S.*

5. Eugene Sandow (1867–1925), British proponent of health and fitness; John L. Sullivan (1858–1918), American boxer.

6. I.e., phthisical, or consumptive.

7. Katherine Turner, a former teacher at Placer Union High School.

[223]   To Donald Wandrei [TLS, MHS]   Sept. 30th, 1938.

Dear Donald:

I received your letter last night, and must reply immediately even though briefly, since the matters of which you write are serious and grave to the last degree.

Knowing you as I have known you all these years, I cannot but believe that you have incontrovertible reasons for what you say. I am, frankly, not unprepared for the revelation of Barlow's rascality. What shocks and astounds me, however, is the thought that Beck, who, from what I have seen of him, struck me as being an honest, somewhat naive and dreamy youth, should be implicated in such scullduggery. Isn't there a chance that he has been used as a sort of cat'spaw by Barlow, and does not realize the moral obliquity involved in taking from Mrs. Gamwell the books, magazines and other matter that would be of such value to her in her present need?

The whole business finds me in a very awkward situation, since I had consented to the issuing of a small edition of my unpublished verse volume, *Incantations,* by the Beck brothers. It is, in fact, possible that work has already been begun on this project by Groo Beck. Even though I believe most publishers, even some of the major ones, to be more or less crooked, I do not relish the idea of having the book brought out by people who could, knowingly, be guilty of such turpitude as you have indicated. Have you any suggestions as to what could be done? Since Groo Beck has my consent to the publication of *Incantations* in a letter, I fear that I could do nothing legally if the Becks wanted to be ugly and hold me to my promise. I believe that I shall try to get the ms. back on the plea of checking it over and making alterations and changes; but they, or Barlow, may possess transcripts.

As to the looting of my own collection, in the case of my sudden and early demise (which seems damned unlikely for such a tough bird as I have grown to be) you can, I think, set your mind at rest. Not long after my father's death, I wrote out a holographic will bequeathing all books, mss., pictures and other art objects to my long-beloved friend, Mrs. Sully. She would take immediate charge in case anything happened to me. (She has, by the way, expressed repeatedly her suspicions of Barlow, and an antipathy toward him, and was in no way surprised when I read your letter to her last night.)[1]

I should write more at length, but have little time, since I am preparing for a week-end in the Sierras with the Sullys. I shall, by the way, take the precaution of placing my holograph *immediately* in G.S.'s hands. It will be safer with her than here in the cabin.

I hope fervently that Scribner's will bring out H. P.'s book.

Please write as quickly as possible, if you can suggest anything anent the Beck proposition.

As ever,
Clark

P.S. A group of my carvings is on permanent display at Gumps in S.F. Five pieces have already been sold, and much interest and admiration around [*sic*].

---

1. HPL had named RHB his literary executor. Upon HPL's death, RHB had gone to Providence to secure HPL's papers and to act on some of the stipulations in HPL's "Instructions in Case of Decease," one of which allowed RHB first choice of certain of HPL's books. DAW, and to some degree AWD, found RHB to be somewhat uncooperative in helping them with the HPL omnibus they were preparing, though that was not entirely the case. Also, because RHB, as a collector, had for the past several years pestered various authors for their manuscripts, he was perceived by those who did not know him well as an opportunist. Many felt he should not have taken the books from HPL's library, but instead have let them be so that HPL's aunt might benefit financially from their sale. DAW had briefly met RHB previously and developed a strong dislike for him, which DAW made evident in his correspondence with CAS, warning CAS against future dealings with RHB.

[224]   To Donald Wandrei [TLS, MHS]   Dec. 10th, 1938.

Dear Donald:

I fear that I have become the most remiss and neglectful of correspondents. Here, at long last (I *should* have returned them weeks—or is it months?—ago) are the various documents relating to the Barlow affair that were marked for return to you. Of late, I have been sojourning so much in the realms of myth, fable, or fantasy, and have had so much of my wildest and most exotic poetry coming to life before me, that I lose all track of terrestrial time. A recent poem, "Wizard's Love,"[1] which I enclose, may suggest a little of what I cannot write, or even tell verbally, in prose.

As to l'affaire Barlow: the ms. of *Incantations* was duly returned to me on my demand, and I am of course holding it permanently. I have not written to the Beck-Barlow outfit, and have no intention of communicating with them, or replying to any possible communications of theirs. Barlow wrote me a card some days ago, saying that they were now ready to begin work on the book. This card I consigned to the stove. I hope sincerely that neither Barlow nor Beck will try to see me in person. If they do, it is probable that I shall run them off the ranch with an old fencing-rapier (a quite formidable-looking object) that was presented to me by the girl for whom I wrote "Wizard's Love."[1] During the recent quail-hunting season, I went around the place with the rapier stuck in my belt, singing bawdy songs or chanting the Dies Irae; and quail-hunters soon began to give it a wide berth!

I hope things are well with you, and that all your literary projects are coming on as per program. As for mine, I think there will soon be more to tell than in years past. At present, I am compelling Wright to buy some of the stories that he has previously refused; these with very minor revisions or excisions. "The Double Shadow" will appear in the next issue of *W. T.*

A number of carvings have been added to my display at Gumps; and a few of my paintings and drawings are now being shown there. It is amusing to recall that I visited G.'s in 1927 with some of these same paintings and tried vainly to interest the art-director in them. The same director received me with deference when I walked into the store during a recent visit in the Bay region. I am sure that he had no recollection of my former visit, or of having seen the pictures before. Life is full of such drolleries; and they seem to multiply as one gets older.

Apart from that, life has become much pleasanter for me than of yore: one reason being a tremendous improvement in my health. I now look ten or fifteen years younger than I did during your visit here in 1934, and have developed the figure of a Greek athlete— 152 pounds of iron muscle. And my 46th birthday is imminent next month!

My best wishes to you, and to all the N.Y. gang, for a happy holiday season. Mine, I hope, will be spent in the demesne of paganry, with fauns and Bacchantes for co-celebrants!

Yours affectionately,
Clark

1. "Wizard's Love" (*The Alchemist*, 1941; *SP*).

---

[225]   To Albert M. Bender [TLS, MCL]   April 29th, 1939.

Dear Albert:

Remembering a request that you made some time ago, I am sending you a few of George's letters for your Mills College collection. Also, a poem of his, "Seismos," which I do not remember to have seen except in manuscript.

You may also like to have these recent verses of my own: "Bacchante," "Resurrection," and "Witch-Dance."[1]

Is there any chance, I wonder, that The California Book Club could bring out another volume for me some time? This could consist entirely of new and uncollected poems. A collection was to have been published for me, without expense to myself, by certain local (I don't mean Auburn) printers; but I have withdrawn the ms. on account of some peculiarly disgusting rascality in which one of the printers got himself involved.

Most reluctantly (since I know the myriad claims that are made upon me) I must ask if you know any admirers of mine who could give me a little financial aid. I should not ask unless the need were urgent. Between the threatened failure of my best magazine market, and the pressure of certain local debts I am, so to speak, "on the spot." If you yourself feel able to loan me some money (I should like a hundred dollars if possible) I can, if you wish, turn over to you some of my rare autographed books and 1st editions as a sort of security. These include Nora May French's *Poems* and George's *Lilith, Rosamund, 35 Sonnets*, etc. I am extremely loath to part with such items to booksellers and should try to redeem them as soon as possible. In case I could not redeem them, they should form a valuable addition to your Mills College collection.

I can give you a few more of George's letters, if you wish. I must have somewhere between 150 and 200 of them, covering 16 years (1911 to 1926)

  With all best wishes and affectionate regards, As always,
   Clark Ashton Smith

 1. "Bacchante"(*WT*, December 1939; *SP* and *HD*); "Resurrection" (*WT*, July 1947; *SP* and *HD*); "Witch-Dance" (*WT*, September 1941; *SP, HD,* and *LO*).

---

[226] To Albert M. Bender [TLS, MCL] Nov. 4th, 1939.

Dear Albert:

 I enclose the dance-program of a young friend of mine who is greatly talented and deserves a world of encouragement and success. You will, I think, remember meeting Madelynne, since she and her husband Eric Barker were with me when I visited your office last fall.[1]

 Madelynne's dancing is of an imaginative interpretative type which should appeal especially to lovers of poetry. She uses facial expression as well as interpretational movement, and has much histrionic ability. Her dance for my "Phoenix" poem is a gorgeous thing, and the one for her husband's poem equally beautiful though of course affording a complete contrast. She *feels* the spirit of poetry and turns it into miraculously appropriate movement. A comic interlude in her program is afforded by *Jimmy Goes to the Dentist*, which depicts with uproarious pantomime the various sensations of a dentist's victim. *Witches' Sabbath* is an eerie and sorcerous thing, and I cannot imagine a better interpretation of the spirit of the old witch-cult. I should know, being something of a wizard myself! It suggested the poem "Witch-Dance," which you fill find among my enclosures.

 I think it would mean much to Madelynne if you could possibly attend her concert. If you cannot, perhaps you know some friend who would be interested. I shall attend myself, if it takes my last dollar—as it probably will!

 All best and kindest regards to you, dear Albert. My gratitude for all past favours as well as for any that you can give in this instance.

  Yours,
   Clark Ashton Smith

 1. CAS refers to the interpretive dancer Madelynne Greene, wife of the poet Eric Barker (1905–1973). His friendship with the Barkers inspired many of the poems in the poetry cycle, *The Hill of Dionysus*.

[227]   To Margaret St. Clair [ALS, private collection]
Feb. 22nd, 1940

Dear Margaret:

I wonder if I can be forgiven the long interim—at least I *fear* that it is long according to temporal notation—since I last wrote you? But I believe you would forgive if you could know all the circumstances. First, there was my father's death (I am quite alone now), and since that, a strange and fantastic history of happenings, some of which, I am convinced, have taken place in the realms of fable and sorcery. So many letters I had meant to write, and should have written, have gone to the bourn of other "good intentions."

I hope all is well with you and Ray, and that the bulb-gardens (of which you wrote and sent me a fascinating catalogue) are flourishing. I can't think of a better avocation or occupation than gardening.

I am explaining to your friend Alberta Dixon the present *Weird Tales* situation. The magazine has two stories and four poems of mine (accepted by Farnsworth Wright) still unpublished, but I think seriously of withdrawing these, even though I need the money like hell and am not likely to find another market for these particular items. Wright was let out by the publishers to cut down expenses, and *W.T.* is now being edited by a woman, who also edits *Strange Stories*.[1] It is to be hoped that Wright will soon secure another editorship, or perhaps even start a rival magazine himself. In the meanwhile, *W. T.*'s best contributors are sticking with him, in the belief that he has had a raw deal.

I enclose a few recent verses.

A huge convent has been built within sight and almost within a stone's throw of my hill-top cabin! It will be occupied soon by fifty nuns and novices. Maybe I'll have to move away—it sounds pretty formidable. Either the atmosphere of holiness will prove too heavy and stifling, or I'll find myself over burdened with complications à la Boccaccio and *Les Contes Drolatiques*. Anyway, I think I'd better stick to young sorceresses, lamiae, vampires, etc. Nuns are an unknown quantity as far as I am concerned.[2]

Perhaps, however, you and Alberta might come up and protect me . . . .

Have I mentioned that some of my carvings are on display at Gumps, in S.F. A few have been sold from time to time.

If you should run over to S.F. some day, why not drop in and see them? Ask for Mr. Dewing (he is an old friend of mine) who will be glad to show you the group.

My best to you and Ray, as always

Clark Ashton

P.S. Can't we start some sort of coven in opposition to that nunnery?

1. WT was sold to William J. Delaney in late 1938. FW remained editor but the magazine was relocated to New York City. Early in 1940 Delaney fired FW and replaced him with *Short Stories* assistant editor Dorothy McIlwraith (1891–1976?) who held the post until the magazine failed in 1954. At the time of FW's dismissal, many WT authors contemplated boycotting the new management in protest.

2. CAS wrote several haiku ("Spring Nunnery," "Nuns Walking in the Orchard," "Impossible Dream") inspired by his new neighbors at the Convent of the Sisters of Mercy (which he called the Nunnery of Averoigne).

---

[228]   To Albert M. Bender [TLS, MCL]   April 4th, 1940

Dear Albert:

Would it be possible for you to help me out again with a small amount of money? I hate to ask, and have put it off in the hope that something would come in, till I am now on the verge of being broke and without necessary food and clothing. Fiction market mix-ups, and the cessation of a small stipend which I have had for many years from Templeton Crocker, have brought about this embarrassment. I am working hard to write stories for new markets, and am finding it necessary to modify my old technique in order to sell them. I believe that I will succeed in this before so very long; but nothing has definitely sold as yet. Twenty or twenty-five dollars, if you can spare it, might tide me over till I receive money due from material reprinted in England.

I am enclosing a few new verses. Also, the open letter to publishers that you suggested my putting in your hands some months ago, together with a good specimen of my published fiction. I am also including a Baudelaire translation, since it occurs to me that one [of] the things I could do would be to make renderings from the French for some book firm interested in translations. I've hesitated to bother you with all this. With any luck, I may be making good money from my magazine stories again in a few months.

I hope this finds you reasonably well, Spring is on the way, and should ameliorate all our troubles.

    Faithfully,
      Clark Ashton Smith

———— • ————

[229]   To Margaret and Ray St. Clair [TLS, private collection]
                                      April 21st, 1940

Dear Margaret and Ray:

I had meant to write before this but have been dreadfully busy with the attempted perpetration of hackwork fiction. A very small income, which I have had for many years, dried up at the source some months ago, and I am now absolutely dependent on writing if I am to eat, let alone drink. None of the present fantasy markets (*Unknown* is the best, I guess) appeal greatly to me; so I am having to compromise more and more with my own tastes and learn new tricks. My latest yarn is a filthy mixture of sex and pseudo science, aimed at one of the "spicy" markets, which won't appear under my own name but under that of a friend, a very successful pulp-writer, who had more commissions on hand than he could get through with.[1]

It was good to hear from you. I have never forgotten you at any time during my cyclic silence. But, for a long time, I wrote no letters at all, except business ones and billets doux.

Glad you liked the recent poems. I'll try to enclose one or two more. "Bond" is the best, I think.[2] It springs out of personal belief and experience. [. . .]

Thanks for the fascinating bulb catalogue. The *variety* of irises is incredible; and some of them are as fantastic as any orchid. They are one of my favorite flowers.

As to leaving Auburn, I want to very badly indeed but am stuck at present for lack of cash. If I can sell my property here (39 acres) (and still retain the use of the cabin), I intend to do so. I understand that the Catholic Sisters (who won't move in till next fall) might be glad to buy it, but the deal couldn't be swung for another year. There is, however, another and more immediate prospect, which I'm going to investigate.

I may visit the Bay Region for a few days next month (contingent on sales to magazines) and should like to see you and Ray.

Also, I'd like to meet Alberta Dixon, whose drawings reveal a temperament much akin to my own artistic disposition.

Do you want to buy any of my books? I'm starting to lighten my library against the extreme possibility, I might say certainty, of a move sooner or later. I enclose a list of items. Maybe some of these would interest you.

As to those nuns, I guess I really wouldn't need a dachshund to protect me. And I don't know what seducing a nun would be like, never having had any experience. Balzac says, somewhere, something to the effect that the pleasure is never so great as when the soul is believed to be in danger of damnation. I fear that my notions of damnation are hardly the orthodox ones. The pleasure would be one-sided in that regard. However . . . even at that . . . .

Faithfully,
Clark Ashton

1. E. Hoffmann Price, "Dawn of Discord" (*Spicy Mystery Stories*, October 1940); Price, "The House of the Monoceros" (*Spicy Mystery Stories*, February 1941) as "The Old Gods Eat." See Steve Behrends, "The Price-Smith Collaborations," *Crypt of Cthulhu* No. 26 (Hallowmas 1984): 32–34. The original mss have been lost.

2. "Bond" (*SP* and *HD*).

---

[230]   To August Derleth [TLS, SHSW]   July 13th, 1941.

Dear August:

You had been in my thoughts quite frequently of late, and I had made up my mind to overcome the inertia or whatever it is that has made me so remiss and dilatory as a correspondent. Then came your announcement and note, which I was delighted to receive.

I do hope the fantasy fans will respond to your projected volume of shorts as well as to the continuation of the HPL trilogy. Your titles for it sound like an excellent selection. Of course I'll be only too glad to have you bring out a volume of my things if circumstances should permit. I'll start looking over my tales for a tentative choice. Would you want typed copies; or will printed ones (magazine clippings) do?

Certainly Whitehead's best stories ought to be reprinted in book form; and a splendid anthology could be made from the finest yarns that have appeared in *Weird Tales*. I hope all of these projects can materialize sooner or later.

Here are some recent poems of mine that you may like to have. I've been away from Auburn much of the time during the past 2 and 2/3 years, and have done more living than writing. Had got to the point where it was absolutely necessary. Now I'm trying to settle down to literary production again.

I trust this finds you well. I celebrated (?) my 48th birthday last January, but do not feel any older—or as old—as I did at 28. For one thing, my health is far better than it was 20 years ago or 10 years either. And in spite of occasional periods of dulness and monotony, I manage to get a lot more fun out of life than I did when I was younger. Youth is often far from being the golden season that it is cracked up to be.

I'm writing to Donald at his home address in St. Paul. Have been owing him a letter for ages. If he is in New York at present, I want him to meet some young friends of mine who went east recently and are now located in Passaic, N.J. I had hoped to go with them but could not raise enough money. Perhaps I can make it later.

> Best regards to you, as always,
> Clark

---

[231]   To August Derleth [TLS, SHSW]   Sept. 5th, 1941.

Dear August:

Thanks for the inscribed copy of *Someone in the Dark*. I think the format is admirable for use in a series of collections of fantasy; the print is beautifully clear, the paper excellent.

I enjoyed renewing my acquaintance with many old friends in your volume. Utpatel certainly did a fine job in the jacket-design.

I had meant to write you before this but ran short of cash about the 1st of August and had to take a job fruit-picking. This is over now. It certainly gave me a more than glimpse into the seamy side of agricultural life, and I could write a novel à la Steinbeck out [of] the experience if I were so minded.[1]

Here are some recent poems. "Swine and Azaleas"[2] was written from a description given me by a friend who, on a trip into the Sierras, came upon the strange scene I have tried to depict.

I've been going over my magazine stories and making a tentative list for the possible volume, as follows:

> The End of the Story
> City of the Singing Flame

The Door To Saturn
The Monster of the Prophecy
A Voyage to Sfanomoë
A Night in Malnéant
The Double Shadow
The Dark Eidolon
The Return of the Sorcerer
The Seven Geases
        or, The Testament of Athammaus
The Chain of Aforgomon
The Last Hieroglyph
Sadastor.

These form an aggregate of about 80,000 words. Choice seems pretty difficult, since, after a few outstanding items such as "The Double Shadow" and "A Night in Malnéant," I seem to find dozens or scores of fairly equal merit. The above list fails to include such popular pieces as "A Rendezvous in Averoigne," "The Vaults of Yoh-Vombis," "The Willow Landscape," etc. If you and Don have other preferences, you could easily outvote me![3]

Best, as always,
        Clark

1. See the fragmentary (and most probably uncompleted) story "Eviction by Night" (*SS*) for CAS's Steinbeckian treatment of "the seamy side of agricultural life."

2. "The Thralls of Circe Climb Parnassus" (*SP*; first title "Swine and Azaleas").

3. AWD has written next to CAS's list the titles "The Second Interment," "The Death of Ilalotha," and "The Uncharted Isle."

---

[232]   To August Derleth [TLS, SHSW]   Oct. 19th, 1941.

Dear August:

I received *The Outsider and Others* some time ago and had been meaning to write and thank you. I do hope it sells out without too much delay. If I get hold of a sum of money that I'm hoping to land, I shall buy two or three copies for gifts.

There is not much here at present. I enclose some recent verses. I seem to be in for a little excitement, however: the local undertaker is proving himself a shark as well as a buzzard by pressing the payment of a claim for $107. I haven't the money and am not quite sure how I'll get it. But here's hoping. My debts have worried me greatly, and I put a valuable collection of letters on sale in the Bay region sometime ago, with the idea that I might realize enough to put myself in the clear. But the sale has not gone through yet.

I won't quarrel with you about the selection of tales for my possible volume. Put in anything that seems advisable.

Tell Donald that I'd like to hear from him. I wrote to him some time ago. I hope he was not offended by my previous silence.

What do you want me to do about my Lovecraft letters? I started typing them years ago but found that my eyesight simply would not stand the strain. I can turn them over to you or Don if and when desired.

  Best, as always,
  Clark

---

[233] To August Derleth [TLS, SHSW] Oct. 22nd, 1941.

Dear August:

I hate like hell to ask this—but can you, or you and Donald, jointly, loan me any cash to meet the emergency mentioned in my last letter? So far I've failed to get the money locally—the people I had counted on are ill in the hospital, out of town, or broke themselves. I'm trying some others today. In the meanwhile, if you can spare anything, will you telegraph it to me. I'll return the money immediately if I get enough elsewhere.

I don't know whether my local creditor, the undertaker, is stalling or not, but he claims that he has been forced by the Federal Government to place *all* his unpaid accounts in the hands of this hellish high-powered collection company, who are evidently prepared to take action against my property if I don't pay them at once. If this is on the level, it looks like a fresh step toward communization on the part of the Government. Half the ranches in this section have already been seized by the California Land Co.

When I get this little mess straightened out, I'm going to place my property on sale for what it will fetch. My isolated life here since the death of my parents has been killing me by inches, and I've got to make a break with it.

Thanks a million for anything that you can do. I'll repay you at the earliest possible moment if I do have to take a loan from you.

  Best, as always,
  Clark

[234]   To Rudolph Blatterer [TLS, JHL]   Oct. 25th, 1941

Dear Rudolph:

I had already consulted an attorney when your note arrived, and found that the debt situation wasn't quite so black and pressing as it seemed on first sight. But I'm anxious to get the business cleared up at the earliest possible moment, and have written the collection co. to this effect. My local creditor claims that the federal government is *forcing* him to collect all overdue accounts!! If this were true, it seems to me it would apply to other business men, and half the population would be languishing in debtors' prisons. I wish to hell the Government would give *me* power to collect what's due me. [. . .]

My whole personal situation, as well as the growing war crisis, has served to crystallize a determination to sell my property here if possible. I have just given a local contractor and builder a thirty day option on the ranch. The sale is problematic, depending on whether or not he decides to use the ridge above my cabin as part of an emergency airport landing for a private airline in which he is interested. If it went over, I will still retain a triangle of land enclosing the cabin, outbuildings, and water-spring, as well as all mining rights. The latter may become valuable at any moment, since tunnels into the ancient river channel under my land are being run from opposite sides, and I hear that some good gravel has been struck in both of them. Of course, there is no certainty about anything, and I don't feel like counting my eggs till they are in the basket.

I'll certainly be grateful for any suggestions you can make.

    Best regards, as always,
        Clark

---

[235]   To August Derleth [TLS, SHSW]   Oct. 29th, 1941.

Dear August:

Please don't worry about me any more—it is perfectly needless. Your letter about my book and advance royalties (thanks a million for the promise of the latter!) is just one item in a general boom. I've gotten all my old Norman and Cavalier blood up, and am working with more speed and energy than ever before in my life. Three of Wright's rejects (maybe I can find more) are being retyped for submission to Miss McIlwraith. I am writing scores of air-mail letters, labelling all my sculptures and making explanatory notes about them. I don't want you to pay me for The Outsider; but you can help me in other ways. Show it to people and tell them that I've made hundreds more, all from materials as unusual as the subjects.

Note the enclosed dance program. Madelynne is the dancer of my poem, "Witch-Dance," published with decorations by Bok in a recent *W.T.* With small capital, alone except for her poet-husband Eric Barker in a huge and strange city, against all manner of obstacles and discouragements, sans manager, she is putting on this recital. She is plucky and highly talented (a natural-born sculptress in addition to her Terpsichorean art) and, if she gets half an audience, should go over. Her dances show a brilliant and diverse technique, ranging from the Satanic abandon to her witch-dance to dream poetic movements in such pieces as "Night Wind," and exuberant humor that even a clod could appreciate in "Jimmy Goes to the Dentist." Will you mail this program immediately, with an urgent recommendation to attend, to someone in NY. who might be interested? I'm taking the liberty of having Madelynne air-mail you a few more programs. You'll note the time is very short. If you do this, I'll appreciate it more than the payment for my sculpture.

I'll get the tear-sheets ready soon. You will by now have received my biographical note. I forgot to put in some colorful bits, such as the fact that I refused a Guggenheim scholarship for study at the U.C. through sheer independence and contempt for education institutions (I *would* take a fellowship—but I simply didn't want the obligation to attend any godblasted school). From the note, you'll get the picture of a fantastic, eccentric, impractical, improvident devil: that well-nigh fabulous being, a poet. My professional story-writing (in 1929) started when my then sweetheart threatened to quit me if I didn't get a job. I failed to get the job, and began spinning yarns for Wright and Gernsback.

Also, I forgot to put in my 8 years of illness (nervous breakdown and incipient t.b.) between 1913 and 1921. This got me out of the 1917 draft—I weighed little more than 100 lbs. at the time; and I'm 5 ft. 11 in height.

My best to you, always,
Clark

[236]   To August Derleth [TLS, SHSW]   Dec. 22nd, 1941.

Dear August:

Here is another letter of HPL's which I recently came across. I had evidently filed it away with a number of others written in appreciation of *Ebony and Crystal.*

I hope you won't mind waiting a little longer for the carvings. I've prepared an exhibit of 41 sculptures (also 25 paintings) to go on at the Crocker Gallery Jan. 1st and have finally gotten them off. Most of my best carvings on hand go into the exhibit but I've kept back one (an elder god whose tentacular appendages evidently relate him to Cthulhu!) and will ship it presently with still another piece. Also, as soon as possible, I'll draw up the lists of stories and carvings that you want. As to carvings, I don't deal in *copies* any more—*every piece* that I now have is an original, and from the differing nature of the material, could scarcely be duplicated in all details. I did make a few casts several years ago but found them unsatisfactory. They were all done in plaster, which is miserable stuff to my way of thinking. The unique nature of the minerals used adds considerably to my sculptures. I have sold many of them at prices which constitute the meagerest kind of day-wage for the work actually done and the time consumed in doing it.

I enclose a write-up from a Sacramento paper. The interviewer, Miss Eleanor Fait, was very pleasant and intelligent.[1] I hope the publicity will be of some use.

I may have a whole gang of weird fans and science-fictionists from Southern California here to see me the Saturday after Xmas. May heaven give me strength![2]

Just at present I'm feeling pretty much under the weather and am laid up with a sore foot, caused by a nail or snag that worked through the sole of an old boot. This letter will be mailed by the first visitor that comes in.

Best wishes for the holiday season and New Year.

        Always,
        Clark

1. E[leanor] F[ait], "Auburn Artist-Poet Utilizes Native Rock in Sculptures" (*Sacramento Union,* 21 December 1941; rpt. *Dark Eidolon* No. 2, July 1989). Fait also mentioned CAS shortly thereafter in "Wide Variety Marks Crocker Loan Exhibit for January" (*Sacramento Union,* 4 January 1942).

2. On 27 December 1941, CAS was visited by Paul Freehafer, Robert A. Hoffman, Henry Hasse, and Emil Petaja, all fans from Los Angeles.

The next day CAS was visited by RHB, a reconciliation having been arranged by E. Hoffmann Price. See R. A. Hoffman, "The Arcana of Arkham-Auburn," *Acolyte* 2, No. 3 (Spring 1944): 8–12; Emil Petaja, "The Man in the Mist," *Mirage* No. 10 (1971): 21–25.

---

[237]   To August Derleth [TLS, SHSW]   April 16th, 1942.

Dear August:

You should have received the typescript of *Out of Time and Space* before this, since I expressed it back to you a week or more ago. I should have written before but have been feeling pretty much under the weather.

You'll notice that I made few alterations in the text, the chief one being the revision of a paragraph in the "City of the Singing Flame." This paragraph was written and interpolated by Walter Gillings, editor of *Tales of Wonder*, to link the original story and its sequel into one tale. I've reworded it for the sake of stylistic unity more than anything else. In your foreword, I inserted *Tsathoggua* for *Yog-Sothoth;* the latter deity being Lovecraft's creation, not mine, and first mentioned, if I remember rightly, in "The Dunwich Horror." *Tsathoggua* was my chief addition to the Lovecraft pantheon. I introduced him in "The Tale of Satampra Zeiros," the earliest written and published of my Hyperborean series. H.P. promptly borrowed him, I recall, for use in "The Mound"!

Of the two specimens of format that you send me, the one with the larger type impresses me as being vastly preferable, and I am glad to note that you express a preference for it yourself. The difference in cost seems inconsiderable. [. . .]

Donald made a good suggestion sometime ago—that is, that I name you and him as my literary executors. Some years ago I wrote a holograph naming Mrs. Sully as the heritor of my books, mss., paintings and art-objects; and I doubt if there will be any reason to change this, except in the case of predecease on Mrs. Sully's part, or the rather remote contingency of marriage on mine. I shall, shortly, write out a new will including the clause of executorship. In the meanwhile, this letter can stand as evidence of my wishes in the matter. I am writing Donald to the same effect.

Here are some snaps of me; one taken in my front yard; the other in the high Sierras, with Mrs. Sully.

My best to you, always,
    Clark

[238]   To August Derleth [TLS, SHSW]   May 9th, 1942.

Dear August:

I hope the proofs will reach me during the next 11 days, since I am going upcountry on the 20th of the month to spend three weeks at a mine owned by a friend near Iowa Hill, an old ghost mining town about 30 or 35 miles from Auburn.[1] If not, I'll leave instructions at the local express office to have the package forwarded. (I presume it will come by express?) It won't take me long to check it over for typographical errors, and I'll shoot it to you at the earliest possible moment.

I've just written out a will, in which you and Donald are named as joint literary executors. Here is a copy of the will, which you can file away. I'm sending another to Madelynne. While I don't anticipate an early demise, there's always an element of danger in underground work (particularly where dynamite is used) such as I'll be doing at Sturmfeder's mine.

I'm writing to Donald at length. All best wishes, always,
            Clark

    1. Franz Sturmfeder (1887–1973), miner, occultist, and friend of CAS.

---

[239]   To August Derleth [TLS, SHSW]   April 31st [*sic*], 1943.

Dear August:

I'm expressing you the statuette today and am hoping you'll like it. In some ways it is my most ambitious effort. As for the price: 10 bucks or pazoors will be o.k.

I hope the Whitehead and Merritt volumes can both materialize.[1] Merritt hasn't done many shorts, but I remember one called "Beyond the Dragon Glass" and another entitled (I think) "Three Lines of Old French."

Here's a tentative title and index for my second, if and when. I'm wondering if you've seen all the stories listed. "The Plutonian Drug" appeared in *Amazing Stories*, Sept. 1934; "The Demon of the Flower" in *Astounding Stories* (can't recall exact date) shortly after it was taken over by Street and Smith. "Flight into Super-Time" (Gernsback's title—my original one was "The Letter from Mohaun Los") was one of my more ironic *Wonder Stories* contributions but I'm sure most of its readers missed the double-barrelled satire. "The Coming of the White Worm" appeared in *Stirring Science Stories,* April 1941. I think it is one of my best-written and most unearthly yarns.

      Best, as always,
        Clark

1. Henry S. Whitehead, *Jumbee and Other Uncanny Tales* (Sauk City, WI: Arkham House, 1944), the company's sixth book. A volume by A. Merritt titled *The Worlds Outside* was planned but never published.

---

[240]   To August Derleth [TLS, SHSW] July 18th, 1943.

Dear August:
    Thanks for the check, which came rather unexpectedly. The continued sale of the book is certainly gratifying, and I hope the *W.T.* ad will bring in many delayed orders.
    I'd have written before but have been picking fruit 10 hrs daily for the past six weeks. The work is monotonous and irksome; but the wages are good (7 bucks a day) and the season promises to be over early. When it's over I should have money enough on hand to settle down to a few months of writing. I'm still paying out on old debts but the end is in sight.
    Please send me five more copies of *Out of Space and Time;* also put aside two of the new HPL volume for me; against my royalties.

      Best always,
        Clark

---

[241]   To Robert A. Hoffman[1] [TLS, private collection]
                         Sept. 14th, 1943.

Dear Bob:
    Voila! Here is the Family Tree of the Old Ones, which I found safely tucked away in the box of Lovecraft letters. Oddly enough, it was the visit of my enchantress which brought the missing papyrus to light: I had gotten out the box to show a few of the letters.[2]
    Derleth writes that the printing of the Lovecraft volume is delayed but he hopes to get enough paper to start distribution by Oct. 1st. My book has now sold 688 copies. D. insists that *Lost Worlds* be retained as the title of my next collection. Personally I

don't think the point worth fighting over: after all there isn't much likeness between my tales and the Conan Doyle yarn.

I guess either of the two dates you mention will be all right for a visit here; since I shan't go to S.F. till after the 3rd of October. Let me know when you can come, as far in advance as possible.

I've done nothing but loaf, write poems and pay visits. I'll type the promised excerpts for Laney[3] before I settle down to story-writing. What you say about the market outlook is certainly depressing; but I'll try to do a little anyway.

As for that picture-poem project, it's hard for me to make a definite promise, since I've never been able to write verse to order. Your pictures might suggest some weird quatrains to me; or they might not. Why don't you do the series of drawings anyway and let me see it? I'll oblige you if I can. If I can't, maybe you could cook up some verses yourself for me to retouch with an eye to metre, technique, etc.

The Wandrei book is probably a reprint of shorts, though I haven't definitely heard yet.[4] I hope it is.

I'd be glad to have you meet a bona fide witch; but unluckily I only know one. She lives in S.F. and doesn't get up here very often. She and her husband spent the last week-end with me.

As ever, C A S

1. Robert A. (Rah) Hoffman, Los Angeles-area SF fan and composer who became friends with CAS when stationed near Auburn during World War II.

2. See letter 189, n.1.

3. Francis Towner Laney (1914–1958), prominent fan. His memoir, *Ah! Sweet Idiocy* (1948) contain an account of his visit to CAS's cabin.

4. Donald Wandrei, *The Eye and the Finger* (Sauk City, WI: Arkham House, 1944), the company's fifth book.

[242]   To August Derleth [TLS, SHSW]   Nov. 30th, 1943.

Dear August:

I have been going over *Beyond the Wall of Sleep*,[1] which certainly contains a vast variety and number of first-rate items in spite of a few uneven and inferior pieces. *The Case of Charles Dexter Ward* (I read this in *W.T.* of course) is one of HPL's greatest; and *The Dream-Quest of Unknown Kadath,* which I read the other night for the first time, is an astonishing and very delightful fantasy, with only the most superficial resemblance to Dunsany. Who but Lovecraft would have thought of bringing in those marshalled armies of cats and cohorts of ghouls, night-gaunts, etc? I don't know of anything more remarkable in the way of dream-literature: the tale is far more coherent and better-knit than I had expected from HP's criticism and that of others.

Nearly all of the shorter pieces are familiar to me. "The White Ship" and the title story are perhaps the topnotchers. Such revisions as "Out of the Aeons," "The Mound," and "The Diary of Alonzo Typer" are genuine Lovecraftian masterpieces. I am sure that everything published by Hazel Heald is 99% Lovecraft.

Laney did a fine piece of work in his "Cthulhu Mythology." Re some of the place-names, however: Price originally dug up the name and legend of Shamballah from theosophic writings, probably those of Blavatsky. My Hyperborea, too, is drawn as much from occult tradition as from the old classic legends. Thule, which Laney seems to think I originated, was merely the name given by the ancients to the extreme north. *The Book of Dzyan,* older than the world, is part of that Theosophic Shamballah legend. But of course all this is rather meticulous, since these names, like Nodens and Dagon and other actual names, are now part of the Mythology anyway.

I'm hoping you'll have an influx of orders for *Out of Space and Time.* Lilith Lorraine[2] writes that she is recommending it to all her students in verse technique "as an aid to vocabulary as well as for the intrinsic merits of the book as great literature."

Don't forget my extra copy of *Beyond the Wall of Sleep.* The one you sent me will go as a slightly overdue birthday gift to Mrs. Sully's daughter Helen (Mrs. Nelson Best) who met Lovecraft through my introduction back in 1933.

> Best, as always,
> Clark

P.S. The jacket photo disappoints me through its loss of fine detail. But I'm not sure that this doesn't make the sculpture seem even more palaeogean and Lovecraftian!

1. The book (published in 1943) contains various minor short stories, two previously unpublished short novels, stories HPL had revised or ghost-written for or collaborated on with other authors, poetry, Francis T. Laney's "The Cthulhu Mythology: A Glossary," and "W. Paul Cook's "An Appreciation of H. P. Lovecraft." The dust jacket featured photographs of CAS's carvings.

2. Lilith Lorraine, pseudonym of Mary Maud Dunn Wright (1894–1967), was a poet, science fiction writer, and founder and editor of the little magazines *The Raven, Different, Challenge,* and *Flame.*

[243]   To August Derleth [TLS, SHSW]   June 9th, 1944.

Dear August:

I have your letters and the returned Lovecraft correspondence. I'm glad you were able to get a few notes out of the latter.

Thanks for your suggestion that a photo of one of more of my carvings be used on the jacket of *Lost Worlds*. I like the idea but think that at least one of the carvings should be directly illustrative of something in the book—some entity from one of my own myth-cycles. I'll try to do something of this sort at the first opportunity and will loan you the result for photographing.

Re my copies of *Lost Worlds:* I'll be glad to sell twelve of the fifteen that I hold to individual purchasers (not book-dealers) but wish to keep the remaining three for future contingencies.

As for that new Poetry league: I know Coblentz quite well and have had much correspondence with Miss Lorraine. Both, I feel sure (I don't know the other committee members) are animated by a sincere desire to uphold the older and main tradition of English poetry amid the chaos of current criteria. Personally I can't follow Coblentz in his wholesale denunciation of all modernistic writing, no matter how distasteful individual examples, such as Cummings, are to me. I haven't joined the league, since, for one thing, I could hardly pledge myself to write letters denouncing a group of authors most of whom I have not even read, nor would I write such letters even if I had read them. Anyway, it seems obvious that poets, like other artists, have the right of experimentation: time will separate the grain from the chaff. One might argue that the experimentalists have the best of it at present, in regard to the support of magazines, publishers and critics, and that it is hard to get a fair hearing for work that is not experimental in form. The League of Sanity (a none-too-fortunate name) may mark the beginning of the inevitable reaction against reaction. But I don't think there is any danger that its activities will result in a literary dictatorship.

          Best, as always,
          Clark

[244]   To August Derleth [TLS, SHSW]   July 26th, 1944.

Dear August:

Thanks for your letter of the 22nd with enclosed check for $25. The photos you send are very striking, and I trust that the one used on the book jacket will turn out well. I still continue to receive inquiries about my sculptures on the strength of the Lovecraft jacket.

I'm sorry that I still haven't any good photos of myself apart from snapshots taken with friends, which wouldn't be suitable for your purpose. My last visit to a professional photographer (about 14 yrs ago!) resulted in the villainous libel that *Wonder Stories* used for several issues with my pseudo-science yarns. But I'll try again some time.

I'm picking fruit at present and will be tied up with this for several weeks. But I'll get to work on a selection of poems as soon as possible—also a list of stories for a third book; and will loan you my volumes of verse. Incidentally I haven't a copy of *Sandalwood* (my third volume) on hand but have a typescript made by Barlow. I'm surprised there should be so much demand for "The Hashish-Eater."[1]

By the way, can you give me an idea as to how much material you would want in this selected verse volume—no. of pages, approximately, and no. of lines to a page?

As for parallelisms between the Cthulhu Mythos and my own cycles, I haven't been able to find that there is really enough for an article, since Laney has now covered my main additions to the Lovecraft Mythology. In common with other weird tales writers, I have borrowed the Necronomicon in more than one of my yarns, and have made a few passing references (often under slightly altered names, such as Iog-Sotot for Yog-Sothoth and Kthulhut for Cthulhu) to some of the Lovecraftian deities. My Hyperborean tales, it seems to me, with their primordial, prehuman and sometimes pre-mundane background and figures, are the closest to the Cthulhu Mythos, but most of them are written in a vein of grotesque humor that differentiates them vastly. However, such a tale as "The Coming of the White Worm" might be regarded as a direct contribution to the Mythos. My tales of Averoigne, it seems to me, are all thoroughly medieval in spirit; but two of them, "The Holiness of Azédarac" and "The Beast of Averoigne," contain suggestions drawn from the Lovecraftian cosmos. Offhand, I would say that there is even less correspondence between the Lovecraft

Mythos and my main cycle, that of Zothique. But perhaps some one else could trace parallels.

Best, as always,
Clark

1. The Arkham House anthology *Dark of the Moon: Poems of Fantasy and the Macabre,* ed. AWD (Sauk City, WI: Arkham House, 1947), the company's twenty-third book, contained twelve poems by CAS. It was the only appearance of "The Hashish-Eater" between the publication of *EC* and *SP.*

---

[245]   To Donald Wandrei [TLS, MHS]   Aug. 13th, 1944.

Dear Donald:

I was delighted to get your letter, which was a little delayed in reaching me, since I am picking fruit at present (a somewhat fatiguing occupation) and don't go to the P.O. every day. Today, Sunday, is my first chance to sit down and write you: the letter, by air-mail, should reach you in care of August.

Derleth had already mentioned a plan for a selected volume of my poems, though with no definite time of publication, and I had planned to start working on [it] as soon as the fruit-season ends, which will be early in September. Needless to say, your project for a *complete* collection thrills and pleases me immensely; yet I am not sure that all the work in my published volumes, nor all the uncollected stuff, is worthy of such preservation. For instance, some of the nature lyrics in the *Star-Treader* seem a bit banal to my present taste. The compiling of the volume will take careful consideration. I doubt if it could run to the size of the Lovecraft omnibus; but it might run to 350 or 400 pages. Like August, I favor a regrouping in regard to general subject matter form, etc: the blank verse poems from T*he Star-Treader* and *Ebony and Crystal* could be grouped together for the first section; then the odes; the shorter poems of fantasy and weirdness under some such subtitle as *Incantations;* the love poems to be grouped together as *The Book of Eros.* But, as you say, the book is still fluid and uncrystallized. It would be splendid if you could use a few of my paintings or drawings: I'll look over what I have with a tentative view to this purpose.[1]

I have *The Eye and the Finger,* which I am enjoying vastly. The title story is new to me, and it is certainly a neat little horror. Gods! but you have an imagination! The ones I have read before seem even better on rereading in book form. Incidentally, I liked your preface too, and was pleased by the high mention you gave me.

Re a preface for my poems. I'd be delighted to have one by you; and it seems to me that Sterling's brief foreword to *Ebony and Crystal,* and a short appreciation by Benjamin De Casseres (which runs to about two pages) could also be included to advantage.

Yes, I think it will be best for me to do the typing: I don't even possess a printed copy of *Sandalwood* (I have a typescript made by Barlow!) and shall want to sift many piles of scattered mss. for some of the stuff to be included.

I've thought many times of our meeting in Sacramento, which was one of those unexpected episodes that do so much to take the staleness from existence. It prefaced a run of unusual Sundays for me: on the following Sunday I had an experience too beautiful and macabre to write about here; on the next, I stole rhododendrons for a girl out in Golden Gate Park.

I'll hunt for some poems to enclose with this.

As ever Clark

My best to August—I'll write him soon.

Life still has its surprises. A charming and unlooked-for brunette is lying close at hand, reading your book, as I write this.

1. CAS worked for five years at preparing his *SP* (tentatively titled *The Hashish-Eater and Other Poems*). The manuscript was delivered in 1949, but the book was not published until 1971, ten years after CAS's death. It was the only volume of poetry published by Arkham House to see a full (rather than limited) print run. Instead of recasting the poems according to subject matter, CAS mostly followed the arrangements of his collections *ST, EC,* and *S,* although he did group the translations in a special category, while adding others, such as *The Jasmine Girdle, Incantations, The Hill of Dionysus,* and others. As CAS suggested, the preface to *EC* served by Sterling was used; Benjamin De Casseres' "short appreciation" served as the preface to *SP.*

---

[246]   To Robert A. Hoffman [TLS, private collection]
                                                      Sept. 9th, 1944.

Dear Bob:

I was about to write you when your letter came, enclosing the check for 3 copies of *Lost Worlds.* Thanks a lot for the order, which I'll fill as per instructions when my first consignment (which should be fifteen copies) arrives.

As you surmised, I've been busy with fruit-picking and didn't finish till last week. Personal correspondence went by the board and I'm just beginning to pick up the threads again.

As for a third volume of stories, I haven't settled on all the titles yet and am hoping that I may have some new work to include by the time Arkham House is ready to publish it. Definitely, however, the book will contain "The Garden of Adompha," "Genius Loci," "The Charnel God," "The Colossus of Ylourgne," "The Disinterment of Venus," "Vulthoom," "The Devotee of Evil," "The Voyage of King Euvoran," "The Willow Landscape," "The Eternal World," "The Black Abbot of Puthuum," "The Witchcraft of Ulua," "The Phantoms of the Fire" and "The Ice-Demon." I haven't a title yet for this volume.[1]

My prose pastels will be included in the collection of my poetry which Derleth and Wandrei hope to bring out in 1945 or 1946.[2] This will be entitled *The Hashish-Eater and Other Poems* and will be uniform in size, format, etc, with the volumes of Tales. For the past week I have been exhuming ancient mss. and am retouching some of them in preparation for the immense job of typing which Wandrei has set me. He wants copies of every poem that I have ever written! Incidentally I can let Laney print some of this old, hitherto-unpublished material if he would care for it. I have found one unpublished prose-poem, "Narcissus," of which I will send you a copy before long together with the musical setting of my poem "Impression," which I promised you some time back.[3]

I've enjoyed Wandrei's book of tales immensely, though most of them were familiar to me. Frank Wakefield did a nice job on the jacket of the Whitehead volume.[4] Personally, I liked some of the Whitehead tales a lot better than I expected to: they have a quiet sort of potency at best.

Yes, my carvings have continued to sell and I dare say the jacket of *Lost Worlds,* which features a photo of several, will bring in fresh inquiries. I've had inquiries about my paintings too and must draw up a list with brief descriptions and prices. Incidentally, Wandrei wants to use a reproduction of one of my paintings (not yet selected) in full color as a frontispiece to *The Hashish-Eater and Other Poems.*

"The Ghoul" has never had professional publication. Should I try it on McIlwraith? Yes? No?

It's been hotter here the past week than Satan's gridiron. I'm going to pack my little handbag Monday morning and take the bus to San Francisco. Probably the consignment of *Lost Worlds* will be waiting when I get back.

Best, as always,
Klarkash-Ton

1. The volume ultimately was titled *Genius Loci and Other Tales* (Sauk City, WI: Arkham House, 1948), the company's thirty-fifth book. It did not include "The Devotee of Evil," "The Voyage of King Euvoran," "The Witchcraft of Ulua," or "The Ice Demon" but did include "The Ninth Skeleton," "A Star-Change," "The Primal City," "The Disinterment of Venus," "The Satyr," and "The Weaver in the Vault."

2. CAS's "prose pastels" had been appearing in the *Acolyte* at this time. None appeared in *SP*, but some were published in *AY*. Many ultimately appeared in *PP*.

3. "Narcissus" (*Acolyte,* Winter 1945; *PP*). The composer Joseph W. Grant published a musical setting of CAS's poem "Impression"(*EC* and *SP*) for "Chorus with Women's Voices with Piano Accompaniment" (New York: Carl Fischer, Inc., 1944).

4. I.e., *Jumbee and Other Uncanny Tales.*

[247]   To August Derleth [TLS, SHSW]   June 10th, 1945.

Dear August:

Thanks a lot for the royalty statement and check, which came several days ago. At present I'm working on a ranch 7 miles out of Auburn and so may not have a chance to cash the check for several weeks (since I can't get to a bank during banking hours.)

I'm pleased that *Lost Worlds* has sold so well. I hope to begin the final typing of my volume of poems after the 1st of July, when this ranch job is wound up. As for the novel mentioned by Price, this must be "The Infernal Star," of which I drafted 12,000 words back in 1935.[1] Somehow the impetus petered out and I never went on with it. But it might be worth finishing some time. I have a idea for another weird tale, short book length, to be called "The Scarlet Succubus," a yarn of Zothique, too erotic for magazine publication.[2] Needless to say, when and if I do finish a book length, I'll give you the option on it. [. . .]

    All best regards,
        Clark

1. Never completed; fragmentary tale printed in *SS*.
2. Never completed.

[248]   To August Derleth [TLS, AH]   April 14th, 1947.

Dear August:

I had meant to acknowledge the copies of *Dark of the Moon* and your letters and check weeks ago and am horrified at the way time has run on.

The anthology is a pretty strong collection and I like it very much. However, I missed many favorites, such as Sterling's "A Wine of Wizardry," Oscar Wilde's "The Sphinx," Browning's "Childe Roland," Tennyson's "Voyage of Maeldune," and Arnold's "The Forsaken Merman."

I'm inclined to leave the omission of or holding-over of stories from *Genius Loci* to you. However, if I must make a choice it seems to me that "The Third Episode of Vathek," "The Devotee of Evil," "The Abominations of Yondo," "The Ice-Demon," and "The Weaver in the Vault" could be held over as well as any.

Frank Wakefield, who did the jacket design for Whitehead's first volume, is living near Auburn at present. He spoke of wishing that he could do a jacket design for *Genius Loci*.[1] If you haven't some one else already in mind, it seems to me that he could do an excellent one. His address is, c/o A. V. SCHENCK, Box 338, Route 1, Auburn, Cal.

I've had a sterile period for weeks but am beginning to pull out of it. The enclosed verses will be new to you.

Best always,
Clark

1. Wakefield did in fact design the dust jacket for *GL*.

[249]   To August Derleth [TLS, AH]   July 3rd, 1947.

Dear August:

I am enclosing a letter from our old friend Ef-Jay Akkamin,[1] which you can read and return to me with your reactions. I haven't answered it too definitely but am pointing out to him that reprint rights would have to be secured from you for some of the tales that he lists: notably "The City of the Singing Flame" and its incorporated sequel; "Flight into Super-Time" ("The Letter from Mohaun Los") and "The Light from Beyond." Also, that two other tales, "The Eternal World," and "The Visitors from Mlok" ("A Star-

Change") are scheduled for use in *Genius Loci and Other Tales.* Moreover, that "Master of the Asteroid" may be included by you in an anthology.

Most of my other sf tales strike me as being second or third-rate. But a volume could conceivably be made up from them if anyone wants to bite.

Yes, I am anxious to do something for the Anniversary No. of *Weird Tales;* also, for the projected Avon House Magazines concerning which Donald Wollheim has written me.[2] Market possibilities are certainly improving and I feel more encouraged than for a long time past.

Your plan for a magazine to publicize supernatural fiction seems a good one to me and you are welcome to use any of my tales, already printed or forthcoming.

The cast will be removed from my leg early next week. The ankle seems pretty strong now and I am hoping that I won't have too much trouble with it. But I am feeling the lack, or comparative lack of exercise woefully, and am still pepless and anemic from the hospital diet of denatured starches. However, the experience should make a good chapter for a realistic novel or, rather, a series of connected sketches about the local milieu, which I have tentatively started to write. I certainly got the low-down on public hospitals!

I'll appreciate your advice on the Akkamin proposition, since I don't want to get drawn into anything without your approval. There certainly seems to be a growing crop of sf and fantasy publishers!

My best to you, always,
Clark

1. I.e., Forrest Ackerman, who was attempting to market a collection of CAS's "scientifiction" stories for another publisher.
2. CAS contributed "The Master of the Crabs" to *WT*'s 25th anniversary issue (March 1948). Wollheim, though, only bought reprints for the series of *Avon Fantasy Readers,* which he edited from 1947 to 1952.

———— ♦ ————

[250]   To August Derleth [TLS, SHSW]   July 9th, 1947.

Dear August:
Thanks for your letter of the 5th, which I appreciated greatly. I had begun to feel more and more the same way myself on thinking the matter over, and have written Ackerman that the idea for a volume of my sf yarns is definitely "out." Apart from your claim

on such work of mine as is worth reprinting, too many of the tales in question are inferior stuff. Perhaps I can salvage some by revision before the time comes for you to put out a fourth volume of my stuff.

I can easily furnish you with some unpublished poems for the quarterly, and will enclose with this several of the pieces that I have been working on for the selected volume. Some of these have been completely rewritten from the original ancient drafts.[1]

With the hospital doctor's permission, I removed the cast from my leg yesterday. The damned ankle is slightly swollen, apart from the inevitable stiffness. I'm afraid the sprain I received was a lot worse than the break, which was confined to one small bone.

My best,
Clark

1. Poems that CAS contributed to the *Arkham Sampler* include "Lamia," "The Nameless Wraith," and "The City of Destruction" (Winter 1948); "Hellenic Sequel" and "The Blindness of Orion" (Spring 1948); "No Stranger Dream" and "On the Mount of Stone" (Summer 1948); "Only to One Returned" and "Anterior Life" (a translation of Charles Baudelaire) (Autumn 1948); "Avowal" (Winter 1949); "Sed Non Satiata" (after Baudelaire; Spring 1949); "Oblivion" (a translation of José-María de Heredia [1842–1905]) and "The Giantess" and "Lethe" (after Baudelaire, Summer 1949); and "Calenture," "Pour chercher du Nouveau," and "The Death of Lovers" (after Baudelaire; Autumn 1949).

---

[251]   To Samuel J. Sackett[1] [TLS, UCLA]   May 13th, 1948

Dear Mr. Sackett:

Thanks for your interesting letter of the first, which I had meant to answer sooner.

Re the tobacco pipes: so far, I have made only a few of these. I have given away several to friends, have sold one (the finest, I think) at $10.00, and am listing two others at $7.50 each for possible sale. To make one of them, with the fitting of the stem, mouthpiece, etc., means at least two days' work. As a special accommodation, I could make you one at $5.00. Or, if you smoke cigarettes, I could carve you a holder (probably in the form of a small fish or reptile) at $3.50; or a grotesque ash-tray at $4.00. I have, so far, made two cigarette holders, selling one and keeping the other for myself.

As to fantasy stories, I think it is rather hard to lay down general rules, since the genre includes so many types and variations. My own work, for instance, falls into several different moods and styles, ranging from grotesque and sardonic humor (as in "The Door to Saturn") to pure horror and unearthly fantasy. I do not have any fixed rules of composition, apart from the establishment and maintenance of what seems an appropriate tone, manner, and style of wording throughout the particular piece in question. In my experience, it often helps to write out a detailed synopsis of a story before beginning the actual composition; even though one may depart from, or vary, the plot and development later.

If you care to send me the ms. of that third fantasy tale of yours, perhaps I could make a few suggestions more to the point than the above generalities. I am wondering which, and how many, magazines, you tried. The fantasy editors are an idiosyncratic lot; perhaps you merely picked the wrong ones for that particular tale.

Sincerely yours,
Clark Ashton Smith

1. Samuel J. Sackett (b. 1928), Professor of English at Fort Hays University, Hays, KS, fan, and science fiction writer.

---

[252]   To Donald Wandrei [TLS, MHS]
6666th autumnal equinox of the black yuga.
[Oct. 27, 1948]

Dear Donaldius:

If you had received all the letters I have intended to write, you would be in possession of a sizable file of correspondence by now!

It was certainly good news to hear that you had finished the editing of the Lovecraft letters. I can well realize the monumental scope of this labor of devotion, and the fabulous and inestimable riches uncovered by it. I can never quite accustom myself to the strangeness, and the sense of irremediable loss, in no longer receiving letters that were to me, as well as to you and others, a stimulus without parallel. Indeed, I shall be most grateful to read some of the volumes if you will loan them to me at your convenience; and am inclined to leave the choice to you.

As for my poems, the remaining labor is largely one of assembling and typing and should not take so long if I could only settle down to it. The heaviest revision, some of it including the partial or entire recasting of poems, has been on the *Star-Treader* group and certain unpublished pieces of the same or a slightly posterior date. These are all typed in triplicate. Revision of old work is a hellish task; but I hope that I have salvaged some poems which, in their original form, were too inferior or uneven. For instance, take the new octave of a sonnet in *The Star-Treader,* called "The Unrevealed," in which only one line remains as originally written:

> What close prenatal palls occlude from us
> Once-prevalent Signs, once-rampant arms! How straight
> The sunless road, suspended, separate,
> That leads from death to birth. Not luminous
> With lodestar, or with star calamitous,
> The past is closed as by the night-black spate
> Of planet-gulfing seas—its keyless gate
> Lost in Avernian shadows cavernous.

The revisions on later work are comparatively slight and minor, apart from my Baudelaire translations, some of which I have retouched considerably. There must be around forty of these in all. I enclose one of the more exotic *Fleurs,* "Sed non Satiata," which has cost me a lot of trouble.

I have made a few changes in "The Hashish-Eater," designed mainly to vary the cadence of the blank verse. And there are three new stanzas for "The Nereid" to be inserted preceding the last stanza:

> The berylline pallors of her face
> Illume the kingdom of the drowned.
> In her the love that none has found
> The unflowering rapture, folded grace,
>
> Await some lover strayed and lone,
> Some god misled, who shall not come
> Though the decrescent seas lie dumb
> And sunken in their wells of stone.
>
> But nevermore of him, perchance,
> Her enigmatic musings are—
> Whose purpling tresses float afar
> In grottoes of the last romance.

There is a considerable mass of uncollected material which has accumulated subsequent to *Sandalwood,* and I shall try to start typing this shortly, leaving the pages unnumbered (as I have done with the earlier poems) until the entire typescript is finished. It will fall into three main sections; one, *Incantations,* including most of my later weird and fantastic poems, as well as miscellaneous material; and the other two, *The Jasmine Girdle* and *The Hill of*

Dionysus, being sequences of love-poems, many of which are in themselves more or less touched with strangeness and fantasy. I have too a few satires, travesties on modernism, vers libre, etc, of which I enclose the most recent specimens, "Surrealist Sonnet" and "Sonnet for the Psychoanalysts." There are also some poems in French, two or three of which seem correct enough in diction, grammar, etc., for possible inclusion.

I hope you will like some of the enclosures—a rather motley lot. Such recent lyrics as "Calenture" and "Some Blind Eidolon" strike me as being probably among my best. The experiments in haiku, the so-called "one-breath" Japanese form, seem to have evoked rather various reactions in those who have read them; some thinking the form too fragmentary, too exotic for domestication in English. However, I believe that others, such as Amy Lowell and John Gould Fletcher, have experimented with it. Personally I like the form, into which almost any sort of single impression or image can be distilled.[1]

Anyway, I am anxious to finish the typing of all this material and get it into your hands; and wish the task were further advanced. The last two years, however, have been rather hellish ones for me, since I have had almost no money to live on, and have been stone broke for weeks at a time. Oct. 1947 was the worst period, and I'm hoping that I can somehow avert another quite as bad.

Anent some of the things in your letter. I *did* receive *The Eye and the Finger,* and thought I had thanked you for it years ago. The book is one of the most highly prized items in my shelf of Arkham House publications. I certainly enjoyed re-reading *The Web of Easter Island,* and think you have improved marvellously on the ms. that you showed me so many years back. It was a pleasure to review the book for *The Arkham Sampler.*[2]

Your idea for a new novel of cosmic fantasy is what the late H.S. Whitehead would have called a "honey-cooler," and strikes me as having infinite possibilities. I wonder if the old ecclesiastical word *energumen,* meaning a possessed person, would appeal to you as a title, or part of a title.

I imagine that Lovecraft derived his information about Shamballah from E. Hoffmann Price, who in turn probably drew the data from Blavatsky or some other theosophical authority. I have some notes that Price gave me, in which Shamballah is mentioned:

"The word came from Shamballah, the Holy City, to destroy Atlantis 850,000 years ago, and overthrow the Lords of the Dark Face. The divine race of Aarab escaped the catastrophe, and in Al Yemen they reared the mighty Himyar palaces, with prodigious bulks, uncounted domes."

S. is supposed to exist, invisible, somewhere in the Gobi desert. It was, I seem to remember, built by the lords of the Flame who came down from Venus. In it is kept the *Book of Dzyan*, older than the world.

I hope fervently that you do come to California this fall or winter. Prices are horribly inflated here; but perhaps a place of settlement could be found.

Yours, under the seal of Dagon and all the Ashtaroth,
Klarkash-Ton

1. Amy Lowell (1874–1925), the well-known Imagist poet. John Gould Fletcher (1896–1950) was also an Imagist, but he later worked in more traditional forms. In *SP* CAS grouped some of his haiku under the heading "Distillations."

2. "CAS, "A Cosmic Novel," under "Books of the Quarter" (*Arkham Sampler*, Autumn 1948; *PD*).

---

[253]   To August Derleth [TLS, AH]   Nov. 6th, 1948.

Dear August:

I'm glad that one of those "duds" passed muster. I like them myself in the same order that you indicate. "Food of the Giantesses" is a punk title—the original one being "Jim Knox and the Giantesses." How about "Genesis of the Giant" or "Tall Man's Tale"?

As for payment, would it be easier to send the money in instalments? I can appreciate your difficulties. I'm stone-broke at the moment, having spent my last money for type-paper.

The books are at the P.O. and I'll get them today.

Here's a new poem (satire) which may amuse you. I'm trying it on a few magazines. Benet *almost* bought it for the *Sat. Review of Lit.*

Best always,
Clark

---

[254]   To Robert A. Hoffman [TLS, private collection]
Jan. 31st, 1949.

Dear Bob:

I trust you received the copy of *Genius Loci,* duly and fantastically inscribed. Thanks for the order. I had meant to write before but the savage cold prevailing here all month (I believe you have had the same in Southern California) just about paralyzed all my activities; and I begin to understand Lovecraft's abhorrence to freezing weather.[. . .]

No, I haven't heard the records of *The Medium*. Ravel's nursery opera sounds enticing, and I'm sure I would like it.[1] Ravel (along with Debussy) is one [of] the comparatively few composers that I seem able to understand. I hear a lot of radio music at the home of certain friends in Auburn, and heard something that I liked the other night by a negro composer named Still. I can't remember the exact title; but it was divided into four parts: Longing, Sorrow, Humor and Aspiration.[2] The first three struck me as being the best: the last one seemed to go on indefinitely without getting anywhere.

I have some new stories under way, and have been working a lot on my volume of selected poems for Arkham House, which is beginning to shape up now. Here is a new poem (suggested by the recent weather!) which may go in to it. I am starting to learn Spanish and may have a few translations of Spanish poetry to include along with the ones that I have made from the French.

Do you know anyone in your area who missed buying *Lost Worlds* and wants a copy of it? I find that I still have a couple of extras, and will sell them at $4.50 apiece. The book was listed at $5.00 in some dealer's catalogue that came to me not long ago.

My best to you, as always,
Klarkash-Ton

1. Gian Carlo Menotti (b. 1911), *The Medium* (1946); Maurice Ravel (1875–1937), *L'enfant et les sortilèges* [*The Child and the Enchantments*] (1920), with a libretto by Colette.
2. William Grant Still (1895–1978), *Symphony No. 1* (premiered 1931). Still was the first African American composer to have a symphony performed by an American orchestra. The movements are as CAS describes.

[255]   To August Derleth [TLS, SHSW]   Feb. 11th, 1949.

Dear August:

Thanks for the new *Sampler,* and the consignment of *Genius Loci*. It is indeed gratifying that the book should be selling so rapidly, and I hope that another six weeks or two months will see you out of the red as far as *Genius Loci* is concerned. By the way, have there been any good reviews of the book? I have not seen any at all, except the brief one by John Haley which you sent me some time back.[1]

I like very much your poem in the *Sampler,* especially the last two lines; and Starrett's is highly amusing. Among the stories, I am inclined to prefer Grendon's "Open Sesame." Bradbury's, for once, failed to "come off" for me—there seemed to be something lacking.[2]

I have read the symposium on science-fiction with great interest.[3] Since you have summed up so ably in your editorial the main deductions to be drawn, I will content myself with a few footnotes, so to speak. For one thing, it struck me that most of the contributors (Dr. Keller being an exception) failed to emphasize sufficiently the historical aspect of the theme and were too exclusively preoccupied with its contemporary development. Yet surely, for the proper understanding of the genre and of fantasy in general, some consideration should be given to its roots in ancient literature, folklore, mythology, anthropology, occultism and mysticism.

I was quite surprised that no one mentioned Lucian, Apuleius and Rabelais among the forefathers of the genre, since all three are of prime importance. Lucian was a satirist and skeptic who, in the form of imaginative fiction, endeavored to "debunk" the religious superstitions and contending philosophies of his time; being, one might say, somewhat analogous to Aldous Huxley, who in his turn has satirised modern science. Apuleius, borrowing a plot from Lucian in *The Golden Ass,* expressed, on the other hand, the power and glamour of a sorcery that was *regarded as science* by the moiety of his contemporaries; and his book, in its final chapter, plunges deeply into that mysticism which is seemingly eternal and common to many human minds in all epochs. The omission of Rabelais is particularly surprising, since he was not only the first of modern satiric fantaisists, but also one of the first writers to develop the Utopian theme (so much exploited since) in his phalanstery of Theleme: which, I might add, is the only fictional Utopia that I should personally care to inhabit!

Another thing that struck me was the ethical bias shown by some of the contributors; a bias characteristic of so many science-fiction fans, as opposed to the devotees of pure fantasy. Such fans are obviously lovers of the imaginative and the fantastic, more or less curbed in the indulgence of their predilections by a feeling that the fiction in which they delight should proceed (however remote its ultimate departure) from what is currently regarded as proven fact and delimited natural law; otherwise, there is something reprehensible in yielding themselves to its enjoyment. Without entering into the old problem of ethics plus art, or ethics versus art, I can only say that from my own standpoint the best application of ethics would lie in the sphere where it is manifestly not being applied: that is to say, the practical use of scientific discoveries and inventions. Imaginative literature would be happier and more fruitful with unclogged wings; and the sphere of its enjoyment would be broader. However, perhaps I am biased myself.

What pleased me most about the symposium was the prominence given to Wells and to Charles Fort, and the inclusion of your anthology, *Strange Ports of Call*.[4] I am looking forward to *The Dark Side of the Moon*.

I could mention books, out of my own far from complete reading of science-fiction, than were missed or slighted by the contributors. Of these, Huxley's *After Many a Summer Dies the Swan*, is perhaps the most salient from a literary standpoint.[5] It is a gorgeous and sumptuous satire on the results of self-achieved immortality. Leonard Cline's *The Dark Chamber* could be mentioned too, since it depicts with singular power the retrogression of a human being to the primal slime. But one could multiply titles without adding anything of permanent literary value and significance. As Wandrei says, the field is peculiarly barren in this respect.

It seems likely, however, that the atom bomb may bring about one desirable result by attracting to science fiction some new writers of genuine power and adequate technique.

I am hoping to write some more yarns of this type, and have many synopses on hand that could be expanded into story form.

My best, as always,
Clark

P.S. Sometimes I suspect that Freud should be included among the modern masters of science fiction!

P.P.S. I forgot to mention Lucian's *True History*, which contains what is probably the first interplanetary tale, a fantastic account of a voyage to the moon.

1. Not located.
2. The *Arkham Sampler* for Winter 1949 contained "The Pool in the Wood" (poem) by AWD; "Travel Talk" (poem) by Vincent Starrett, "Open Sesame!" by "Stephen Grendon" (pseudonym of AWD), and "The Spring Night" by Ray Bradbury.
3. "A Basic Science Fiction Library," a symposium containing contributions by Forrest J. Ackerman, Everett Bleiler, David H. Keller, Sam Merwin Jr., P. Schuyler Miller, Sam Moskowitz, "Lewis Padgett" (pseudonym of Henry Kuttner and C. L. Moore), Paul J. Payne, A. Langley Searles, Theodore Sturgeon, A. E. van Vogt, and DAW, appeared in the same issue of the *Sampler*.

4. AWD, ed., *Strange Ports of Call* (New York: Pellegrini & Cudahy, 1948).

5. Aldous Huxley (1894–1963), *After Many a Summer Dies the Swan* (1939).

---

[256]   To Samuel J. Sackett [TLS, UCLA]   June 30th, 1949.

Dear Mr. Sackett:

Thanks for your letter and the enclosed check. I was indeed glad to hear from you. I haven't any ash-trays at the moment but will cut you one as speedily as possible and send it on.

As to biographical data for your sketch, I'm glad to give you what I can, which isn't really a tremendous lot. To begin with, I was born on Friday the 13th, Jan. 1893 at a ranch-house belonging to my maternal grandfather, Hiram Gaylord, in Long Valley, Cal., only a few miles from my present dwelling-place. The Gaylords are an old New England family, descendants of Huguenot refugees who left Normandy late in the 16th century and settled for a generation or two in Somerset and Devonshire; later (1630) emigrating to Massachusetts. The name was Anglicized from Gaillard. The family claims descent from an armigerous Norman house dating back to the Crusades, and has a published genealogy. My grandmother was of Scotch-French Canadian extraction; my first name, Clark, being her family name. My father, Timeus Smith, was the son of a rich Lancashire iron-master who had married into the local gentry; and I got my second name, Ashton, from my paternal grandmother. My father did a lot of globe-trotting (Brazil, Australia, etc.) before he finally settled in California.

My childhood was happy enough, apart from rather frequent illnesses which made my school attendance intermittent. All told, I doubt if I really spent more than four years at the old red school-house! But I did acquire an early taste for reading, and began to scribble fairy tales, modeled on Andersen and the countess D'Aulnoy,[1] at the age of eleven. A little later, I branched into long and involved narratives derived from the Arabian Nights, Beckford's *Vathek* and the Indian tales of Kipling. Then I began to write verse, including, I remember, some rather lame imitations of the *Rubaiyat*. Gradually I acquired a feeling for meter and rhythm; and at sixteen or seventeen was able to sell a few poems to magazines. At the same time several of my short stoires (contes cruels with Oriental themes) were accepted by the *Black Cat* and the *Overland Monthly*. In spite of such encouragement, I abandoned fiction for a number of years and wrote only poetry, of which four volumes were in print by 1925. Then, incited by Lovecraft, with whom I was corresponding, I wrote my first weird story, "The Abominations of Yondo," which appeared in the revived *Overland* and drew many howls of wrath and derision from readers. But I did not really settle down to fiction-writing for another four years; when the partial failure of a small income made it necessary for me to earn some sort of living.

My experience of journalism, concerning which you inquire, was limited to the writing of a column for a local weekly paper, *The Auburn Journal*. In 1922 the Journal Press published my third volume of poems, *Ebony and Crystal;* and the column was written and continued more or less for several years, to discharge part of my indebtedness to the printer. It consisted of epigrams, translations from the French, and original poetry; sometimes containing merely a single short poem; and bore a variety of names, such as "Cocktails and Creme de menthe," "The Devil's Note-Book," "Paradox and Persiflage," and "Points for the Pious." I fear that it was not universally popular with readers: some of my epigrams were considered a bit too pointed. I enclose a few clippings, which you are welcome to keep. Most of the stuff seems rather cynical and flippant; but I still like some of the more serious apothegms.

I have taken various workaday jobs, lasting from a few days to a few weeks or months; the longest being intervals of ranch-work during the first years of the 2nd World War, when such labor really counted as war-work. The hardest labor I have ever done was well-digging and cement-mixing by hand (the well was dug for the local nunnery) and the nastiest was the spraying of fruit-trees with such infernal chemicals as arsenic, bluestone and sulphur. And once, for a whole week, I typed bills in a water-company's office. But I fear that I have little taste for honest labor. No doubt I have missed some promising opportunities: the rag-picker at the local city dump once offered to take me on as assistant!

For a period of ten years (from 1918 to 1928) I made numerous paintings and drawings, ranging from the weird and grotesque to the decorative and semi-naturalistic. Some of these pictures were exhibited in various Coast cities and in New York; a few were sold and many given away. Since that period I have done little pictorial work, apart from a few illustrations for my own stories that were used in *Weird Tales*. These were hardly representative of my best, since my real forte lies in color rather than in black and white line-work. Lately I have felt an urge to resume painting and have started by retouching some old pictures. Also, I have begun to experiment with the possibility of making pigments from local earths and minerals and have made various tints, mostly browns, yellows, reds, purples and greys, which can be used with a tempera medium such as white of egg. Blues and greens are harder to get; but certain copper minerals, such as azurite, bornite and malachite, should afford them.

Sculpture is the most recent of my several arts or endeavors—I began it almost by accident. In 1934 I enjoyed a visit from E. Hoffmann Price, who wished to secure some mineral specimens for a museum curator in the East.[2] So Price and I paid a visit to an old copper mine of which my uncle was then part owner. We came back with an auto-load of various rocks, ores and minerals; and from among these I kept a few specimens for myself. After the stuff had been lying around the cabin for a year, it suddenly occurred to me that I might carve something from a lump of it; the result being the head of a hybrid grotesque something between a hyena and a horned toad. I don't know just how many carvings I have done since; but the total must be climbing toward the 2 hundred mark. I don't seem able to keep many for myself, since the pieces now sell about as fast as I can make them, or sometimes faster. Some have been shipped as far afield as Hawaii, England and South Africa.

My sculptures are nearly all cut from solid materials; though I have done some experimental casting (not too successful) in plaster and clay; and have recently modeled one piece, a fountain-figure of Dagon, from potter's clay. Some of my materials are in the nature of fossils, or technically to be classified as such: that is to say, they are part of a "cast" of mineral matters which still retains the form of an herbiforous dinosaur! The creature was buried in ancient days by volcanic mud, and was exposed by the excavation of a local railroad cut. Whatever bones there were have long since been removed. I suppose what is left could be classed as dinosaur steak. Anyway, it winds diagonally upward for 18 or 20 feet in the wall of the cut. Climbing for hunks of it is a rather tricky business, since most of the wall is rotten shale; but recently I secured a fresh supply with the help of some friends. Incidentally, the bowl and mouthpiece of your pipe were cut from these materials; and I shall make your ash-tray from a piece of the same.

As for authors who were formative influences, I think Poe should head the list. Baudelaire and George Sterling in regard to poetry, and Lovecraft and Dunsany in respect to prose, should be added; though I think some critics tend to exaggerate the Dunsany influence. A poetic influence that no one seems to have pointed out is that of Oscar Wilde's fantastic masterpiece, "The Sphinx"; but it seems evident in many of the poems of *Ebony and Crystal*. Lafcadio Hearn, Gautier and Flaubert (the latter at least in *The*

Temptation of St. Anthony) have all helped to shape my prose style. I do not think that my paintings and carvings show any perceptible influences; whatever resemblance they have (if any) to other art is purely coincidental. One critic said that my carvings showed a study of pre-Columbian art—of which I have seen almost nothing! And having seen only two or three of Odilon Redon's paintings, I am still unable to decide whether there is any basis for comparing my pictures with his.

Do you need any bibliographical information for your article? If so, let me know. My poems and stories have gotten into many anthologies, some of which I have never seen and whose names I can't remember; and some have even been included in school-text books.[3] If you get the Arkham House booklists, you will have seen the announcement of three future volumes, *Selected Poems, The Abominations of Yondo,* and *Tales of Science and Sorcery.* And I have a part-written book-length fantasy, "The Infernal Star," which I hope to finish some day; also, numberless plots and synopses for short stories.

I have received some fine British write-ups recently, by Walter Gillings [*sic*] in *The Fantasy Review.* And the current *Famous Fantastic Mysteries* has me among its Masters of Fantasy with a nicely worded blurb and a villainous drawing.[4]

Well, I hope this rambling and desultory discourse will be of some use to you.

      Cordially,
      Clark Ashton Smith

1. Marie-Catherine Le Jumel de Barneville, Countess d'Aulnoy (1650/1651–1705), French noblewoman and author of fairy tales.

2. I.e., HPL's colleague James F. Morton.

3. *California State Series; Sixth Year Literature Reader,* comp. Le Roy E. Armstrong (Sacramento: California State Printing Office, 1916); *Today's Literature. An Omnibus of Short Stories, Novelettes, Poems, Plays, Profiles, and Essays,* ed. D. C. Gordon, V. R. King, and W. W. Lyman (New York: American Book Co., 1935).

4. Arthur F. Hillman, "The Lure of Clark Ashton Smith" (*Fantasy Review,* February–March 1949), a review of *GL;* and "The Poet of Science Fiction" (*Fantasy Review,* April–May 1949); [Forrest J. Ackerman,] "Clark Ashton Smith—The Star Treader" (*Famous Fantastic Mysteries,* August 1949).

[257]   To Samuel J. Sackett [TLS, UCLA]   Dec. 1st, 1949.

Dear Sam:

[. . .] My *Selected Poems,* on which I have spent infinite labor, go forward to the publishers today; but I've no idea just *when* the book will see print. If all the poems are used, it will run around four hundred pages. Ten of the titles are in French: I enclose copies of four specimens, each followed by a literal English rendering, and would be obliged if you were to show them to the French teacher or teachers at the University. I'm anxious for criticism, particularly in regard to any flaws that they may contain. The English translations, I might add, are not offered as finished poems —they merely give the bare sense.

I'll send you some more poems later, since I have any number of surplus copies lying around.

> Cordially,
> Clark

---

[258]   To August Derleth [TLS, AH]   March 31st, 1950.

Dear August:

I have been intending to write for a long time past and send you the enclosed carbon of "The Dweller in the Gulf," which is listed for use in *The Abominations of Yondo.* Please use this copy when you have the volume typed. The story, printed as "Dweller in Martian Depths" in *Wonder Stories,* came out with an emasculated ending, since Gernsback considered the original one too horrible. Also, the butchering was badly done.

I've exhausted my supply of *Genius Loci* and would like you to send me another five copies. Also, another of *Something About Cats,* since I have given away the copies originally purchased.[1]

Would it be worth your while to handle some copies of my old pamphlet, *The Double Shadow,* etc? I have been selling some recently at 75¢ per copy to individual purchasers, and believe that a demand could be worked up if fantasy readers knew that the book was still obtainable. I must have at least 400 copies left. If you care for the idea, I could supply you with some of them at the usual discount. Probably ninety cents or a dollar would not be too much to ask for the book.

I'll try to do the preface for *The Abominations of Yondo* shortly.[2] Am pulling out of a bad physical slump and have not done too much work, apart from the writing of poems in Spanish, some of which I hope to place sooner or later with Latin-American periodicals. They have been checked over by a good Spanish professor, who did not find too much to correct.

Here is a bit of mythological japery. I can probably sell it somewhere; though the Shakesperean [*sic*] "wappened" will no doubt have to be replaced with some word more familiar to the general reader.[3]

All best, as ever,
Clark

1. HPL, *Something about Cats and Other Pieces* (Sauk City: Arkham House, 1949).
2. *AY* does not have a preface.
3. "The Twilight of the Gods" (*DC*): "All the satyrs have been dehorned, / And wappened are Mohammed's houris;" ll 1–2.

---

[259]   To Samuel J. Sackett [TLS, UCLA]   July 11th, 1950.

Dear Sam:
Thanks for the sketch,[1] which I have read over carefully, checking several obvious errors made by the typist.

Your data are substantially correct, apart from a few minor points. Poe, *not* Omar Khayyam, was the first poet who impressed me, and I'll never forget the thrill of finding his poems in a grammar-school library at the age of thirteen. I remember too that the librarian commented reprovingly on my morbid and unhealthy taste in reading-matter!

Arthur F. Hillman is in error on one or two points. The changes in "Dweller in Martian Depths" were not made by me but by the editor, David Lasser, and were made without my knowledge. The original text of this tale, under its original title, "The Dweller in the Gulf," will appear in my next volume of tales. The worst thing about the alterations was, that they were crudely done.

Also, it is hardly true that I was forced to discontinue writing fiction, since there has been no time when my tales were not in request among editors and readers. The chief reason was my own growing disgust with pulp fantasy and with the restrictions imposed upon writers.

James Blish's critique is new to me, and I find parts of it quite astounding.[2] No doubt a wider scholarship on Mr. Blish's part would enable him to assemble a much longer list of alleged "influences," including writers that I have never read! He has missed some of my favorite poems, including Keats and Beddoes, and apparently does not take Huysmans or Ambrose Bierce into account in tabulating sources (?) for my prose! For the bane of every new creative artist, the world is full of people with Mr. Blish's turn of mind—that is to say, people who can see nothing but resemblances either real or fancied (usually the latter) and who can always be depended upon to miss or ignore the essential *differences* between a new talent and its predecessors.

Incidentally, the phrase "superterrestrial fairylands accurst" which Blish quotes as being from Lovecraft, is really taken from an appreciation of my poetry written by Benjamin De Casseres.

Blish, too, is obviously one of those who refuse to admit the ornate literary style (such as that of Sir Thomas Browne) as a legitimate form of art. On this point, I might quote Lytton Strachey, who thoroughly appreciated Browne and wrote a fine essay upon him. "There is a great gulf fixed between those who naturally like the ornate and those who naturally abhor it." As Strachey points out, argument is useless. . . .

As to my own employment of an ornate style, using many words of classic origin and exotic color, I can only say that [it] is designed to produce effects of language and rhythm which could not possibly be achieved by a vocabulary restricted to what is known as "basic English." As Strachey points out, a style composed largely of words of Anglo-Saxon origin tends to a spondaic rhythm, "which by some mysterious law, reproduces the atmosphere of ordinary life." An atmosphere of remoteness, vastness, mystery and exoticism is more naturally evoked by a style with an admixture of Latinity, lending itself to more varied and sonorous rhythms, as well as to subtler shades, tints and nuances of meaning—all of which, of course, are wasted or worse than wasted on the average reader, even if presumably literate.

Among writers who have praised my poetry highly, you might add to your list Ambrose Bierce, Vachel Lindsay, Robert Haven Schauffler, Stanton Coblentz, Lilith Lorraine, and the late British poet, Alice Meynell.

I enclose some reviews and appreciations, including the one written by De Casseres, which you have probably not seen. There have been many others, but unfortunately I have not kept all of them and have mislaid others. For instance, there was a fine write-up by Stanley Mullen in *The Gorgon* about three years back; and another, written by one Richard Stockton (who really showed some understanding of my work) appeared in *The Acolyte*.[3]

As to coinages, I have really made few such, apart from proper names of personages, cities, countries, deities, etc, in realms lying "east of the sun and west of the moon." I have used a few words, names of fabulous monsters, etc., drawn from Herodotus, Maundeville, and Flaubert which I have not been able to find in dictionaries or other works of reference. Some of these occur in "The Hashish-Eater," a much-misunderstood poem, which was intended as a study in the possibilities of cosmic consciousness, drawing heavily on myth and fable for its imagery. It is my own theory that if the infinite worlds of the cosmos were opened to human vision, the visionary would be overwhelmed by horror in the end, like the hero of this poem.[4]

I hope I have made it plain that my use of rare and exotic words has been solely in accord with an esthetic theory, or, one might say, a technical theory.

I had intended to write and thank you some months back for your letter returning my French verses with the criticism of your Lithuanian professor. Curiously enough, he, not I, was in error in two instances out of three—the third being due to my own carelessness in not actually checking up on a word.

Incidentally, some of my French, and also my Spanish, verses have been praised by scholars deeply grounded in these languages. Latterly I have concentrated on the study of Spanish. I'll enclose a specimen or two of Spanish verse, which has been checked over by a local professor.

I hope that you and your wife will be able to come up during the summer. Let me know beforehand, since I may be away for a week or two, at a date not yet determined. [. . .]

My best to all of you,
Clark

P.S. I'm not sure when my poems will appear, since publication is being held up by the exorbitant cost of printing. My next prose volume, *The Abominations of Yondo,* is evidently scheduled to precede the poems, and should be out early next year, if not sooner.

1. S. J. Sackett, "The Last Romantic" (*Fantasy Sampler,* June 1956; rpt. *Nyctalops* No. 7, August 1972).

2. James Blish, "Eblis in Bakelite," *Tumbrils* No. 2 (June 1945).

3. Stanley Mullen, "Cartouche: Clark Ashton Smith" (*Gorgon,* July 1947); Richard Stockton, "An Appreciation of the Prose Works of Clark Ashton Smith" (*Acolyte,* Spring 1946).

4. This explanation of "The Hashish-Eater" is presented in greater depth in "The Argument of the Hashish-Eater" (*SS*).

[260]   To L. Sprague de Camp[1] [TLS, JHL]   Oct. 24th, 1950.

My dear De Camp:

Re your card of the 18th: the name *Zothique* was constructed on the analogy of *antique* and therefore rhymes with it. However, the sounding of the mute e (Zotheek´ee) is allowable as an alternative.

Your forthcoming book sounds most interesting.[2] As to the literary angle, my own impression is that much, if not most, of the modern fiction written about Atlantis, etc., has drawn its inception from Theosophic sources, and am wondering if you have come to the same conclusion.

Incidentally, it should be noted that Zothique as I have conceived it belongs to the future rather than the past, and lies at the other end of the time-cycle from Hyperborea, Mu, etc. The peoples of Zothique, one might say, have rounded the circle and have returned to the conditions of what we of the present era regard as antiquity. The idea of this last continent was suggested by the "occult" traditions regarding Pushkara, which will allegedly become the home of the 7th root-race, the last race of mankind. However, I doubt if Theosophists would care for my conception, since the Zothiqueans as I have depicted them are a rather sinful and iniquitous lot, showing little sign of the spiritual evolution promised for humanity in its final cycles.

Rosicrucianism seems to have some similar traditions regarding the lost continents. But perhaps you have gone into all this. I don't know how much claim to "ancient wisdom" any of it has, but have my apprehensions.

        Cordially yrs,
        Clark Ashton Smith

1. L[yon] Sprague de Camp (1907–2000), science fiction writer; author of short biographies of various fantasy writers, including CAS; see *Literary Swordsmen and Sorcerers* (Sauk City, WI: Arkham House, 1976).

2. *Lost Continents: The Atlantis Theme in History, Science and Literature* (New York: Gnome Press, 1954).

[261]   To August Derleth [TLS, AH]   June 16th, 1951.

Dear August:

Herewith a selection of additional poems for *The Dark*

Chateau—enough to make up a total of around 65 pages. I have included a poem in French (one of my best, I think) followed by a fairly literal English translation. This poem, and the two short ones in Spanish previously sent, have been carefully overhauled by language experts.

I should have sent the poems before, but have been away from home most of the time for several weeks, working on a ranch job. Now that it is over, I can get down to my own work.

I haven't yet received the new Arkham House catalogue, and am wondering if it appeared.

Did you ever receive any particulars about Barlow's death?[1]

    All best, as always,
        Clark

P.S. Mindful of your injunction, I have selected for the most part pieces of weird or fantastic interest, several with a humorous or satiric tinge. "Hesperian Fall" is non-weird but has been a favorite with people reading it in ms.

        C.

1. RHB committed suicide by an overdose of barbiturates on 1 January 1951, despondent over the possible revelation of his homosexuality.

---

[262]   To August Derleth [TLS, AH]   Oct. 7th, 1953.

Dear August:

Herewith my formal okeh on the use of "The Metamorphosis of Earth" in that British edition of *Beachheads in Space*.[1]

I have finished eleven new carvings and want to do about a dozen more for quick sale to build up my lowering reserve of cash. Thanks to the check-list that you published several years back in *The Arkham Sampler,* I still get letters of inquiry from prospective purchasers and could no doubt make a full-time occupation out of sculpture if I so desired. So far, I haven't done anything about most of the recent letters, of which there must be dozens lying around.

I have put aside for you a new head of Shub-Niggurath, and am listing hereunder, with descriptions and prices, the other new carvings, all of which strike me as being successful and nicely finished:

Hyperborean totem-pole (top section, two heads). Upper head rather bird-like, with enigmatic ironic expression and long snaky neck. Lower head burly and bellicose with flat tentacles or feelers running downward to the base and upward on the neck of the superimposed head. Talc, bluish and flecked and mottled with rusty brown. $7.00.

One-horned Venusian Swamp-dweller. Humanoid and slightly toadlike head with long three-sectioned horn. Face broader than cranium. A beautiful piece of work, in which a prolonged firing has brought out the whitish and reddish coloring of the talc, slightly suggesting porcelain. Diagonal stripes across the face give it a tigerish look. Tip of the horn is bluish, with a little fire-black at the back. $7.00

The Early Worm. Figurine, rather humorous. A fat, cocky little reptile in an attitude of defense, head thrown back, mouth open, and tail sticking straight up. Probably a tough mouthful for anything but a road-runner or secretary-bird. Material seems to be a porphyritic silicate of alumina, in which the firing has brought out a warm terra-cotta coloring. $7.00

The Voyeur (or The Sexologist). Brown silicate animal head with tilted snout and humanoid mouth and eyes with inquisitive prurient expression. Suggests Dr. Kinsey pursuing his usual investigations. $6.00

Newly hatched Dinosaur. Head, mouth open and toothless, eyes shut. Leaden-colored talc. $4.00

Reptile of the Prime. Fat reptile on four stumpy legs or feet, tail curling upward. Leaden bluish-black talc. $7.00

The Mysteriarch. Head, three-lobed cranium, slitted eyes and elongated concave face. A strange sculptural form, somewhat triangular at the back, but flowing in modulated curves. Resembles The Inquisitor Morghi a little. Glossy fire-black talc, showing a hint of dark red in the face. $6.00

The Goblin. Head with small pointed cap. Face rather bird-like, wicked staring eyes and short curved beak wide open as if cackling or screeching. Pale whitish-blue talc, rusty flecks and mottlings. Goblin might have stepped out of Andersen or Hoffmann. Small but finely executed piece. $5.00

Prehistoric Bird. Head in rather heavy relief on block of talc about two by three and one half inches. Base an inch thick in part, so that piece can be set upright if desired. A wicked-looking fowl, beak open and equipped with saw-like teeth that curve backward at the points. Through a trick in firing, the upper ground and top of head are lighter-colored than the rest, so that the head seems to [be] emerging from or sinking into shadow. $5.00

Waterfowl. Head in talc. Almost that of a duck, except for the barbs or pointed hackles at the back. Less fantastic than any other of my new pieces but nicely done. $5.00

Shub-Niggurath. Goatish, leering head, curved horns, ears and muzzle slightly formalized, the former drooping close to the head, the latter almost vertical in profile. Brownish silicate with small black spots. $6.00

I hope to do some other Lovecraft pieces, and of course will give you first option on them.

If you feel like taking on any of the above-listed pieces at present, or want to examine them, let me know and they will go forward, or, if you want to purchase any particular subjects later, I could list them for duplication. In that case, the material might have to be a different one, since I am running out of talc and am not likely to get any more of it at the present time.

My best of all to you,
Clark

I haven't yet received the contract for "Phoenix," but suppose it will be coming on before long.[2]

1. AWD, ed., *Beachheads in Space* (1952; London: Weidenfeld & Nicolson, 1954).
2. "Phoenix," *Time to Come* (New York: Farrar, Strauss & Young, 1954); OD.

———————————◆———————————

[263]   To L. Sprague de Camp [TLS, JHL]   Oct. 21st, 1953.

Dear Sprague:
I have your letter of Oct. 17th, and feel a little embarrassed in answering by the paucity of autobiographical detail that would be suited to your purpose. (I'm not nearly old enough yet to write my Confessions!)

As for my education, that's easy enough to answer, since it has been mainly self-conducted, highly irregular, and largely a matter of following my own vagrant and varying inclinations. I did grad-uate from grammar school and register for entry into high school. But my real education began with the reading of *Robinson Crusoe* (unabridged), *Gulliver's Travels,* the fairy tales of Andersen and the Countess D'Aulnoy, *The Arabian Nights* and (at the age of 13) Poe's *Poems.* Poe seems to have confirmed me in a more or less permanent slant, which led later to Baudelaire and the French Romantic School. Beckford's *Vathek,* read at the age of 15, was another early influence. I did a lot of boyhood scribbling, imitations of Omar, lurid Oriental romances, etc;, and at 17 sold several pseudo-Orientales to the *Black Cat* and the *Overland Monthly.* Curiously enough, after that I wrote little but poetry for a number of years, and dabbled a lot in painting and drawing, the pictures being mainly grotesques and fantastic exotic landscapes. I think it was mainly Lovecraft's interest and encouragement (I began to correspond with him in 1922) which led me to experiment with Weird fiction. My first genuinely weird tale, "The Abominations of Yondo," was written in 1925 and appeared in the *Overland Monthly,* evoking, I was told, many protests from the readers. In the fall of 1929 I began an intensive campaign of fiction-writing, both weird and pseudo-science, for which, I am going to confess frankly, the influence and coercement of a woman-friend was largely responsible. The bulk of my published tales were written between that time and 1936. I might add that out of my total fictional output (probably around 110 completed stories) very little has remained unsold, and this little is mediocre—which, I fear, applies to some of the published yarns also.

As for other occupations, these have been largely seasonal or part-time jobs, such as orchard work and garden work-fruit-picking, thinning, pruning, etc. I have done a little mining but dislike working underground. And I did take a flier in journalism for awhile: the contributing of a column of epigrams, verse, etc., to a local newspaper. The epigrams were a little too sophisticated for their audience and I was no doubt lucky to escape incarceration in the county jail. Also I have dabbled a lot in small grotesque sculptures and, to my surprise, I have sold nearly my entire output. But I am giving up such work for the present because of the heavy eye-strain entailed and, for the first time in years, have gone back to fiction-writing. Two shorts, written since the middle of September, are in the mails, and I am going ahead on a third. The tales are quite varied—one, "Schizoid Creator," being a fantastic satire that mixes black magic with psychiatric shock-treatment (the patient being a demon!) and the second, "Morthylla," a tale of Zothique, concerning a pseudo-lamia who was really a normal woman trying to please the tastes of her eccentric poet-lover. The one that I am writing at present, "The Theft of the Thirty-Nine Girdles," is told by the Hyperborean thief Satampra Zeiros whom you may remember if you have read *Lost Worlds.*[1] The theme is the stealing of the golden and jeweled chastity girdles worn by the virgins (!) of a Hyperborean temple. Satampra has taken on a moll, an ex-virgin of the temple, who is really quite a help to him in this delicate enterprise.

Re your other questions. I never met Lovecraft, and have never been very far east of the Sierras. However, I corresponded with Lovecraft till within six weeks of his death. I've met a few other fellow-practitioners—Price, Wandrei, Williamson, Fritz Leiber Jr., and Edmond Hamilton; and every so often one or two or three or four "fans" drift into Auburn. I enclose a rather good snap of myself taken some years back with a couple of the latter. The youth in the middle is Laney, who edited *The Acolyte*. I look about the same now (a pretty healthy object on the whole) with the addition of a small imperiale.

No, I don't run, and hardly expect to run, a motel. On the other hand, I am not the recluse that certain current fables have represented me as being. I do *not* live in a remote part of the Sierras; and I do *not* keep "a pack of savage dogs to ensure my privacy." In fact, I've kept nothing but cats for a number of years. The last one, a tom, disappeared some time back; and I haven't tried to replace him, since I do too much catting around myself to make a good master of cats, who find it increasingly hard to live on the land in this game-depopulated section.

That unfinished novel must have been "The Infernal Star," which I began a number of years back as a prospective three-part serial for *W.T.* I drafted the first part (around 12,000 words) but somehow never went on with it. The hero was an innocent biblio-phile who, through an amulet found behind the cracked binding of a volume of Jane Austen, was drawn into a series of wild and sorcerous adventures leading to a world of the star Yamil Zacra, the center from which all cosmic evil, sorcery, witchcraft, etc., emanate. I'll try to finish it if I can sell enough shorts to finance myself for awhile. A better idea, though, is "The Scarlet Succubus," a projected short novel of Zothique, which I'm carry-ing in my head. The conception takes a hint from Balzac's terrific yarn, "The Succubus," in *The Droll Stories*, and will exploit the imaginative and mystic possibilities of sex—an angle that seems rather neglected in this day of raw and mundane realism.

As to reading—I do *not* read any set number of books a year and would hate to undertake any such feat. In fact, I have a way of passing up what most of the world is reading. I buy an occa-sional fantasy or science fiction magazine to get a general idea of the current trend, or trends. Of books that I have read at all recently, I might instance *The Spear in the Sand*, by Raoul Faure, and *The Adventures of King Pausole* by Pierre Louys as being among those that have most impressed me.[2] Among living writers, probably I admire Aldous Huxley and Walter de la Mare as much as any. But my tastes are fairly eclectic, running as they do from Lovecraft to John Collier, from Maupassant and Flaubert to Fritz Leiber Jr.

Among other dabblings that I have neglected to mention is the translating of French and Spanish poetry, and also a few attempts to write verse of my own in the aforesaid languages. Among my few unpublished masterpieces is a short play in blank verse, "The Dead Will Cuckold You,"[3] which could easily be turned into a prose yarn of Zothique for *Weird Tales*.

I might add that I write slowly and painstakingly, with much recasting and revision. Much of my old work strikes me as being hasty, over-verbose and sometimes hackish. I have a number of ideas, also many written synopses, which I hope to work out. But I believe that my tendency will be away from horror of the Poesque or Lovecraftian type, toward fantastic satire, drollery and what-have-you. Also, there should be room for some good inter-planetaries that would avoid the current glibness, dryness and matter-of-factness.

I have enjoyed the fantastic humor of your own tales, and must buy *The Rogue Queen*, which sounds most alluring. And I'll look forward to *The Tritonian Ring*.[4] Will gladly autograph any copies of my own books that you send on.

Hope this medley will be of a little use. I'll look forward to seeing you when you reach California. Don't forget!

Klarkash-Ton

I enclose an astoundingly complete bibliography of my published fiction, compiled by a New Zealand admirer.[5]

1. "Schizoid Creator" (*Fantasy Fiction*, November 1953); "Morthylla" (*Weird Tales*, May 1953; *RA*); and "The Theft of the Thirty-nine Girdles" (*Saturn Science Fiction and Fantasy*, March 1958); all in *TSS*.

2. Raoul Cohen Faure (b. 1909), *The Spear in the Sand* (1946); Pierre Louys (1870–1925) *The Adventures of King Pausole* (1919).

3. "The Dead Will Cuckold You" (*SS*).

4. L. Sprague de Camp, *The Rogue Queen* (1951) and *The Tritonian Ring* (1953).

5. T. G. L. Cockcroft, *The Tales of Clark Ashton Smith* (Melling, Lower Hutt, New Zealand: privately published, 1951).

[264]   To L. Sprague de Camp [TLS, JHL]   Nov. 3rd, 1953.

Dear Sprague:

Thanks for yours of Oct. 27th.

I'd like to oblige Mr. Kessler, but, unfortunately, have never drawn a map of Zothique nor any other of my mythical regions and continents. To do so would involve going over all the stories I have written concerning such regions; and large sections would have to be labeled Terra Incognita.

However, I can give you (and Lyle Kessler) some data on Zothique as it exists in my own conception.

Zothique, vaguely suggested by Theosophic theories about past and future continents, is the last inhabited continent of earth. The continents of our present cycle have sunk, perhaps several times. Some have remained submerged; others have re-risen, partially, and re-arranged themselves. Zothique, as I conceive it, comprises Asia Minor, Arabia, Persia, India, parts of Northern and eastern Africa, and much of the Indonesian archipelago. A new Australia exists somewhere to the south. To the west, there are only a few known islands, such as Naat, in which the black cannibals survive. To the north are immense unexplored deserts; to the east, an immense unvoyaged sea. The peoples are mainly of Aryan or Semitic descent, but there is a negro kingdom (Ilcar) in the north-west; and scattered blacks are found throughout the other countries, mainly in palace-harems. In the southern islands survive vestiges of Indonesian or Malayan races.

The science and machinery of our present civilization have long been forgotten, together with our present religions. But many gods are worshipped; and sorcery and demonism prevail again as in ancient days. Oars and sails alone are used by mariners. There are no fire-arms—only the bows, arrows, swords, javelins, etc., of antiquity. The chief language spoken (or which I have provided examples in an unpublished drama) is based on Indo-European roots and is highly inflected, like Sanskrit, Greek and Latin. I quote an example, the last line of a sorcerer's invocation, from the afore-said drama:

Vachat pantari vora nagraban (Finished (or made) is the spell by the necromancer.)

To this the sorcerer's assistant answers: Ze, mozadrim, vachama vongh razan. (yes, master, the vongh (corpse animated by a demon) will do the rest.)

Following Grimm's law, the ancient roots are not too hard to detect; pantari, for instance, coming from the Sanskrit *mantra*. [. . .]

Yes, I knew that del Rey was no longer editing *Fantasy Fiction*. I hope the magazine will be able to survive, since I'd like to do more stories for it. "Schizoid Creator" has not yet been paid for. *Weird Tales*, too, seems to be having its troubles, doubtless due to the change in format, and is far behind in payment.

I've done a science fiction story ("Phoenix") for a book anthology that Derleth is compiling. Also, some new carvings, for which I can usually get quicker cash than for anything else that I do. The work is fun, and at least provides me with frijoles, pane, carne, pescado, leche, manteca, legumbres, tabaco y vino.

Cordially,
Klarkash-Ton

---

[265]   To George Haas[1] [TLS, private collection]
Feb. 1st, 1954.

Dear George:

Your letter was a poignant reminder that I have not answered the one last fall and thanked you for the excellent photos. I have been intending to do so for ages—but the intention has somehow gone to pave the place that is notoriously paved with all good intentions.

Your book-dealer down in Compton certainly must be good— or else have preternatural resources. I had begun to think that a copy of *Sandalwood* was quite unobtainable! The edition was the smallest of any of my books, and much of it, curiously enough, was distributed locally; and local purchasers seem canny enough to hang on to it, as I have found from vain efforts to re-purchase one. You should not have so much trouble in procuring a copy of *Nero and Other Poems*.

There was only one binding used for *Sandalwood*—a dark green pebbled art-paper. You were lucky to get one in good condition.

It is good news that my "fourth dimension of Enchantment," as your dealer calls it, is appealing to more readers. Such appreciation is always reassuring, especially in one's darker moments.

As to poetry in general, I think that one usually has to cultivate, through more or less reading, an appreciation of its nuances and finer values. And many readers never do develop such appreciation, stopping at the surface-thought or reducible idea-content— which is often the least of it. The real magic is another thing—and often too elusive for definition in crude prose.

I hope you will not have to wait for spring before coming up again. It would be best, however, to come in good weather, and perhaps another high-pressure area, keeping out rain, will develop or is [in] process of developing now. All you need do is write me, or send a telegram or night-letter a couple of days beforehand, which would be put in my P.O. box. And your friend Mr. Johnson would be very welcome to come along.[2] [. . .]

    With all best regards, cordially yours,
       Klarkash-Ton

P.S. I'll keep an eye out for that poem, "Sandalwood."

    1. George Haas (1906–1978), science fiction fan and friend of CAS. His extremely interesting life is documented in Don Herron, *Echoes from the Vaults of Yoh-Vombis* (St. Paul, MN: Dawn Heron Press, 1976). He wrote two memoirs of CAS which are collected in *BB*.
    2. Robert Barbour Johnson (1909–1979), *WT* author. A photograph of CAS, Haas, Johnson, and Howard Stanton LaVey (aka Anton Szander LaVey) (1930–1997) appears in Blanche Barton, *The Secret Life of a Satanist* (1990).

------

[266]   To George Haas [TLS, private collection]
                   117 Ninth St.,
                   Pacific Grove, Cal.
                   April 11th, 1955.

Dear Ji-Ech:
    I have been meaning to write for ages, but fear that a prolonged honeymoon has led to the neglect of correspondence.[1]
    I hope you and your mother are both in better health than at last hearing. This beautiful spring weather, almost summer-like, should banish any lingering remnants of winter colds.
    How about coming down to spend a week-end with us? It seems high time to renew the invitation. Any week-end would do; except over the 23rd and 24th of April, when we will probably run up to Auburn briefly, riding with a local friend who took us up for the best part of the Easter vacation. I wanted to check on the cabin and make fire-breaks. These I did not finish owing to overmuch sociality, so another visit seems advisable. We had no chance to go through Berkeley.
    I have about a dozen new carvings, of which Carol has taken photos, and am now starting to offer most of them for sale. All but two are cut from a new material, a sort of diatomite, which I

have found in the hills back of Carmel and Monterey. It is white or greyish in color, but various tints of pink, buff, grey-blue etc are brought out by firing.

I enclose a photo of the whole group, ranged on the back fence of our patio, and close-ups of two smaller groups, but must ask their return at your convenience. We have also taken kodachromes but have not yet received the developed prints.

Some of the pieces strike me as being among my best. Because of the increased cost of production, photographs, fuel, etc., I am having to up the prices somewhat. Even with the increase, I doubt if these prices give me more than a dollar an hour for the actual work spent.

I have listed titles on the backs of the photos. Herewith the prices:

Atlantean High-Priest	$ 9.00
Pixy	7.00
Dagon	11.00
The Guardian	14.00
Octopoid Entity	14.00
Terminus from Zothique	12.00
Crawler from the Slime	12.00
The Sorcerer Transformed	12.00
Mercurian Beast	9.00
Charnadis.	9.00

After typing this, I have remembered that Dagon, the latest, has not been photographed. It is a bust, with reddish, bluish, grey and buff mottlings, a short comb on the head, ears ending in fins, tentacle-like whiskers attached to the nostrils and bulging eyes. I started to make an inhabitant of Innsmouth, but think Dagon a better title.

Carol is so fond of the piece called One-horned Martian Dog that I am not offering it for sale. She thinks it resembles a rather monstrous and destructive bull-dog that she once owned!

Do you feel like buying any of these pieces at an early date? It will be better of course if you can come down and look them over. In view of our income, recently curtailed, I am anxious to raise money on them as soon as possible. I have had letters of inquiry from several possible customers, including a young admirer in Copenhagen, but have not answered them as yet.

Our affectionate regards to yourself and your mother,
Klarkash-Ton

P.S. The pixy came out worst in the group photo, owing to a shadow cast by the tilted pose, giving the appearance of a hole.

The Kodachromes have just come in, and I'll send one or two of them forward tomorrow.

1. On 10 November 1954 CAS married Carol Jones Dorman, whom he met while visiting his friend the poet Eric Barker. They honeymooned on the Monterey peninsula, and ultimately set up residence in Pacific Grove, whence all CAS's subsequent letters were written.

---

[267]   To Donald Wandrei [TLS, private collection]
Aug. 12th, 1955

Dear Donald:

I have been meaning to write you for ages, but time has been scant and broken—partly through the adjustments entailed by marriage—adjustments rather to the general changed set up and my wife's three teen-age children than the woman herself. Carol is all that I could ask or dream for—a good sport, a thoroughbred, intelligent, sensitive, sympathetic—and a lusty wench with an Elizabethan verve and tang. Curiously enough, she is descended from a minor Elizabethan poet, one Sir Thomas Overbury. She is fifteen years younger than I by the calendar. We were married within three weeks of our first meeting, after jumping over the broomstick— surely a witch's broom,—more or less publicly. Her whole story would give points and situations to Boccaccio or Balzac.

One of many things that the marriage has brought is a chance to live close to the sea, as I have always wanted. Our house is only half a block from Monterey Bay, and we look out from our dormer room upstairs over house-tops, some as quaintly gabled as those of Arkham, to flying sea-gulls and surf and fishing boats.

Carol's children, two boys, thirteen and fourteen respectively, and a sixteen year old girl, were violently opposed to me at the start, but have now become reconciled. Unruly puppies, all of them, but we get on, and oddly enough, they seem to obey me better than they do their mother when I am forced to exert authority. I must pause to chuckle over finding myself in a parental position—surely the last thing I ever bargained for, and more fantastic even than legal marriage.

What are you doing? What have you written? I feel so out of touch and would like to hear from you.

I wrote, and sold, several stories last year, and had a number of others started or worked out in synopsis. Due to the upheaval of marriage, etc., I have not yet resumed fiction-writing but believe I will be able to do so this fall when the children go back to school.

I have managed to write several poems, and have finished a number of carvings, many of which have already been bought by Derleth and other collectors of the sculptural weird and grotesque. Apart from that, I have been taking some part-time garden jobs, which pay from 1.50 to 1.75 per hour, to help out on the family income, which was cut down by Carol's rich bitch relatives after she married me. Carol herself is working on the revision of a book based on her own experiences at bringing up the children after her divorce from their father years ago. The experiences were varied and dramatic, and I think she has a far better chance of doing a best seller than I. Of course I am helping all I can with criticism, insisting on strict chronological order, attention to story and character values, etc., etc. [. . .]

> Faithfully,
> Clark

————————— • —————————

[268]   To August Derleth [TLS, SHSW] May 12th, 1956.

Dear August:

I enclose P.O. order for $2.05, for which please send to us your book on Ignatius Loyola.[1]

Hope all is well with you and yours. At this end, there is both good and bad news. The good news is, that I am to give a poetry reading (for which I will receive the gate receipts) in Carmel the last Thursday of this month. I will also read a short paper on the sources of science fiction motifs in mythology, ancient literature, etc. This will be followed by a week's showing of such sculptures and paintings as I have on hand.

The bad news is, that my Auburn cabin has been so thoroughly vandalized that it will seem almost hopeless to put the place in order again for such brief occupancy as Carol and I can give it. One motive was plainly robbery (the depredators took about everything useful—except books, which they merely strewed on the floor and, in some cases, shot holes in.) The other was malice— they even dumped a can of tar on my sitting-room-and-work-table! And poor Carol had looked forward so much to the place for a week or two of refuge from domesticity and her brood of voracious, nagging teen-agers. It looks as if Auburn were about washed up for us.

Has it occurred to you that a selection of my best (or most popular stories) might perhaps be placed with one of the pocket-book companies, such as Ballantine? If you and I can make a selection of perhaps ten or twelve stories, Carol will be glad to prepare the typescript.

Looking over *Genius Loci* the other day, it occurred to me that a story such as "The Satyr," if slightly pruned of its purple verbiage, might appeal as a reprint to such magazines as *Playboy* and *Escapade*. We'll be glad to re-type the yarn if you would care to submit it.

Best always,
Clark

1. *St. Ignatius and the Company of Jesus* (1956).

---

[269]   To August Derleth [TLS, SHSW]   July 3rd. [1956]

Dear August:

Herewith, at last, a slightly revised and snapped-up typescript of "The Satyr," which might possibly have reprint interest for *Playboy* or others of its ilk.

Carol and I were in Auburn for more than a week last month, checking on the vandalized cabin and cleaning it up to the best of our ability—an Augean task. In some ways, though, the damage was less than I had feared, books, letters, scripts, etc., having been littered about but not otherwise molested. Among other things I recovered the box containing my letters from Lovecraft which, with much else, I had to store with local friends against the time when we can get up with a car (we traveled by bus and could not handle more than our suit-cases and sleeping-bags.)

One thing that burns me up is that the vandalizing and theft went on after the local sheriff was apprised that the place had been broken into. A week, at least, elapsed before he went out to fit the door with a new padlock to replace the one that had been shot off. During that week, according to our check, the cook-stove was removed bodily, together with every other piece of sizable iron; and an oil portrait of me, done many years back, was filled with bullet holes and apparently also slashed with my rapier, of which I found the broken-off point on the floor.

I have made a tentative list of titles from my books for a possible pocket reprint, with the possible title, *Far from Time*. You might check it over at leisure.[1] Alternate titles are indicated with brackets. Probably the collection shouldn't have more than twelve stories, which, roughly, would aggregate around 80,000 words. The first seven, the longest stories, are science fiction or science fantasy.

Could you give me Sam Loveman's address, which I have lost? And do you know anything about Michael DeAngelis or his present whereabouts? DeAngelis did a little amateur printing from my verse about six years back,[2] and also planned to print my one-act play, "The Dead Will Cuckold You," of which I loaned him my only extra copy. Since that time, my original copy was damaged by fire, so that complete reconstruction would be a hellish task. Friends to whom I have read the piece, minus the charred gaps, believe it could be presented locally. Therefore I'd like to get in touch with DeAngelis, if he is still available.

All best to your and yours,
Clark

1. A table of contents for *Far from Time* is reprinted in *Klarkash-Ton* No. 1.
2. *The Ghoul and the Seraph* ([New York]: Gargoyle Press, 1950).

---

[270]   To August Derleth [TLS, SHSW]   Sept. 7th, 1957.

Dear August:
Re your letter to Carol, mentioning the possibility of a new volume of my verse. I have made and typed a selection under the tentative title *Spells and Philtres,* which I am mailing herewith. None of the poems has appeared in book form before, though many have had magazine publication. I think the proportion of fantasy is about the same as in *The Dark Chateau.* If publication becomes feasible, you can deal freely with the selection by omitting any that you wish.

This is a very hasty note, since I wish to mail the collection this morning. The p.o. closes by noon for the week-end.

Best to all of you, as ever,
Clark

---

[271]   To August Derleth [TLS, AH]   [c. 5 February 1958]

Dear August:
Herewith the first 12,000 words of "The Infernal Star," the short novel that I started to write in 1935 or 1936. Unluckily, I have not been able to find any notes about the continuation of the story, which was originally designed as a three-part serial for *W.T.*

However, I recall enough, or can devise enough, to bring the tale to 25,000 or 30,000 words. I am also enclosing the detailed complete synopsis of another tale, The Master of Destruction, of pseudo-scientific interest. Would you please read and return them, indicating which you would prefer to have me work on for the proposed novella?

It is good news that my *Spells and Philtres* will appear in late March.

Sorry to have delayed so long in writing. I had to search through endless boxes for the material enclosed. And Carol's daughter has kept us upended with her nebulous changing plans for marriage to an Army Language School student from Pennsylvania. We sincerely hope that the plans come off without hitch.

We hope to return to Auburn for a month or two toward the end of February, where I can work in comparative peace. I have, by the way, applied for an old age pension, which has meant endless irritating red tape. Wish me luck!

I was shocked to see, in last night's local newspaper, a brief notice of the death of Henry Kuttner at Santa Monica.[1] Do you know anything about the details?

Best from both of us, as always,
    Clark

1. Kuttner died of a heart attack on 4 February.

———————— • ————————

[272]   To George Haas [ALS, private collection]
                                                      June 16th, 1959
Dear Ji-Ech:
    Yes, your letter and check of May 21st were finally relayed to us in P. G. I am profoundly sorry that no acknowlgement was made in the state of confusion about the property near Auburn into which we were plunged. Evidently each of us thought that the other had written you.

I am glad your mother has gone for a stay in Healdsburg. May she return refreshed and strengthened. It is good to learn that you are both well.

In all probability, we will remain here for considerable time, and let the kartle of would-be lawyers, bidders, etc., simmer itself down. Any buyers who have so far come forward, want to jew us down to the ultimate. They can stew in their own greed.

Let us hear from you when convenient.
  Our love to both of you.
      Klarkash-Ton

P.S. I am decorating our patio gate with such inscriptions as *no admittance, no pasaran* (they shall not pass), *cave canem* (beware the dog) etc. I wonder if you could give me the German (German lettering) for something like *keep out,* or *go to the devil, you beat-niks.* All this applies only to bores, time-wasters, salesmen, etc!

---

[273]   To August Derleth [ALS, SHSW]   Feb. 8th, 1960.

Dear August:
    The front jacket and back-strip of my book arrived Saturday. I think they are admirable. Dagon and the High Cockalorum suggest an art unknown to history or archaeology and should arouse interest and speculation.
    Donald's little essay for the book-jacket is fine, and I thank him. And Ackerman's photo, I am sure, will reproduce well on the jacket-paper.
    Would it be possible to let us know (a card would be enough) a little in advance of publication?
    Carol has been unwell—a near migraine.
    She joins me in best wishes and affectionate regards.
        As ever,
        Clark

---

[274]   To George Haas [ALS, private collection]
                                    April 27, 1961

Dear Ji-Ech:
    Carol may have dropped you a line about our having to go to Auburn suddenly, on a peremptory order from the D.A, telling me to fill a hole on my Auburn property—or else go to jail at the end of April. We went up, an expensive proceeding, and returned here a week ago. The mission was finally accomplished, with the aid of a bulldozer belonging to the son of an old family friend (now dead) down in Long Valley. You will remember the hole—the water-spring and old mining shaft behind it which I used for a cellar in hot weather. It took about half an hour to push in the ancient

dump. We thought of you and Mrs. Boyd, very regretfully, when we passed Berkeley. We had met with no end of trouble and expense, delays, false leads, etc., and our budget was far over-passed. [. . .]

Our love to Mrs. Boyd and yourself.

As ever,

Klarkash-Ton

---

[275]   To Donald Sidney-Fryer[1] [ALS, UCLA]   June 5th, 1961

Dear Don:

Here, at long last, is an alexandrine sonnet which I hope that you and Cockcroft can use.[2] I wrote it yesterday, in the midst of the Sabbat pandemonium of dogs, brats and autos. I'm sure I've written lousier stuff.

Well, I must get this off. I enclose two typed copies, and two in ms., of which the pencil draft was the first written.

Pardon my haste. I received the magazine *Fantasy Fiction,* and the typed copies of "Schizoid Creator," which you were more than good to make. Believe me, I appreciate it.

As ever,

CAS.

1. Donald Sidney-Fryer, poet and writer, commissioned CAS to write a poem for inclusion in a comprehensive bibliography of his work, later published as *Emperor of Dreams: A Clark Ashton Smith Bibliography* (1978). Sidney-Fryer is the pre-eminent scholar of CAS's work.

2. "Cycles," CAS's last poem (*BB* and *LO*).

---

[276]   To T. G. L. Cockcroft[1] [ALS, private collection]

[Postmarked July 28, 1961]

Dear Mr. Cockcroft:

It lies heavily on my conscience that I have not written you long ago. I received your addition to the bibliography (probably from Fryer) sometime back. Your publications proved invaluable in making up a list for Derleth (dates and magazines in which stories appeared) against my next volume, *Tales of Science and Sorcery,* since I had lost, given away or had stolen so many of my own copies. I could not have located the tales without your bibliographies.

I have a story, "The Root of Ampoi" (which first appeared in the *Arkham Sampler*) in the current August issue of *Fantastic Stories*. And I have just finished writing a new story, "The Dart of Rasasfa,"[2] for use in the same magazine. It was done against a definite time limit; and should appear around the end of 1961— if the Russians don't blow everything into cosmic smithereens before that. Personally, I doubt if they will.

My wife has not been very well. And I have heard that you too are, or have been, ill. Here's wishing better days for all of us. Anyway, I manage to keep on, in spite of a neighborhood full of brats, muts, autos, and planes from Fort Ord across the bay.

Here's wishing you the best with all cordial good regards and wishes,

 Yours,
  Clark Ashton Smith

1. Thomas G. L. Cockcroft, New Zealand collector and bibliographer who compiled *The Tales of Clark Ashton Smith* (1951) and *Index to the Weird Fiction Magazines* (1962).

2. CAS's last story, written around a cover illustration for *Fantastic Stories*. The story was not used; it appears in *SS*.

Selected Bibliography

I. Primary Sources

    A. Poetry

The Star-Treader and Other Poems. San Francisco: A. M. Robertson, 1912.

Odes and Sonnets. San Francisco: The Book Club of California, 1918.

Ebony and Crystal: Poems in Verse and Prose. Auburn, CA: Printed by The Auburn Journal Press, 1922. Preface by George Sterling

Sandalwood. Auburn, CA: Printed by The Auburn Journal Press, 1925.

Nero and Other Poems. Lakeport, CA: The Futile Press, 1937.

Selected Poems. Sauk City, WI: Arkham House, 1971. [Prepared September 1944 to November 1949.]

The Dark Chateau and Other Poems. Sauk City, WI: Arkham House, 1951.

Spells and Philtres. Sauk City, WI: Arkham House, 1958.

The Hill of Dionysus: A Selection. Pacific Grove, CA: Roy A. Squires and Clyde Beck, 1962.

Poems in Prose. Sauk City, WI: Arkham House, 1964. Introduction ("Clark Ashton Smith: Poet in Prose") by Donald S. Fryer.

¿Donde Duermes, Eldorado? y Otros Poemas. As by "Clerigo Herrero." Glendale, CA: Roy A. Squires, 1964. [La Imprenta de Rojo Escuderos.]

The Fugitive Poems of Clark Ashton Smith. Zothique edition. Glendale, CA: Roy A. Squires.

The Tartarus of the Suns. First fascicle. 1970.

The Palace of Jewels. Second fascicle. 1970.

In the Ultimate Valleys. Third fascicle. 1970.

To George Sterling: Five Poems. Fourth fascicle. 1970.

The Fugitive Poems of Clark Ashton Smith. Xiccarph edition. Glendale, CA: Roy A. Squires.

    The Titans in Tartarus. First volume. 1974.

    A Song from Hell. Second volume. 1975.

    The Potion of Dreams. Third volume. 1975.

    The Fanes of Dawn. Fourth volume. 1976.

    Seer of the Cycles. Fifth volume. 1976.

    The Burden of the Suns. Sixth volume. 1977.

The Hashish-Eater; or, The Apocalypse of Evil. Ed. Donald Sidney-Fryer. [Sacramento, CA: Donald Sidney-Fryer, 1990.]

Nostalgia of the Unknown: The Complete Prose Poetry of Clark Ashton Smith. Ed. Marc Michaud, Susan Michaud, Steve Behrends, and S. T. Joshi. West Warwick, Rhode Island: Necronomicon Press, 1988.

The Last Oblivion: Best Fantastic Poetry of Clark Ashton Smith. Ed. S. T. Joshi and David E. Schultz. New York: Hippocampus Press, 2002.

B. Fiction

The Double Shadow and Other Fantasies. Auburn, CA: Clark Ashton Smith, 1933. Contains: The Voyage of King Euvoran; The Maze of the Enchanter; The Double Shadow; A Night in Malnéant; The Devotee of Evil; The Willow Landscape.

Out of Space and Time. Sauk City, WI: Arkham House, 1942. Contains: Clark Ashton Smith: Master of Fantasy, by August Derleth and Donald Wandrei. *Out of Space and Time:* The End of the Story; A Rendezvous in Averoigne; A Night in Malnéant; The City of the Singing Flame (includes sequel, Beyond the Singing Flame); The Uncharted Isle. *Judgments and Dooms:* The Second Interment; The Double Shadow; The Chain of Aforgomon; The Dark Eidolon; The Last Hieroglyph; Sadastor; The Death of Ilalotha; The Return of the Sorcerer. *Hyperborean Grotesques:* The Testament of Athammaus; The Weird of Avoosl Wuthoqquan; Ubbo-Sathla. *Interplanetaries:* The Monster of the Prophecy; The Vaults of Yoh-Vombis; From the Crypts of Memory; The Shadows.

Lost Worlds. Sauk City, WI: Arkham House, 1944. Contains: *Hyperborea:* The Tale of Satampra Zeiros; The Door To Saturn; The Seven Geases; The Coming of the White Worm. *Atlantis:* The Last Incantation; A Voyage to Sfanomöe; The Death of Malygris. *Averoigne:* The Holiness of Azédarac; The Beast of Averoigne. *Zothique:* The Empire of the Necromancers; The Isle of the

Torturers; Necromancy in Naat; Xeethra. *Xiccarph:* The Maze of Maal Dweb; The Flower-Women. *Others:* The Demon of the Flower; The Plutonian Drug; The Planet of the Dead; The Gorgon; The Letter from Mohaun Los; The Light from Beyond; The Hunters from Beyond; The Treader of the Dust.

Genius Loci and Other Tales. Sauk City, WI: Arkham House, 1948. Contains: Genius Loci; The Willow Landscape; The Ninth Skeleton; The Phantoms of the Fire; The Eternal World; Vulthoom; A Star-Change; The Primal City; The Disinterment of Venus; The Colossus of Ylourgne; The Satyr; The Garden of Adompha; The Charnel God; The Black Abbot of Puthuum; The Weaver in the Vault.

The Abominations of Yondo. Sauk City, WI: Arkham House, 1960. Contains: The Nameless Offspring; The Witchcraft of Ulua; The Devotee of Evil; The Epiphany of Death; A Vintage from Atlantis; The Abominations of Yondo; The White Sybil; The Ice-Demon; The Voyage of King Euvoran; The Master of the Crabs; The Enchantress of Sylaire; The Dweller in the Gulf; The Dark Age; The Third Episode of Vathek; Chinoiserie; The Mirror in the Hall of Ebony; The Passing of Aphrodite.

Tales of Science and Sorcery. Sauk City, WI: Arkham House, 1964. Contains: Clark Ashton Smith: A Memoir, by E. Hoffmann Price. Master of the Asteroid; The Seed from the Sepulcher; The Root of Ampoi; The Immortals of Mercury; Murder in the Fourth Dimension; Seedling of Mars; The Maker of Gargoyles; The Great God Awto; Mother of Toads; The Tomb-Spawn; Schizoid Creator; Symposium of the Gorgon; The Theft of the Thirty-Nine Girdles; Morthylla.

Other Dimensions. Sauk City, WI: Arkham House, 1970. Contains: Marooned in Andromeda; The Amazing Planet; An Adventure in Futurity; The Immeasurable Horror; The Invisible City; The Dimension of Chance; The Metamorphosis of Earth; Phoenix; The Necromantic Tale; The Venus of Azombeii; The Resurrection of the Rattlesnake; The Supernumerary Corpse; The Mandrakes; Thirteen Phantasms; An Offering to the Moon; Monsters in the Night; The Malay Krise; The Ghost of Mohammed Din; The Mahout; The Raja and the Tiger; Something New; The Justice of the Elephant; The Kiss of Zoraida; A Tale of Sir John Maundeville; The Ghoul; Told in the Desert.

Strange Shadows: The Uncollected Fiction and Essays of Clark Ashton Smith. Ed. Steve Behrends with Donald Sidney-Fryer and Rah Hoffman. New York: Greenwood Press, 1989.

The Unexpurgated Clark Ashton Smith. Series editor, Steve Behrends. West Warwick, RI: Necronomicon Press. Comprises: *The Dweller in the Gulf* (1987); *Mother of Toads* (1987); *The Monster of the*

Prophecy (1988); *The Vaults of Yoh-Vombis* (1988); *The Witchcraft of Ulua* (1988); *Xeethra* (1988).

A Rendezvous in Averoigne. Sauk City, WI: Arkham House, 1988. Contains: The Sorcerer Departs (poem). Introduction, by Ray Bradbury. *Averoigne:* The Holiness of Azédarac; The Colossus of Ylourgne; The End of the Story; A Rendezvous in Averoigne. *Atlantis:* The Last Incantation; The Death of Malygris; A Voyage to Sfanomöe. *Hyperborea:* The Weird of Avoosl Wuthoqquan; The Seven Geases; The Tale of Satampra Zeiros; The Coming of the White Worm. *Lost Worlds:* The City of the Singing Flame (restored text); The Dweller in the Gulf; The Chain of Aforgomon; Genius Loci; The Maze of Maal Dweb; The Vaults of Yoh-Vombis; The Uncharted Isle; The Planet of the Dead; Master of the Asteroid. *Zothique:* The Empire of the Necromancers; The Charnel God; Xeethra; The Dark Eidolon; The Death of Ilalotha; The Last Hieroglyph; Necromancy in Naat; The Garden of Adompha; The Isle of the Torturers; Morthylla.

The Black Diamonds. Ed. S. T. Joshi. New York: Hippocampus Press, 2002. A juvenile novel.

C. Nonfiction

Planets and Dimensions: Collected Essays of Clark Ashton Smith. Ed. Charles K. Wolfe. Baltimore: Mirage Press, 1973.

Grotesques and Fantastiques. Ed. Gerry de la Ree. Saddle River, NJ: Gerry de la Ree, 1973. Previously unpublished poems and drawings.

Klarkash-Ton and Monstro Ligriv. Ed. Gerry de la Ree. Saddle River, NJ: Gerry de la Ree, 1974. Previously unpublished poems, drawings, and letters.

The Black Book of Clark Ashton Smith. Ed. Donald Sidney-Fryer. Sauk City, WI: Arkham House, 1979. Foreword by Marvin R. Heimstra. Contains two memoirs by George Haas, "As I Remember Klarkash-Ton" (from Chalker, 1963) and "Memories of Klarkash-Ton" (from Morris, August 1972).

The Devil's Notebook: Collected Epigrams and Pensées of Clark Ashton Smith. Compiled by Donald Sidney-Fryer. Ed. Don Herron. Mercer Island, WA: Starmont House, 1990.

II. Secondary Sources

The following books and articles, in addition to those cited in the notes, may be useful to the student of Clark Ashton Smith:

Ambrose, Michael E. "The Poetry of Clark Ashton Smith: An Introduction." *Dragonbane* No. 1 (Spring 1978): 48–51. Brief but cogent general essay on Smith as a poet.

Behrends, Steve. *Clark Ashton Smith.* Starmont Reader's Guide 49. Mercer Island, WA: Starmont House, 1990. The only full-length study to date.

———. "The Song of the Necromancer: 'Loss' in Clark Ashton Smith's Fiction." *Studies in Weird Fiction* No. 1 (August 1986): 3–12.

———, ed. *Klarkash-Ton: The Journal of Smith Studies* No. 1 (June 1988); as *The Dark Eidolon: The Journal of Smith Studies,* Nos. 2 (July 1989) and 3 (Winter, 1993). Published originally by Robert M. Price's Cryptic Publications, then by Necronomicon Press, this regrettably defunct journal provided a forum for both new articles on Smith as well as a source for reprinting important material from the past.

Bell, Joseph, and Roy A. Squires. *The Books of Clark Ashton Smith.* Toronto: Soft Books, 1987. Updates Sidney-Fryer et al. (1978).

Brandenberger, Mary Ann. "Poetic Devices in 'The Empire of the Necromancers'." *Niekas* No. 45 (1998): 87–9.

Buchanan, Carl Jay. "Clark Ashton Smith's 'Nero'." *Central California Poetry Journal* 96, No. 61(2001): 01a2. <http://www.solopublications.com/jur01a2.html>.

Chalker, Jack, ed. *In Memoriam: Clark Ashton Smith.* Baltimore: Anthem, 1963. Contains articles and tributes by Fritz Leiber, Ethel Heiple, George Haas, Ray Bradbury, Theodore Sturgeon, L. Sprague de Camp, and others.

Clore, Dan. "The Babel of Visions: The Structuralization of Clark Ashton Smith's 'The Hashish-Eater'." *Studies in Weird Fiction* No. 18 (Winter 1996): 2–12.

———. "Loss and Recuperation: A Model for Reading Clark Ashton Smith's 'Xeethra.'" *Studies in Weird Fiction* No. 13 (Summer 1993): 15–18.

Connors, Scott. "An Arthur Machen Review of Clark Ashton Smith." *Faunus: The Journal of the Friends of Arthur Machen* No. 6 (Autumn 2000): 31–38.

———. "Gesturing Toward the Infinite: Clark Ashton Smith and Modernism." *Studies in Weird Fiction* No. 25 (Summer 2001): 18–28.

de Camp, L. Sprague. "Sierran Shaman." *Literary Swordsmen and Sorcerers: The Makers of Heroic Fantasy.* Sauk City, WI: Arkham House, 1976, pp. 195–214.

Ellison, Harlan. *"Out of Space and Time* by Clark Ashton Smith." In *Horror: 100 Best Books.* Ed. Stephen Jones and Kim Newman. New York: Carroll and Graf, 1998, pp. 135–9.

Goodrich, Peter H. "Sorcerous Style: Clark Ashton Smith's *The Double Shadow and Other Fantasies." Paradoxa* No. 13–14 (1999–2000): 213–25.

Guillaud, Laurie. "Fantasy and Decadence in the Work of Clark Ashton Smith." *Paradoxa* No. 13–14 (1999–2000): 189–212.

Herron, Don. "Collecting Clark Ashton Smith." *Firsts* 10, No. 10 (October 2000): 26–37.

Hilger, Ronald S. *One Hundred Years of Klarkash-Ton: The Clark Ashton Smith Centennial Conference.* N.P.: Averon Press, 1996. Record of a conference held in Auburn to commemorate the 100th anniversary of Smith's birth. Includes color reproduction of paintings and carvings by Smith. Also includes memoirs by Violet Nelson Heyer and Robert B. Elder.

Hitz, John Kipling. "Clark Ashton Smith: Master of the Macabre." *Studies in Weird Fiction* No. 19 (Summer 1996): 8–15.

Lyman, William Whittingham. "Clark Ashton Smith." Unpublished ms., Lyman Family Papers, Bancroft Library, University of California at Berkeley. Brief memoir of Smith and his family in the late 1920s by a friend not associated with fantasy fandom.

Marigny, Jean. "Clark Ashton Smith and His World of Fantasy." Trans. S. T. Joshi. *Crypt of Cthulhu* No. 26 (Hallowmas 1984): 3–12.

Morris, Harry, ed. *CAS-Nyctalops.* Albuquerque, NM: Silver Scarab Press, August 1972. Special issue (No. 7) of this important and long-running fanzine, with contributions by Robert Bloch, Marvin K. Hiemstra, Frank Belknap Long, George Haas, Dennis Rickard, Charles K. Wolfe, S. J. Sackett, T. G. L. Cockcroft, and others.

Petaja, Emil. "The Man in the Mist." *Mirage* No. 10 (1971): 21–25. Memoir.

Price, E. Hoffmann. *Book of the Dead: Friends of Yesteryear: Fictioneers & Others.* Ed. Peter Ruber. Sauk City, WI: Arkham House, 2001, pp. 94–125. Contains expanded version of Price's memoir from *TSS.*

Rickard, Dennis. *The Fantastic Art of Clark Ashton Smith.* Foreword by Gahan Wilson. Baltimore: Mirage Press, 1973. Contains many photos (unfortunately, black and white) of Smith's paintings and carvings.

Ruber, Peter. "Clark Ashton Smith." In *Arkham's Masters of Horror.* Ed. Peter Ruber. Sauk City, WI: Arkham House, 2000, pp. 53–61.

Sidney-Fryer, Donald. *Clark Ashton Smith: The Sorcerer Departs.* West Hills, CA: Tsathoggua Press, 1997. Reprint of biographical-critical article from Chalker, 1963.

———. *The Last of the Great Romantic Poets.* Albuquerque, NM: Silver Scarab Press, 1973. Essay-review of Smith's *Selected Poems.*

———. "A Memoir of Timeus Gaylord: Reminiscences of Two Visits with Clark Ashton Smith, &c." *The Romantist* No. 2 (1978): 1–19.

———. "A Statement for Imagination: George Sterling and Clark Ashton Smith." *The Romantist* No. 6–7–8 (1982–83–84): 13–23.

Sidney-Fryer, Donald, et al. *Emperor of Dreams: A Clark Ashton Smith Bibliography.* West Kingston, RI: Donald M. Grant, 1978. Also contains memoir-letters by Eric Barker, Madelynne Greene, Rah Hoffman, Genevieve K. Sully, Ethel Heiple, and others, plus letters of appreciation by such writers as Harlan Ellison, Ray Bradbury, Fritz Leiber, and Avram Davidson. The foundation upon which all Smith scholarship rests.

Stableford, Brian. "Outside the Human Aquarium: The Fantastic Imagination of Clark Ashton Smith." In *American Supernatural Fiction: From Edith Wharton to the Weird Tales Writers,* ed. Douglas Robillard. New York: Garland Publishing Co., 1996, pp. 229–252.

Index

Three thousand copies of this book have been printed by the Vail-Ballou Mfg. Grp., Binghamton, NY from Sabon typeface on 50# Maple Tradebook Antique. Binding cloth is Arrestox B. Typesetting by The Composing Room, Inc., Kimberly, WI.